Television and Political Advertising
Volume 1:
Psychological Processes

COMMUNICATION

A series of volumes edited by:
Dolf Zillmann and **Jennings Bryant**

Television and Political Advertising

Volume 1:
Psychological Processes

edited by

Frank Biocca

Center for Research in Journalism and Mass Communication
University of North Carolina at Chapel Hill

LEA LAWRENCE ERLBAUM ASSOCIATES, PUBLISHERS
1991 Hillsdale, New Jersey   Hove and London

Lawrence Erlbaum Associates, Inc., Publishers
365 Broadway
Hillsdale, New Jersey 07642

Library of Congress Cataloging-in-Publication Data

Television and political advertising.

   Contents: v. 1. Psychological processes —
v. 2. Signs, codes, and images.
   1. Advertising, Political.   2. Advertising,
Political — Psychological aspects.   3. Television
in politics.   I. Biocca, Frank.
JF2112.A4T46   1990   659.1′932   89-71468
ISBN 0-8058-0655-5 (v. 1)
Printed in the United States of America
10 9 8 7 6 5 4 3 2 1

Contents

Part III:
Differential Processing of Positive and Negative Advertising

Part IV:
The Psychological Contexts of Processing

Preface

The sizzle, sputter, and hiss of political discourse is increasingly confined to 30-second barrages. The television "spot" is the haiku of political thought. Much must be crammed into 30 seconds, but even more must be inferred when the message is received and unpacked in the mind of the voter.

The chapters in these volumes examine the artifice of the televised political ad and attempt to peer into the minds of the voters who view them. This work is the labor of the National Political Advertising Research Project (NPARP). NPARP's mission was to study the psychological and symbolic processing of political advertising.

Back in the spring of 1987, I felt that we needed a better understanding of how these ads structure political information and how that information is represented in the minds of voters. Through the generous assistance of the Gannett Foundation, funding was obtained to support research projects at universities and research centers around the country. The project was administered by the Center for Research in Journalism and Mass Communication at the University of North Carolina at Chapel Hill.

The NPARP focused solely on television advertising. Television is the most influential political advertising medium. We reasoned that to better understand the psychological processing of political advertising, it was first necessary to better understand the processing of television as a medium.

From a pool of over 80 research proposals, a group of 17 was chosen for funding. They constituted a team whose research goals were most focused on the mission of the project. The project sought research that was theory driven and would advance our fundamental understanding of how political ads interact with cognitive structures and what role the medium of television plays in those cognitions. It was also important to understand the social circulation of the codes of representation found in ads and political discourse. It was clear that progress toward a better understanding of the political ad could only come about through the simultaneous application of various theoretical and methodological paradigms. The contents of volumes 1 and 2 reflect this philosophy.

A project like this always involves the assistance and good graces of a number of bright and supportive people. I know all the participants are very grateful that support of their research was made possible through the help of Gerald Sass of the Gannett Foundation and Richard Cole, Dean of the School of Journalism at the University of North Carolina. I personally would like to acknowledge the assistance of a number of colleagues and research assistants, who at one time or another helped keep me from sinking in a sea of paper: Rich Beckman, Tom Bowers, Sara Carpenter, Prabu David, Juming Hu, Joe Keefer, Phil Myers, Jane Rhodes, and Mary Alice Sentman. I also want to acknowledge the help and patience of my most treasured colleague, Zena Biocca.

Frank Biocca
Project Director
National Political Advertising Research Project
Center for Research in Journalism and Mass Communication

I

Viewing Political Television: Models and Theories

1

In Search of the Model Model: Political Science Versus Political Advertising Perspectives on Voter Decision Making

John Boiney
David L. Paletz
Duke University

Voting is at the heart of democracy. Naturally and inevitably, various political thinkers have long labored to identify and explain the crucial determinants of Americans' voting decisions. From the Columbia school in 1940, down to the present, social scientists have sought not only to unravel but also to model the processes by which voters make their choices.

Certain political activists have been struggling with the same task even longer, attempting to influence election outcomes by using the media to communicate with the voters. Known nowadays as campaign consultants or perhaps more colloquially as "media gurus," they too possess, at least implicitly, models of the voters' decision-making processes.

Surprisingly, the models of these two groups have never been compared, nor their differences and similarities mapped and explained. It is to such a comparative task that this chapter is devoted.

To facilitate comparison of the models, we need to establish common terms. There are five elements found in most political science models that are of continuing theoretical importance. These are partisan identification, candidate issue positions, candidate image, voter group membership, and retrospective voting. These have also been explored, although more indirectly and sporadically, in the political advertising literature. We deploy them to organize analysis throughout the chapter and directly to compare the political science to the political advertising models.

The chapter is divided into three sections. First, we review the major

3

political science models, drawing conclusions about the current state of the literature regarding each of the five factors. Second, we survey the political advertising literature that, although extensive, does not attempt specifically to outline a model of the process by which voters decide for whom to vote. Nonetheless, some of the work is related closely enough to our task that a review is appropriate and conclusions possible.

Finally, having revealed a number of gaps in the political advertising literature, we attempt to fill some of them in with our own original research. We present and discuss the findings of our exploratory study coding the content of 196 political advertisements in terms of the five elements. In effect, we outline the current model of voter choice held implicitly by political consultants as represented in the ads they devise.

The chapter culminates with a discussion of how this consultants' model compares to that of political science. A modicum of modesty tempers our conclusions, but does not deter us from suggesting future lines of research.

POLITICAL SCIENCE

There are four variables common to most models of voter choice. First is some form of partisanship, usually understood as partisan identification or *party ID*. The term originated with *The American Voter* (Campbell, Converse, Miller, & Stokes, 1960) and was defined as a psychological attachment to one of the two major parties. Since then, the understanding of party ID has changed considerably, with concomitant change in the variable's centrality to voter decision making.

The second major factor is voter assessment of candidate—or party—issue positions. The common assumption regarding what we simply call *issues* is that voters care about what candidates or parties have done and propose to do about particular policy issues, certain economic and social problems, subjects of concern, and so forth.

A third variable we dub *candidate image* or simply *images*. This stands for the attitudes and feelings voters have toward the individuals running in a given race. Measurement of this element has varied widely over time, ranging from the open-ended likes/dislikes questions of the Michigan team to Rahn, Aldrich, Borgida, and Sullivan (1990) effort to identify three particular factors as comprising overall candidate image.

Fourth is what we call *groups*. Most prominently associated with the Columbia studies of the 1940s, this element refers to the tendency for some individuals to define themselves as members of a group—such as racial, religious, or economic—and to be influenced in their voting by that membership.

In addition to these four variables is the idea of retrospective voting. This refers to the argument that voters judge the incumbent alone (Key, 1966), or incumbent and challenger (Downs, 1957; Fiorina, 1981) by past events and actions with which these candidates are identified or associated.

The form and importance of the four variables and retrospective voting have varied considerably from the earliest voter models to the present. They can therefore be used to organize a roughly chronological review of the major models. Beginning with the Columbia school's 1940 and 1948 studies and concluding with the most recent published effort (Marcus, 1988), we sketch the development and changing status of the five elements.

The Major Models

One of the earliest attempts to model voter behavior came out of the Columbia school. Lazarsfeld, Berelson, and Gaudet (1948) conducted a panel study of 6,000 voters in Erie County, Ohio from May to November 1940.

The analysis presented voting as very stable because voters erect a "sort of protective screen" to shield out any information that might conflict with their pre-set decision. One of the most basic and primary forms of that screening is an individual's partisanship. A related major finding is that people vote "in groups," meaning they tend to follow those with whom they work, play, worship, and so on. Thus, a person's demographic characteristics provide a stable predictor of the vote. The researchers linked the two findings in an "index of partisan predisposition," constructed from such demographic dimensions as religion, residence, and socioeconomic status (SES).

Thus, at this early stage of voting study research, partisanship was an important variable not only because of its screening function, but because the Columbia scholars characterized voting as a choice between parties, not candidates. However, group membership is ultimately the central variable: It produces partisanship.

Although Downs (1957) also constructed his model in terms of the parties, it is quite different from that of the Columbia scholars. He posited a rational voter who compares what he or she believes are two programmatically consistent parties in an effort to maximize the utility he or she would receive were each in office. The voter weighs the incumbent's performance against what the challenger would have done, deriving an "expected party differential" (p. 40). If it is positive the individual votes for the incumbent, if negative, for the challenger.

Thus, although Downs' model too represents a partisan choice, it says nothing about partisanship. And an individual unmoved by group ties makes that choice. He or she uses the past in rational, issue-based terms to choose for the future.

The American Voter (Campbell et al. 1960) represents the pinnacle of the partisan approach to voting. The Michigan researchers introduced the concept with which they have become identified: partisan identification. This concept is significant for three reasons. First, it is explicitly psychological, a decided departure from both the Columbia group and Downs. Second the Michigan men determined it to be a durable and stable measure. Third, they assumed party ID represented a "perfect distillation of all events in the individual's life history that have borne upon the way in which he relates himself to a political party" (p. 34). Here, then, was a single, easily measured variable that seemed to allow scholars to tap the voter's mind.

The Michigan scholars also initiated systematic inquiry into the influence of attitudes toward the candidates. They used questions tapping likes and dislikes of parties and candidates, and categorized responses across six dimensions of "partisan attitudes." This approach heralded the coming of a new and significant variable—candidate evaluation. Although voter choice is still primarily a function of partisanship, it is no longer purely a choice between parties. The questions in the likes–dislikes survey place equal emphasis on attitudes toward candidates as toward the parties.

Kelley and Mirer (1978) extended this reasoning. They argued that voting is a simple act with a single rule: Voters tally their likes and dislikes for each party and candidate, then vote for the candidate with the highest positive number. If the tallies are equal, the voter follows his or her party identification. Applying this simple rule to SRC data for presidential elections from 1952 through 1968, the authors were able to account for voting and election outcomes much more successfully than any previous model.

It is important to note that for both the Michigan studies and Kelley and Mirer's work, issues can exert an influence. Because the original SRC questions were open-ended, the final attitudes yielded by coding ranged widely in content and sophistication. Some represented simple gut reactions, whereas others spoke specifically of stances taken on particular issues. Attitudes may, as Kelley and Mirer expressed it, "implicate issues of policy" (p. 573).

In 1966, Goldberg brought together for the first time all four major variables in one schematic model of voter choice. His recursive model had a series of causal paths all leading toward the vote. At the head of each path was a variable roughly corresponding to one of the four we have adumbrated. Party ID was once more the central element standing at the crossroads for all the other variables. It exerted the most substantial direct impact on voting, as well as considerable indirect impact via issues and candidate evaluation. Goldberg also found candidate evaluations exerted a much stronger influence than issues.

Goldberg's model was the most sophisticated yet because demographics affect partisanship, and party ID affects issue positions and candidate evaluations. Pomper (1975) extended that model by adding two crucial links. He suggested that issue positions are affected not only by party ID but by the voter's partisan predispositions (SES). More importantly, he argued that issues affect candidate evaluation. These links have two implications: a weakening of the impact of party ID, and an increase in the impact of issues.

Using data from several presidential elections, Pomper found the direct and indirect effect of party ID on the decline, issues on the rise, and the independent influence of candidate evaluations also increasing. Because transmission of party ID seemed to be weakening, Pomper concluded that voting was not a group dynamic, not a "dependent act" (pp. 200–202).

The recursive model, because it suggests that causation runs only one way, was problematic. Political scientists asked, for example, how realistic it was to suppose that issues could affect candidate evaluations without the reverse also occurring. Jackson (1975) responded with the first nonrecursive model. He simultaneously related the endogenous variables of people's issue preferences, their evaluations of the parties' positions, and the strength of their party identifications to one another. Using data from the 1964 presidential election, Jackson determined that party identification is derived not so much from social characteristics as from issue positions. He thus became the first researcher to offer evidence for the suggestion that party ID can change as easily as issue positions.

Although issues took on renewed prominence in this nonrecursive model, party ID remained the central variable. Jackson's model used four simultaneous equations, each of which was either based on or determined party identification. Party ID is an integral element of issue positions, party evaluations, and the vote. The same cannot be said for any other variable. Noteworthy, too, is the fact that candidate evaluations are nowhere in sight.

Page and Jones (1984) followed Jackson with their own nonrecursive model. Three variables—current party attachment, comparative policy distances, and comparative candidate evaluations—are endogenous.

Among the exogenous variables are demographic characteristics, past party voting, and family predispositions.

The authors took two important theoretical steps. They argued that voters compare the candidates. Then they made candidate evaluations virtually synonymous with the vote: It is the only variable having a direct impact. Page and Jones consequently continued the trend toward characterizing the voter's choice in terms of candidates rather than parties; and they place new emphasis on the voter as an individual rather than as a group member. Also worth noting is the transformation of partisan identification into *current partisan attachment,* a term making voters' relationship with their parties more transient than durable. Indeed, using data from the 1972 and 1976 presidential elections, Page and Jones found that partisan attachment (which is measured in the same way as party ID) did not exert consistent or particularly strong influence on voting.

More importantly, there was a strong reciprocal relationship between comparative policy distances and comparative candidate evaluations. Surprisingly, voters clearly alter their perceptions of the candidates' issue positions to accord with their evaluation of those candidates. The reciprocal relationship between these two variables basically shunts party attachment aside as an explanatory variable. Issues and candidate evaluations dominate party ID.

Markus and Converse (1984) were the first to model the lagged impact of party identification, issue stands, and vote on current levels of those variables. They also measured voters' perceptions of candidate personality, accelerating the trend toward personalizing the voting process. Like Page and Jones, they found that any candidate evaluations differential will largely determine the vote. Unlike Page and Jones, they revived party ID by emphasizing its pervasive, albeit indirect, role. "While partisan predispositions are unlikely to dominate the process completely . . . these loyalties appear to make repeated inputs of substantial magnitude throughout the process" (pp. 151–52).

In summary, the nonrecursive models rather dramatically changed political science's view of voting. Party ID loses its centrality, its direct influence on the vote. Candidate evaluations become the most important variable, although a link is identified between evaluations and issue positions that appears to be significant. And Markus and Converse begin to echo voices heard long ago concerning retrospective voting.

Fiorina (1981) did not echo, he shouted, by reviving retrospective voting. His model—comprising retrospective evaluations, future expectations, and previous party ID—is an attempt to test Key's (1966) "throw-the-rascals-out" theory along with Downs' notion of a rational issues voter. It also represents the culmination of the trend in party ID definition. He exorcised the psychological demons by making it a "running tally of retrospective evaluations," providing both "an explicit political basis" and "mechanism for change in party ID" (p. 90).

Fiorina's results indicate that future expectations have the strongest impact on vote choice. Retrospective evaluations can also matter, as in 1976 when then-President Gerald Ford's performance significantly affected the vote. But voter behavior generally accords more with the Downsian than with the Key model.

Fiorina represented an island in the stream of thought on voter models. Although others tend away from expressing models in terms of the parties he placed party ID at the center, in general making parties the crucial figures. Voter attitudes toward the parties as economic managers, guardians of world peace, and overseers of domestic tranquility consistently overwhelm other direct influences on the vote.

Rahn et al. (1990), although assigning a strong role to party ID, are part of the stream rushing past Fiorina. They assumed that "overall affect about the candidates summarizes judgments and feelings about issues, parties, and . . . the candidates" (p. 142). This understanding of affect is strikingly reminiscent of that held of partisan identification in *The American Voter* (Campbell, 1960), and underscores the rather dramatic shift in thinking about voter behavior.

Rahn et al.'s model represents the triumph of candidates over party not only by its assumptions and complete construction in terms of candidates, but also by the finding that the direct influence of affect toward the candidates accounts for half the variation in vote (see their Table 5). Still, party ID retains a vital role: It exerts an indirect effect on vote through competence, personal qualities, and affect; and its direct effect approaches that of affect (Table 5 also).

Like Markus and Converse, Rahn et al. frame the voting decision as a comparative one: The voter compares the two candidates to each other and to him or herself in terms of issue positions. Thus, issue positions exert influence on the vote, but indirectly (i.e., through candidate evaluation).

The final attempt to deal with the decision-making process of individual voters we discuss comes from Marcus (1988). His main goal was to characterize the emotional reactions of individuals to presidential candidates. He identified two dimensions: threat, referring to anger, fear, unease, and reactions of disgust; and mastery, referring to feelings of hope, pride, and sympathy.

Marcus found that issue appraisals have no influence on the mastery dimension, a significant one on threat. Mastery, however, more strongly influences the vote than does threat. His conclusion in terms of the elements being examined in this chapter was straightforward: "elections turn more on moral leadership and leadership competence and less on issues" (p. 775).

Marcus also found partisanship exerting a significant influence on the vote, although it lags behind personal evaluations. He thus echoed the findings of Rahn et al., although partisanship is a less important part of his scheme.

The Five Elements Appraised

Based on our review of representative and distinctive political science models of voter choice from the 1940s to 1988, we derive the following contemporary composite model.

1. Partisan identification remains a central variable significantly affecting the vote, but its importance has declined rather steadily.
2. Candidate image has grown in significance as party has declined. Models are now constructed in terms of candidates and there is strong, consistent evidence that image is the primary factor affecting the vote.
3. Candidate issue positions contribute to candidate evaluations. Indeed, issues and personal evaluations are hard to separate empirically. What is clear is that issue positions are secondary in influence to candidate image.
4. The firmest finding regarding retrospective voting seems to be Fiorina's that it conforms to the Downsian model (i.e., voters use retrospective evaluations to make prospective judgments in a comparative voting act).
5. The assumption of most models seems to be that voters act as isolated individuals, relatively free of both partisan and group influences. However, conclusions about group influence must be tempered by the recognition that models do not explicitly argue group membership is unimportant.

THE POLITICAL ADVERTISING LITERATURE

Evidence from the political advertising literature about the determinants of voting is sporadic and generally indirect. Most of it concerns the relative proportions of issue and image material in advertising.

The issues-versus-image debate has usually arisen in response to the prominence of ads in particular campaigns and elections, and has focused around the ads' supposed manipulation of voters and assumed deleterious effects on U.S. democracy. Fueling the controversy have been a spate of "how-to" political consulting books (Napolitan, 1972; Schwartz, 1973; Wyckoff, 1968) and such notorious ads as the "Daisy Spot" for Lyndon Johnson in 1964 and the George Bush 1988 campaign revolving door ad. There is concern that ads can and do ignore or trivialize serious issues, helping instead to create or at least facilitate the election of candidates who are more fantasy than substance. At their worst, the ads are alleged to seduce the public and to rape democracy. The first scholarly attempts to measure the menace generated some surprising results. Patterson and McClure (1976), comparing the content of television news broadcasts and political spot ads, asserted that although the latter had more issue content, they had virtually no impact on the public's evaluation of candidate image. Instead, ads appeared to serve an informative function.

Patterson and McClure's findings were quickly substantiated by other studies: Hofstetter, Zukin, and Buss (1978), that ads increased viewers' levels of information; Hofstetter and Zukin (1979), that news provided less issue material; and Joslyn (1980), that mentions of issues were more prevalent in the ads than candidate qualities.

More recent studies, however, feed anxieties. Chagall (1981) titled his study of consultants *The Kingmakers,* returning on several occasions to consultant Joseph Napolitan's quote that "emotions control every campaign." Diamond and Bates (1988), after surveying several hundred ads used between 1952 and 1984, concluded that soft, emotional appeals have replaced issue-oriented, hard-sell ads. Benze and DeClercq (1985) found image content more prevalent than issues for candidates of both sexes.

Joslyn (1986) generated similar results with his typology of advertising "approaches." In his analysis, ads can contain four types of elements: prospective, focusing on issue content and position taking; retrospective, which is less "responsible," focusing on credit claiming and blame placing; benevolent leader, emphasizing candidate qualities; and election-as-ritual, with melodramatic appeals that push agreeable values or political symbols. Much to his dismay, the most issue-oriented type, prospective, is least prevalent. Retrospective ads dominate, followed very closely by benevolent leader.

Symptomatic of the gulf between the political scientists constructing models of the voting process and those writing about election campaigns and the actual doings of campaign consultants, the issues-versus-image debate has missed a crucial point made repeatedly by practitioners: Issues not only can be, but are consistently used to sell candidate image (Napolitan, 1972; Schwartz, 1973; Wyckoff, 1968). This point was recently reiterated by Rudd (1986). After working inside a 1982 gubernatorial campaign as creative consultant, he noted that several ads were designed to suggest a candidate's concern about an issue without revealing specific stances. The concern was framed to improve the candidate's image in basic human values, personality, or leadership.

A final issue in the issues–images controversy is their respective content. What issues are most prevalent? Which candidate qualities are most commonly used to convey image? Although the "Red Menace" was a significant issue in the 1950s and early 1960s and intermittent thereafter, domestic themes dominate. Issue ads raise concerns close to home, commonly the economy (Shyles, 1983). Image content too tends consistently to stress the same attributes, with a wider range than for issues. Leadership, honesty, competence, and strength appear to be primary (Joslyn, 1980; Nimmo & Savage, 1976; Shyles, 1983a), although the lack of consensus among researchers about which set of attributes to investigate precludes definitive conclusions.

Beyond issues versus image, few political advertising studies bear on the five elements examined in this chapter. Although the mass media are used to gain the attention of large numbers of people and can be easily targeted to specific segments of the population, surprisingly few studies have discussed the nature of group appeals in ads. Joslyn's (1980) content coding revealed that references to groups were quite common, falling just behind issues and images. Diamond and Bates (1988) pointed out that "high-tech" developments have allowed advertisers to direct their ads more effectively and to conclude that targeting is increasingly common.

The theory of retrospective voting has also received remarkably little attention. Joslyn's 1986 study is the only one explicitly to look at ad content in retrospective terms. As noted, he found it to be the most widely employed among his four types, with 60% of all ads in his sample containing some kind of retrospective appeal.

Partisan appeals have also been neglected. Joslyn (1980) did find that ads have over time become less partisan, less issue-oriented and more group-oriented. Candidates using group-oriented ads, moreover, were more likely to win than those whose ads relied on partisan or personal qualities appeals.

We do not mean to suggest by the brevity of this review that the political advertising literature is sparse. The field abounds with historical, descriptive, and experimental studies. To those already cited, we would add the contributions of Nimmo and Savage (1976), Spero (1980), and Jamieson (1984). In particular, Lynda Lee Kaid (1986) stands as a prominent researcher and editor, talents most notably displayed in the invaluable collection, *New Perspectives on Political Advertising*.

Generalizations

Our survey of the limited political advertising literature on our five elements permits the following generalizations:

1. Image appeals have become increasingly prominent, made either directly in the form of candidate qualities or conveyed indirectly using issues.
2. Advertisers assume that retrospective voting is the norm, with prospective voting virtually nonexistent. But this conclusion is based on just one study.
3. Group appeals are quite prevalent, although less than issue and image ones. Advertisers apparently believe that targeting groups via ad content and placement can be an effective strategy.
4. Ads rely less and less on issue appeals, which suggests advertisers believe voters have become less concerned with, or at least are not easily swayed by, candidates' issue positions.
5. Advertisers seem to feel partisanship is, like issues, a cue relied on less and less by voters. The limited data available suggest it is the least important of the four model variables.

The political advertising and political science literature concur on some important points. Partisan identification is a decreasingly important variable, whereas candidate image is increasingly significant. Ads are becoming less issue-oriented as time goes on. Retrospective voting appears to be the dominant mode of voter decision making.

The two literatures also diverge significantly. That of political advertising continues to see group appeals as significant. Conversely, it provides an even weaker contemporary role for party ID than do the political science models.

The political advertising literature has one debilitating shortcoming: It never derives an integrated theory or model of people's voting decision processes and calculations out of its findings on each of the five elements in question. There have been no attempts to distill from the content of political advertising the assumptions about voter behavior—about what people think is important in deciding to vote for one candidate rather than another (or not to vote at all)—that would seem to underlie that content. Our study is a first step toward this essential and desirable project.

A NEW STUDY OF POLITICAL ADVERTISING

Our goal in designing this exploratory study was to identify and outline the model of voter behavior held by political advertisers through an analysis of the actual ads they produce and show. By coding the content of ads in terms of issues, candidate image, partisanship, group references, and retrospective voting we hoped to discover the prevalence of each element in ads in general and hence how salient and important advertisers feel each is to the voters.

We created and applied our code, then, to answer two heretofore unexplored questions: Is there a model of voter behavior by which political advertisers guide their efforts and, if so, how does it compare to the composite model we have derived from political science?

Procedures

We acquired 196 televised political advertisements from 1984 general election races for three electoral levels: presidential (Ronald Reagan vs. Walter Mondale), U.S. Senate (North Carolina race between Jesse Helms [R] and Jim Hunt [D], and U.S. House (Connecticut third district race between Bruce Morrison [D] and Larry DeNardis [R]). This set of ads, with the exception of those from the Hunt–Helms race, was procured from the University of Oklahoma archives and represents, to the best of our knowledge, all ads televised on behalf of the candidates (see Table 1.1).

We developed an elaborate content-analysis scheme and coded a wide range of items. Here we limit our discussion to the relatively small subset directly relevant to this study. These are divided into five sections corresponding to the five voter model elements as follows:

Issues: Primary and secondary policy areas mentioned in each ad; specificity of stance taken by candidate on mentioned policy; and primary content of each ad.
Candidate Evaluations: Personal qualities assigned to candidate; primary content of each ad.
Retrospective Voting: References to past conditions, statements, behaviors, performance; references to the future; and number of references to candidate and opponent.

Table 1.1 Number of Ads and Length, by Candidate

	Ads	$<=15$ sec.	15–30 sec.	31–60 sec.	1–2 min.	longer
Reagan	46	0	32	11	0	3
Mondale	28	0	25	0	0	3
Helms	56	12	43	1	0	0
Hunt	45	1	38	4	1	1
Morrison	11	0	11	0	0	0
DeNardis	10	0	10	0	0	0

Partisanship: Number of references to candidate's and opponent's party.
Groups: Groups represented in or targeted by the ad.

Two graduate students, one in political science the other in marketing, and an undergraduate experienced in analyzing film, were hired to do the coding. Coding was completed within 2 weeks. For the items just listed on which this chapter is based, reliability percentages were respectively 93 for intracoder, 80 for intercoder.[1]

This reliability level, although acceptable, could be better. Coding, however, was extremely complex, as we asked our assistants to code 82 items for each ad. We also attempted not only to tap hitherto unexamined areas but also to measure content of previously examined areas more completely. So, although we expect to perfect the content-analysis code and procedures in the future, we candidly acknowledge that the results of this study are more suggestive of potentially fruitful lines of future endeavor than definitive.

To generate the most useful data, we compiled the coding of each variable and recorded the frequency with which each option was selected. We thus realized a set of data showing the relative frequencies of all coding options. For instance, the procedure revealed that for all ads, of the policy areas mentioned, 56% dealt with the economy, 16% with redistributive programs, and so on. These data then enable us to determine if the relative importance assigned each element in the political advertising model is the same as that for each in the political science model.

We confronted an intriguing dilemma, however. Most of the political science model conclusions are based on analyses of data from voting at the presidential electoral level only.[2] Our data, on the other hand, represent advertising for candidates in presidential, U.S. Senate, and House of Representatives' races. But is voter behavior constant across electoral levels? Do voters use the same elements in the same way when they select a president as when they select a congressman?

Rather than assume an affirmative answer to those questions, we present data for all ads, and also for each electoral-level subset. If this

---

[1]Reliability was determined using a subset of 19 ads (17 for intracoder). Coding for each variable was compared and the number of differences for each across the 19 ads were totalled. Reliability = 1-(NDIF/NVARS/NADS), where NDIF represents the total number of differences, NVARS the total number of variables, and NADS the number of variables on which the procedure is based. This method is a variation on that discussed by Holsti (1969).

[2]Fiorina (1981) and Kelley and Mirer (1974) are exceptions, both having applied their models in part to Congressional elections.

approach reveals important differences in the structure of ads at different electoral levels, it indicates that political scientists are missing much of the voting picture by looking only at presidential data. If not, it suggests something even more important, namely that voter behavior is quite consistent and predictable across election levels—at least as measured by our set of ads.

We look at two dimensions of the five elements. One involves partisanship, issues, candidate evaluations, and groups as they compete in effect against one another for influence on the individual voting decision. The second concerns how those elements are used by voters. One way is retrospectively, by evaluating the candidates based on past events, actions, outcomes? Another is, as Downs suggested, to compare the candidates in a forward-looking evaluation of each.

Results

We present the results of our analysis of the ads as conclusions about voter behavior. A significant summary conclusion is followed by a series of supporting conclusions and data concerning each of the five model elements.

Summary Conclusion: Ads from all electoral levels can be represented by one model of voter behavior.

Supporting Conclusions and Data: 1. Most Citizens Vote Retrospectively. They look to past conditions, statements, behaviors, and performance in reaching the vote decision. Whether this voting conforms more with Key's or Downs' theory is unclear, although indirect evidence tends to support Downs.

Ads at all electoral levels refer primarily to the past. Conversely, few ads refer *primarily* to the future. But, if Downs is right that voters use information from the past as a guide to making future-oriented evaluations, advertisers, although devoting much of a given ad to the past, should use its contents as a basis for alluding to the future. So indeed they do: Although few ads refer *primarily* to the future, many make at least some reference to it (see Table 1.2).

Table 1.2 Percentage of Ads Referring to the Past, to Future

	All	Presidential	Senate	House
Primarily to past	75	60	81	91
Primarilily to future	18	27	14	5
At all to future	68	87	54	71

Table 1.3 Percentage of Ads Referring to Candidate and Opponent

	All	Presidential	Senate	House
Mention both	47	31	57	52
Mention both equally	22	19	21	29

Table 1.4 Percentage Assigning Personal Qualities to the Candidate

	All	Presidential	Senate	House
At least one quality	71	89	55	91
At least two qualities	51	53	46	67
Three or more qualities	35	26	41	43

Downs also argued that voters compare the two candidates in a general election, rather than evaluating only the incumbent, as Key proposed. Based on our sample of ads, it is clear that the advertisers encourage such candidate comparisons in favor, obviously, of the sponsoring candidate. Almost half of the ads mentioned both candidates, and some 22% explicitly compare them, mentioning both with approximately the same frequency, generally concerning their positions on some policy (see Table 1.3).

Ads also invite comparison in different ways. Some merely mention the opponent. Others follow a litany of charges against that antagonist with a saccharinely favorable characterization of the sponsoring candidate. Even ads devoted to promoting a candidate may elicit comparison with a tagline that in effect asks, "Isn't the choice obvious?" Or, as in many of the 1984 Republican ads, "Why would we ever want to return to where we were less than 4 short years ago?" And ads mentioning neither candidate may still be clever enough to elicit comparison of the two on a wide range of concerns.

2. Of the Other Four Elements, Candidate Evaluations (Image) are Most Important to the Vote. Some 71% of all ads across all levels assign at least one personal quality to the sponsoring candidate, and 51% allocate two. As shown in Table 1.4, that "image" content is wide and deep.

In contrast, issue content is wide but not nearly so pervasive: Ads devoted exclusively to personal qualities are always more prevalent than those devoted to issues (see Table 1.5), and very few ads at any level have secondary policy content (see Table 1.6).[3]

---

[3]Coders were instructed to identify as the primary policy area that to which the most time was devoted. To qualify as secondary, the area needed to consume at least one quarter of the ad's time. The one quarter guideline is an approximation only. No attempt

Table 1.5   Percentage of "Exclusive" Ads

	All	Presidential	Senate	House
All image	18	14	16	38
All issues	5	6	4	5

Table 1.6   Percentage of Ads With Policy Content and Stances

	All	Presidential	Senate	House
Primary policy	76	84	73	57
Stance taken	60	65	51	92
vague	61	66	58	55
specific	8	8	10	0
Secondary policy	10	13	9	5

Thus, although advertisers clearly recognize the importance or at least the necessity of invoking a few policy issues, their attempts to bolster, if not create, candidate image are more complex and persistent.

3. Voters are Quite Concerned With Certain Issues and Attend to the Positions the Candidates Take on Them. Table 1.6 shows that the majority of ads at all levels have a primary policy area. Further, when a primary policy exists, candidates take a position on it more often than not.[4] But most of those stances are vague. Viewers encountering one of our 196 ads when watching television stood about a 50–50 chance of hearing a candidate take an issue position—the chance of that stance being specific was practically zero.[5]

Advertisers, and no doubt candidates, obviously believe that some issues are or can be made important to voters. They therefore invoke such issues but vaguely or vacuously enough so that the maximum

---

was made to actually determine how much time was devoted to each policy area. Generally speaking, it was very clear which policy area was primary and which secondary. In fact, most ads did not even have a secondary policy area.

[4]The fact that a greater percentage of Senate ads have a primary policy than assign at least one personal quality to the candidate suggests for those ads that personal evaluations are secondary to policy stances. However, the magnitude of policy's "advantage" over personal qualities is diminished considerably because the personal qualities content is more pervasive than that of policy. And for the Senate as for all other ads, those exclusively devoted to personal qualities far outnumber those exclusively devoted to policy.

[5]Stances were coded as "vague" if they did not include a means for taking action on an issue. Such stances constitute little more than acknowledgment that a need exists (i.e., "I will work for better health care"). A specific stance is a detailed policy proposal, a promise the candidate will have to keep, or a claim the accuracy of which can be confirmed (i.e., "To keep the system afloat, I would tax the social security benefits of the rich").

Table 1.7 Percentage of Ads Mentioning Partisanship

	All	Presidential	Senate	House
Of candidate	2	4	1	0
Of opponent	6	13	2	0

number of voters can encounter material favoring the sponsoring candidate in the message.[6]

4. Citizens Tend to Vote as Part of a Group, but the Influence of Group Membership is Secondary to Issue Concerns. Ads usually attempt to target societal groups. Some consciously target "everybody." They are populated by people emblematic of major segments of society. Thus, a single Reagan ad contained a Black woman, a young White woman, an older White woman, a young Black man, a young White man, a Hispanic man, a construction worker, and a farmer. A plurality of ads at all levels engaged in this kind of targeting, ranging from 35% of House ads to 49% of presidential.

A minority of the ads were narrower, directed at specific groups. Most of those attempts across all levels focus either on the elderly (their fears of cuts in Social Security benefits), or economic classes.

We rank groups second in importance to issues because the ads seemed to assume, no doubt correctly, that group influence is exerted through policy preferences. It could be argued, for example, that Jews vote overwhelming Democratic because they believe Democratic candidates share their policy preferences. Similarly, voters overwhelmingly vote for candidates who are known to support, even identify with, programs favorable to their interests. No need for ads to make the connection explicit. Some voters moreover, gravitate to candidates of similar ethnic background, particularly if that candidate is the only such one in the race. In the 1984 and 1988 Democratic presidential primaries, Jesse Jackson was the overwhelming benefactor of Black support.

5. Partisanship Seems to Exert Little Influence on How Citizens Decide for Whom to Vote. Most ads make no mention at all of the candidate's party and are only slightly more likely to mention the opponent's party (see Table 1.7).

THE MODELS COMPARED

Deriving a model of voter decision making from a set of advertisements is not without problems. Nonetheless, we believe our results are sugges-

---

[6]Page (1978) labeled this incentive structure "emphasis allocation theory" (p. 178).

tive, if not compelling. For, the way we have represented each of the five model elements in the ads is plausible; and the data we have presented are strong enough to counter doubts about coding reliability.

How then do our composite models, representing 1984 political advertising and political science respectively, compare? The two are intriguingly close in many respects. Both tend to support Downs' rather than Key's theory of retrospective voting. Both agree on the pre-eminence of candidate evaluations. The political science literature is moving steadily in the direction exemplified by Rahn et al. (1990), who constructed their model in terms of candidates rather than parties, and who found evaluation exerting the strongest influence on the vote.

The models also agree on the secondary importance of issues and stances. Clearly these matter to many voters, but how distinct a dimension they represent is unclear. Are they instead an integral part of candidate evaluations? Our data do not answer this question.

The models appear dramatically to diverge on the importance of partisanship. Party ID, although its significance has fluctuated over time and diminished somewhat in recent years, is the most constant element of the political science models. By contrast, in the advertisers' model of voter calculations we have derived from our set of ads, partisanship is unimportant.

The divergence in the significance of partisanship leads to differences in the importance of appeals to groups in the two models. Based on our ads, groups are quite important to the voting decision, even if only indirectly through issues positions. Advertisers go to great lengths to appeal to, or at least avoid alienating, societal groups. The status of groups in political science models is less clear, but they do not enjoy the attention accorded any of the other major elements we have discussed.

The Differences Considered

First groups. Clearly, political science models tend to underestimate the extent to which candidates appeal to societal groups. On the other hand, appeals to group allegiances in the ads may be fewer than our analysis admits. One could argue that inhabiting ads with emblems of various elements of American society is not really synonymous with making specific group appeals.

Nonetheless, our detailed examination of the 1984 ads indicates that group appeals are pervasive and often subtle. For example, one Mondale ad attempted to elicit anxiety among property owners by picturing a home shrouded in darkness, being slowly closed in on by the camera whilst a somber voice related the perils of ownership under the Reagan administration. The ad attempted to expose what it viewed as the dark side of the nation's economic health by suggesting to the nation's stable, property-conscious middle class that things are less than idyllic.

A less subtle tactic adopted by both presidential campaigns was to duplicate the "pictures" of an ad, backing one with an English script and the other with a Spanish one in an effort to target the burgeoning Spanish-speaking electorate.

Finally, although we were unable to examine this factor, it is well known that campaigns have at their disposal increasingly sophisticated methods for targeting ads. They can selectively purchase time slots on television and radio, knowing certain groups watch at certain times. They also direct certain ads to particular geographic areas in an effort to tap narrower regional or local interests.

As for party identification, we suspect that it is a more important determinant of voting than the political advertising model allows. One reason for its relative absence from ads in 1984 may have been because the consultants assumed the electorate knew the candidates' party affiliations. The ad-makers may also believe that partisanship is a particularly stable attitude, more emotionally based, deeply held, and more impervious to change by direct advertising appeals through the mass media, than many other attitudes. It is thus either a factor working in favor of or against the advertiser. Because advertisers devote their resources to susceptible aspects of the voting decision, a frontal assault on partisanship becomes an unwise investment.

So our model of advertising may not accurately reflect the importance of partisanship to voting. But, if advertisers continually attempt to influence voting by not talking about partisanship, they could be reducing party ID's importance to voting. As the election dialogue takes place more and more through mass media and paid advertising, the absence of partisanship from that dialogue is likely to contribute to its further decline among those who depend on that dialogue for information. That party identification is atrophying is acknowledged by most recent political science models. The absence of partisanship in political advertising may be a herald and a cause, influencing, in turn, both the electorate's voting decision processes and the models of these processes devised by researchers.

There is one other (at least) very important difference between the political advertising and political science models. The former contain all the elements of the latter, but the reverse is not true. This discrepancy is crucial. One point that emerges vividly from the publications containing consultants' comments on their means and motives, tactics and techniques, is that advertising targets viewers' emotions. "Hot buttons":

everyone has them and advertising attempts to press them.[7] Ads are designed for the client's benefit in a wondrous variety of ways to manipulate viewers' actual and latent emotions.

The power of these appeals, and the reason political scientists have not yet adequately attempted, let alone succeeded, in capturing and quantifying their influence, lies in the ways the ads tap and use emotions nonverbally. Particularly through visual images, sound tracks, camera angles, editing, and colors, advertisers consciously attempt to paint a picture, tell a story, create a feeling with which many viewers can resonate or, even better, identify. The intent is to give each ad a "feel" to which the voter can emotively react; which capitalizes on voters' emotions in ways benefiting the candidate.[8]

As one example, a 1984 Mondale ad contained footage shot from step level of a stereotypical bureaucratic structure of a horde of briefcase-toting professionals trotting down to their waiting limousines. Meanwhile, the narrator intoned about the perils of lobbyists living high off the hog fattened by Ronald Reagan's policies. The camera angle gave viewers the impression they were being overrun, even stomped on, by those lobbyists, whose faces were never shown even as they entered their limos that seemed to drive off over the camera (and viewers). The clear intent was to arouse apprehension and fear, and to identify Mondale's opponent with them.

Even more emotive is "Morning in America," a classic from Ronald Reagan's 1984 campaign. It exemplified how ads can involve viewers in a story, encouraging them to identify with the protagonist, and reach the pro-Reagan conclusion designed. A typical American, probably a farmer, took off in his truck at daybreak. That image faded into a rolling montage of American symbols like the Grand Canyon and the Statue of Liberty. It also showed construction abounding, manned by all races and sexes. And it was backed by a warm voice and music. The ad closed with the same truck returning home at dusk after a long day touring the nation's attractions and saying hello to hardhats. As it presented its idealized if not mythical America, the ads provided access and identification for the viewer/voter. Impact was enhanced by adroit camera angles and the "plot's" visual and logical symmetry: the farmer departs, the farmer returns.

The most recent political science models, notably Rahn et al. and Marcus are beginning to tap into emotion by using more sophisticated scaling techniques to assess voter reactions to candidates. Still, these techniques automatically delimit the range of responses for the voter.

---

[7] Diamond and Bates (1988), passim.
[8] Sabato (1981) made this last point.

Furthermore, they attempt to attach words to reactions that resist such categorization, which the voter is unwilling to share, or that function only in the voter's subconscious.

CONCLUSIONS AND FUTURE DIRECTIONS

Political science models tend to be based on voters' behavior in the most recent elections and then modified to incorporate or reflect voters' decisions and what seems to influence them in subsequent elections. In other words, the models follow voting trends, especially those in presidential elections.

Following such trends may represent periodic detours along an otherwise progressive journey toward Truth. Our analysis indicates, however, that the political science models have failed to identify the underlying dynamics of voter behavior. Thus, future research on political advertising could help achieve a more complete model of voter behavior. In this section we briefly indicate four major directions for such research.

Political science models of voter decision-making processes could be compared to political advertising over time. This will require creating a series of models that reflect the political science voting literature from its establishment, through modifications and revisions, to its current assumptions and elements. This similarly necessitates expanding the database of ads to develop a set of "advertising models" over time parallel to the political science models. These advertising models will need to be sensitive to the election context, the candidates involved, and economic and social conditions, all of which obviously influence, if not determine, political advertising's approaches, subjects, and foci.

Our data hint at variations in advertising across electoral levels, despite interesting similarities. Future work should sample more extensively from each level, allowing factors such as candidate status, gender, and party to vary more definitively.

Analysis of the logical structure of particular advertisements could examine how they attempt to implicate viewers into their lines of reasoning and capitalize on emotions and attitudes. This analysis likely takes advantage of schema theory. It would also be fruitful to explore the logical structure of entire campaigns, for example the extent to which ads in a given campaign are sequenced.

Finally, and most importantly, emotion clearly fulfills an integral function for political advertising. Political ads can be remarkably clever and complex in invoking emotion, yet researchers and practitioners understand surprisingly little about the process. Research devoted to assessing the prevalence and targeting of emotion in ads, categorizing emotional appeals, identifying patterns of usage, and trying to determine effects is vital.

Our search for the model model has caused us to doubt the truism that academics reside in ivory towers, out of touch with the reality of politics. For there is considerable agreement on the fundamentals of voter behavior between those who are a part of and those who study the political scene. Nonetheless, the differences we found between political advertising and models of voter behavior, the gaps in knowledge about the nature and effects of the ads themselves, reveal the necessity and the abundant opportunities for future research.

ACKNOWLEDGMENTS

The authors wish to acknowledge The National Political Advertising Project directed by Professor Frank Biocca and funded by the Gannett Foundation for essential funding; Murray Jardine, Peter Nye, Gabriel Michael Paletz, and Chris Graham for their contributions towards development of the coding scheme and coding itself; Julian Kanter, Curator of the Political Commercial Archive at the University of Oklahoma for providing many of the advertisements; Professor John Aldrich, for continuing comments; Professors Jan van Cuilenburg and Marten Brouwer, and Jan de Ridder and Karin Mulie-Velgersdijk, of the Communications Institute of the University of Amsterdam for providing facilities and support.

REFERENCES

Benze, J. G., & DeClercq, E. R. (1985). Content of television political spot ads for female candidates. *Journalism Quarterly, 62,* 278–283.

Campbell, A., Converse, P. E., Miller, W., & Stokes, D. E. (1960). *The American voter.* New York: Wiley.

Chagall, D. (1981). *The new kingmakers.* New York: Harcourt, Brace & Jovanovich.

Diamond, E., & Bates, S. (1988). *The spot* (rev. ed.). Cambridge, MA: The MIT Press.

Downs, A. (1957). *An economic theory of democracy.* New York: Harper & Row.

Fiorina, M. P. (1981). *Retrospective voting in American national elections.* New Haven, CT: Yale University Press.

Goldberg, A. S. (1966). Discerning a causal pattern among data on voting behavior. *American Political Science Review, 60,* 913–922.

Hofstetter, C. R., & Zukin, C. (1979). TV network news and advertising in the Nixon and McGovern campaigns. *Journalism Quarterly, 56,* 106–115.

Hofstetter, C. R., Zukin, C., & Buss, T. F. (1978). Political imagery and information in an age of television. *Journalism Quarterly, 55,* 562–569.

Holsti, O. R. (1969). *Content analysis for the social sciences and humanities.* Reading, MA: Addison-Wesley.

Jackson, J. E. (1975). Issues, party choices and presidential votes. *American Journal of Political Science, 19,* 161–185.

Jamieson, K. H. (1984). *Packaging the presidency.* NY: Oxford University PRess.

Joslyn, R. A. (1980). The content of political spot ads. *Journalism Quarterly, 57,* 92–98.

Joslyn, R. A. (1986). Political advertising and meaning of elections. In L. L. Kaid, D. Nimmo, & K. R. Sanders (Eds.), *New perspectives on political advertising* (pp. 139–183). Carbondale, IL: Southern Illinois Press.

Kaid, L. L., D. Nimmo and K. R. Sanders (eds.) (1986). *New perspectives on political advertising.* Carbondale, IL: Southern Illinois University Press.

Kelley, S., & Mirer, T. W. (1974). The simple act of voting. *American Political Science Review, 68,* 572–591.

Key, V. O., Jr. (1966). *The responsible electorate.* Cambridge, MA: Harvard University Press.

Lazarsfeld, P., Berelson, B., & Gaudet, H. (1948). *The people's choice.* New York: Columbia University Press.

Marcus, G. E. (1988). The structure of emotional response: 1984 presidential candidates. *American Political Science Review, 82,* 737–761.

Markus, G. B., & Converse, P. E. (1984). A dynamic simultaneous equation model of electoral choice. In R. G. Niemi & H. F. Weisberg (Eds.), *Controversies in voting behavior* (2nd ed., pp. 132–153). Washington, DC: CQ Press.

Napolitan, J. (1972). *The election game and how to win it.* New York: Doubleday.

Nimmo, D., & Savage, R. L. (1976). *Candidates and their images.* California: Goodyear.

Page, B. I. (1978). *Choices and echoes in presidential elections.* Chicago: University of Chicago Press.

Page, B. I., & Jones, C. (1984). Reciprocal effects of policy preferences, party loyalties and the vote. In R. G. Niemi & H. F. Weisberg (Eds.), *Controversies in voting behavior* (2nd ed., pp. 106–131). Washington, DC: CQ Press.

Patterson, T. E., & McClure, R. D. (1976). *The unseeing eye: Myth of television power in politics.* New York: Putnam.

Pomper, G. M. (1975). *Voter's choice.* New York: Dodd, Mead.

Rahn, W. M., Aldrich, J. H., Borgida, E., & Sullivan, J. L. (1990). A social–cognitive model of candidate appraisal. In J. Ferejohn & J. Kuklinski (Eds.), *Information and democratic processes,* (pp. 136–159) Urbana, IL: University of Illinois Press.

Rudd, R. (1986). Issues as image in political campaign commercials. *Western Journal of Speech Communication, 50,* 102–118.

Sabato, L. J. (1981). *The rise of political consultants. New ways of winning elections.* NY: Basic Books.

Schwartz, T. (1973). *The responsive chord.* Garden City, NY: Anchor Press/Doubleday.

Shyles, L. C. (1983a). Defining the "images" of presidential candidates from televised political spot advertisements. Paper presented at the International Communication Association Convention, Dallas.

Shyles, L. C. (1983b). Defining the issues of a presidential election from televised political spot advertisements. *Journal of Broadcasting, 27,* 333–343.

Shyles, L. C. (1987). *Profiling candidate images in televised political spot advertisements for 1984.* Paper presented at the meeting of the Speech Communication Association, Boston, MA.

Spero, R. (1980). *The duping of the American voter.* NY: Lippincott and Crowell.

Wyckoff, G. (1968). *The imagecandidate: American politics in the age of television.* New York: MacMillan.

2

Viewers' Mental Models of Political Messages: Toward a Theory of the Semantic Processing of Television

Frank Biocca
University of North Carolina at Chapel Hill

The battle of political commercials is a battle over meaning. Political spots struggle to realign the meanings of candidates, issues, and groups constructed in the mind of the voter. To fully grasp the function and effectiveness of the political commercial, it is necessary to better understand the interaction between the commercial and the voter. Viewed in cognitive terms, the struggle over the candidate's image is the struggle over the semantic processing of political commercials by voters. In the mind of the viewer the imagery of the political commercial is represented by networks of semantic nodes and markers radiating from a central concept, the candidate. In other words, viewers construct *mental models* (Johnson-Laird, 1983) of information presented in the commercials.

This chapter outlines a framework for studying the viewer's mental representations of political commercials. The approach points to ways in which we might better understand the viewer's moment-to-moment processing of commercials as well as the viewer's long-term memory for commercials. The approach is encapsulated in a theory of *schematic frames* presented here. This theory is also a first step toward a more general approach to the semantic processing of television.

As a content area of television, political commercials provide excellent "texts" to study. Political commercials are neat 30 second units of television. They are a distinctive genre of television content, a closed universe of styles and techniques with predictable and relatively stable structures. Their short duration allows us to more easily analyze the moment-to-moment processing of the form and content units within the ad and infer and test how these units are modeled in the mind of the viewer. Although of short duration, the political commercial is complete; it stands alone as a slice in the flow of television content. Because of this, we may more clearly see how the moment-to-moment processing of a commercial's parts might relate to the long-term memory or mental representation of the commercial. Without minimizing the enormous complexity of the psychological processes involved in the viewing of even a single frame of television, the short duration of political commercials can allow us to more easily theorize the relationship between mental processes such as inference making and the long-term traces of those processes, memory for television content.

From the communicator's viewpoint, the attempt to engineer the meanings absorbed by viewers is deliberate, sophisticated, and critical to the political process (Jamieson, 1984; Sabato, 1981). The elaborate structure of the commercial is an act of semantic engineering that attempts to connect, displace, or rearrange the network of links that connects candidates to each other and to the "issues" in the web-like structure of semantic memory.[1] The communication goals of these units of television content are clear (often), the work sophisticated (mostly), and the stakes high (very).

This chapter will a) introduce the concept of schematic frames, and b) develop a theory of how the semantic processes of the viewer are organized to construct a mental model of the political message. The end of this chapter and the chapter that follows will show how this approach to the semantic processing of political commercials can help a researcher find out how different groups of voters are reacting to the political commercial by first constructing a distribution of various possible mental models of the message, and then measuring and testing for evidence of the presence of these various mental models in specific audiences.

---

[1]Attempts have been made to represent aspects of a voter's semantic universe using traditional attitude measures and multidimensional scaling (Woelfel & Fink, 1980). This representation captures some of the relationships within categories and concepts (Rips, Shoben, & Smith, 1973). For example, if all the issues have some relationship to each other, they may be displayed in a multidimensional space.

But such multidimensional representations are not what is meant by the semantic structures discussed here. The semantic network is an individual level concept, and it is questionable whether these networks can be aggregated into a "semantic space for the electorate," assuming we could reliably and validly measure the semantic space at the individual level. But there is no reason to believe that the category, "politician," does not have a categorical structure that is definable at the level of "political culture" and whose overall structure is relatively stable and shared by most voters.

THE VOLATILE POLITICAL MESSAGE

A number of theoretical areas have observed that viewers *read* into a message. For example, this is an often repeated tenet of semiotic theory (Eco, 1976; Fiske, 1987; Harteley, 1982). The preference for this term is not accidental. The word "read" implies an active engagement with the message. The meaning of a message is not "received," it is extracted, inferred, worked on, and constructed. The audience member always "reads into" the message. In a very psychological sense, the television audience is an "active audience" (Biocca, 1988a; Levy & Windahl, 1984).

The viewers contain within them a range of possible decodings. To say this another way, a viewer's interpretation of the message is not fixed, it will vary with mood, the viewer's situation, and the programming context of the message. An often replicated finding shows how processing varies according to contexts of viewing.

It is a presupposition of psycholinguistics—a presupposition that advertising research supports (i.e. Burke reports, see also, Jacoby, Hoyer, & Sheluga, 1980; Jacoby & Hoyer, 1987)—that the meaning of a message is highly unstable and variable. These variable meanings are "read" or modeled within the mind of the viewer. The variations in viewers' psychological models ("readings") of the message may be due to:

1. socio-cultural variations in the use of codes including those used to process television. [For example, this is described in literature on "cultural schema" (Kintsch & Greene, 1978), "interpretive communities" (Lindlof, 1988; Morley, 1980a) and the presence of "sociolects" (Labov, 1972)];
2. individual differences in knowledge of the rules of reference, that is viewers vary in their competence[2] in using and trans-

---

[2]The number, specificity, and depth of codes accessed depends on the semiotic competence of the viewer. *Semiotic competence* refers to the extent to which a viewer has learned the syntactic, referential rules, and declarative knowledge base of the codes employed by a genre of communication, in this case, political commercials.

Let us use an extreme but realistic example to illustrate. When a recent immigrant with limited English language skills processes a political commercial, he or she will leave out the processing of spoken text with the exception of non-lexical information such as tone, pace, and rhetorical style (see Petty & Cacioppo, 1986, on the influence of speech variables). The individual may focus on the codes with which he or she is more familiar, the nonverbal codes of the candidate's presentation, for example. For this instantiated viewer,

lating television's codes [For example, see the discussion of "competence" and "cognitive skills" (Salomon, 1979), or the accessibility of schema (Fiske & Kinder, 1981; Fiske, Kinder, & Larter, 1983)];

3. knowledge based differences in the extent and nature of viewers' inference making [For example, schema instantiation in news and political communication (Conover & Feldman, 1986; Gunther, 1987); and

4. factors in the viewing situation that influence the allocation of attention or vary the context of semantic processing for the viewer (see discussion of "context effects," e.g., Higgins & King, 1981).

These factors represent only a subset of the variables that can influence and change the meaning of political commercials. We should expect significant variation in the meaning of the political commercial across segments of voters.

But context effects and the changing knowledge of the voter suggest that the commercial's meaning may also vary across exposures. The same viewer may "get" something different out of the political message upon repeated viewings. Each viewing will constitute a *different mental model* of the message. Each mental model would appear to be the interaction of the (a) model intended by the communicator, (b) the evolving abilities and knowledge of the individual viewer, and (c) the transient mental states of the viewer. This gives us a more dynamic and realistic view of the process of "viewing," though a slightly more complex one.

We could also benefit from talking about the video message not as some unchanging piece of digital tape but as dynamic mental phenomena. Maybe the concepts of "communicator," "message," and "viewer" could be reconceptualized so that we can more easily talk about them as *processes.* A more process oriented theory would need a theoretical vocabulary that can more easily accommodate the instability of the meaning of television messages.

Figure 2.1 presents some of the initial parameters in this reconceptualization. The message and the viewer's semantic memory are structures, but the instantiated viewer will be described as a process so that we can account for the various forces that shape the moment-to-moment mental

---

the semiotic competence of the viewer leads to major deviations from the model reader. With varying degrees and for different reasons, some limitation in the processing of the codes of a political commercial is extremely common as any advertising researcher who has tested these commercials can attest (See Jacoby, Hoyer & Sheluga, 1981).

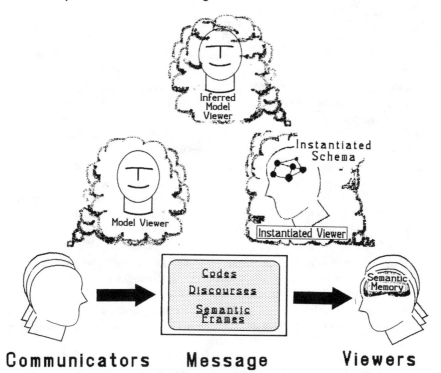

Communicators   Message   Viewers

FIGURE 2.1   At the very beginning of creating a message, communicators start with a mental model of the viewer, called the model viewer. Their assumption influences their selection of codes, discourses, and semantic frames. In a way the model viewer is embedded as a kind of program within the message.

A viewer's mental model of the message will vary across viewers and within the same viewer at different times. An instantiated viewer is constructed from the schema activiated at the time of the processing of the message. The instantiated viewer will be a product of the structure of viewer's semantic memory, the structure of the message, and viewer's inferences regarding the intended model viewer of the message.

representations of political commercials. The advantage to this approach will be that all three: the model viewer, the instantiated viewer, and the viewer's semantic memory are all psychological phenomenon. They are just three aspects of the psychological representation of the political commercial.

The Model Viewer

Many variations in the meaning of a political messages are not intended by the communicator. The communicator anticipates certain decodings by psychologically generating a model of the ultimate viewer of the commercial. This model we can call the *model viewer* (see Figure 2.1).[3]

The psychological character of the model viewer can best be appreciated by considering a similar mental model used in interpersonal communication. For example, in face-to-face communication our speech and non-verbal behavior is directed towards our theory (model) of who we are speaking to, what that person knows and believes, and how best to communicate our message (generate a specific mental representation in the mind of the listener). This model is used to predict affective reactions and anticipate the meanings (representations) the listener will decode from our words, gestures, and general rhetorical strategies. Therefore, in the very process of constructing our message, we start with a model of the other person we are about to address. The model, which is translated into a set of psychological "plans," is implicitly embedded in the structure of the message (see Clark & Clark, 1977). The feedback of face-to-face communication allows the speaker to continuously test the validity of his or her model of the listener by monitoring non-verbal cues and by searching for verbal cues of the desired interpretation of his or her statements (For example, signs of agreement or understanding such as head nods, facial expressions, eye contact).

All communication requires this kind of modeling. Similarly, at the organizational level of television programming and commercials, a great deal of time and research may be dedicated to generating a model of the "target audience." Both psychologically and organizationally, the message is designed to communicate to a communicator's model of the "typical" audience member.

While the traditional concept of the "target audience" and the text based concept of the "model reader" share some properties, there are critical differences between the two. The target audience is primarily a sociological entity defined by statistical averages of demographic, behavioral, and psychographic variables (Garreau, 1981; Wells, 1974). During the construction of the political commercial, the model viewer can be thought of as a prototype of the viewers. But it is worth underlining that the model viewer is not just some passing image in the mind of the communicator nor is it some sociological construct.

The model viewer is a psychological model in the mind of the communicator that is inserted as a *communication strategy* into the

---

[3]The phrase *model viewer* is derived from the notion of "model reader" found in semiotic theories of text processing (Eco, 1979). The medium specific term viewer is preferred here in the interest of clarity, over the more common, global application of the term reader to the processing of all media and texts.

structure of the political message. The model viewer is *implicitly embedded* in the structure of the commercial. The message is a kind of program for activating the model viewer and the processing associated with the model viewer in the mind of physical individual watching the commercial.

The Model Viewer As A Cognitive Process Within the Individual Viewer

Figure 2.1 shows the model viewer both in the mind of the communicator and in the mind of the viewer. To understand the message created by a communicator, the viewer constructs two models: (a) a model of the communicator (i.e., the communicator's intentions, motivations, and knowledge), and (b) a model of the model reader (i.e., the intended recipient of the message).

To further describe this process, let's consider the example of a message that is not working. The viewer may realize the message is not intended for him or her: i.e., it is in a different language, it makes false assumptions about his class or attitudes, it refers to things he or she does not understand, and so on. Most of us have had the experience of viewing commercials and television programs that seem directed "at someone else." How then do we process such messages? To understand "where the message is coming from" we try to decode it *as if we were the model viewer.* We make assumptions about the model viewer's reactions (For example, "This is supposed to be the sad part," or "some people probably believe this."). We can only carry out this kind of activity, if a fundamental facet of receiving communication is the construction of a model of the model viewer. It may very well be a fundamental facet of communication reception, that receivers attempt to align their decodings to what they perceive to be the intended "reading."

The Viewer Looks at the Political Commercial Through Schemata

The individual brings a great deal of pre-existing knowledge to the semantic processing of the political commercial. The meaning(s) of the message will be determined by what existing knowledge is activated and how it is activated. But the processing of the political message is influenced not just by "units" of knowledge but the way the knowledge is structured in the mind of viewer. The concept of *schema* (Rumelhart, 1980, 1983) has come to be used extensively to describe these cognitive structures.

Political commercials most often present their information within short discursive or narrative structures. It is interesting to note that much of schema theory has grown out of work on the processing of short sentences and stories (Bower & Cirilo, 1985; Mandler, 1978; Rumelhart, 1977; Schank & Abelson, 1977). Based on schema theory we can hypothesize that the viewer brings a number of schemata to bear on the processing of the semantic structure of televised messages (Brewer & Nakumura, 1983; Fiske & Taylor, 1984; Garramone, 1986; Hamil & Lodge, 1986; Lau, 1986).

From our point of view, the importance of an individual viewer's schemata comes from how the schemata influence the processing of television. Schema theory suggests that viewers automatically use social, political, and textual schema as "grids" for the processing of television. The cells of these "grids" are like variables. When a schema is activated, it determines what kind of information ("values" for the variables) will be sought and how the information will be organized (the "structure" of the grid). When information (a value for a variable) is "missing," it may be inferred from existing knowledge and placed by default into the grid (Minsky, 1975). This supply of default values is important in determining the interpretation of the message, inferences made by viewers, and ultimately the meaning of the message.

The Instantiated Viewer is the Activation of Some of the Viewer's Schemata

For any specific exposure, the actual "reading" (path of semantic activation) of a political message is defined as the *instantiated viewer* (see Figure 2.1). The concept of the instantiated viewer follows Rumelhart's (1980, 1983) usage of "instantiated schema" to describe the cognitive activation of a schema. Here, the instantiated viewer is defined as the specific set of schemata activated in one viewing of the message by an individual viewer at any one time. Viewed from "within" the mind of an individual viewer, the instantiated viewer is a pattern of semantic activation or a specific path through semantic memory taken during the processing of a specific exposure to the commercial.

This brings up an important point about our attempt to understand and measure the cognitive processing of political advertising. We are not really studying individual viewers per se, but *specific patterns of semantic activation within individual viewers*. To understand how televised political messages work we need to study television viewing not television viewers. Why should we insist on separating individuals from the patterns of semantic activation within individuals? When we look at the interaction of messages with individual viewers, we see that individual viewers do not correspond to specific or fixed patterns of semantic activation but to families of patterns. This is because these patterns of semantic activation ("meanings") vary within individuals across time points. This variation is due to the variety of contextual and maturation factors discussed above. Therefore, the *unit of analysis* is a pattern of semantic activation, not an individual.

Patterns of semantic activation, that we call the instantiated viewer, should also be the object of theories of television viewing. That pattern is, of course, not random but shaped by cognitive procedures for the application of semantic knowledge to the decoding of the political message.

To appreciate how viewers use the framing mechanisms within schema to organize semantic processes, we need to briefly consider how the structure of the typical television segment works with cognitive processes to guide the viewer's understanding of the message.

The Political Message is Composed of Codes and Semantic Frames

The political commercial is a set of codes, discourses, and semantic frames (Biocca, in press-a, in press-b). A code is a set of rules of coreference between sign units and meanings (Eco, 1976). The creation of a code is a social process (Eco, 1976), but the process of decoding is a psychological process (van Dijk & Kintsch, 1983). The encoding and decoding of a message involves the utilization of procedural knowledge (i.e. syntactic rules) and declarative knowledge, (i.e. rules of coreference between signs and referents in the semantic memory of the viewer). Television programs and messages access a great many codes including all those associated with the English language (Clark & Clark, 1977; Garnham, 1985); the syntax of television form: images, camera movement, and montage (Bordwell & Thompson, 1986; Carroll, 1980; Metz, 1974; Monaco, 1977); codes of video narrative (Bordwell, 1985); nonverbal behavioral codes (Ekman, 1974; Ekman, 1985; Kendon, 1977) (see also Fiske, 1987; Sebeok, 1986).

The semantic structures of television are guides for cognitive procedures in the mind of the viewer (see Figure 2.2). These procedures activate semantic links between a sign and concept and, more broadly, whole networks of concepts in semantic memory. Therefore, considered as a whole, the political message can be seen as a procedural map for generating a semantic process in the viewer.

In creating this procedural map, the communicator's selection of code elements (signs) is based on a set of elaborate and often unanalyzed assumptions about the isomorphism between the codes utilized in the

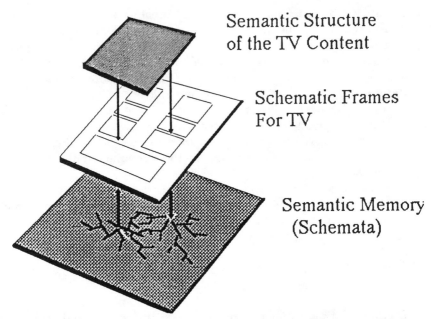

Semantic Structure
of the TV Content

Schematic Frames
For TV

Semantic Memory
(Schemata)

FIGURE 2.2. Schematic frames are sets of cognitive procedures that organize the decoding of the message. They involve the application of schemata to the semantic structure of the message.

message and the codes in the mind of the viewer. These assumptions constitute the model viewer. Codes and specific signs (i.e. a specific word, a particular facial expression, and so on) are selected on the basis of the communicator's assumption that they will activate target schema as well as the desired networks of denotations and connotations in the mind of the model viewer. Therefore, the message is a *set of strategies* to activate certain meanings, or networks of nodes in the semantic memory of the viewer.

When we look at the political message in this way, we see it as a procedural map guiding the viewer to correct selections (i.e. code selections, inferences) in a kind of giant "decision tree." What we can temporally call a "decision tree" is more aptly described as various paths of semantic activation (Collins & Loftus, 1975) through the semantic memory of the viewer. Figure 2.2 depicts this pattern of activation as a set of jagged lines extending within semantic memory.

For any single frame (shot, scene) or for any spoken word, a great many meanings are possible. To put it another way, a viewer may take various paths or decisions at each intersection of the large decision tree that constitutes the message. This condition of the message is sometimes referred to as *polysemy* (Clark & Clark, 1977; Fiske, 1987). The communicator uses strategies to not just "communicate" meaning but to *constrain* the many possible meanings (paths of semantic activation) of a picture or word and to guide the *sequencing* of meanings and associations (prime the correct sets and sequences of semantic nodes).[4]

Some psycholinguistic research uses the word *frame* to refer to the opening phrase of a sentence which orients the processing and which the rest of the text further constrains (Chafe, 1974; Clark & Clark, 1977, p. 34). For example, an establishing shot is commonly used to define a physical space prior to taking the viewer through that space. A topic sentence in a script is used to activate certain topical schema (discursive frames) in the mind of the reader. Along the way specific signs are selected because they activate certain meanings and somehow link up with the overall frame of the message (i.e. message "macrostructures": van Dijk, 1980; van Dijk, 1988a; van Dijk, 1988b). For example, words are selected over others because they evoke (activate) the right connotations (semantic structures).

In an attempt to conduct research on how a message is framed, one

---

[4]The semantic strategy that a communicator may take can vary dramatically based on the intent and semiotic skill of the communicator. One distinction identified in literary theory and the semiotic literature is the difference between "open" and "closed" texts (Eco, 1979). Texts incorporate message strategies that assume a closed or open reading by the model reader. A closed text picks a model reader, and makes strong assumptions as to the exact decoding of its various signs. It operates with a set of narrow correspondences. When it encounters aberrant decodings, these can lead to a major breakdown of authorial strategy/intent. In a contradictory way, a closed text can inadvertently lead to very open "readings" (Eco, 1979).

Open texts have a more open strategy toward their model reader. The communicator consciously or unconsciously builds into the text the possibility of the many paths in the generation of the instantiated content. The author does not attempt or assume one reading, but prepares or anticipates multiple decodings. These may be left open for aesthetic play and enjoyment. A semantic vacuum is inserted into the text to allow space for the construction of the viewer/reader. Or loose connections are made at the connotative level of the signs and less control exercised at the denotative level.

In the case of the political advertising text, openness is only relative. An attempt is made to anticipate a variety of model viewers and decoding strategies among instantiated viewers, but the goal is control over the reading and a certain amount to semantic closure. Nonetheless, many political messages flirt with openness by avoiding unambiguous statements of issue positions and policy. Image commercials may embed the major actant, the candidate, within a set of polysemic discursive frames or a possible world filled with the social mythology of nation, country, and power. This strategy assumes an open reading of the connections between the concepts and the candidate. Closure assumes and attempts to guarantee that the connotative semantic association (semantic markers) will be marked positive. If we agree with Osgood, Suci, and Tannebaum (1957) that a major dimension of meaning is the evaluative dimension, then the message strategy seeks only to fix the meaning of the commercial along this dimension. But it assumes that other dimensions of the meaning will vary in the instantiated viewer.

could begin to analyze the television message by trying to define all the codes a message carries and isolate all its signs. But given the enormous range of codes contained in a single video frame of television and the limited development of our understanding of non-linguistic and pictorial codes, this atomistic approach may not be possible or, maybe, even desirable (See Metz, 1974). A better research and theory building strategy might proceed by collapsing the plethora of codes contained even in a single video frame and to consider the message more broadly as a set of *semantic frames* (Biocca, in press-d).[5]

A semantic frame is defined as a textual or message strategy for the activation of desired schema in the mind of the viewer. The strategy is embedded[6] in the text and present in the selection, use, and sequencing of the codes of the message (van Dijk, 1988a). The semantic frame is a cue for the activation of schema in the viewer. As Reeves, Chaffee and Tims (1982) have noted in the area of political communication, "Advertisements and political rhetoric are replete with allusions to widely shared schemata that are counted upon to set in motion a predictable sequence of cognitive linkages that would produce mass behavior desired by the communicator" (p. 299). But a semantic frame is only a cue for a viewer who already possesses (has internalized) a set of television codes as part of a schema (Salomon, 1979).

The structures of the message, the use and juxtaposition of codes and signs, reveals sets of semantic frames, "gestalts" for guiding processing. As film theorists point out, "Cues are not simply random; they are organized into systems" (Bordwell & Thompson, 1986; p. 24). How the viewer uses these cues determines the meaning of the message. The viewer has cognitive structures that have been developed to use these cues.

---

[5]Van Dijk (1988b) used the term news schemata to describe the existence of the structural properties of mass media messages. But I find this use of the term schemata to be potentially confusing. Here and in the work on schema theory (Rumelhart, 1980), the term schemata refers only to psychological structures, and does not refer to structures of texts and messages. In the interest of clarity and theoretical specificity, it is probably desirable to distinguish between structural semantic properties of the message (semantic frames), semantic knowledge structures of viewers (schemata), and structural properties of moment-to-moment semantic processing (schematic frames).

[6]I am not stating here that everything in the structure of the message is part of some conscious intention of the author, communicator, agency, and so on. Some of the structure of the ad is generated by the conventions of the genre. Nonetheless, the structure is assumed to address the model reader. In the mind of the communicator, the model reader/viewer can only be perceived at any moment as an individual. But in political speech, the model reader/viewer must be a social construct. This leads much political discourse towards self-contradictory structures, terminal banality, and empty generalities.

Why the Model Viewer Never Equals the Instantiated Viewer

The goal of the communicator to activate a model viewer for the message is never achieved perfectly. That is the model viewer never perfectly equals the instantiated viewer. For this to occur exactly, the flesh and blood individual viewing the message would have to perfectly embody all the assumptions of the communicator. There would have to be a perfect alignment between the assumptions present at the encoding of the message and inferences made by individual viewer during the decoding of the message. This is unlikely.

Let us use a computer analogy to make the concept a little more intuitive. The content of the message can be discussed as an embedded cognitive program (a syntax and semantic frames). Continuing our computer analogy, we see that the message is an instruction set intended to run on a particular machine, the model viewer. The programmer (communicator) makes assumptions about the structure of the machinery, assumptions about the presence of resident programs (viewer competence with codes), and the presence of resident data (semantic knowledge). If those assumptions are not met—they are never perfectly met—the program still runs (it is instantiated) on the target machine (the viewer's mind—semantic memory). It does not precisely yield the predicted results (i.e. aberrant decodings, Eco, 1979). Communication always fails to some degree.

Nonetheless, the communicator must construct a model viewer to generate a message (even if the model viewer is but a model of himself). But the communicator's model viewer is always a bit off target, especially in mass communication. Using a statistical analogy, we can think of the model viewer as a statistical estimate with a wide confidence interval and a variable confidence level. Like the apocryphal "average American family" with 2.5 children, the model viewer may never be embodied in any instantiated viewer. For any group (interpretive community) of viewers, a specific pattern of semantic activation (set of instantiated viewers) will be more statistically probable than the others. The message's semantic frames constrain semantic activation, but they do not define it.

The Advantages of Theoretical Distinctions Between the Model Viewer, the Individual Viewer, and the Instantiated Viewer

The distinction between the model viewer, the individual viewer, and the instantiated viewer offers a number of theoretical advantages. All aspects of the communication process, the initial formulation of the political message, the message itself, the knowledge of the viewer, and final decoding of the political message can be easily discussed as psychological processes. The communicator and receiver exist as psychological constructs at each pole of the communication link.

The approach suggests that the message is not just information or a set of codes, but a cognitive program for generating a model viewer. This suggests that for a communicator to construct a successful message, he or she must make correct assumptions about the existence of cognitive procedures and data in the mind of the receiving viewer. This further suggests that an interesting topic of communication research should be the gap between the assumptions of competence and knowledge contained in the message, and the presence or absence of this competence and knowledge in the various viewers.

The approach points out that we should look at how the political message changes when those assumptions are not met. "Errors" in decoding may be more revealing about psychological processes than information "successfully" retained. This suggests related questions such as: Which incorrect assumptions are most fatal to successful communication? Are "open messages," those that make fewer assumptions about the cognitive processes of the viewer, best insulated against aberrant decoding by first assuming that these will occur (see Eco, 1979)?

The distinction between the individual viewer and the instantiated viewer is also useful. The message becomes just one pattern of semantic activation in the mind of the individual viewer. Contexts, mood, and other variables known to influence processing are assumed by the model. For any individual viewer, there will be more than one instantiated viewer depending on the context of viewing, the transitory states inside the individual viewer, and the frequency with which the message has been seen.

A further elaboration of the dynamic tension between the model viewer and instantiated viewer allows us to better model the moment-to-moment cognitive processing of the viewer. We can do this by elaborating the relationship of the semantic frames of the political message with the schematic frames of the viewer. This will be outlined in the following sections.

By looking at differences in the schemata and code competence of various viewers, we can better address how the meaning of messages vary across individuals. The gap between the model viewer and the instantiated viewer assumes that the message is unstable and varies from viewer to viewer. Variation is built into the process. Communication is not seen as the transportation of information but as the construction of mental models in the mind of the communicator and the viewer.

Finally, this approach suggests that communication and television viewing is a fascinating process of mental modeling, that communication is inherently probabilistic, and that the interpretation and meaning of television messages is varied and unstable because of the very nature of the mass communication process.

THE VIEWERS' SCHEMATIC FRAMES GUIDE THEIR
PROCESSING OF POLITICAL COMMERCIALS

Television viewing is a continuous process. The stimulus is ever changing. Cognition responds to the structure of stimulus (Carroll, 1980; Hochberg, 1986). Therefore, the cognitive processes of the viewer must also continuously change.

If the structure of the political commercial is not arbitrary and the viewer makes use of these structures, then we can hypothesize that viewers have developed cognitive procedures for processing and organizing information presented on television. The viewer's understanding of the conventions and structure of television is organized into a system adapted to the processing of television. The elements of these cognitive procedures are probably not unique to television. The system no doubt incorporates modes of understanding used to process other media and everyday experiences. For example, knowing how to follow the plot of a mystery drama must make use of skills shared with deducing plots from mystery novels or following a sequence of causally related events.

The viewer must use well learned procedures to activate schema for processing television form and content. Using the theory building approach of cognitive functionalism (Fodor, 1968; Johnson-Laird, 1983), we might be able to generate a theoretical model that can specify the high-level semantic "programs" that appear to be operative in the processing of television. Figure 2.3 depicts such a theoretical model. Each box depicts a set of cognitive procedures which text, discourse, and film processing research suggest are active in generating mental models of television messages and programs. We can call these structures *schematic frames.* They are called schematic because they access the viewer's schemata. They are frames because each extracts and and arranges specific information from the semantic frames of the message. Schematic frames are cognitive processes that organize the application of the viewer's schemata to the semantic frames (codes) of the political message.

Each frame represents a set of psychological operations. The frames in the model are suggested by existing cognitive research. The upper set of frames (see Figure 2.3) is suggested by research in the areas of psycholinguistics and discourse processing (Bower & Cirilo, 1985; Eco, 1979;

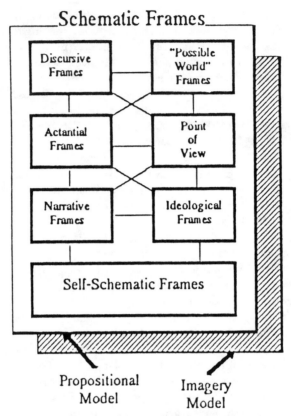

FIGURE 2.3. The schematic frames represented here are theorized to be active in the processing of television content, including political messages.

Kintsch & van Dijk, 1978; Petolfi, 1971). The ideological and self-schematic frames at the bottom have been introduced to integrate relevant findings from persuasion research on the self-referential aspects of involvement (Petty & Cacioppo, 1981, 1986; Petty, Ostrom, & Brock, 1981). Some additional features of the schematic frames are introduced to reflect the theoretical insights and research findings of film theory (Bordwell & Thompson, 1986; Branigan, 1984; Carroll, 1980; Metz, 1974).

I will proceed by first laying out the function and structure of the schematic frames, then I will discuss the operation of each frame individually.

Some General Properties of Schematic Frames

Schematic frames are "problem spaces" for calculating semantic values from the codes of television. During the viewer's moment-to-moment processing of television's many codes, larger semantic constructs are generated to model the message. Genetically determined abilities such as perceptual processing, and the viewer's learned responses to television's codes (Salomon, 1979) quickly and imperceptibly integrate information regarding the spatial structure of the represented environment, characters, events, and themes of the programming (van Dijk & Kintsch, 1983). These processes add up to the "meaning" of the political message for the viewer.

To incorporate this multilevel semantic processing, the theory posits a set schematic frames. These are conceptually similar to "problem spaces" in artificial intelligence (e.g., Newell, 1981). Problem spaces are areas (subroutines) where specific processing tasks are carried out. Here schematic frames are problem spaces used to model various dimensions of the political message.

Each schematic frame generates semantic values either from data driven processing of the codes of programming and/or schema-driven processing in which values are inferred. The different schematic frames are posited to work in parallel (Hinton & Anderson, 1981) or, using a slightly different terminology, synchronically (Sebeok, 1986).

The values calculated for the "lower" schematic frames involve deeper processing. The model shows a slice of processing time rather than a linear sequence involving the movement of processing from one frame to another. But the vertical dimension of the model suggests a hierarchy among the frames. Deeper levels of processing (Cermak & Craik, 1979) are assumed to occur in the frames "lower" down. Values in the "deeper" frames, such as the ideological frame and self-schematic frame, are generated from greater involvement and elaboration of the message (Greenwald & Leavitt, 1985; Greenwald & Pratkanis, 1984; Petty & Cacioppo, 1986).

The values in the schematic frames are calculated in cycles. The values in the schematic frames continuously change as the political message is processed. It is hypothesized that television is processed in cycles (Kintsch & van Dijk, 1978). The cycling is strongly influenced by the syntactic structure of the message (Carroll, 1980; Jarvella, 1975). A cycle is often equivalent to a scene or other "phrase" or "sentence" of video.

Semantic work carried out within the schematic frames results in lasting memory traces for the message. The semantic work is composed of decoding, semantic priming, schema activation, and inference making. The resulting memory trace will reflect the structure of schematic frames, rules of inference making (discussed later), and the pattern of activation during the cycles of semantic processing.

Viewers use both propositional and imagery models of the political messages. Although at the "machine level," that is at the level of neurons, there may be a single uniform code (Anderson, 1978), the mind appears to use different mental media to model the world and to make cognitive calculations (Johnson-Laird, 1983). Language, for example, is both an external means of communication and an internal medium for mentally modeling relations in the world (Clark & Clark, 1977; Olson, 1976; Vygotsky, 1978).

In the processing of television, it is hypothesized that viewers make use of different mental media to model the television programming. At this stage in the research, these can be divided into two general classes: (a) propositional models, and (b) imagery models.[7]

Propositional models seem well suited for much of the information contained in news and commercials. Propositional models are in fact a class of conceptual models (Johnson-Laird, 1983). They are used to capture abstract relations such as identity/non-identity, set membership, entailment, and causal relation.

Television is also rich in visual and non-linguistic aural information. The viewer must model this information. Imagery models are used to capture perceptual properties such as spatial, temporal, kinematic, dynamic, and imagistic relationships (Johnson-Laird, 1983, p. 422ff).

But how is the imagery information used and stored? The theory hypothesizes that visual imagery is stored and used as a set of key frames (Reeves, et al., 1982; Wyer & Gordon, 1984). Wyer and Gordon (1984) suggest that subjects use key frames to code continuous event sequences. The key frames capture non-propositional relations in the form of visual (or acoustic) imagery. These are used to compute relations in the moment-to-moment processing of the programming and are stored as part of the implicit memory for the programming. Key frames may store prototypical features of a scene, object or person (Wyer & Gordon, 1984, p. 104). Key frames may also be stored and used to derive further propositions about the plot, events, and characters in the programming when later processing demands necessitate a memory retrieval of the imagery models (Kosslyn, 1980).

The imagery models must somehow be linked to the propositional models of the programming. The key frames may be referred to by pointers (networked links) in propositions about political messages. The

---

[7]The propositional and imagery models should not be translated too narrowly into a popular distinction between stored "political issues" and "political images." For example, propositional models are used to store evaluative propositions about the "political image" of a candidate. Imagery models, on the other hand, can also store key frames that may be used as nodes to infer candidate "issues" and "beliefs."

pointer refers to the frame in a proposition about the message. Through the use of pointers the key frames become part of propositions about event sequences, causal attributions, and trait inferences. The possibility of some kind of key frame coding is supported by evidence that subjects better remember static images that occur close to "break points" in filmed sequences of events (Newtson & Enquist, 1976).

Viewers begin with early "bracketed models" of the message and recalculate these continuously.   All message processing involves the making of inferences and some modeling of the "intended" message, the viewer's representation of the message's *model viewer.*

> Understanding, then, may be regarded as a process whereby a listener or viewer attempts to infer the knowledge structure of a speaker or writer by using the available linguistic message, contextual information, and his own knowledge as "data structures" for which the inference is to be made (Frederiksen, 1975; cited in Jacoby & Hoyer, 1987, p. 35).

Starting in the very first milliseconds of the programming, the viewer constructs an early mental model of the overall message. The viewer does this automatically by calculating values in some of the schematic frames. This in turn primes and instantiates selected schema, leading the viewer to infer default schema consistent values (Minsky, 1975) to the other schematic frames. For example, the viewer makes inferences about the setting of the programming and the topic of the program. This may activate inferences about the type of people typical of the world of the program, and some projection about how the story of the program or commercial "will turn out."

An early model is constructed to handle and structure the incoming information. This early model is *bracketed* (Eco, 1979). The default schema and the values set for the various frames are temporally in "brackets." Their truth value or utility is tested for consistency against the incoming information (Rumelhart, 1977). This model is continuously remade as the values in the various schematic frames vary with each cycle of processing of the incoming codes of the message and with the activation of new schema (Schank, 1982). "A comprehender continually tests input propositions against the contents of the short-term memory buffer . . ." (Kintsch & van Dijk, 1978, p. 371).

Foregrounding a schematic frame will influence the values calculated in other frames.   Some of the values for the frames will be provided from the decoding of the message (data driven) whereas others will be inferred (schema driven). Modeling and inference making will lead to temporary hierarchies in the top-down processing of the schematic frames (see Figure 2.4). For any message and for any specific viewer, some of the frames may be more salient than others. The more salient frames will drive the activation of schema. This leads to the activation of schema consistent default values in the other frames (Bower & Cirilo, 1985, p. 95). For example, if an instantiated viewer believes a program segment is about "urban crime" (discursive schematic frame) the viewer may automatically make inferences about scenes he or she will see (possible world frame) and the motivations and behaviors of persons shown on the screen (actantial frame).

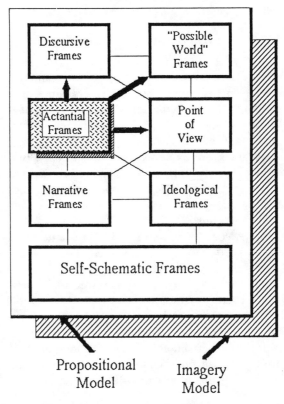

FIGURE 2.4. Goals, processing sets, or semantic priming may lead to the foregrounding of one of the schematic frames. When a schematic frame is foregrounded, it influences the calculation of semantic values in the other frames.

The term foregrounding[8] is used to describe hierarchies in semantic processing whereby a calculated value within a specific frame influences the activation of default values in the other schematic frames. The temporary foregrounding of a schematic frame may emerge from a number of causes. Enduring psychological states such as processing goals can influence the foregrounding of a frame, so can the selective processing of message channels and codes. Foregrounding may ultimately influence the structure of the memory trace of the message (Cohen, 1981).

Consider the following two examples of processing goals during the viewing of political commercials. A viewer's goal may be to understand more about the issues in a commercial or, an alternative goal, to get a general image of the candidate. An "issue set" may foreground the discursive frame and the propositional model of the commercial. Work by Garramone (1983; see also Garramone, 1986; this volume) shows that subjects adopting an issue set attend to the commercial's audio track so as to better model the linguistic propositional structure of the message. The instantiated viewer may foreground the discursive frame of the message. On the other hand, subjects whose processing goal is image formation ("image set") seek to use imagery modeling strategies. They may foreground the actantial schematic frames and rely primarily on the video track of the political ad.

Semantic priming (Carr, McCauley, Sperber, & Parmelee, 1982; Meyer & Schvaneveldt, 1976) can influence foregrounding (Biocca et al., 1987). For example, if a political commercial follows a news story about taxes, this may result in the semantic priming of the discursive frame with values related to the economy, even though that may not be a central topic of the commercial.[9]

The syntactic structure of the message (e.g., subject position in a sentence) can make some of the information more salient and result in foregrounding. An experiment by Hornby (1974) demonstrates how sentence syntax highlights information as "given" or "new," and how

---

[8]Bower and Cirilo (1985) use the concept of "subschema" to advance a similar notion of schematic hierarchy and foregrounding. But the notion of subschema does not make clear how the hierarchy might be initiated, nor is it clear what structural factors might determine superordinate and subordinate positions in schema activation.

[9]The group of schematic frames presented assumes complex inference making by the viewer. These inference making processes result in the rich and varied meanings viewers derive from commercials, but they are potential sources of major mis-communication and message distortion when schema driven inferences lead to major misalignments between the model viewer of the message and the actual instantiated viewer (Jacoby, Hoyer, & Sheluga, 1980; Jacoby & Hoyer, 1987).

this significantly influences the processing of related pictures. Subjects listened to sentences such as, "It is the BOY who is petting the cat," or, "It is the CAT which the boy is petting." Drawings of a boy or girl petting a cat or dog were shown for 1/20 of a second. Subjects had to indicate whether the sentence was true or false. The allocation of attention within the picture and the processing of the pictorial codes appeared to be driven by the syntax of the sentence. This lead to almost twice the number of errors when the contradictory detail (i.e., a dog instead of a cat) was part of the implied "given" part of the sentence.

The relative hierarchy of the schematic frames is likely to change during the processing of a program or commercial. But when the "deeper" levels of the schematic frames are activated and foregrounded (such as ideological frames or self-schematic frames), they are likely to provide stronger and more enduring top-down, schema driven processing (see Petty & Cacioppo, 1986).

HOW EACH SCHEMATIC FRAME ORGANIZES THE VIEWER'S UNDERSTANDING OF POLITICAL MESSAGES

The Possible World Frame

To the degree that a television viewer recognizes a set of characters and a spatial environment, he or she must assign the incoming stimulus to some "possible world." This concept has been introduced to cognitive psychology from the area of logical semantics (Linsky, 1971). Possible worlds are social-psychological constructs with scripted values for spatial, temporal, and actantial variables. For example, script theory's discussion of the "restaurant script" represents the kind of inferences made about people, events, and behaviors of the possible world of restaurants (Schank & Abelson, 1977).

The spatial and temporal semantic information of the possible world frame situates the message and helps decode both linguistic and non-linguistic information. Even in the first frame of a video, a great deal of semantic information is virtually present. Cognitive efficiency requires a limitation of semantic values. The information in news stories and dramas must be assigned to some context to be understood. A bracketed schematic frame assigning the context of a possible world to the incoming message helps to guide (frame) the decoding.

Political commercials, for example, make frequent reference to social worlds with predictable properties: the candidate in the world of the "farm," walking the "streets of the nation" shaking hands, or walking in the "offices of government." To process even a single frame of such an image requires the activation of a set of scene consistent scripts or schema (Schank & Abelson, 1977). Note that a possible world is not just a spatial setting for the action, it also includes a number of values for "possible" actions, characters, and behaviors appropriate in that "possible world."

"Violations" of the social or spatio-temporal code can lead the instantiated viewer to (a) reconsider his or her inference or "bracket" the possible world, (b) identify the violation as an aesthetic device, use of metaphor, or contrast used for humor (thereby, altering or further "bracketing" the possible world activated in the frame), or (c) jump to the foregrounding of an ideological frame or self-schematic frame, assign a negative truth value to information based on discrepancies, and scrutinize, criticize, or otherwise elaborate on the message.

Lest we believe that "possible worlds" for programming are relatively limited and stable, it must be remembered that programs and commercials regularly invoke various "possible worlds" that violate the physical properties of the viewer's "real" (default) world. It is common in our everyday processing of television to model worlds in which inanimate objects such as products speak; people undergo physical transformation; and where all manner of spatial, temporal, and cultural rules are varied, transformed, or violated.[10]

Discursive Schematic Frames

When a viewer encounters the information codes in a single shot, there is potentially an infinite set of meanings that can be calculated. Experiments in semantic priming (Collins & Loftus, 1975; Marcel, 1983a, 1983b) suggest that cognitive processing undergoes a rapid, highly interconnected pattern of semantic activation. Marcel (1983a, 1983b) found that *all* the meanings of a polysemic word such as "palm" (i.e. palm tree, palm of your hand, and so on) are primed in the first few *milliseconds* of processing as the cognitive system attempts to isolate one of its meanings (maximally activating a specific set of denotative and connotative nodes in a concept's semantic network of nodes). Although it is difficult to specify the precise nature of the brain's neural networks (Rumelhart, et al., 1986a, 1986b), the analogy that semantic memory is

---

[10]When viewers' original inferences regarding the possible world of the message are violated, the viewers may increase their attention to the surface structure of the message. Researchers may be able to detect evidence of increased processing effort directed towards identifying the "correct" possible world by measuring increased attention and retention of executional properties of a message when possible world inferences are in doubt and being "recalculated."

like a highly cross referenced encyclopedia (Eco, 1976, 1979) captures the interdependence and hierarchy suggested by the research into semantic processing.

In the early history of film, classic experiments on shot sequencing (Pudovkin, 1954) demonstrated how a single shot can have multiple interpretations. Meaning depended on the shot's placement in a sequence of shots. Of course, all the semantic properties of a particular shot or syntagma are not foreseen or actualized in a video sequence. But many meanings are virtually present and can be instantiated as aberrant or idiosyncratic decodings of the programming by certain viewers (See Eco, 1976, p. 139–142).

In an effort to activate the model viewer, the structure embedded by the communicator may guide the spread of semantic activation in the instantiated viewer through a series of what Eco (1979) refered to as *semantic disclosures*. The semantic disclosures assist the viewer in activating the communicator's intended semantic branching when processing specific lexemes or shots. According to Eco, "Semantic disclosures have a double role: they *blow up* certain [semantic] properties (making them textually relevant or pertinent) and *narcotize* some others" (1979, p. 23)."

Discursive schematic frames "blow up" or "narcotize" the various semantic branches of association radiating from a concept. Every message has a discursive structure, a sequence of "topics." It introduces the themes and topics as a sequence of semantic disclosures to guide semantic processing (Jacoby & Hoyer, 1987, p. 42; van Dijk, 1988b, p. 41ff). Communication conventions are set up for this process—paragraphs begin with topic sentences, and so on. Television has a discursive structure that guides the instantiated viewer through the processing of the message.

Like any complex text, a segment of television programming can have parallel discursive structures ("levels of meaning").

According to Eco (1979):

> It is imprudent to speak of *one* textual topic. In fact, a text can function on the basis of various embedded topics. There are first of all *sentence* [shot] topics; *discursive* topics at the level of short sequences [syntagmas and scenes] can rule the understanding of microstructural elements, while *narrative* topics [the commercial's "issues"] can rule the comprehension of the text at higher levels. Topics are not always explicit. Sometimes these questions are manifested at the first level, and the reader simply cooperates by reducing the frame and by blowing up the semantic properties he needs. Sometimes there are topic-markers such as titles. But many times the reader has to guess [infer] where the real topic is hidden. (p. 26)

Discursive topics can be established by the reiteration of certain words, e.g. "the economy," or by redundant use of shot sequences from the "same" semantic field: e.g., a dirty river, drains, chemical drums, or dead animals, to underline a larger discursive topic of "pollution."

There is an unwritten contract between the communicator and the viewer that a sequence of shots is united around a common theme. It is important to note that the sequence of shots comes from the "same" semantic field only because the viewer picks out a common semantic path from the semantic priming set in motion by the sequence. The viewer begins with the assumption of communication intent and semantic coherence, and seeks to uncover the discursive structure using what he or she knows (code competence) about the conventions of film and the genre of programming. It is a curious fact that a communicator could assemble a random sequence of shots and that the video could still generate a "discursive topic" for an instantiated viewer. Because of the presupposition of communication intent and structure, the viewer would make semantic connections between the random images, blowing up or narcotizing the properties of various semantic frames to emerge with a value (meaning) in the discursive schematic frame.

There is often an openness of design in the semantic frames of programming, especially commercials. A tacit assumption exists that in the ambiguous presentation of images of people and situations, the viewer will infer a set of connections, often personal ones. In commercials there is the assumption (hope?) that these positive and personal associations will be semantically linked to the concept of the brand. In this way the ambiguous commercial attempts to activate and reconfigure a network of semantic markers attached to the product.

Actantial Frames

Programming segments are sequences of propositions referring to agents, objects, and relations in some possible world. Consider the typical political commercial, that often combines the devices of news shows and product commercials. A central "agent" in almost all political ads is, of course, the candidate. A script for a political commercial might contain the following sentence, "Concerned voters vote for Harrison, a leader." During the parsing and semantic processing of this sentence, viewers may organize the information around two central nodes represented in Figure 2.5. The nodes are labelled X and Y and are connected by relation R. X node has the following subject-predicate relations attached to it: (a) X is a voter, (b) X is concerned, and (c) X is plural. Y node might be represented by the following propositional set: (a) Y is a

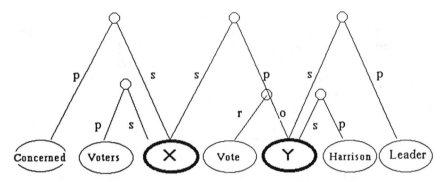

FIGURE 2.5. Nodes representing how information about a candidate presented within a single sentence might be organized in semantic memory (following Anderson, 1976).

"Harrison," and (b) Y is a "leader." These propositional sets and the diagram in Figure 2.5 represent the kind of parsing and organization (modeling) that is suggested by some sentence and text processing theories (Anderson 1976, 1980, 1981; Bower & Cirilo, 1985).

The many scenes and propositions of television programming may be organized around a similar set of referent nodes to which are attached sets of propositions. I will use the term *actant* (Greimas, 1986; Greimas & Courtes, 1982) to designate these central nodes. The concept actant is derived from linguistic and literary theory. It has properties that recommend it to an analysis of the visual and verbal cues that designate the agents and objects of political ads.[11]

The word actant is derived from the same root as the Latin word for "to do" and for "actor," one who does. But actants are not synonymous with the cast of a television segment. It is a common mistake to confuse the notion of actant with the notion of actor or character. In the "story" of a video segment, the agents and objects of propositions are picked from a typically limited set.

Let's use the example of a news story. Major political figures and celebrities are often actants within the news story. But in many news stories collective non-human entities such as "the economy," "the

---

[11]This part of the conceptual apparatus of literary theory has a number of advantages and its use here is suggested by precendents from psycholinguistic research. Many psycholinguistic terms are borrowed directly from linguistics (e.g., subject, objects, and so on). This allows researchers to easily connect psychological processes to linguistic structure. In our case, using terms from literary theory allows us to more easily make use of the theoretical tools of literary theory, and allows us to more easily connect the structures of semantic frames (the systems embedded in the message) and schematic frames (the processes activated in the mind of the viewer).

military," "Iran," can be actants. They are actants ("actors") within the news story because they are the agents or objects of casual narrative relations or central referents of sequences of propositions. Similarly, more than one actor may represent the same actant.[12]

While attempting to generate a mental model of a political commercial, the viewer will construct an organization of the actants, an *actantial structure* (Eco, 1979; Greimas, 1986). In the propositional model of the commercial, the agents and objects of the propositions constitute the actantial structure of a program (see the related notion of referential coherence graph in Kintsch & van Dijk, 1978; and propositional structures in commercials, Thorson & Synder, 1984). The viewer must construct an actantial structure (a set of referents) with which he or she organizes the propositions and relations that constitute a large part of the message of a video segment.

The importance of using the agents and objects of propositions in modeling information is indicated by the fact that 98% of the worlds languages use sentence structures where the subject occurs before the object. In 79% the subject is presented before the verb (Ultan, 1969, cited in Anderson, 1980). This suggests that the message structure has evolved to suit the kinds of processes assigned to the actantial schematic frame.

There is substantial evidence in text processing research to support the idea that the viewer models an actantial structure for the program. It appears that the modeling of each new actant (referent) takes time. For example, it takes longer to read a sentence that contains new referents (actants) than one that refers back to referents for which a node already exists (Haviland & Clark, 1974). Similarly, Kintsch and his colleagues (1975) found that given two very similar passages, the one that contained a greater number of referential repetitions (i.e. pronouns referring to previously introduced nouns) took significantly less time to read.

Research also suggests that the reader/viewer keeps a running model of the actantial structure (referential connections) in short term memory and uses this information to decode new propositions. The most recently used referents remain active in short term memory, whereas referents not currently in use are stored in long-term memory and have to be "reinstated" (Bower & Cirilo, 1985) to be used in semantic

---

[12]Take for example, a commercial involving on the street interviews with "real Americans." The individual speaking into the camera and to the viewer is rarely identified by name. In such cases, the viewer may model the actantial structure of the ad in such a way that the individuals are actantial roles for the actant, "voters," "concerned Americans," and so on. Here the actant (type) is "concerned Americans," while the individual actor is simply a token of the type. These tokens can be subsumed under the concept of actantial roles presented here.

processing. Clark and Sengul (1979) found that the time it took to understand a new sentence was related to the distance (in sentences) between the sentence when the referent was last mentioned and the new sentence. The integrating of new propositions to existing actants is elegantly revealed in text processing by patterns of regressive eye movements linking pronouns to their referents (Carpenter & Just, 1977).

Actantial Roles

The organization of information about a central actant may not be unified. This suggests that a further distinction should be made between an actant and actantial roles (Greimas, 1986; Greimas & Courtes, 1982). The actant may not be unidimensional. Evidence indicates that individuals maintain significant amounts of contradictory information within their conceptions of people such as candidates (Wyer & Gordon, 1984). Individuals may group trait and behavior information about the candidate into situationally specific dimensions (for example, specific to the context of certain possible worlds, i.e., Washington, home, sports, and so on).

In a similar fashion, an actant may have more than one actantial role in a political commercial. The key actant in a commercial, often the candidate, may play a variety of social roles: "leader of the free world," "father to Chris," "representative of the farmers," and so on. It can be easily observed that when characters are first mentioned in narrative texts, they are often introduced with a linguistic marker that foregrounds a specific actantial role, i.e., "the neighbor, Leslie" or "John, her lover."[13] The public debate in the 1988 presidential election over the "face" of Willy Horton was, in some interesting ways, an issue of the relationship between actants and actantial roles.[14]

Consider the example of political commercials. The candidate or opponent may not represent "himself" during the course of a commer-

---

[13]It is perhaps revealing of some of the points I am making in this sections, that the typical reader (my model reader) would probably have made a connection between the word "Leslie" and the pronoun, "her", and inferred (possibly visualized) a relationship between John and Leslie, although in a strictly linguistic sense, they could just as easily be processed as completely unconnected and separate examples.

[14]In the 1988 campaign the face of Willy Horton was a very good example of shifting actantial roles. A debate was launched as to whether the commercial was "racist." The debate over this commercial could be defined as, "What actantial role did the face of Willy Horton play in the Bush commercials?" The Bush campaign claimed that the face of Willy Horton merely represented a specific individual who had committed a gruesome crime of sexual violence. This argues that for the model reader, the face of Willy Horton represented nothing more than its simple denotation.

Others argued that the social schema instantiated in the mind of the viewer was not that of a relatively insignificant individual but that of the actantial role, "urban black." It would

cial. Through metaphorical or indexical semantic associations, he may play the actantial roles of "the President," "America," "an oil man," and so on. Within any specific commercial, an actant, such as the candidate may take on more than one actantial role.

In some ways, the actant is the *type,* while the actantial role is the *token* linked to specific context, and therefore, to a foregrounded subset of semantic markers. For example, when the candidate's face first appears on the screen all the semantic properties of the concept, "George Bush," can be virtually present: that he "is a" man, a Texan, an oil man, a president, married, rich, etc. Only some of these possible semantic markers will be "blown up"; the others, to use Eco's phrase, will be "narcotized." For example, in a scene from a Bush commercial called "Family" (see Biocca, this volume), Bush bent down to pick up a child. With the camera in soft focus and slow motion,[15] he raised her to the sky. In this simple semantic disclosure, a specific set of semantic nodes should be activated in the instantiated viewer. This opening scene presents a set of semantic disclosures highlighting an actantial role for the candidate/concept, "George Bush." The semantic properties linked to the actantial roles, "grandfather," "patriarch," are blown up as schema related to these roles are instantiated. This is the decoding that the model viewer should take, but, as always, it is not necessarily an automatic relation in the representation of this scene in the mind of the instantiated viewer.[16]

Another reason that the concepts of actantial role and actantial structure are useful to a theory of the semantic processing of television,

---

be unlikely that the communicators framing the commercial would be unaware that the face with its matted afro-haircut and its threatening features might activate, through its connotative connections, the broader concept of "black menace" in the minds of key groups of viewers, the white middle-class viewer. If this reading was truly the model reading, Jesse Jackson's accusation that the commercial was racist would be entirely correct. Although it may be difficult to trace the model reading of the communicator, in this case Bush's media consultants, it is possible to predict and measure the most likely decoding of an image for any interpretive community (i.e., white voters). It could be determined if the average instantiation of the actantial role of the "face of Willy Horton" was "objectively" racist.

[15]The use of soft focus and slow motion as stylistic devices is likely to trigger references to other texts (films) and to the "typical" applications of this technique. As a filmic device used in many films, soft focus is often used to connote human warmth, tenderness, a teary wistfulness. Slow motion is used to either underline a physical movement or to suggest memory or mental imagery.

[16]That same piece of film might, for example, be used as part of a physical therapy documentary on how to pick up children, or on a *60 minutes* piece on "retarded" children. The semantic branching activated in the physical therapy film would be on the movement of picking up the child. The semantic branching in the *60 Minutes* piece would be on the child and tragedy, rather than joy expressed in the shown sequence. Many segments of political commercials and other video are essentially ambiguous and take on specific meaning only in the context of other film segments and discursive structures.

is that they allow us to consider how semantic markers might be transferred from one actant to another within a commercial, as well as to how the commercial might be remembered. It is hypothesized that actants are linked (a) as terminal nodes in the proposition (see Figure 2.5), or (b) by sharing an actantial role. The latter is less obvious and requires that we consider the overall actantial structure. So we now turn to the discussion of actantial structure.

Graphing the Actantial Structure

How then might the actantial structure of a political commercial or program be modeled? Research into person perception and text processing can give us some clues as to the key components of the structure.

Figure 2.6 shows the hypothesized structure for a single actant. Note that actantial roles are seen as mediating the links between an actant and the more specific set of traits, motivations, and behaviors (semantic nodes or markers) associated with the actantial role. In a review, Wyer and Gordon (1984) concluded that, ". . . subjects may not only encode the behaviors in terms of traits but may form direct associations among the behaviors within each category. However, trait-behavior clusters may not be organized into a single configural representation of the target" (p. 132).

Information about an individual person is apparently not organized into a single configural representation of this person. Information, therefore, may not be organized around a central actant but may be organized around actantial roles. Each actant is perceived through the roles it plays. These may be differentiated on the basis of schematic links to possible worlds (i.e., his "office" roles) or sociocultural categories such as lawyer. Work by Gordon (reported in Wyer & Gordon, 1984) suggests that person information such as traits and behaviors are situationally specific and are not generalized across situations. Because information may not be organized around actants, viewers may report traits that are on the surface inconsistent but may appear more consistent when grouped by actantial role [i.e., for example, former president Reagan the gentle, private man (possible world = home, family) who cries at sentimental movies; Reagan the public man (possible world = governmental Washington), tough bomber of Libya, heartless "killer" of children].

Inferred traits/motivations[17] appear to be important in the organiza-

---

[17]The terms "motivation" and "trait" are just two words for the same inference making process in the viewer. "Motivation" and "trait" distinguish between a temporary state or a lasting predisposition. A trait is simply an enduring motivation (e.g., "greedy" as a temporary state or enduring characteristic of a person). And reciprocally, a motivation is simply a trait that is perceived to be temporary.

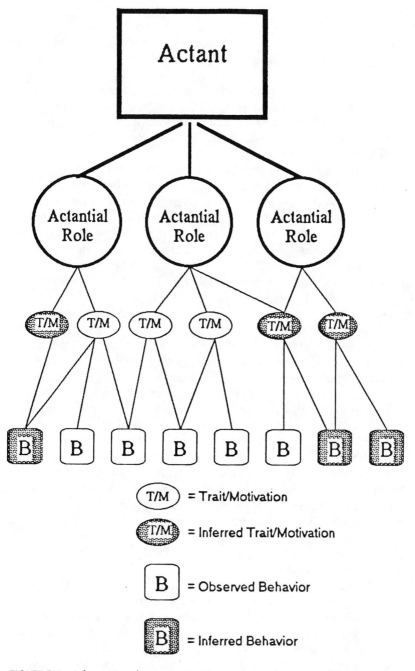

FIGURE 2.6. Information about an actant in a message (e.g., a candidate) may be organized into actantial roles. Observed or stated behaviors, traits, and motivations are organized around the actantial roles and are used to infer further traits, motivations, and behaviors of the actant.

tion and memory for observed behaviors (see Lichtenstein & Bower, 1978). The representational conventions of film and television further support the use of a cognitive procedural rule to infer traits from behaviors. In television's dramatic narratives, behaviors of actors are scripted as a means of "revealing" (semantic disclosure) the character traits of those actors. Because the behaviors of actors (actants) are used to infer traits, they may be stored in memory using links to a central node for the inferred trait.

An experiment by Brewer and Dupree (1983) supports the claim that inferred traits/motivations organize memory for behaviors. Brewer and Dupree showed two videotapes of an actress paced through a series of mundane behaviors in her apartment. In some conditions an opening sequence showed that the behavior was motivated by a goal (i.e. setting a clock). In other conditions the behaviors did not appear to be motivated by a goal. While immediate recall for behaviors was the same for each condition, delayed recall was significantly higher when the behaviors could be organized under a motivation (goal).

During data driven processing, behaviors in a videotape may be used to infer traits or motivations, but in schema driven processing viewers may use given traits (i.e. "candidate X is a farmer," "candidate X is warm and open") to infer behaviors. Viewers may use the given trait information to infer behaviors or other correlated traits. During testing, traces of these inferences may be detected as schema intrusions (the "added" information resulting from inferences) in free recall protocols of viewers.

Parallel Semantic Structures, Shared Actantial Roles, and the Use of Metaphor. Probably one of the most interesting issues is the need to explain how verbal and visual metaphor is modeled by the viewer. Determining the mechanism for comprehension of metaphor is a difficult problem for theories of cognitive processing (Ortony, 1979). The notion of actantial roles does not resolve the problem. But incorporating the use of metaphor under a theoretical discussion of actantial roles allows us to at least hypothesize about metaphoric substitution within television programming.

The actants of a political commercial can be linked in a variety of ways. They may be linked by (a) a causal relation as the agents and objects of some action, (b) as the referents of linked propositions, and (c) by sharing actantial roles. Figure 2.7 represents the latter kind of semantic link. The semantic markers of one actant (i.e. traits, motivations, behaviors) may be transferred to another actant through semantic association in a shared actantial role. These parallel actantial roles, a common device in literature, link two actants (characters) so that one becomes metaphorically associated to the other.

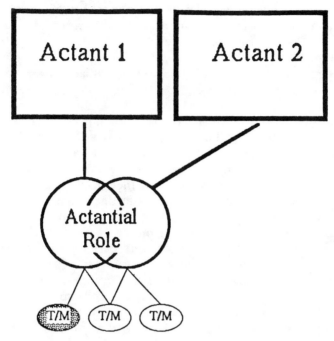

FIGURE 2.7. Two actants within a message may share an actantial role. This sharing of actantial roles leads the viewer to take traits and motivations identified with one actant and associate them with the other actant.

For example, a program may establish an actantial link between a young boy and a puppy through the actantial role of "child" (i.e. child in the possible world of humans; child in the possible world of dogs). Through the use of cuts or parallel narratives, some of the traits of the puppy are transferred to the child. The actantial link can also be used to advance the narrative. For example, harm to the puppy might be used to foreshadow harm to the child.

Similarly, political commercials may be designed so that the candidate shares an actantial role with some famous and well-respected figure so that the perceived traits of the famous figure may be transferred through association to the candidate. This is a common strategy in presidential commercials where candidates may be linked to previous popular presidents using some parallel structure. In 1988 the "Massachusetts-Texas" axis of the Dukakis-Bentsen ticket (a reference to the previous Kennedy-Johnson Democratic ticket) was a blatant rhetorical use of such a device.

In commercials the sharing of actantial roles can be an important device in transferring meaning (traits) from a product endorser to the product or from a narrative character (e.g., continuing central character) to the product. Commercials may be designed so that the product shares an actantial role with some famous and well respected figure. The perceived traits of the famous figure may be transferred through association to the product.

The sharing of an actantial role can be initiated by a variety of structural devices in a message:

(a) Actants may play the same actantial roles in parallel narratives. For example, a script might show President Roosevelt leading the country out of the depression, and establish a parallel problem where candidate X leads the nation to better times. A link is establish between these two actants by the actantial role they share.

(b) Syntactic devices such as cuts associating one image with another are also used to establish actantial links. A common device in non-narrative films establishes semantic links between adjacent images by the judicious juxtaposition of shots with purely formal or structural similarities (Bordwell & Thompson, 1986).

(c) Groups of actants may be presented so as to appear to be members of a common category. Category membership ends up being the shared trait linking the actants and a device for semantic transfers. Perceived category membership might lead the viewer to transfer traits and motivations from one actant to another. Viewers may engage in deeper processing to establish categorical links among the set of presented items (Brewer & Nakumura, 1984).

There are a number of semantic-processing phenomena that the concept of actantial roles allows us to address. Most deal with how the political commercial achieves its fundamental goal, linking semantic nodes (positive or negative "associations" regarding traits and behaviors) and transferring meaning from one concept to the candidate (or, in "attack" commercials negative semantic transfers to the opposing candidate).

Metaphor often links an actant to an actantial role. It is a special case where the actantial role is radically foregrounded. This foregrounding often leads the viewer to instantiate schema linked to the metaphor and calculate new values in the other schematic frames. An example, might help illustrate this use. The area of political advertising provides a paradigmatic example. The infamous "Bear in the Woods" commercial from the 1984 Reagan campaign featured shots of a bear walking in the woods and a hunter with a gun by a hillside. A voice over mused how "some people" were not sure whether or not there is a bear in the woods and whether he is dangerous.

The key to the comprehension of the commercial was the correct modeling of its actantial structure. The commercial required calculating the parallel actantial role of Russia = bear and using this association as a key to infer other shared actantial roles, i.e. Reagan = hunter. This commercial rested on the assumption that the model viewer would have, as part of his or her semiotic competence, easy access to the central metaphoric link between the visual image, "bear," and its referent, the "Soviet Union." It was possible to indirectly access the model reading of the commercial by activating the discursive frame of "defense spending." But this was not foregrounded in the semantic framing of the message. Note that the commercial also includes a semantic parallel between the possible world of forest and hunter, and the world of super power hide-and-seek.

When Republican strategists tested the "Bear in the Woods" commercial in focus groups, it became immediately apparent that the key metaphorical connection was not activated in the minds of many viewers. This failure lead to the instantiation of a variety of aberrant decodings. Some viewers inferred the discursive topic of "environmentalism" by making the wrong metaphoric link between actantial role and actant (represented bear = "Smokey Bear"). Others decoded it by using the representation of a gun to infer a discursive frame of "gun control laws" and, by foregrounding this value read the ad as a defense of the right to bear arms (no pun intended, of course). Nonetheless, the commercial was aired. It benefited from repeated exposure. Its metaphorical structure led many viewers to pay more attention upon second and third exposures. This additional attention may have led to deep processing of its structure and, subsequently, to high recall for the ad and its macropropositions regarding danger, safety, and defense.[18]

Summing up, viewers identify actants and use them as referents (nodes) for propositions about television programs and messages. Actants are modeled as a set of actantial roles to which are attached observed or inferred traits, motivations, or behaviors. The set of actants in a political commercial is organized into an actantial structure. Each actant may play one or more actantial roles. The political commercial may be structured so that two or more actants may share an actantial role. In such cases semantic nodes (perceived traits, motivations, and behaviors) associated with one actant may become associated with the other actant.

---

[18]Talk by political consultant, Donald Ringe during a plenary session on Political Advertising and the 1988 Campaign at the meeting of the American Association for Public Opinion Research, Toronto, May 1988.

Point-of-View

All television is seen from a point-of-view. This is one of the more interesting aspects of the cognitive processing of television. Point-of-view allows the viewer to see the possible world of the program "through the eyes" of some actant or for the viewer to have some external voyeuristic role relative to the actants.

Point-of-view in television has two interacting dimensions: (a) mode-of-address and (b) position of sight. Because of these dimensions, point-of-view in television and film is significantly different than it is in literature.[19]

Mode-of-address is part of the semantic framing of the television sequence. The structure of a narrative or the use of rhetorical codes will invite the viewer to occupy a specific point-of-view. A number of cues play a part in guiding the viewer to hold the point-of-view of the model viewer. These include actants directly addressing the camera, active or passive camera movement, camera angles suggesting the position-of-sight of various actants within the scene.

Position-of-sight means quite literally the position of the viewer in space as cued by the camera's position in space.[20] Position-of-sight is not "given," it is modeled like everything else in the commercial or program. It is a psychological perceptual process determined by the pictorial and visual spatial cues (Gibson, 1979; Marr, 1982). Position-of-sight, therefore, is an important part of the processing of the instantiated viewer and has definite semantic properties and effects (see below).

We can categorize the following points-of-view as determined by the mode-of-address and position-of-sight codes of television:

---

[19]The degree to which point-of-view is different in texts as opposed to film is arguable. One has to consider the role of mental imagery and the influence of film genre on the "reading" of texts. There is no doubt that reading can generate a great deal of visual imagery. This visual imagery will often include the "position-of-sight" effects that one sees in television and film.

There is also the question of the interaction of cognitive training resulting from exposure to television and film with reading processes. Subjects have been trained by film to occupy a position-of-sight in scenes and bring this perceptual training to the reading of narratives. They may be reading narratives with the imaginal eye of film. Reciprocally, it has been argued that writers weaned on the conventions of film and television embed the "eye of the camera" into the structure of their writing, seeking to evoke film-like position-of-sight effects in the readers.

[20]We traditionally refer to the "camera's position" in space but with the increased use of computer graphics, the point-of-sight is determined by mathematical rules of perspective (digital point-of-sight) rather than the camera (analog point-of-sight).

"First Person" Viewer's Identity. Programming, which cues the viewer with a first person, viewer identity point-of-view, usually addresses the viewer directly. The actants, may directly speak to and establish "eye contact" with the camera, seeking to "interact" with the viewer.

The most common format features an actant engaged in "straight talk" with the viewer. The camera's point-of-sight is usually close to eye level, suggesting that the actant is directly speaking to the viewer. The camera distance is usually close up or medium close up, suggesting regular conversational distances.

The message structure may cue the viewer to model an active or passive actantial role for himself or herself. Typically, the viewer's role is passive (didactic modes-of-address). This appears to be true of 90% of political commercials using the first person, viewer identity point-of-view. On the other hand, other cues may signal the viewer to become more psychologically engaged in the narrative or action. Active viewer point-of-view is usually signalled by a moving, "subjective" camera point-of-sight position, as well as indications that the movement in space has causal effects. Actants within the sequence appear to react to the viewer's "movement." Objects may move as a result of camera movement (e.g., branches in a forest scene). The early perceptual system must not only model this movement, but semantic processing necessitates that the instantiated viewer model the narrative and causal relations with himself or herself as the causal agent in the propositional representation. The most dramatic form of first-person viewer identity point-of-view is found in interactive video or video games.

"Second Person" Borrowed Identity. Second person or borrowed identity point-of-view shares many of the properties of viewer identity except for one significant semantic processing feature. The programming may cue the viewer to instantiate him or herself as an actant in the mental model of the program, but the identity (traits/motivations) of that actant are determined not by the empirical viewer's "real world" identity (self-schema) but by an actantial role in the instantiated "possible world." The instantiated viewer occupies an actantial role provided by a schema for that role in the possible world.[21] Although not

---

[21]A borrowed identity point of view can also result from an ideological rejection of a message structured for a first person, viewer identity point-of-view. In this case the viewer idiosyncratically rejects the "contract" to take a "first person" point-of-view because he or she perceives the position as a violation of his selfschema (i.e., "this commercial doesn't speak to me"). The viewer may model the position of the model viewer and use that role to "read" the message, while keeping the ideological or self-schema foregrounded.

that common in political commercials, it is found in one of the examples discussed in Biocca (chapter 3, this volume).

Borrowed identity is a common semantic framing approach in television programming and interactive video and video games. For example, in many corporate interactive videos the empirical viewer is often cued to role play (e.g., play the role of the "boss"). In that actantial role the instantiated viewer interacts with the actants of the possible world framed by the video, but uses an instantiated schema for that role (i.e. occupational role schema for "boss").

"Third Person" Nomadic Identity. This is the most common point-of-view in television and film. The instantiated viewer sees the possible world from, quite literally, a variety of perspectives. He or she looks at the possible world through the eyes of the various actants or as a passive voyeur (see below). The point-of-sight is continuously changing with classic point-of-sight reversals for dialog, scene pans, etc. The viewer is not cued to take on any specific identity within the possible world. The propositional and imagery mental models will most likely not contain self-schematic nodes indicating a role for the individual viewer.[22]

"Third Person" Voyeur. In this case the point-of-view is consistently that of an outsider to the narrative. Sequences of images and scenes flow by on the screen, but at no time do the point-of-sight cues suggest the "perspective" of an actant within a narrative nor does it engage in some causal relation within the possible world ("diegetical space," see Bordwell & Thompson, 1986) of the film or program. Political commercials vary to the degree to which they initiate changes in the viewer's point-of-view.[23]

Basically, the viewer is psychologically putting him or herself in "someone else's shoes" while self-consciously reflecting on "what it's like."

[22]We must remember that the viewer is free to engage in idiosyncratic or aberrant decoding. Instantiated viewers may strongly "identify" with actants or actantial roles and may even foreground self-schematic framing (i.e., the classic "Walter Mitty" phenomenon). In such cases the instantiated viewer models the propositional structure of a commercial with a self-schematic actant, but mediated through an actantial role in the possible world of the film. Therefore, the viewer pushes the program or commercial into a "second person, borrowed identity" point-of-view even though the semantic framing of the commercial or program is structured for a model viewer adopting a third person, nomadic identity point-of-view.

[23]There are some sections of the commercial that have points-of-view that are "separate" from the rest of the commercial. For example, party identification frames at the end of the commercial are usually used for cueing a first person passive point-of-view or the even more passive, third person voyeur point of view. This may be separate from the point-of-view used in the main body of the commercial.

There is evidence that the point-of-view adopted by a viewer influences what information is attended to in a message, perceived causes for events, and memory for the message (Bower & Cirilo, 1985; Strange & Black, 1989; Wyer & Gordon, 1984). Point-of-view appears to have this effect by altering the mental imagery and inference making of readers and viewers (Strange & Black, 1989), leading them to make attributions about the motivational causes of events (Taylor & Fiske, 1978). In a similar fashion, point-of-sight can have definite effects on semantic processing by influencing the traits inferred about actants when they are viewed from a specific point-of-sight (see Kepplinger, chapter 6, this volume; Kraft, 1987).

Narrative Frames

The cognitive processing of narrative has received a significant amount of study as researchers in the areas of psycholinguistics, literary theory, discourse processing, text linguistics, film studies, and artificial intelligence have converged on an intense analysis of the structures of narrative. It is clear that the comprehension of text involves the instantiation of narrative schema that help guide the mental modeling of the narrative (Bower, 1976; Rumelhart, 1977; Schank & Abelson, 1977; van Dijk, 1988b). Learning how to process television appears to involve the acquisition of narrative schema to guide the parsing, inference making, and the modeling of much of the content of television (Collins, 1979). The fact that narratives appear to have consistent structures both within and across cultures (Labov, 1972; Propp, 1968) suggests that their structure reflects the application of fundamental mental processes.

There are a number of interesting issues regarding the psychological interaction of the narrative structure of the message with the instantiated narrative schema of the viewer. In general, many researchers in this area have tried to specify elements of a "deep structure" of narrative processing. Theorists differ as to what constitutes a "deep" structure and how a reader/viewer transforms elements of the narrative in the process of creating a model of its structure. Some emphasize structural properties of stories such as "story grammars" (Kintsch & van Dijk, 1978; Mandler, 1978; Mandler & Johnson, 1977; Rumelhart, 1977). Others concentrate on how "real world" knowledge and the reader's everyday use of plans and goals structure the reader's interpretation of narratives (Schank & Abelson, 1977). Still others see the processing of narratives as part of more general processes of mental modeling that are operative in the comprehension of texts (e.g., Johnson-Laird, 1983).

Some general principles emerge from these various attempts to understand the cognitive processing of narratives:

1. narrative texts have some underlying structure that is cognitively salient and used to guide processing;
2. narrative schema operate like other schema, providing a set of variables, for which values are sought or inferred;
3. the modeling of narrative leads to a hierarchical representation. Some macropropositions emerge from the organization (deletion, substitution, etc.) of the narrative. The macropropositions are more likely to be the most salient elements of memory for the narrative; and
4. modeling has some element of linear organization that is episodic or some other form of causal or sequential "left-to-right" branching of events and episodes.

Adapted from Rumelhart (1977), Figure 2.8 displays one of the simpler structures for representing narratives. The figure represents a theory of the processing of narratives that has been tested using mass media messages (Thorndyke, 1977). It shows a hierarchical structure that Rumelhart suggested is used in the modeling of narratives (see also

Mental Representation of Narrative

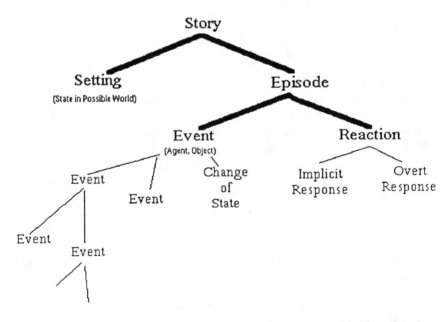

FIGURE 2.8.   A schematic for the representation of narratives contained in political messages (following Rumelhart, 1977).

Clark & Clark, 1977). The hierarchy appears to reflect not only structuring during comprehension but memory for the narrative (Rumelhart, 1977; Thorndyke, 1977). Simply stated, units higher in the hierarchy are more likely to be remembered.

To discuss the structure, I will use the outline suggested by Rumelhart (1975) and (Clark & Clark, 1977).

Narrative = setting + episode

At its very basic level, a narrative is a combination of setting and episode.

Setting = state + state. . . . + state (in possible world).

Setting for a narrative is usually some state of a possible world. The state is a partial (foregrounded) representation of states of the possible world. For example, in the possible world, "cities," a state of that world might be indicated by semantic frames that foreground "drugs in the street," "gang murders," "street crime," and so on.

Episode = event + reaction

An episode is made up of an event and a reaction. This is the basic causal relation. For example, event = "election of candidate" leads to a reaction that is either internal (e.g., "joy," "sadness") or external (e.g., "celebrate," "protest").

Event = change of state, or
= action, or
= event + event . . . , or
= (episode)

An event can be a change of state from the initial state framed by the setting, an action by an actant, an enabling or preceding event, or a complete embedded episode. Therefore, the model can be recursive.

Reaction = internal response + overt response.

A causal relation (reaction) may be set up between an event and some internal or overt response of an actant.

Viewers appear to use narrative schema to organize incoming information. Even when a story is in a random order, readers and viewers will reconstruct the original order by apparently making use of narrative schema (Mandler & Johnson, 1977). Agent, object, instrument, and other information are not essential to the modeling of the narrative and, along with enabling events, are often deleted when a reader summarizes a narrative or stores it in memory (Rumelhart, 1977; Thorndyke, 1977).

The problems of time limitations in a commercial need not limit the complexity of the narrative schematic framing. The schema activated by the viewer provides an elaborate pre-existing structure. A common device for filling in literally volumes of missing informa- tion is intertextual semantic frames. Intertextuality, as it is called in semiotic and literary theory, is one of many types of semantic disclosure (Fiske, 1987; Kristeva, 1969), but appears to function like a schema. Intextextual references activate not "real" world information but information drawn from other "texts" or films. When commercials or programs make use of genres such as "westerns," "cops and robbers," and the like, they are using intertextual semantic frames that activate existing knowledge about a genre and the sequence of events and causal relations associated with it. The reference to some other "text" allows the communicator to activate various fields of information (semantic networks) which can supply default values for many of the schematic frames. Because of this, intertextual reference is not limited to the activation of narrative schematic frames, but can be used to quickly reference possible worlds, actantial roles, and ideological frames.

Ideological Schematic Frames

When the viewers instantiate their ideological schema, they are not just examining the message but quite literally how the message is framed.[24] The viewers do not simply decode a message but analyze the codes to infer the ideology of the communicator or, indirectly, the ideology of the model viewer. To use a popular phrase, the instantiated viewer "reads between the lines" not to find what is not said but to infer the unspoken ideological assumptions of what is said.

Because of how the genre, "television advertising," is categorized, members of our culture immediately activate the semantic marker, a "message whose intent is to persuade." The political ad is doubly marked. It is both an ad and its discursive frame, "politics," underlines its persuasive intent.

When the ideological schematic frame is foregrounded a processing sub-goal becomes not the processing of the message but the modeling of the world view and ideology of the message/communicator. The inferred communicator becomes a major actant ("actant of communication"; Greimas, 1986; Greimas & Courtes, 1982) in the schematic framing of the instantiated viewer. Ideological decoding is the perfect phrase to describe the goal of the modeling. The viewer attempts to construct the "logic of the ideas" of the communicator or the message.

The cognitive procedures accompanying ideological schematic framing may include attempts to match schema of specific ideologies to the incoming message to determine its ideological structure. The procedure may be, to a large degree, a categorization task as the viewer

---

[24]In the terminology of semiotics, attention to the structure of the message is a dimension of metasemiotic processing (see Eco, 1976).

attempts to identify the ideological category to which the message or communicator belongs. For example, the schema for various ideologies might have a link between the discursive topic, "Jews" (with negative semantic markers) and the ideology, "anti-Semitism."

For many American voters, the selection of relevant schema might involve a simple dichotomous categorization, labelling the ideology of the communicator-message as "conservative" or "liberal." The complexity of the decision tree will vary broadly with the knowledge and competence of the viewer. Expert (politically engaged) viewers may have highly elaborated schema for the reading of political ideology (Fiske & Kinder, 1981; Fiske, Kinder, & Larter, 1983; Lau, 1986).

The ideological schematic frames used by the viewer will vary according to the subculture and culture in which the viewer has been socialized. A politically engaged viewer processing a political message in Italy, for example, will certainly require more elaborate schemata for ideological structures because the evolution of political discourse has given rise to a splintering of institutionalized ideological voices.

It would be a mistake to think of ideological schematic framing too narrowly in terms of traditional political ideologies. In any communication process, ideological schemata are activated to determine the intent of the communicator. In interpersonal communication, a significant amount of schematic and propositional inference making goes into determining "where the other person is coming from." To determine "where the person is coming from" is to infer from the message and non-propositional cues the world view or, in the broad sense, the communicator's personal ideology. For example, a rebellious teenager may perceive that a message has the worldview of his parents, and, therefore, reject it.

The default stance of the viewer is likely to be one of commonalty between the world view/ideology of the message and his or her own.[25]

---

[25]There is likely to be a great deal of interpersonal variation in the default assumptions about the ideological stance and world view of messages. Individuals who are harmoniously socialized with the dominant ideology and world view are most likely to assume commonalty. There is no doubt that there are conditions in which the individual default will be one of ideological distrust and, therefore, bracketing of the message. Individuals who are highly alienated from the political system are likely to immediately adopt a stance that brackets the truth value of a message. The immediate response is "this message is not for me," "it doesn't speak to my world." This is certainly the immediate psychological response of many disenfranchised subcultural groups to most political messages. There is also likely to be a great deal of ideologically framing of messages from other cultures. For example, when a typical American viewer looks at a communist political video he or she immediately brackets the truth value. This ideological stance is cued by the possible world of the video. Attention is paid to the codes (i.e., "style" "slant") of the message and a search is initiated for clues of ideology. This too is a form of "oppositional decoding."

Detection of discrepancies between expectations of ideological stances towards significant referential objects may lead to the suspension of that commonality, and a bracketing of the message and its truth value as the viewer attempts to model or categorize the alternative ideology of the message.

The foregrounding of the ideological schematic framing is more likely to occur when persuasion is failing than when it is successful. If ideological schematic framing is foregrounded during the message, the viewer is likely to engage in a bracketing of the whole message while he or she "reads between the lines" and determines its ideological intent. During bracketing, the truth value of the message (statement) is suspended, as the viewer searches for the ideological foundations of the argument. This "bracketing" can be the initial phase of negative elaboration associated with message counterarguing (Petty & Cacioppo, 1986). The propositions of the message are also analyzed at the metasemiotic level, that is to say that just as much attention is paid to their form as to their content. During negative counterarguing, the viewer brackets the proposition, tests for its truth value by referring to his or her self schema, and searches for weaknesses and counter examples.

Traces of the semantic processing associated with foregrounding of the ideological framing can be found in free recall protocols (Ericsson & Simon, 1985). Viewers are more likely to engage in metastatement (metacommentary) during recall. A researcher is likely to see more commentary of an evaluative nature (e.g., "I didn't like the way they presented . . .") The protocol will reveal more inferences of communicator intent (e.g., "They're trying to sell the notion of a clean environment"). The protocol is also likely to have more comments that reflect inferences about the model viewer for the message (e.g., "This message seems intended for people who believe in a strong defense. . . ."; or, "That's what they want you to believe . . ."). In general, the protocols reveal traces of previous semantic processing that have led to (a) inferences about and some distancing from the model viewer (rejection of the implied contract of the message), and (b) increased negative evaluative comments. If the viewer is taking a highly oppositional and defensive approach to the message, the protocol will also reveal, (c) attention to the surface structure of the message and the testing of truth values of the message (e.g., "The people didn't seem realistic . . ."; or, "The ad was pretty slick but . . ."). Highly oppositional strategies are likely to result from the strong activation of self-schematic frames and the negative foregrounding of the ideological frames.

Self-Schematic Frames

One of the primary goals of many political ads is to push a "hot button" and to "hit them where they live." These colloquial expressions are ways in which the professional refers to commercials that generate a great deal of audience "involvement," "self-referential" thought, or self-schematic processing.

Research suggests that individuals possess well defined self-schemata (Markus, 1977; Markus & Sentis, 1982), that is prototypical concepts of the self (Kuiper & Derry, 1981). Self-schemata exhibit properties similar to other schemata. But there are significant differences. Self-schemata are constructed from self-observation, information that is readily and consciously available. Because of the immediacy of the information and the pervasiveness of its construction, the self-schema is more complex, salient, and easily retrievable.

What is in the self-schematic frame? How does it influence semantic processing? In some ways it is close to the ideological frame. The self-schema of the viewer is posited to be the key part of a viewer's primary ideology. It is ideological in the very core sense that it is a "logic of cherished ideas," concepts that stem from some fundamental model of how the individual fits into the world. The self-schema is the core of an individual's world view: "the world as it looks from where I stand." It is the activation of the self-schematic frame that Krugman (1965) wanted to distinguish with his schema-driven conceptualization of involvement. He referred to "the number of conscious 'bridging experiences,' connections, or personal references per minute that the viewer makes between his own life and the stimulus" (p. 355).

It is well established that messages that generate self-referential thinking receive qualitatively and quantitatively different levels of processing (Borgida & Howard-Pitney, 1983; Petty & Cacioppo, 1979, 1981, 1984; Petty, Cacioppo, & Goldman, 1981). Much of the work of the elaboration likelihood model (ELM) and its "central route" to persuasion is built on the manipulation (activation) of self-schematic processing (Petty & Cacioppo, 1986; Waszak, 1988). Self-schematic processing has been characterized as more complex, elaborated, and requiring greater cognitive effort. Greenwald and Leavitt (1985) similarly define what they call, a "self system" as the "deepest" level of their cognitive processing hierarchy.

Because the self-schematic frame involves the activation of the viewer's primary world view, it is the locus of the assignment of truth values to propositions about the "real world" or a "possible world". This suggests an executive function[26] for this schematic frame as well as an

---

[26]This executive function is restricted solely to conscious, attentive, and elaborated evaluative thought. Work on parallel distributed processing (PDP) models of cognitive processing (Rumelhart, et al., 1986a, 1986b) throws into question notions of a general executive found in a number of information processing models (See Lachman, Lachman, & Butterfield, 1979).

evaluative dimension to the semantic processing. The evaluative dimension requires complex judgments and generates the high amounts of message elaboration that Petty and Cacioppo (1986) report. The consumer behavior notions of "decisional" or "product" importance that are linked to "involving" cognitive processing, support the assertion of an evaluative dimension in self-schematic processing (Sentis & Markus, 1986).

It is important to think of the word, "self," in self-schema as an expansive concept. It is highly connected or "networked" to many concepts in semantic memory. There is a danger of too narrowly conceptualizing the self-schematic frame as self-referential in a purely egoistic or corporeal sense.

The activation of the self-schematic frame is accompanied by a strong form of hierarchical, top-down processing. It is hierarchical because self-schematic considerations are likely to drive the instantiation of the schema in the other schematic frames. It is likely that this foregrounding contributes to the observed resistance to counter-attitudinal persuasion when a message activates self-schematic ("involving" or "central") processing (e.g., Sherif & Hovland, 1961).

More than any of the other frames just described, the activation of the self-schematic frame is most clearly an interaction between the semantic frames of the message and schema of the viewer. Whether or not a message will activate a significant amount of self-schematic processing cannot be reliably predicted from the structure of the message itself.[27] Although the semantic frames embedded in a message may "cause" self-schematic processing, it is clear that pre-existing variables related to situational, goal schema, and personality factors play a much larger part in the activation of self-schematic framing (Lastovicka & Gardener, 1979).

HOW CONTEXT AFFECTS THE VIEWER'S SEMANTIC PROCESSES

The semantic processing of a political commercial is by no means totally driven by the influence of its structure on the processing of the

---

[27]Greenwald and Leavitt (1985) stated that "the level of involvement required of an audience varies as a function of the complexity of the advertising message" (p. 235). Note that the key word is "required." Rephrased in terms of the model just discussed, this can be translated into "the level of involvement of a model viewer is assumed to be greater for complex messages." The actual level of involvement of the instantiated viewer cannot be predicted but the "preferred" reading of the message assumes a certain "level of processing" in Greenwald and Leavitt's model.

instantiated viewer. While the instantiated viewer is defined as a product of the interaction of the schemata of the viewer and the semantic frames of the message, pragmatically, we must recognize that a variety of environmental, situational, and contextual variables can influence the instantiated viewer for any political message. Some of these variations are subsumed under the concept of *processing set.* Processing set is defined as preexisting or residual patterns of schematic framing (semantic activation) that the empirical viewer brings to the processing of the message.[28] Basically, it must be recognized that an instantiated viewer is already partially "preformed" before the political message starts. In the continuum of "watching television" an instantiated viewer is continuously being made and the "momentum" of that processing helps determine the instantiated viewer for a specific political commercial. The pre-existing pattern of schematic frame activation cannot be defined as the enduring semantic competence of the empirical viewer but, rather, as temporary variations in the use and activation of that competence.

The Effect of Viewing Situation

The focus of semantic processing (the schematic frames and schema likely to be activated) will be influenced by situational variables. For example, a viewer may be viewing alone or with friends. In the latter case, the political ad may serve as a source of discussion or the object of derision. If ideologically opposed, the viewer may attend carefully (especially to the audio track), looking for gaps in arguments or flaws in the presentation so as to use them for later discussion. In a similar group viewing situation, the viewer may search for points of potential humor where the meaning of the communicator/message can be subverted. The viewer may focus on the physical flaws of the candidate as sources of humor, (i.e., Paul Simon's ears or bow tie, etc.), or look for points where the credibility of the message can be challenged or its sincerity mocked. These are forms of oppositional decoding (Hall, 1980b). In this case the instantiated viewer is a long cry from the model viewer of the message but the points of subversion are still to some degree "framed" by the structure of the message. But the message is reconstructed to serve the processing goals of the empirical viewer as set by situational and attitudinal factors.

---

[28]Of course, processing set can be experimentally manipulated to establish more general principles such as the influence of processing set on channel attention, code selection, and memory (e.g., Garramone, 1983).

The Effect of Programming Context

The semantic processing of the ad may also be influenced by its context within the programming as well as by the commercials that precede it. Programming context can affect the processing of the commercial by generating positive or negative affect in the viewer, increasing attention or arousal, and by semantically priming appropriate or inappropriate schema (Aaker, Staymen, & Hagerty, 1986).

For example, it is clear that processing set for a political ad will be more favorable when it is embedded within television news programming as opposed to humorous programming like the Cosby show. The viewer is more likely to have instantiated schema and processing strategies favorable to activating the model viewer appropriate for decoding the intended message.

Chance factors can also increase the motivation to process. For example, the author observed that during the 1988 campaign a Bush commercial on the economy followed a favorable television news story on the economy. This serendipitous juxtaposition, no doubt greatly increased the attention to that commercial and boosted its credibility.

The schematic framing that constitutes the pattern of semantic activation of the instantiated viewer will reflect the influence of stimuli other than the commercial itself. The commercial and its semantic frames are but one of the forces shaping the processing of the instantiated viewer at any point in time.

TESTING ALTERNATIVE MENTAL MODELS: ISSUES OF RESEARCH DESIGN AND MEASUREMENT

The model of schematic framing has been presented as a (a) theoretical tool intended to guide the framing of theoretical questions about political commercials, (b) means of reinterpreting and integrating findings on the semantic processing of television, (c) structure to guide hypotheses about the processing of particular variables and commercials, and (d) practical means to model and test hypotheses about viewers' mental models of television form and content. This section will concentrate on the last issue. In a review of the social cognition and mass media research literature, Reeves et al. (1982) pointed out the need for a theory of cognitive models and ways to test the empirical constraints of such models:

> The major research task becomes one of discovering empirical constraints
> on classes of cognitive models that are plausible and that adequately

describe the interactions among messages, channels, information processing, and response. The task inevitably places cognition in the central role
and implies a need for more than "black box" descriptions of intervening
mental processes (p. 292).

In attempting to explore the "intervening mental processes" described in the schematic frame model, we should consider how we
might measure the semantic processing of political advertising or television.

Variable Selection

From a research design viewpoint, part of the purpose of the schematic
frame model, is to *turn processes into forms.* Or, to put it another way,
to vary and measure the *mental forms of television content.* The
viewer's mental models are the results of processes, automatic computations. The processes and their results have forms or structures that
reflect the computations, and that are theoretically measurable.

The Choice of Dependent Variables. The mental model of something like a short political commercial is a dynamic system; change one
element, especially if you alter a foregrounded frame, you change all the
other elements. Knock over one domino and the others around it begin
to fall in the same direction, forming a pattern. "It is the total structure
of a set of cognitions that determines what simplified structure will
result" (Reeves, et al., 1982, p. 290). The interactive nature of semantic
processes and activation has implications for how we might define
dependent variables when attempting to measure the semantic processing of television.

Let us take a traditional measure like "recall of content." The model
suggests that any gross measure of recall may be inadequate. The
question must be asked, "Recall of what?" Gross measures of recall,
implicitly conceptualize the message as a quantity of information, rather
than a process or structure. A researcher measures how much information was acquired. Such an approach suggests that the message is a set of
units and that the researcher need simply count the number of units
retained. This implicitly assumes that the units are roughly equal and
that communication is simply a transportation process in which so many
units are transferred to the viewer.

In this "unit" approach to recall, the structure of what is recalled is
often not adequately conceptualized. Recall of a macroproposition of a
political commercial is treated as equal to recall of a microproposition
(see Kintsch & van Dijk, 1978; van Dijk & Kintsch, 1983, for suggestions

on how this is clearly problematic). Gross recall (especially in the form of multiple-choice tests) also favors recall for the propositional model and leaves out tests of the imagery model of the commercial (Rossiter & Percy, 1983). And finally, gross recall does not address the "meaning" of what is recalled, which is to say, it does not measure the semantic structure of what is recalled.

This suggests that the dependent variables should be structural variables. If a researcher is manipulating a message variable (i.e., a semantic frame) then one needs to look at how various manipulations lead to structural changes in the actantial framing, discursive framing, point-of-view, narrative framing, self-schematic framing, and so on. Dependent measures of memory would need to be measures of structures. For example, a researcher might generate a set of hypothesized structures as the outcomes of some change in the semantic framing of a political commercial. This might be specified, for example, as various potential actantial structures of a message, specifying the actants, the actantial roles, the sharing or parallelism of actantial roles between actants, potentially inferred traits, and the like. Following the manipulation the researcher might attempt to measure the presence, absence, and form of the actantial structure in specific groups of viewers. Similarly, a researcher might look for schema activation by attempting to detect "intrusions" of schema-consistent information during recall.

How those structural variables are defined and operationalized will depend on whether the research will be measuring the semantic processing (instantiated viewer) in real time or whether one is measuring the long-term memory traces of the semantic processing. For example, if one is using postexposure protocols as a dependent measure, then trace evidence of variations in schematic framing may be present in the structures of those protocols. Therefore, the process of schematic framing often needs to be defined as a set of alternative structures (different paths of semantic activation) and the researcher needs to look for evidence of the presence of alternative structures.

The Choice of Independent Variables. I have put a discussion of independent variables after the discussion of dependent variables for a reason. A sophisticated, theory-driven approach to the selection of independent variables requires a theory and model of semantic frames or codes, something that has not been attempted here (see Biocca, in press-a,b,c,d; van Dijk, 1988, 1989). Just as psycholinguistics is implicitly dependent on a theory of linguistics, a theory of schematic frames is implicitly dependent on a theory of semantic frames. Of course, we can always continue to manipulate independent variables like camera angle, message length, or pacing, but doing so without understanding the systems within which these variables exist too often leads to problems of generalization and inconsistent results (see the Herculean but disappointing effort of Stewart & Furse, 1980, for an example of serious problems with such an approach).

Measuring Changes in Viewers' Mental Models.

Semantic processing of television, film, and commercials has, until recently, been mostly addressed through interpretive and hermeneutic techniques (e.g., Fiske, 1987; Hartley, 1982; Leymore, 1975; Rowland & Watkins, 1984; Williamson, 1978). While a great deal of insight can and has been gained by some of the more sophisticated introspective approaches, they alone cannot answer the fundamental questions at the basis of the schematic framing model (Biocca, 1990). At best, introspective approaches can suggest the semantic processing of the "Model-Reader" or suggest theoretical questions, but they cannot satisfactorily map out the range of semantic processing variations and aberrant decodings in the mind of the viewer, nor can such techniques satisfactorily explore the changing paths of semantic processing caused by everyday phenomena such as multiple exposure. To understand the "meaning" of television's "texts," we must directly engage the actual viewer and explore the instantiated viewer.

But how does one look "inside" to trace the movements of the instantiated viewer down the paths of semantic memory? How does one test hypotheses about foregrounding, the influence of various codes, group differences in schema instantiation, and so on?

There are a number of measures that are being used to explore the cognitive processing of television form and content. All have strengths and weaknesses. The design and choice of measures will be different if a researcher is exploring more general theoretical questions regarding the schematic framing of television or if one is interested in a means of practically testing the frequency and prevalence of alternative mental models of a specific political ad or campaign. As always, the selection of measures needs to be preceded by a clear and rich set of theoretical or practical questions.

Protocol Analysis. To trace semantic processes over long time spans (30 seconds is a very long amount of cognitive time), one needs semantically rich data. The only way yet devised to obtain this is protocol analysis. The classic work in this area is still Ericsson and Simon's (1985) *Protocol Analysis.* The methods of protocol coding have achieved some popularity in consumer research (Brock & Shavitt, 1983). This approach is grounded on the classic method of examining the structure of a "black box"; the researcher looks at semantic inputs and semantic outputs to infer intervening processes.

The application of the approach of van Dijk and Kintsch (1983; Kintsch & van Dijk, 1978) to the analysis of television seems promising. The approach has been used to study the processing of advertising copy by Thorson and Snyder (1984), though only to test how linguistic structure can be used to predict recall. With some additional work it may be possible to apply elements of Kintsch and van Dijk's approach more broadly to include larger issues of the semantic processing of propositions in texts and images.

Kintsch and van Dijk analyze subjects postexposure protocols and assign each proposition to the following categories to search for traces of cognitive processes during the processing of the text:

Reproduction. Here they look for the reproduction of the explicit propositions of the text noting frequency and order. The reproduction of propositions about episodes in the text reveal: "(a) traces from various perceptual processes and linguistic processes involved in text processing, (b) traces of comprehension processes, and (c) contextual traces" (Kintsch & van Dijk, 1978, p. 375).

Reconstruction. Reconstructions provide evidence of the application of rules of inference to the text. They suggest schema driven additions, deletions and substitutions. Here Kintsch and van Dijk (1978) look for: "(a) addition of plausible details and normal properties, (b) particularization and (c) specification of normal conditions, components, or consequences of events" (p. 375).

Metastatements. In the process of producing a protocol, the subject will produce comments (metacomments) on the content or the structure of the text. (In the case of schematic framing, these can provide insight into the activation of ideological framing and self-schematic framing.)

Unclassifiable statements and errors. Some propositions will not be classifiable.

The Kintsch and van Dijk analyses are strictly for verbal texts. Although such an approach can be used to analyze the protocols for the audio track of a commercial, it is not clear how it can be used to analyze the propositional information and inference making generated by the video track. Nonetheless, recognizing the methodological difficulties (including just its application to linguistic text), the approach provides a potentially valuable heuristic.

Overall, the analysis of protocols can provide evidence of foregrounding, inference making, and schema activation as well as traces of propositional modeling in the various schematic frames.

Moment-to-moment Audience Response Measurement. Computerized audience response systems (Biocca & David, forthcoming) have been used for commercial, film, and television research for a long time (Levy, 1982). But in some ways this has been a measure in search of a theory. By this I mean that it has been a moment-to-moment measure of an audience's semantic judgements during a period of television research when there was little theory of moment-to-moment processing of television. The case that it can provide insight into semantic processes is supported by the fact that the data produced by such systems have long been used as a means to probe and guide focus groups in the interpretation of their own responses to programming (Merton, 1956). Therefore, it can be used along with protocol analysis.

Using multiple semantic differential scales, a researcher can generate real time patterns of semantic judgment that are correlates of underlying semantic processes (Biocca & David, 1989). The automated subgroup analysis can reveal group differences in semantic processing. By varying the subject's task, the research can try to probe processing activity in some of the schematic frames. Similarly, statistical analyses of the moment-to-moment data can be used to derive an indicator of attention to television (see Biocca & David, forthcoming).

Psychophysiological Measures. Various psychophysiological measures have been used to analyze the processing of commercials (Alwitt, 1985; Fletcher, 1971; Lang, in press; Reeves et al., 1985; Rothschild & Thorson, 1983; Schleuder, in press; Stewart & Furse, 1982). The advantage is that these are also moment-to-moment measures of moment-to-moment processes. But there is some question as to the degree to which the measures are sensitive to subtle semantic processes (Hillyard & Kutas, 1983). Connecting a specific change with some aspect of the stimulus sometimes leads to problems of interpretation (Price, Rust, & Kumar, 1986; Rothschild & Thorson, 1983; Stewart & Furse, 1982). Nonetheless, the measures have provided valuable insight into the global effects of some structural variables of television presentations (Lang, in press; Reeves et al., 1982). It remains to be seen whether they can assist us in understanding the kind of processes covered by the model of the schematic frames.

Reaction Time. This popular measure is used to probe semantic processing within a variety of measurement paradigms: (a) semantic priming/inhibition paradigms, (b) perceptual detection and judgement tasks, (c) and secondary task or probe reaction time paradigm (see Bower & Clapper, 1990; Carroll, 1980; Carroll & Bever, 1976; Schleuder, in press). While the specific measure may vary (i.e. simple reaction time, choice reaction time for a perceptual judgement or semantic judgement), the approaches all use these measures to detect cognitive effort or, similarly, the effect of the stimulus on semantic facilitation or inhibition within the viewer. Such techniques are useful to explore stimulus parsing and cycling (Carroll, 1980; Carroll & Bever, 1976) and can be used to detect the "involvement" that accompanies deep processing activated by self-schematic framing (Petty & Cacioppo, 1986).

Speeded recognition measures using choice reaction time remain one of the few ways to explore the structure of the imagery model of the commercial. One can test for the memory for key frames and through these measures make inferences about cognitive processing. The measure is sometimes included in a semantic facilitation or inhibition paradigm.

Eye Movement Measures. Eye movement measures have provided valuable insight into the semantic processing of texts (Carpenter & Just, 1976a; Just & Carpenter, 1977) and pictures (Carpenter & Just, 1976a; Fleming, 1969; Loftus, 1976; Rayner, 1984). They reflect higher cognitive processes including inference making and schema activation (Sender, Fisher, & Monty, 1978). Although much commercial work is regularly done on the relationship of eye movements to the processing of commercials, there is less systematic, theoretically driven work though there are some notable exceptions (e.g., Flagg, 1978; Sheena & Flagg, 1978; Wolf, 1970).

Eye movement measures can provide insight into how viewer's construct video sentences as they select various aspects of image. We would expect different processing strategies to be reflected in different eye movement patterns, especially on larger screens.

AI modeling. The outline of the schematic framing approach is by no means specified in enough detail to allow us, any time soon, to be able to produce even a primitive artificial intelligence (AI) model of the semantic processing of television. But Johnson Laird (1983) in a book titled *Mental Models* strongly advocated the use of AI modeling to define and test theories of mental models. The complexity of television stimuli makes this impossible for much more than the processing of verbal scripts. Nonetheless, specifying theories in such a way that they can eventually enter an AI model of the process can lend some vigor and specificity to the theory, and prepare for later integration into AI models that may emerge from work in psychology and computer science (Hinton & Anderson, 1981; Rumelhart et al., 1986a, 1986b).

Summary and conclusion.

During the course of the cognitive processing of television, it is hypothesized that the viewer models the flow of information and imagery using molar structures similar to the schematic frames described earlier. In the mind of the viewer, schematic frames organize information and inferences about places and social situations (possible worlds); people, causes, and agents (actants); topics (discursive frames); as well as inferences about ideologies and how the programming relates to the viewer (ideological and self-schematic frames).

With each second—or even millisecond—of processing, there will be slight changes in the values calculated in each of the schematic frames. The way a television program or message introduces information and topics (strategy of semantic disclosures embedded in the semantic frames of the message) will influence which schematic frames are foregrounded by the viewer (which information is attended to and how it guides the viewers' inferences). Foregrounding, like assertion and supposition in sentences, creates a relative hierarchy among the schematic frames, and, therefore, influences the default values assigned to the frames during the processing of a scene (i.e., processing cycle). For example, the instantiation of a narrative schema might influence the range and selection of actants and actantial roles assigned to the actantial frame.

By tracing the pattern of semantic disclosures in a political message and hypothesizing the potential patterns of schema instantiation and frame activation in the minds of viewers, it may be possible to plot not only the semantic path of the model viewer but the likely points of inferential activity or communication failure for various groups of instantiated viewers. For any television program or message, there are likely to be key points in the course of the semantic disclosure where inferences based on values in the schematic frames are critical to the processing of the message. By looking at how each shot and scene presents its information, it may be possible to (a) model the semantic path of the model viewer. By altering assumptions regarding the code competence of the viewer, the research can create models of alternative semantic processing that (b) anticipate likely points of interpretive failure, and (c) predict likely points where some viewers may instantiate alternative or oppositional schema.

For any message there will be a path or pattern of semantic activation expected of the model viewer. For that same message there will be varying partial, distorted, and oppositional decodings of its meaning. Based on some knowledge of the average code competence of various audiences or the universe of schema likely to be activated, an analyst may be able to model (a) the various "meanings" of the message (paths of semantic activation) for different audiences, and (b) the changing meaning of a message over the course of various exposures.

To watch television is to create meaning, to create mental models of the world on the screen. All discussion of the effects of television rests on our understanding this fundamental process. If an increasingly major part of a voter's political thinking is defined within the boundaries of the political commercial, it is very important to understand how thought is modeled within these 30-second bites. The mind of the viewer is generating mental models of television, all of television. The content area of the political commercial is but one set of frames in the endless stream of frames that constitutes the psychological experience of television. In the final analysis, it is clear that to understand the mental representation of political commercials, it is necessary to first understand the mental representation of television.

REFERENCES

Aaker, D. A., Staymen, D. M., & Hagerty, M. R. (1986). Warmth in advertising: Measurement, impact, and sequence effects. *Journal of Consumer Research, 12,* 365–381.

Alwitt, L. (1985). EEG activity reflects the content of commercials. In L. F. Alwitt & A. A. Mitchell (Eds.). *Psychological processes and advertising effects: theory, research, and application* (pp. 201–220). Hillsdale, NJ: Lawrence Erlbaum Associates.

Anderson, J. (1976). *Language, memory, and thought.* Hillsdale, NJ: Lawrence Erlbaum Associates.

Anderson, J. (1978). Arguements concerning representations for mental imagery. *Psychological Review, 85,* 249–277.

Anderson, J. (1980). *Cognitive psychology and its implications.* San Francisco: Freeman.

Anderson, J. (1981). *Cognitive skills and their acquisition.* Hillsdale, NJ: Lawrence Erlbaum Associates.

Baddeley, A. (1986). *Working memory.* Oxford: Clarendon Press.

Biocca, F. (1988). Opposing conceptions of the audience: The active and passive hemispheres of mass communication theory. In J. Anderson (Ed.). *Communication Yearbook 11* (pp. 51–80). Beverly Hills: Sage.

Biocca, F. (1990). Semiotics and mass communication: Points of intersection. In T. Sebeok & J. Umiker-Sebeok (Eds.), *Semiotic web 1990.* The Hague: Mouton Press.

Biocca, F. (in press-a). Looking for units of meaning in political ads. In F. Biocca (Ed.), *Telvision and Political Advertising: Vol. 2. Signs, Codes, and Images.* Hillsdale, NJ: Lawrence Erlbaum Associates.

Biocca, F. (in press-b). Determining the role of communication codes in political ads. In F. Biocca (Ed.), *Telvision and Political Advertising: Vol. 2. Signs, Codes, and Images.* Hillsdale, NJ: Lawrence Erlbaum Associates.

Biocca, F. (in press-c). The analysis of discourses within the political ad. In F. Biocca (Ed.), *Telvision and Political Advertising: Vol. 2. Signs, Codes, and Images.* Hillsdale, NJ: Lawrence Erlbaum Associates.

Biocca, F. (in press-d). The orchestration of codes and discourses: Analysis of semantic framing. In F. Biocca (Ed.), *Television and Political Advertising: Vol. 2. Signs, Codes, and Images.* Hillsdale, NJ: Lawrence Erlbaum Associates.

Biocca, F., & David. P. (1989). *The use of semantic scales for continuous audience measurement.* Beverly Hills: Quick Tally Corporation (technical report).

Biocca, F., & David, P. (forthcoming). Computerized audience response systems: Theory, methods, and technology. In J. Schleuder (Ed.), *Measures of the psychological processing of television.* Hillsdale, NJ: Lawrence Erlbaum Associates.

Biocca, F., Neuwirth, K., Oshagan, H., Zhongdang, P., & Richards, J. (1987, May). *Prime-and-probe methodology: An experimental technique for studying film and television.* Paper presented to the International Communication Association, Montreal.

Bordwell, D. (1985). *Narration in the fiction film.* Madison: University of Wisconsin Press.

Bordwell, D., & Thompson, K. (1986). *Film art.* New York: Knopf.

Borgida, E., & Howard-Pitney, B. B. (1983). Personal involvement and the robustness of perceptual salience effects. *Journal of Personality and Social Psychology, 45,* 560–570.

Bower, G. H. (1976). Experiments on story understanding and recall. *Quarterly Journal of Experimental Psychology, 28,* 511–534.

Bower, G. H., & Cirilo, R. K. (1985). Cognitive psychology and text processing. In T. A. van Dijk (Ed.), *Handbook of discourse analysis.* (Vol. 1, pp. 71–106). New York: Academic Press.

Bower, G. H., & Clapper, J. P. (1990). Experimental methods in cognitive science. In M. Posner (Ed.), *Foundations of cognitive science* (pp. 245–300). Cambridge, MA: MIT Press.

Branigan, E. (1984). *Point of view in the cinema.* New York: Mouton.

Brewer, W., & Dupree, D. (1983). Use of plan schemata in the recall and recognition of goal-directed actions. *Journal of Experimental Psychology: Learning, Memory and Cognition, 9,* 117–129.

Brewer, W. F., & Nakumura, G. V. (1983). The nature and function of schemas. In R. Wyer & T. K. Srull (Eds.). *Handbook of Social Cognition* (Vol. 1, pp. 119–159). Hillsdale, NJ: Lawrence Erlbaum Associates.

Brock, T., & Shavitt, S. (1983). Cognitive-response analysis in advertising. In L. Percy & A. G. Woodside (Eds.). *Advertising and consumer psychology* (pp. 91–116). Lexington: Lexington Books.

Carpenter, P. A., & Just, M. A. (1976). Linguistic influences on picture scanning. In R. A. Monty & J. W. Senders (Eds.), *Eye movements and psychological processes* (pp. 459–72). Hillsdale: Lawrence Erlbaum Associates.

Carpenter, P. A., & Just, M. A. (1977). Reading comprehension as the eyes see it. In M. Just & P. Carpenter (Eds.). *Cognitive processes in comprehension* (pp. 459–472). New York: John Wiley & Sons.

Carr, T. H., McCauley, C., Sperber, R. D., & Parmelee C. (1982). Words, pictures, and priming: On semantic activation, conscious identification, and the automaticity of information processing. *Journal of Experimental Psychology: Human Perception and Performance, 8(6),* 757–77.

Carroll, J. M. (1980). *Toward a structural psychology of cinema.* The Hague: Mouton.

Carroll, J., & Bever, T. (1976). Segmentation in cinema perception. *Science, 191,* 1053–1055.

Cermak, L., & Craik, F. (1979). *Levels of processing in human memory.* Hillsdale, NJ: Lawrence Erlbaum Associates.

Chafe, W. (1974). Language and consciousness. *Language, 50,* 111–133.

Clark, H. H., & Clark, E. (1977). *Psychology and language.* Chicago: Harcourt Brace Jovanovich.

Clark, H., & Sengul, C. (1979). In search of referents for nouns and pronouns. *Memory and Cognition, 7,* 35–51.

Cohen, C. (1981). Goals and schemata in person perception: making sense from the stream of behavior. In E. Cantor & J. Kihlstrom (Eds.), *Personality, cognition, and social interaction* (pp. 119–144). Hillsdale, NJ: Erlbaum Associates.

Collins, A. (1979). Children's comprehension of television programs. In E. Wartella (Ed.), *Children communicating: Media and development in thought, speech, understanding.* Beverly Hills, CA: Sage.

Collins, A., & Loftus, E. (1975). A spreading activation theory of semantic processing. *Psychological Review, 82,* 407–428.

Conover, P. J., & Feldman, S. (1986). The role of inference in the perception of political candidates. In R. Lau & D. Sears (Eds.), *Political cognition* (pp. 127–158). Hillsdale, NJ: Lawrence Erlbaum Associates.

Ebbesen, E. (1980). Cognitive processes in understanding ongoing behavior. In R. Hastie, E. Ostrom, D. Wyer, D. Hamilton, & D. Carlston (Eds.), *Person memory: The cognitive basis of social perception.* Hillsdale, NJ: Erlbaum Associates.

Eco, U. (1976). *A theory of semiotics.* Bloomington, IN: Indiana University Press.

Eco, U. (1979). *The role of the reader.* Bloomington, IN: Indiana University Press.

Ekman, P. (1974). *Unmasking the face.* Englewood Cliffs, NJ: Prentice-Hall.

Ericsson, K. A., & Simon, H. (1985). *Protocol analysis: Verbal reports as data.* Cambridge: MIT Press.

Fiske, J. (1987). *Television culture.* London: Methuen.

Fiske, S., & Kinder, D. (1981). Involvement, expertise, and schema use: Evidence from political cognition. In N. Cantor & J. F. Kihlstrom (Eds.), *Personality, cognition, and social interaction* (pp. 171–192). Hillsdale, NJ: Lawrence Erlbaum Associates.

Fiske, S., & Kinder, D., Larter, W. (1983). The novice and expert knowledge based strategies in political cognition. *Journal of Experimental Social Psychology, 19,* 381–400.

Fiske, S., & Taylor, S. (1984). *Social cognition.* New York: Random House.

Flagg, B. (1978). Children and television: Effects of stimulus repetition on eye activity. In J. W. Senders, D. Fisher & R. Monty (Eds.), *Eye movements and the higher psychological functions* (pp. 279–291). Hillsdale, NJ: Lawrence Erlbaum Associates.

Fleming, M. (1969). Eye movement indices of cognitive behavior. *Audio-visual communications review, 17,* 383–398.

Fletcher, J. E. (1971). The orienting response as an indication of broadcast communication effect. *Psychophysiology, 8,* 699–703.

Fodor, J. A. (1968). *Psychological explanation.* New York: Random House.

Garnham, A. (1985). *Psycholinguistics: central topics.* London: Methuen.

Garramone, G. (1983). Image versus issue orientation and effects of political advertising. *Communication Research, 10,* 59–76.

Garramone, G. (1986). Candidate image formation: the role of information processing. In L. Kaid, D. Nimmo & K. Sander (Eds.), *New perspectives in political advertising.* Carbondale, IL: Southern Illinois University Press.

Garreau, J. (1981). *The nine nations of north America.* Boston: Houghton-Mifflin.

Gibson, J. J. (1979). *The ecological approach to visual perception.* Boston: Houghton. Mifflin.

Greenwald, A., & Leavitt, C. (1985). Cognitive theory and audience involvement. In L. F. Alwitt, & A. A. Mitchell (Eds.), *Psychological processes and advertising effects: theory, research, and application* (pp. 221–240). Hillsdale, NJ: Lawrence Erlbaum Associates.

Greimas, A. A. (1986). Actant. In T. Sebeok (Ed.), *Encyclopedic dictionary of semiotics.* (Vol. 1, pp. 7). Berlin: Mouton de Gruyter.

Greimas, A. A., & Courtes, J. J. (1982). *Semiotics and language: An analytical dictionary.* Bloomington: Indiana University Press.

Hall, S. (1980a). Recent developments in theories of language and ideology: a critical note. In D. H. A. L. and Paul Willis Stuart Hall (Eds.), *Culture, media, language* (pp. 117–121). London: Hutchison.

Hall, S. (1980b). Encoding/Decoding. In S. Hall, D. Hobson, A. Lowe, & P. Willis (Eds.), *Culture, media, language* (pp. 127–138). London: Hutchison.

Hartley, J. (1982). *Understanding news.* London: Methuen.

Haviland, S., & Clark, H. (1974). What's new? Acquiring new information as a process of comprehension. *Journal of Verbal Learning and Verbal Behavior, 13,* 512–521.

Herbner, G., Van Tubergen, G. N., & Whitlow, S. S. (1979). Dynamics of the frame in visual composition. *ECTJ, 27*(2), 83–88.

Higgins, E., & King, G. (1981). Accessibility of social constructs: Information processing consequences of individual and contextual variability. In N. Cantor & J. F. Kihlstrom (Eds.), *Personality, cognition, and social interaction* (pp. 69–122). Hillsdale, NJ: Lawrence Erlbaum Associates.

Hillyard, S., & Kutas, M. (1983). Electrophysiology of cognitive processing. *Annual Review of Psychology, 34,* 33–61.

Hinton, G., & Anderson, J. (1981). *Parallel models of associative memory.* Hillsdale, NJ: Lawrence Erlbaum Associates.

Hochberg, J. (1986). Representation of motion and space in video and cinematic displays. In K. Boff, L. Kaufmann & J. Thomas (Eds.), *Handbook of perception and human performance* (Vol. 2, pp. 21-1–21-64). New York: Wiley.

Hornby, P. (1974). Surface structure and presupposition. *Journal of Verbal Learning and Verbal Behavior, 13,* 530–538.

Jacoby, J., & Hoyer, W. (1987). *Comprehension and miscomprehension of print communications: An investigation of mass media magazines.* Hillsdale, NJ: Lawrence Erlbaum Associates.

Jacoby, J., Hoyer, W., & Sheluga D. (1980). *Miscomprehension of televised communications.* New York: American Association of Advertising Agencies.

Jacoby, J., Hoyer, W., & Sheluga D. (1981). Miscomprehension of televised communication: A brief report of findings. *Advances in Consumer Research, 8,* 410–413.

Jamieson, K. H. (1984). *Packaging the presidency. A history and criticism of presidential campaign advertising.* New York: Oxford University Press.

Jarvella, R. (1975). Syntactic processing of connected speech. *Journal of Verbal Learning and Verbal Behavior, 10,* 409–416.

Johnson-Laird, P. (1983). *Mental models: Towards a cognitive science of language, inference, and consciousness.* Cambridge, MA: Harvard University Press.

Just, M. A., & Carpenter, P. A. Eds. (1977). *Cognitive processes in comprehension.* New York: John Wiley & Sons.

Kendon, A. (1977). *Studies in the behavior of social interaction.* Bloomington, IN: Indiana University Press.

Kintsch, W., & E. Greene. (1978). The role of culture-specific schemata in the comprehension and recall of stories. *Discourse Processes, 1,* 1–13.

Kintsch, W., Kozminsky, E., Steby, W. J., McKoon, G., & Keenan, J. M. (1975). Comprehension and recall of text as a function of context variables. *Journal of Verbal Learning and Verbal Behavior, 14,* 196–214.

Kintsch, W., & van Dijk, T. (1978). Toward a model of text comprehension and production. *Psychological Review, 85*(5), 363–393.

Kosslyn, S. (1980). *Images and mind.* Cambridge, MA: Harvard University Press.

Kraft, R. (1986). The role of cutting in the evaluation and retention of film. *Journal of Experimental Psychology: Learning, Memory, and Cognition, 12,* 155–163.

Kraft, R. N. (1987). The influence of camera angle on comprehension and retention of pictorial events. *Memory & Cognition, 15,* 291–307.

Kristeva, J. (1969). *Semiotike: Recherches pour une Semanalyse* (Semiotics: Research for a semioanalysis). Paris: Seuil.

Krugman, H. (1965). The impact of television advertising: Learning without involvement. *Public Opinion Quarterly, 29,* 349–356.

Kuiper, N., & Derry, P. (1981). The self as a cognitive prototype: An application to person perception and depression. In N. Cantor & Kihlstrom, J. (Eds.), *Personality, cognition, and social interaction* (pp. 56–59). Hillsdale, NJ: Erlbaum Associates.

Labov, W. (1972). *Sociolinguistic patterns.* Philadelphia: University of Philadelphia.

Lachman, R., Lachman, J., & Butterfield, E. (1979). *Cognitive psychology and information processing.* Hillsdale, NJ: Lawrence Erlbaum Associates.

Lang, A. (in press). Involuntary attention and physiological arousal evoked by formal features and mild emotion in TV commercials. *Communication Research.*

Lastovicka, J., & Gardener, D. (1979). Components of involvement. In J. Maloney & B. Silverman (Ed.). *Attitude research plays for high stakes* (pp. 143–178). Chicago, IL: American Marketing Association.

Lau, R. R. (1986). Political schemata, candidate evaluations, and voting behavior. In R. Lau & D. Sears (Eds.), *Political cognition* (pp. 000). Hillsdale, NJ: Lawrence Erlbaum Associates.

Levy, M. (1982). The Lazarsfeld-Stanton program analyzer: An historical note. *Journal of Communication,* 30–38.

Levy, M. R., & Windahl, S. (1984). Audience activity and gratifications: A conceptual clarification and exploration. *Communication Research, 11*(1), 51–78.

Leymore, V. (1975). *Hidden myth: Structure and symbolism in advertising.* London: Heinemann Educational Books.

Lichtenstein, E., & Bower, G. H. (1978). Memory for goal-directed events. *Cognitive Psychology, 9,* 111–151.

Lindlof, T. (1988). Media audiences as interpretive communities. In J. A. Anderson (Ed.), *Communication Yearbook 11* (pp. 81–107). Beverly Hills, CA: Sage.

Linsky, L. (1971). *Reference and modality.* London: Oxford University Press.

Loftus, G. (1976). A framework for a theory of picture recognition. In R. A. Monty & Senders, J. W. (Eds.), *Eye movements and psychological processes* (pp. 499–513). Hillsdale: Lawrence Erlbaum Associates.

Mandler, J. (1978). A code in the node: The use of story schema in retrieval. *Discourse Processes, 1,* 11–35.

Mandler, J., & Johnson, N. (1977). Remembrance of things parsed: Story structure and recall. *Cognitive Psychology, 9,* 11–151.

Marvel, A. J. (1983a). Conscious and unconscious perception: An approach to the relations between phenomenal experience and perceptual processes. *Cognitive Psychology, 15,* 238–300.

Marcel, A. J. (1983b). Conscious and unconscious perception: Experiments on visual masking and word recognition. *Cognitive Psychology, 15,* 197–237.

Markus, H. (1977). Self-schemata and processing information about the self. *Journal of Personality and Social Psychology, 35,* 63–78.

Markus, H., & Sentis, K. (1982). The self in information processing. In J. Sols (Ed), *Social psychological perspectives on the self* (pp. 98–126). Hillsdale, NJ: Erlbaum Associates.

Marr, D. (1982). *Vision: A computational investigation in the human representation of visual information.* San Francisco: Freeman.

Merton, R. K. (1956). *The focused interview, a manual of problems and procedures.* Glencoe, IL: The Free Press.

Metz, C. (1974). *Film Language.* New York: Oxford University Press.

Meyer, D., & Schvaneveldt, R. (1976). Meaning, memory structure, and mental processes. In C. Cofer (Ed.). *Structure of human memory.* San Francisco: Freeman.

Minsky, M. (1975). Frame-system theory. In R. C. Shank & B. Nash-Webber (Eds.). *Theoretical issues in natural language processing.* Cambridge, MA: MIT press.

Monaco, J. (1977). *How to read a film.* New York: Oxford University Press.

Morley, D. (1980). *The nationwide audience: Structure and decoding.* London: British Film Institute.

Newell, A. (1981). Reasoning, problem solving and decision processes: The problem space as a fundamental category. In R. Nickerson (Ed.), *Attention and Performance.* Hillsdale, NJ: Lawrence Erlbaum Associates.

Newtson, D., & Enquist, G. (1976). The perceptual organization of ongoing behavior. *Journal of Experimental Social Psychology, 12,* 436–450.

Olson, D. (1976). Culture technology and intellect. In L. L. Resnick (Ed.), *The nature of intelligence* (pp. 23–56). Hillsdale, NJ: Lawrence Erlbaum Associates.

Osgood, C., Suci, G. & Tannenbaum, P. (1975). *The measurement of meaning.* Urbana, IL: University of Illinois Press.

Ortony, A., Ed. (1979). *Metaphor and thought.* Cambridge: Cambridge University Press.

Petolfi, J. (1971). *Transformationsgrammatiken und eine kotextuelle textheorie* (Transformation grammar and a contextual theory). Frankfurt: Athenaeum.

Petty, R., & Cacioppo, J. (1979). Issue involvement can increase or decrease persuasion by enhancing message relevant responses. *Journal of Personality and Social Psychology, 3,* 1915–1926.

Petty, R., Cacioppo, J. (1981). *Attitudes and persuasion: Classic and contemporary approaches.* Dubuque: Brown.

Petty, R., & Cacioppo, J. (1984). The effects of involvement on response to argument quality: Central and peripheral routes to persuasion. *Journal of Personality and Social Psychology, 46,* 69–81.

Petty, R., & Cacioppo, J. (1986). *Communication and persuasion: Central and peripheral routes to attitude change.* New York: Springer-Verlag.

Petty, R., Cacioppo, J., & Goldman, R. R. (1981). Personal involvement as a determinant of argument-based persuasion. *Journal of Personality and Social Psychology, 41,* 847–855.

Petty, R., Ostrom, T., & Brock, T. (1981). *Cognitive responses in persuasion.* Hillsdale, NJ: Lawrence Erlbaum Associates Associates.

Price, L., Rust, R., & Kumar, V. (1986). Brain-wave analyses of consumer response to advertising. In L. Percy & A. G. Woodside (Eds.). *Advertising and consumer psychology* (pp. 17–34). Lexington: Lexington Books.

Propp, V. (1968). *The morphology of the folktale.* Austin: University of Texas Press.

Pudovkin, V. (1954). *Film technique and film acting.* London: Vision.

Rayner, K. (1984). Visual selection in reading, picture perception, and visual search. In H. Bouma, & D. Bouwhuis (Eds.), *Attention and performance X: Control of language processes* (pp. 67–96). Hillsdale, NJ: Lawrence Erlbaum Associates.

Reeves, B., Chaffee, S., & Tims, A. (1982). Social cognition and mass communication research. In M. Roloff & C. Berger (Eds.), *Social cognition and communication,* (pp. 287–326). Hillsdale, NJ: Lawrence Erlbaum Associates.

Reeves, B., Thorson, E., Rothschild, M., McDonald, D., Hirsch, J., & Goldstein, R. (1985). Attention to television: Instrastimulus effects of movement and scene changes on alpha variations over time. *International Journal of Neuroscience, 28,* 241–263.

Rips, L. J., Shoben, E. J., & Smith, E. E. (1973). Semantic distance and the verification of semantic relations. *Journal of Verbal Learning and Verbal Behavior, 12*, 1–20.

Rossiter, J. R., & Percy, L. (1983). Visual communication in advertising. In R. J. Harris (Ed.), *Information processing in advertising* (pp. 83–125). Hillsdale, NJ: Lawrence Erlbaum Associates.

Rothschild, M., & Thorson, E. (1983). Electroencephalographic activity as a response to complex stimuli. *Proceedings of the second annual advertising and consumer psychology conference*, 239–251.

Rowland, W., & Watkins, B. (1984). *Interpreting television: Current research perspectives.* Beverly Hills, CA: Sage.

Rumelhart, D. (1977). Understanding and summarizing brief stories. In D. Laberge & M. Collins (Eds.), *Basic processes in reading: Perception and comprehension* (pp. 265–304). Hillsdale, NJ: Lawrence Erlbaum Associates.

Rumelhart, D. (1980). Schemata: The building blocks of cognition. In R. Spiro, B. Bruce & W. Brewer (Eds.), *Theoretical issues in reading comprehension: Perspectives from cognitive psychology, linguistics, artificial intelligence, and education* (pp. 33–58). Hillsdale, NJ: Lawrence Erlbaum Associates.

Rumelhart, D. (1983). Schemata and the cognitive system. In R. Wyer & T. Srull (Eds.), *Handbook of social cognition*, (pp. 161–188). Hillsdale, NJ: Lawrence Erlbaum Associates.

Rumelhart, D., McClelland, J., & PDP-Research-Group (Eds.) (1986a). *Parallel Distributed Processing: Explorations in the microstructure of cognition. Vol. 1. Foundations.* Cambridge, MA: MIT Press.

Rumelhart, D., McClelland, J., & PDP-Research-Group (Eds.) (1986b). *Parallel Distributed Processing: Explorations in the microstructure of cognition. Vol. 2. Psychological and biological models.* Cambridge, MA: MIT Press.

Sabato, L. J. (1981). *The rise of political consultants.* New York: Basic Books.

Salomon, G. (1979). *Interaction of media, cognition, and learning.* San Francisco: Jossey-Bass.

Schank, R. (1982). *Dynamic memory: A theory of reminding and leaning in computers and people.* Cambridge: Cambridge University Press.

Schank, R., & Abelson, R. (1977). *Scripts, plans, goals, and understanding: an inquiry into human knowledge structures.* Hillsdale, NJ: Lawrence Erlbaum Associates.

Schleuder, J. (forthcoming). The use of reaction time to measure attention. In J. Scheluder (Ed.), *Psychological measures of television viewing.* Hillsdale, NJ: Lawrence Erlbaum Associates.

Sebeok, T. (Ed.). (1986). *Encyclopedic dictionary of semiotics.* Berlin: Mouton de Gruyter.

Senders, J. W., Fisher, D., & Monty, R. (1978). *Eye movements and the higher psychological functions.* Hillsdale, NJ: Lawrence Erlbaum Associates.

Sentis, K., & Markus, H. (1986). Brand personality and self. In J. Olson & K. Sentis (Eds.), *Advertising and consumer psychology.* (Vol. 3, pp. 132–148). New York: Praeger.

Sheena, D., & Flagg, B. (1978). Semiautomatic eye movement data analysis techniques for experiments with varying scenes. In J. W. Senders, D. Fisher & R. Monty (Eds.), *Eye movements and the higher psychological functions* (pp. 65–76). Hillsdale, NJ: Lawrence Erlbaum Associates.

Sherif, M., & Hovland, C. (1961). *Social judgement: Assimilation and contrast effects in communication and attitude change.* New Haven, CT: Yale University Press.

Stewart, D., & Furse, D. H. (1980). *Effective television advertising: A study of 1000 commercials.* Lexington: Lexington Books.

Stewart, D. W., & Furse, D. H. (1982). Applying psychological measures to marketing and advertising research problems. In J. H. Leigh & C. R. Martin (Eds.), *Current issues and research in advertising* (pp. 1–38). Michigan: University of Michigan.

Strange, J. J., & Black, J. B. (1989). *Imagined point of view. Causal inference and mental models of narrative events.* Paper presented to the Information Systems Division of the International Communication Association. San Francisco, California, May, 1989.

Taylor, S., & Fiske, S. (1978). Salience, attention, and attribution: Top of the head phenomena. In L. Berkowitz (Ed.), *Advances in experimental social psychology* (Vol. 11, pp. 250–287). New York: Academic Press.

Thorndyke, P. (1977). Cognitive structures in comprehension and memory of narrative discourses. *Cognitive Psychology, 9,* 77–110.

Thorson, E., & Snyder, R. (1984). Viewer recall of television commercials: Prediction from the propositional structure of commercial scripts. *Journal of Marketing Research, 21,* 127–136.

van Dijk, T. (1980). *Macrostructures.* Hillsdale, NJ: Lawrence Erlbaum Associates.

van Dijk, T. (1988). *News Analysis: Case studies of international and national news in the press.* Hillsdale, NJ: Lawrence Erlbaum Associates.

van Dijk, T. (1988). *News as discourse.* Hillsdale, NJ: Lawrence Erlbaum Associates.

van Dijk, T., & Kintsch, W. (1983). *Strategies of discourse comprehension.* New York: Academic Press.

Vygotsky, L. L. (1978). *Mind and society* (M. Cole, V. V. John-Steiner, S. S. Scribner & E. E. Souberman, Eds.). Cambridge, MA: Harvard University Press.

Waszak, C. (1988). *The role of self-schema in persuasion: An examination of the elaboration likelihood model.* Unpublished paper, Dept. of Psychology, University of North Carolina at Chapel Hill, Chapel Hill, NC.

Wells, W., (Ed.). (1974). *Life style and psychographics.* Chicago: American Marketing Association.

Williamson, J. (1978). *Decoding advertisements: Ideology and meaning in advertising.* London: Marion Boyars.

Woelfel, J., & Fink, E. (1980). *The measurement of communication processes: Galileo theory and method.* New York: Academic Press.

Wolf, W. (1971). Perception of visual displays. *Viewpoints.* 112–140.

Wyer, R., & Gordon, S. (1984). The cognitive representation of social information. In R. Wyer & T. Srull (Eds.), *Handbook of social cognition* (Vol. 2, pp. 73–150). Hillsdale, NJ: Lawrence Erlbaum Associates.

3

Models of a Successful and an Unsuccessful Ad: An Exploratory Analysis

Frank Biocca
University of North Carolina at Chapel Hill

This chapter provides a set of examples, exploratory analyses of two political commercials using the conceptual framework of the schematic-framing approach (see Biocca, Chapter 2, this volume). The analyses are intended to illustrate some of the issues that might arise in the initial phase of generating hypothesized mental models for political commercials. The analyses are further illustrated by reference to some computerized audience response data, focus group interviews, and in-depth interviews. The data were collected from uncommitted voters in focus groups conducted in the final 2 weeks of the 1988 presidential election.[1]

---

[1]Note on method: The data were collected by the author and a team of researchers and journalists on Tuesday, October 16, 1988 in Springfield, Ohio. The data collection was part of a study designed as a test of political ads for a *USA TODAY* article and, therefore, was not designed to test the schematic framing model. Some of the results were subsequently reported in *USA TODAY* (Katz, 1988a, 1988b).

Subjects

Thirty-five undecided voters were randomly selected from the Springfield, Ohio community because Ohio was a "swing state" and Springfield was a "bellwether" community that had tended to vote for the winning presidential candidate in past presidential elections. Subjects were paid $30 to participate. The political makeup of the group included 10 Republicans, 13 Democrats, and 12 independents. The 35 subjects were divided into two focus groups.

Stimuli

Subjects viewed a videotape containing 20 political commercials embedded within programming and nonpolitical commercials. Half the test commercials were Bush ads and

In the following discussion, the data are used *solely* to illustrate rather than to confirm the analysis.

The chapter proceeds by examining each commercial using the schematic frames discussed in Chapter 2. The analysis attempts to outline: (a) the inferential activity of the model viewer, (b) key points of likely inference making on the part of the instantiated viewer, and (c) structural properties that facilitate or interfere with the activation of the model viewer. Semantic-processing issues considered are the kinds of structural considerations that can lead the analyst/researcher to posit various mental models of the ad prior to testing their prevalence in a population of viewers.

SCHEMATIC FRAMING AND AN EXAMPLE
OF A SUCCESSFUL AD

Table 3.1 contains the script for a George Bush image commercial titled "Family" from the 1988 presidential campaign. The commercial tested well on computerized audience response systems, focus groups comments, and was noted by professionals as a successful commercial (Katz, 1988a, 1988b).

The analysis that follows uses abbreviations that make reference to the following items numbered in the script: (a) shots (Shot #), (b) video propositions (VP #), (c) audio propositions (AP #), and (d) audio cues (AC #).

---

half were Dukakis ads. The order of the commercials and programming was counterbalanced with different presentation orders for the two focus groups.

Procedure

Subjects were told that the study was designed to test *USA TODAY* programming. Subjects were instructed to respond to the programming and commercials using a computerized audience response system (Biocca & David, in press) and were told to return the response device to neutral before each commercial or programming segment. The input device had a 7-point dial representing a semantic differential scale of: (1) strongly dislike, (2) moderately dislike, (3) slightly dislike, (4) neutral, (5) slightly like, (6) moderately like, and (7) strongly like. Audience opinions were collected every 2 seconds by an IBM computer.

Following the first exposure, subjects were shown the political commercials again without the programming. At the end of each reviewing they were asked whether the commercial made them (1) more likely, (2) less likely to vote for the candidate, or whether it made (3) no difference in their voting preference for the sponsor. Subjects were also asked whether they thought the ad was fair or unfair.

In the final phase of the study, a traditional focus group was conducted. Some of the ads were replayed to the audience and subjects were probed to elicit their verbal analyses of the ads and their thoughts about how the ads made them feel about the candidates.

Let us start by looking at an aspect of the semantic macrostructure (see types of macrostructure in van Dijk, 1988a) of the commercial (see Fig. 3.1). Looking at the overall structure, we find that the commercial is semantically framed by a combination of narrative and discursive structures (syntagmas) (see Bordwell & Thompson, 1986; Metz, 1974). The opening shot and the final action shot are combined by common form (matched possible world, matched point of sight) and subject matter into a simple episode. Most of the commercial uses a discursive frame within which are linked associated images, one half is connected by the voice over of Barbara Bush, the other half organized by the voice of a male announcer. As we see later these structural divisions appear to frame some of the semantic processing of the commercial.

"Possible-World" Schematic Framing.

According to the schematic framing model discussed in the previous chapter, the opening shot will lead audience members seeing the commercial to assign the incoming information to some bracketed "possible world." Shot 1 of the running child is in soft focus and slow motion. There is a common cinematic code that has associated this type of shot with an actant's internal imagery or "thoughts" and, especially, "memories" (Pudovkin, 1954). The slow, wistful, reflective music also cues the viewer to activate a schematic possible world frame for "mental image" or "memory." This is an "intertextual" schematic frame assembled from the average viewer's years of experience with many other films and TV programs ("texts") that used this cinematic code. The instantiation of this possible world frame, which appears to match the processing of the model viewer, should be automatically activated for a certain percentage of the actual viewers and can be explored and tested by simply stopping the commercial at this point and recording subject protocols.

If the instantiated viewer activates the schematic frame for a possible world of an actant's mental image or memory, the viewer will be automatically "testing" this "bracketed" inference against incoming information from the commercial. Confirmatory semantic disclosures are soon present in the introspective comments of Barbara Bush. Her comments begin with a highly personalized voice-over. Confirmatory linguistic information that the viewer should infer "reflection" or "memory" from this scene is presented on the audio track in the form of Barbara Bush's reflection on George Bush AP2 "as I see him" and AP4, "I'll always love the *time when* . . .". The video and audio semantic cues interweave to direct the model viewer toward instantiating a possible world of "memory" and "mental image" as well as borrowed identity point-of-view (see later).

Table 3.1 Bush 1988 Political Commercial: "Family"

	Video	Audio
SHOT 1 	Fade from black to opening shot (*VP1*) of smiling, blond-haired child running across a field. Camera pans left-to-right to follow running child.	Music: (*AC1*) Up (Slow piano playing what sounds like a practice piece).
SHOT 2 	(*VP2*) Dissolve to see Bush and wife with three grandchildren. They are holding hands. The movement continues from left-to-right.	Music: . . . (Music continues) . . .
SHOT 3 	Dissolve to pick up child running. She reaches Bush as he appears on right of screen. He reaches down to pick her up. (*VP3*) Smiling he raises her into the air and leans her on his shoulder.	Music: Under as (*AC2*) mournful horn comes into solo. Barbara Bush: (voice over) (*AP1*) I wish people could see him . . .

SHOT 4

(*VP4*) Dissolve to close up of Barbara Bush speaking. Eyes are directed off camera to interviewer.

Barbara Bush: . . . (*VP2*) as I see him and as (*AP3*) thousands of people see him . . .

SHOT 5

(*VP5*) Dissolve to medium long shot of Bush at outdoor cooking scene. Viewer sees him through group of relatives. Camera slowly zooms in as he puts hamburger on the plate of a relative.

Barbara Bush: (voice over) . . . And you know (*AP4*) I'll always love the time when (*AP5*) someone said to George. . . . .

SHOT 6

Dissolve to (*VP6*) Bush, surrounded by kids, playing umpire at home plate of picnic baseball game. Signals "strike out."

Barbara Bush: (voice over) . . . (*AP6*) "How can you run for President . . . .

(continued)

Table 3.1 (continued)

	Video	Audio
SHOT 7	 Dissolve to (VP7) medium close up of Bush in kitchen. Opens up large stew pot. Turns around to face left of screen, he smiles and is apparently talking to someone off screen.	Barbara Bush: (voice over) . . . (AP7) You don't have a constituency."
SHOT 8	 Dissolve to (VP8) Bush on ground surrounded by young grandchildren. Blond child with back to viewer approaches him. He makes a welcoming and comforting facial expression.	Barbara Bush: (voice over) . . . George said, "Well, you know, (AP8) I've got a great big family . . .
SHOT 9	 Dissolve to long shot of picnic scene. (VP9) Bush seated, eating, surrounded by young relatives.	Barbara Bush: (voice over) . . . and (AP9) thousands of friends.

SHOT 10

Dissolve to medium close up of (*VP10*) Bush with young granddaughter, arms clasped around his neck, head leaning against his. He is smiling and appears to be speaking to someone as he raises a piece of food to his mouth.

Barbara Bush: (voice over) . . . And . . . uh . . . (*AP10*) that's what he has."

SHOT 11

Cut to medium close up (*VP11*) of grainy black and white footage of Bush as a young fighter pilot. Camera is looking down immediately above him as he looks up, makes eye contact with camera, and walks towards right of screen.

Announcer: (voice over) (deep, "authoritative" male voice) (*AP11*) For more than forty years, (*AP12*) George Bush has met every challenge . . .

SHOT 12

Dissolve to long shot of (*VP12*) Bush seated at what appears to be the UN. Camera pans slowly from left-to-right.

Announcer: (voice over) . . . (*AP12*) his country and (*AP13*) the world have offered up to him.

(continued)

Table 3.1 (continued)

	Video	Audio
SHOT 13	Dissolve to medium close up of (*VP13*) Bush taking oath at inauguration. Bush is on left of screen, wife is looking up at him admiringly to his right.	Announcer: (voice over) . . . (*AP14*) The truth is that (*AP15*) the more you learn about George Bush, . . .
SHOT 14	Dissolve to (*VP14*) Bush with Margaret Thatcher. Bush is in same half of screen looking right. Thatcher is on his right.	Announcer: (voice over) . . . (*AP16*) the more you realize that . . .
SHOT 15	Dissolve to (*VP15*) Bush hugging sister Teresa. Camera zooms in on Teresa who appears joyful and tearful. He is on the left, she is on right.	Announcer: (voice over) . . . and (*AP17*) perhaps no one in this century is better prepared . . .

SHOT 16

Dissolve to medium long shot of (*VP16*) Bush geting off plane, waving to camera. Lech Walesa appears to be on his right.

Announcer: (voice over) . . . (*AP18*) to be president of the United States . . .

SHOT 17

Dissolve to close up of (*VP17*) young, blond female grandchild running as Bush bends down to pick her up. Scene is in slow motion as he raises her into the air. Most of her body is outside the frame as he raises her. Camera is focused on his face as he keeps eye contact with her. There is a broad, open mouthed smile on his face. Camera moves up slightly as (*VP18*) Bush pulls the child towards him, presses the side of her face against his, and he gives her a kiss on the cheek. The child is facing the camera and breaks out into warm smile.

Music: (*AC3*) up.

SHOT 18

Slow dissolve to (*VP19*) superimposition of name "George Bush" on white background. Two seconds later, the (*VP20*) sentence "Experienced Leadership for America's Future" is superimposed below the name. Fade to black.

Music: Fades out.

Abbreviations: S# = shot number, VP# = video proposition number, AP# = Audio proposition number, AC# = acoustic cue number.

Linear "Chunking" of Visual Propositions in Bush's "Family" Political Ad

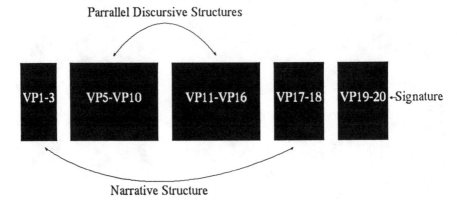

Parrallel Discursive Structures

VP1-3   VP5-VP10   VP11-VP16   VP17-18   VP19-20 ←Signature

Narrative Structure

FIGURE 1   The macrostructure of the commercial is divided into two major groups (syntagmas) of shots (visual propositions). One group at the beginning and end is connected into a very short and simple narrative. The shots in between are organized around the discursive topic of George Bush's "Private" (VP5-10) and "Public" (VP11-16) families.

"Bracketed" Discursive Frames

The mental modeling of the discursive schematic frame should begin with the opening shot. The agency's title for the commercial, "Family" suggests an intended discursive frame (topic) for the commercial. The "title" of the commercial is, of course, not a part of the commercial and must be inferred by the instantiated viewer from cues and codes present in the commercial.

The opening shot of the child is likely to activate this discursive frame for the commercial. Some circumstantial but supportive evidence for this can be found in the quick, positive, computerized audience response for female audience members[2] (see Fig. 3.2). Alternative paths of semantic activation are possible at this point, but the distribution of social codes and the seamless "realism" of the commercial work to constrain aberrant or oppositional paths of semantic activation.[3]

---

[2]This requires that we assume that the present socialization of females makes this discursive frame more salient and tags it with more positive markers than it does for the "interpretive community" of male audience members.

[3]At this point, we could begin to construct a parallel and alternative mental model of the semantic processing by hypothesizing code switching behavior on the part of some audience members. For example, for some audience members the opening shot could have negative semantic markers and therefore generate negative connotations. Although this

Further cues of the discursive semantic framing of "family" is provided in VP2, which shows the Bushs with three children. We have a set of three sequential shots of children and two with a casually dressed George Bush engaged with the children. Using Eco's (1979) terminology, this is likely to "blow up" the semantic frame for family initiated by the semantic activation of the first shot and "narcotize" bracketed aberrant schematic frames potentially instantiated by the first shot in some audience members (e.g., "child running in the playground," the possible result of aberrant schema selection of possible world and discursive schematic frames). In the first three shots and visual propositions (VP1–VP3) the message introduces and attempts to constrain the possible readings of the commercial. (Some other issues related to the discursive schematic framing of this ad are discussed in the section on actantial framing.)

A Note on Parsing

Shots 1–3 are likely to constitute a processing *cycle* for this commercial. That is, the shots represent a video "sentence," and instantiated viewers are likely to be processing this sequence of shots as a scene. A number of cues signal the "end of the sentence" or cycle much like a period does in texts: The music is lowered (AC2), there is the onset of a voice over (AP1), and finally, the video track switches from the slow motion to normal speed with the onset of Shot 4. Because these shots are likely to be parsed as a scene and modeled as a semantic processing cycle, we would predict that just prior to the onset of Shot 4, subjects are likely to be engaged in what Carroll (1980) unceremoniously called "gobbling," that is, cognitive integration of the material. This semantic integration could be detected using probe measures (see section on measurement in chapter 2, and Carroll, 1980).

Point-of-View

Looking at the schematic framing of point-of-view, we find that the commercial has some interesting dimensions that highlight the cognitive influence of point-of-view.

---

instantiation is possible, it is not highly probable for the community of viewers given the social ascendance of the dominant codes of family.

In a similar fashion, the opening scene could encounter oppositional decoding if the nonverbal behavior of the actants or the editing of commercial would make the artificiality of the commercial (its surface structure) more salient. The professionalism of the opening shots and seemingly "unrehearsed" nature of the interaction work to inhibit the foregrounding of ideological frame or to disrupt the construction of a borrowed identity point-of-view.

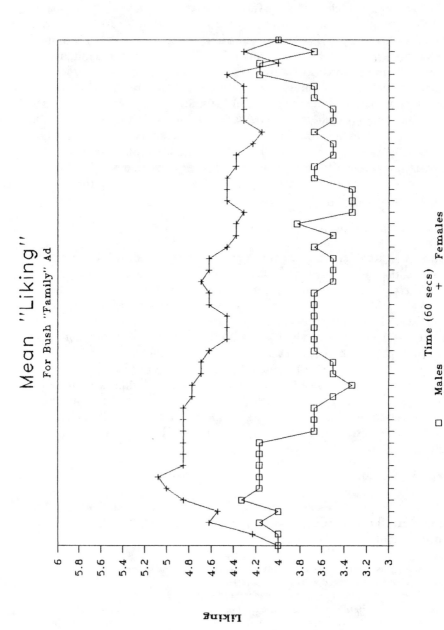

FIGURE 3.2. Mean liking for every 2 seconds of the commercial by males ($n = 15$) and females ($n = 20$).

If the possible world schematic frame of mental imagery ("imagining") is foregrounded in the opening shots, then the instantiated viewer is likely to adopt a second-person, borrowed identity point-of-view. That is, the viewer will position him or herself as "looking through the eyes of another." But the cues are weak. Although the possible world frame suggests a world of mental imagery, the instantiated viewer does not have, up to the end of Shot 3 an obvious actantial node with which to model the mental images. The actantial structure is not developed enough to prime and activate a second-person point-of-view, which in this case would be more cognitively demanding. There are also no position-of-sight cues that suggest that the viewer is taking on the visual perspective of an actant. This and the non-interactive nature of the first four visual propositions is likely to lead to the instantiation of a default, third-person, voyeur point-of-view in the larger percentage of actual viewers.

But the audio track of Shot 4 makes a strong attempt to semantically frame and activate a second-person, borrowed identity point-of-view. Viewers are directly addressed and semantically primed by AP1 "I wish people could *see* him," AP2 "as I *see* him," and AP3, "as thousands of people *see* him" to adopt a borrowed point-of-view defined by the viewer's modeling of the actant's, Barbara Bush's, point-of-view. The commercial dissolves to a sequence of video propositions, VP5 to VP10 of slow motion, soft-focus images of George Bush as a Barbara Bush voice-over reminisces about memories (see AP4, "the time when"). The semantic framing is so well structured, that we would predict that the message successfully leads many of the viewers to instantiate a borrowed identity point-of-view.

We would also predict that adopting the actant's, Barbara Bush's, point-of-view includes the modeling of her affective response (Strange & Black, 1989) and, therefore, likely increases the affective response to video propositions VP5–VP10, viewed "under" this point-of-view. It may also tend to "mute" tendencies to negative ideological schematic framing in terms of cognitive elaborations in the form of counterarguments or deprecation of the images.

Keep in mind that the perceived social distance between the actual viewer and the actant, whose point-of-view the viewer must adopt, will mediate the ability of the viewer to accept the "contract" and adopt that point-of-view (Strange & Black, 1989). Therefore, point-of-view effects in terms of increased affect may be less for males than females. The moment-to-moment audience response data suggests precisely such an effect (see Fig. 3.2). The drop occurring between the 12 and 19 data points occurs when Barbara Bush's point-of-view is semantically foregrounded in the commercial. The drop is far less pronounced for female viewers during this same period.

Actantial Framing

This commercial has a very interesting actantial structure. Because this is a political ad, let us first look at the most important actantial representation in this commercial, the representation of the candidate/concept, "George Bush" (see Fig. 3.3).

The foregrounding generated by the clear priming of the discursive frame of "family" instantiates the actantial role of "family head/patriarch" for the actant "George Bush." There are a great many redundant semantic cues clearly foregrounding this role. The opening scene (Shots 1–3) of Bush casually dressed enjoying his grandchildren foregrounds this role. Bush is quoted by his wife as saying (AP8) "you know I've got a great big family. . . ."

But there is more to this commercial than the simple foregrounding of Bush in the role of "family head/patriarch." The discursive framing of this commercial is divided so as to create a parallel version of the actantial role of "family head." A parallel structure of actantial roles is generated by a discursive frame that distinguishes and associates the roles of "patriarch-private world" and "patriarch-public world."

A number of syntactic and semantic cues lead to the organization of this structure of parallel actantial roles. The actantial role "family head-private sphere" is framed by visual propositions VP1–VP10. This is the section of the commercial where Barbara Bush provides the voice-over. The parallel actantial role of "patriarch-public sphere" is organized syntactically by VP11–VP16. Redundantly, the division overlaps a break in the possible world schematic frames. The first set of visual propositions frames George Bush in a private world. The second group of visual propositions frames George Bush in the public world of AP12, "his country and the world." Both are united by the "memory," point-of-view of Barbara Bush. The parallel structure is further primed by the verbal discourse of Barbara Bush's voice-over. These two spheres are separated and united in Barbara Bush's quote of her husband, (AP8) "I've got a great big family" ("family" in his private world) and (AP9) "thousands of friends" ("family" in the public world). Propositionally, these two worlds are linked together under the linguistic propositions specifying them as Bush's "constituency" (AP7).

One additional detail in the actantial structure of this commercial facilitates the semantic linking of the private and public versions of the actantial role of patriarch. Shot 13 brings Barbara Bush back into the "public world" of George Bush. Because she is the foregrounded actant

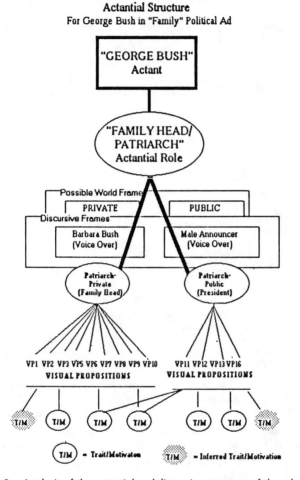

Actantial Structure
For George Bush in "Family" Political Ad

FIGURE 3.3.   Analysis of the actantial and discursive structure of the ad suggests a parallel semantic structure organized around two actantial roles. In one role, the actant George Bush is represented as a "patriarch" of his "private" family. In a parallel actantial role, he is presented as "patriarch" (president) of a "public family." The structure guides the instantiated viewer to semantically associate traits from his or her mental representation of Bush's private family life to Bush's public persona, the political candidate.

in this commercial, she is active in the short-term memory of the viewer. This reference within the *public world* makes her salient, especially in her admiration (George Bush as seen through her eyes).

The shot shows Bush at his inauguration. Within this frame the public and private patriarch are temporarily united in the same video frame. Following this is a set of two shots that share a parallel graphic structure.

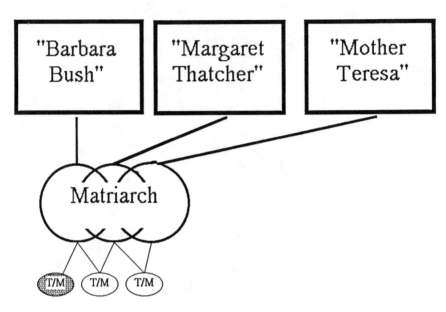

FIGURE 3.4. A segment of the commercial semantically primes the viewers to connect three shots that share a similar graphic structure. The shot sequence and structure semantically bridges the private and public roles of George Bush by priming a shared actantial role for Mrs. Bush, Margaret Thatcher, and Mother Teresa. This helps unite the parallel semantic structure of Bush's two patriarchial roles, private "father" and public "president."

Bush is on the left and a woman is on his right. The smooth dissolve and parallel structure of these three successive shots are likely to be linked by semantic priming and activation. From VP13 of George (left)–Barbara Bush (right), the viewer is shown VP14 George Bush (left)–Margaret Thatcher (right), and then VP15, George Bush (left)–Mother Teresa (right).[4] Figure 3.4 depicts the semantic parallelism that is established between patriarch (George Bush) and matriarch-private (Barbara Bush), matriarch-public (Margaret Thatcher), super matriarch-public (Mother Teresa).[5]

---

[4]As a mental exercise, I suggest that the reader reverse the left–right arrangement or substitute the presence of Helmut Kohl for Thatcher or Mother Teresa. Does the pattern work as well? The former would be syntactically and perceptually jarring (see Hochberg, 1986); the latter would be semantically jarring.

[5]Note that the effect will not be seriously harmed if the instantiated viewer is unable to identify (semantically activate a verbal label and person schema) for Thatcher or Mother Teresa. In such cases, the instantiated viewer will model them as various actantial roles of an actant, "female public figures."

The sequence of shots ends with Bush waving to the viewer, sur-rounded by people (children again?), in a classic presidential pose on top of the stairs beside an airplane, as an audio track intones AP 19 "to be president of the United States." Because of the pattern of semantic activation generated by the structure, the sentence "perhaps no one in this century is better prepared to be *president of the United States*" can, at the level of connotative semantic activation, be modeled as "perhaps no one in this century is better prepared to be *father of our family.*" This is *not* a neo-Freudian connection but a probable activation of connotative markers that can emerge from the pattern of semantic activation generated by the commercial.

As Fig. 3.3 suggests, this parallel structure, like most shared or parallel actantial roles, helps transfer positive semantic markers (traits/motivations) from the private actantial role of the candidate/concept "George Bush, the family patriarch" to the pubic actantial role of "George Bush, the President." This helps extend the notion of "family" into the public sphere. Some of the comments from the focus group study we conducted for *USA TODAY* indicated that some participants clearly revealed trace evidence in their protocols of these patterns of semantic activation. As one subject said after seeing the family commer-cial, "To me, it means he has *all of us* in his heart, I just have a warmer feeling" (see Katz, 1988b). For her, the notion of family was extended into the public sphere and embraced her within Bush's extended "family."

It is important to understand the relationship between semantic framing and the schematic framing of the instantiated viewer. The instantiated viewer does not sit there and say "Yes, public–private" or "Aha, three matriarchs!" These are terms of analysis and the language of semantic frames. The instantiated viewer need not cognitively elaborate these connotative connections, and even the actual creator of this commercial may not be fully aware of its underlying semantic structure. He or she might just intuitively feel as a commercial artist that "it seems to work" just as the speaker of an English sentence may not be fully aware of its underlying structure.

The description of semantic frames suggests *potential* patterns of schematic activation and *testable* alternative mental models of the commercial. If some of the connections are being made connotatively through semantic activation, we might find, for example, that following the commercial the word "president" would prime and facilitate the processing of the word "father" or "family" (see Marcel, 1983; Meyer & Schvaneveldt, 1976). The comments like the one just mentioned from focus group members, suggested that the connections were being made

connotatively, although none of the viewers could sit down and immediately sketch Fig. 3.3 to explain their "feeling."[6]

But *if* such connections were being made by empirical viewers, then
one could only conclude that the Bush "Family" ad was an elegant, even
brilliant piece of semantic "engineering."

Narrative Framing

Using Rumelhart's (1977) structure for the memory representation of
narratives, Fig. 3.5 shows a diagram representing the structure of the
simple narrative of this commercial. It is a brief episode made up of VP1,
VP3, and VP17, VP18. The shots are linked by common camera angle,
content, and linear sequence of actions. According to Rumelhart (1977)
memory involves a kind of editing where narrative is reduced to
essential events. Contributing events, agents, motives, and so on will be
deleted, substituted, or generalized. If narrative structure is related to
memory, than event deletion should lead to a node representing VP17 as
the event (key frame) most likely to emerge as representative of the
narrative.

There is some circumstantial but supportive evidence for the validity
of the structure. For example, when a newspaper editor had to select a
single frame to represent all of Bush's family commercial, he or she
chose a single frame from VP17 (Katz, 1988a). Memory for the ad
appeared to be built around this key frame. As one focus group
participant reported, "the ads I liked were the ones . . . (that) showed
the family and made you feel good . . . I remember more of those from
George Bush" (Katz, 1988b).

Ideological Framing

Negative ideological framing will occur when the instantiated viewer
activates and foregrounds oppositional ideological schema when processing the political commercial. The foregrounding of ideological
schema is often characterized by highly involved processing, elaboration
in the form of counterarguing, message or source deprecation, or code
switching and code inversion (see Hall, 1980, on "oppositional codes";
Petty & Cacioppo, 1986).

There was some indirect evidence of ideological schematic framing
among members of a focus group viewing the Bush "family" commer-

---

[6]Similarly, instantiated viewers make extensive use of language and film grammar to
process the commercial, yet none of them could easily sit down and describe the rules and
connective processes they had been using moments earlier.

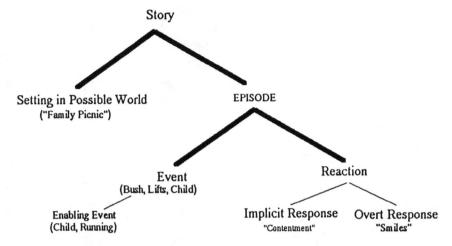

FIGURE 3.5. A representation of the very simple narrative part of the Bush commercial using Rumelhart's (1977) schematic for narratives.

cial. An oppositional stance to the semantic framing of the commercial can be found in the moment-to-moment computerized audience response data. Some subjects indicated an ideological stance by switching to 1 on their semantic scale to indicate "strongly dislike" immediately upon determining that this was a Bush commercial. The significant gap between Republicans and Democrats, especially in the second half of the commercial where the notion of "family" enters the public sphere (see Fig. 3.6), suggests that ideological schematic framing played a part in the reception of this commercial. The quick dip found in the last data point in the Democratic curve appears to be caused by the superimposition of the Bush name on the screen.

Self-Schematic Framing

Self-schematic framing can occur when the viewer elaborates on the ad and makes numerous connections between the ad and concepts of the self. Trace evidence of self-schematic framing of the ad can sometimes be found in self-referential comments (use of personal pronouns in relation to ad content) in the viewer's verbal protocols following an exposure to an ad. For example, we can find some evidence of self-schematic framing in the verbal protocols of focus group members following their exposure to the Bush "family." For example, when a viewer reported, "To *me,* it means he has all of *us* in his heart, *I* just have a warmer feeling," we could infer that there was some self-schematic framing in the instantiated viewing of the ad.

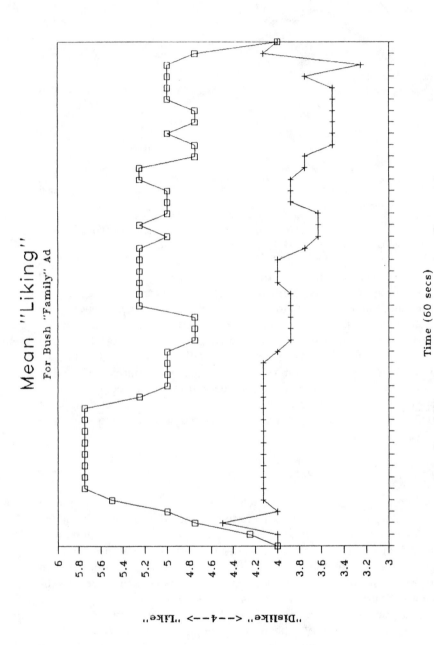

FIGURE 3.6. Mean liking for every 2 seconds of the commercial by Republicans ($n = 10$) and Democrats ($n = 13$).

SCHEMATIC FRAMING AND AN EXAMPLE
OF AN UNSUCCESSFUL AD

To illustrate how a schematic-framing approach can assist in modeling communication failures and deviating paths of semantic processing, we look at an example of one of the Dukakis ads. Table 3.2 contains the script for the Dukakis ad titled the "Packaging of George Bush." This was one of a series of ads that shared a similar macrostructure. The series was roundly criticized by professionals (McCabe, 1988). In a focus group conducted by the author for *USA TODAY,* this ad and its companion scored very badly on a postexposure measure of persuasion, scoring well below the mean for this group of tested ads (Katz, 1988a). Subjects reported confusion, suggesting to us that the semantic structure of the ad invited or did not constrain sources of aberrant decoding and deviating inference making. Also, the moment-to-moment computerized audience response to the ad that is discussed here indicated possible sources of problems with the ad. Using the schematic-framing approach, the analysis looks for possible sources of aberrant semantic processing whereby the model viewer was not instantiated by the ad and for points (cycles) in the path of semantic processing that may have led to aberrant decodings.

Early Discursive Framing

The commercial attempts to restrain the range of interpretations of the opening scenes of this commercial with a clear semantic disclosure. Shot 1 foregrounds the discursive frame. A discursive semantic frame in the unusual form of a "title" attempts to instantiate the semantic associations for its model viewer. The superimposed title (VP2), "The Packaging of George Bush" activates an actant, "George Bush," in the actantial frame. The thematic cue from the word "Packaging" attempts to activate the discursive associations captured by concepts such as "merchandising" and "surface appearances." At this point, certain themes should be "blown up" for the model viewer and other potential paths of semantic activation "narcotized."

On the audio track, semantic disclosure in AP1—"another TV commercial about this furlough thing"—appears intended to activate memory traces and negative associations regarding the "controversy" over the Bush campaign commercials on Dukakis' prison furlough program. The structure requires that the instantiated viewer makes this inference from the weak, vague cue, "furlough thing," when the related referent and actant "Dukakis" has not yet been activated in the commercial. The reference also assumes that the model viewer has pre-

Table 3.2 Dukakis 1988 Political Commercial: "The Packaging of George Bush"

	Video	Audio
SHOT 1 	Fade from black to (*VP1*) shot with large balding man (Man 1) shuffling papers. Camera pans slowly to the left and down. Super: (*VP2*) "The Packaging of George Bush" on the bottom of the screen. (*VP3*) Man #1 leans and speaks to Man #2 seated beside him.	Man 1: (*AP1*) Well, I think we need another TV commercial on this furlough thing.
SHOT 1(b) 	Super: (*VP4*) "Thursday 3:55 p.m." (*VP5*) Man #2 points to paper, looks to right of screen (towards Man #1 now off screen) as camera continues to pan to the left.	Man 2: (emphatically). (*AP2*) No way! (*AP3*) They're beginning to write about Dukakis' real crime record. Man 1: (off camera). (*AP4*) Nobody reads any more.
SHOT 1(c) 	(*VP6*) Man #3 holds booklet in hand. Camera pan pauses. (*VP7*) Man #3 makes hand motion with right hand and points to booklet as he speaks.	Man 3: (*AP5*) Let's hope not. (*AP6*) Well, first of all, Dukakis changed that furlough program. (*AP7*) Now, look at this. (*AP8*) More cops on the street. (*AP9*) More drug offenders behind bars. (*AP10*) Crime down by 13% in Massachusetts.

SHOT 1(d)

(*VP8*) Camera begins slow pan from bottom-left to top-right. (*VP9*) Man #2 gestures with hand as he speaks.

Man 2: (*AP11*) That's what I mean, (*AP12*) how long do you expect to get away with this furlough thing.

SHOT 1(e)

(*VP10*) Man #1 comes into the frame, (*VP11*) turns head to right to speak to character off camera.

Man 3: (*AP13*) How many more weeks till the election, Bernie?
All Men: (*AP14*) (Laughter)

SHOT 2

Dissolve to black frame
Super: (*VP12*) "They'd like to sell you a package."

Announcer: (voice over) (*AP15*) They'd like to sell you a package.

SHOT 3

Dissolve to black frame with (*VP13*) *small lower picture of Dukakis and*
Super: (*VP14*) "Wouldn't you rather choose a President."

Announcer: (*AP16*) Wouldn't you rather choose a president.

Abbreviations: S# = shot number, VP# = video proposition number, AP# = Audio proposition number, AC# = Acoustic cue number.

113

existing knowledge of the controversy. An assumption of semantic competence that may not have been true for a significant percentage of empirical viewers, especially apathetic and undecided voters.

Possible Word Framing

In the very first shot of the commercial, instantiated viewers will attempt to infer a "bracket," a possible world for the incoming information. Problems with the semantic processing of this commercial appear to begin with the manner in which the commercial attempts to activate its possible world and the apparent assumptions about the viewer's knowledge (semantic competence) that have been incorporated into its semantic structure.

The commercial presents a possible world for which there is only a very weak code among typical viewers, the world of "political consultants." It is unlikely that the average empirical viewer had developed a schema for the physical world of the "political consultants." If in the context of a study, the commercial was stopped and the subjects probed in the very first seconds of the commercial, we would predict that a significant portion of the viewers would not yet have clearly identified the possible world of this commercial.

This assumed discursive reference to the world of "political consultants" comes from "inside the beltway," that is, a discursive community more familiar among the interpretive community of Washington insiders and political "junkies" than among the typical, undecided viewer/voter. We must assume that the "target audience" for a commercial aired in the final weeks of a presidential campaign is the undecided voter and not political activists. Therefore, there appears to be a misalignment between the assumed semantic competence of the model viewer of the message and the actual semantic competence of the target audience (empirical viewer). Instantiated viewers will, nonetheless, assign the incoming information to some possible world. We would predict that a significant percentage of instantiated viewers may have begun processing this commercial by instantiating deviant possible world schema connected semantically to the actant "George Bush," for example, White House (staff), Congress (members), and so on.[7]

In the very first frames of the commercial when the viewer is attempting to construct a bracketed possible world for this commercial,

---

[7] If the instantiated viewer infers the value "White House" for the possible world frame, than he or she will most likely assign the trait "White House Staff" or "Bureaucrat" to the unidentified actants (man 1, 2, 3) of the commercial amplifying an aberrant decoding of the commercial.

VP4 leads a percentage of the instantiated viewers to blow up misleading possible world frames. The superimposed video proposition states "Thursday 3:55." This semantic disclosure appears to refer to a specific point in time and it is semantically foregrounded by the commercial through the use of superimposition and its location at the beginning of the commercial. Because of the communication contract that semantic disclosures are intentional cues intended to advance and situate a narrative, a number of the instantiated viewers would probably allocate attention and automatically search their memory for information about the time and date. If the instantiated viewer activates a context for this foregrounded semantic cue, the activated schema is likely to deviate from the model viewing of this commercial. The cue is meaningless for modeling the narrative, and appears to be an intertextual cue for a model viewer to activate the genre for "documentary." The probability of the model viewer reliably activating the appropriate frame associated with this cue may be statistically very low.

Attention allocated to the processing of the ambiguous visual cue, VP4, draws attention away from the processing of the audio track. This adds to the probability of aberrant schematic activation because a *critical, orienting semantic disclosure,* AP1 "this furlough thing," occurs on the audio track at the exact same time as the onset of VP4. At a time when viewers must make essential inferences about the discursive structure of this commercial, instantiated viewers are provided with a weak audio cue, AP1, in competition with a prominent but semantically misleading video cue, VP4.

Actantial Framing

The schematic framing model hypothesizes that viewers immediately begin to construct an actantial structure by which they organize the agents and objects of video and audio propositions and to model causal and narrative relationships between actants.

The opening semantic disclosure in VP1 introduces the actant "George Bush" as the *object* of the relation, "Packaging." The *agent* of this proposition must be inferred. The model viewer should infer the agent as the individuals on the screen at the time the visual linguistic proposition is presented. Failure to make that inference may lead the empirical viewer to instantiate inappropriate schema and engage in aberrant decoding.

Linguistically, George Bush is presented as an actant in the object position of the very first proposition, but the propositions that follow all refer to the actant "Michael Dukakis," who is only implicitly introduced by AP1 and AP3. Short-term memory retention of George Bush as an actant for the decoding of the early propositions by instantiated viewers does not advance a model viewing of the commercial. This invites some confusion as to which actantial node to use to organize the incoming information. Evidence that for some viewers George Bush is retained as the agent and actant in this commercial come from reports that Bush headquarters were called by partisans to complain about these commercials and to ask *Bush* campaign staffers to remove them. That is, some viewers, processed these *as George Bush's commercial* and not Mike Dukakis'. This aberrant schematic framing of the commercial is supported by its structure that shows Dukakis as the actantial *object* of verbal propositions and never as an actantial *agent*. This is the actantial structure a viewer would find in a *Bush attack commercial* on Mike Dukakis. Support for the hypothesis that the opening structure of this ad leads subjects to model it as an attack ad against Dukakis is found in the moment-to-moment audience response data presented in Fig. 3.7. The data indicate that Republicans like the Dukakakis commercial *more* than the Democrats in the opening seconds. Furthermore, Democrats slightly dislike the commercial in its opening moments. The analysis of the actantial structure of this ad in its opening sequence suggests why there might be some aberrant decoding of the opening scenes and why incorrect inferences made in the opening scenes may have led some viewers to recall this commercial as a George Bush commercial.

The introduction of other actants may have also contributed to the potentially aberrant schematic framing of this commercial. AP3 introduces a pronominal reference to an actant that has not been previously activated by the commercial. Text-processing research (Bower & Cirilo, 1985; Haviland & Clark, 1974) indicates that AP3, "They're beginning to write, . . ." will lead to a search of active actant (referents). Assignment of an active actant to this proposition (i.e., the "men," "George Bush's staff") will lead to an aberrant schematic framing. But the model viewer should infer the "press" or "media" from this proposition, yet there are absolutely no verbal or visually supportive cues. The actor in the commercial combines the phrase with a verbal gesture to a report booklet. The "they" is represented visually (indexically) by the booklet. Note this is an ambiguous semantic clue and not a newspaper or other semantically redundant and appropriate cue.

The actantial structure of this commercial provides an example of cases where more than one *actor* represents a single *actant*. Figure 3.8 shows that the three actors, "man" 1, 2, & 3, represent differential actantial roles of the actant, "political consultant." This also provides an example of how actantial roles can represent conflicting tendency in a single actant just as different actantial roles (foregrounded traits) of an

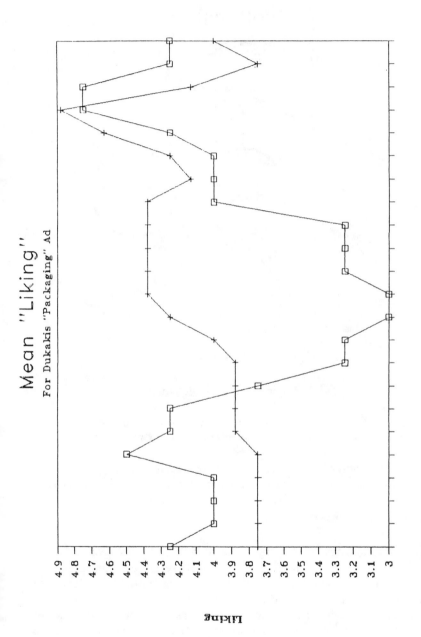

FIGURE 3.7. Mean liking for every 2 seconds of the commercial by Republicans ($n = 10$) and Democrats ($n = 13$).

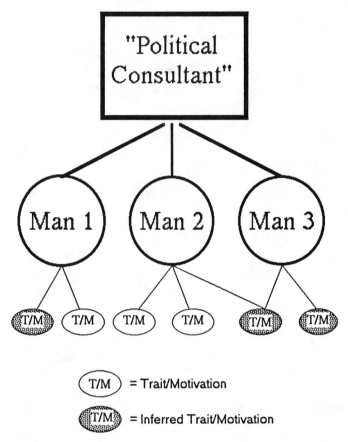

FIGURE 3.8. The three men represented in the commercial are likely to be processed as three versions (actantial roles) of one actant, the "political consultant."

individual character are often used to represent conflict within an individual or personal transformation during the course of a narrative.

Later Discursive Framing

AP3 introduces a new discursive topic to be entered as a value in the discursive schematic frame. The proposition refers to "Dukakis' real crime record" as something that "they're writing about." For the naive empirical viewer trained on the intertextual codes of "cops and robbers" dramas, this has two probable readings. The first is the model reading, "the governor's (actantial role for "Dukakis") legislative record on criminal justice." But an alternative pattern of connotative activation seems equally likely for a percentage of empirical viewers, "Dukakis' (the private individual's) record as a criminal." Activation of this second value should be corrected by AP6 but would nonetheless disrupt the construction of the intended model in these early seconds and lead to weakened and fragmentary memory traces.

Point-of-View

Two probable point-of-views are likely to be instantiated by the majority of empirical viewers. Because of the structure of the message, the activation of either point-of-view can lead to different mental models (Biocca, chapter 2, this volume).

A second-person, borrowed identity point-of-view can be activated from the structure of the message. The camera's position-of-sight would be a strong cue for activating this point-of-view. The commercial is filmed as one continuous shot. The point-of-sight of the camera is at the level of someone sitting at the table along with the actants, a group of three "political consultants." The camera slowly pans along the participants as if the viewer is moving his or her head and following the conversation. If this point-of-view is activated, the instantiated viewer appears "inside" this circle of consultants. Any resulting identification with the characters by the viewer adopting the role of actant within the boiler room should serve to diffuse the negative, distancing apparently intended by the commercial. The viewer would be inclined to see the "world" through the eyes of the actants and join in their laughter (AP14) rather than be appalled by their cynicism as the model viewing appears to intend. In Fig. 3.6 the spike of positive response during the moment of humor at the end suggests that the viewers may be sharing in the Bush political consultants' glee. Note that the Republicans in the audience appear to enjoy the humor a little longer while the humor quickly sours for the Democrats. A tendency for the viewers to share and possibly identify with the political consultants indicates a point-of-view that is likely to contribute to the actantial confusion as to the sponsorship of this commercial.

The model viewing of this commercial would appear to require a third-person voyeur point-of-view. The instantiation of this point-of-view is more likely to lead to the psychological distancing necessary for the activation of the model ideological stance (the position apparently intended by the communicator) relative to the actants.

Ideological Framing

This commercial appears to require a relatively complex activation of the ideological frame. Although the commercial is sponsored by the

Dukakis campaign, its model viewing requires that the viewer take a negative ideological position to the actants in the commercial. In simple terms, the viewer, potential Dukakis supporters, must be hostile to the actants in this Dukakis commercial for the commercial to work. There is one danger to this approach. If the ideological schematic framing is foregrounded and the semantic processing of this commercial includes source deprecations and counter arguing with the actants in the commercial, there is the possibility that this will prime a deprecation of the *real* source of the commercial, Mike Dukakis.

Self-Schematic Framing

Self-schematic framing can rarely be reliably hypothesized from an analysis of the semantic framing of a commercial. Nonetheless, it would appear unlikely that a representation of a somewhat distant squabble between political consultants over the esoterica of Bush's "furlough" ads would activate much self-schematic framing among the majority of the undecided voter/viewers.

CONCLUSION

The analyses presented here are purely exploratory and intended to suggest the kind of analytical issues that might come into play when analyzing the structure of the political ad and when constructing hypothesized models of the semantic processing. Finer and more detailed analyses are possible depending on the nature of the question asked. For example, audio propositions can be broken down into finer and more complex discursive structures (Kintsch & van Dijk, 1978; van Dijk, 1988a, 1988b).

The data presented here provide some illustration but are not to be interpreted as paradigmatic of the measurement approach to schematic framing. The data had been collected for other purposes by the author. An adequate testing of general properties of schematic framing would require the fuller complement of measures presented in Biocca (chapter 2, this volume) along with a research design intended to measure mental models of the commercials or the influence of structural variations in semantic framing.

But nonetheless, this exploratory analysis of these two commercials should have demonstrated ways in which the model reader is embedded in the structure of the ad. But ads will vary in their ability to instantiate their model viewer. Meaning is always unstable and more so when the structure of the message potentially activates various deviating paths of semantic processing. Although viewers are always free to instantiate all sorts of alternative and deviating paths of semantic activation, the actual paths taken by empirical viewers have probabilities that are determined by the constraints imposed by cultural uses of codes and by semantic cueing of those codes by a message. To understand how an ad is represented in the mind of the actual viewers, it is necessary to first analyze its structure and construct a path for the model viewer, identify points of critical inference making, and model alternative paths of semantic processing. Only by variously measuring patterns of semantic activation through multiple indirect techniques can a distribution of probable mental models of the ad be estimated for a community of viewers processing the ad within a specific window of time.

REFERENCES

Biocca, F. (1989). *"Reading" the video screen: Psychological measurement of spatial attention and perceptual biases within television, video, and computer monitors.* Unpublished doctoral dissertation, University of Wisconsin—Madison, Madison, WI.

Biocca, F. (1990). Semiotics and mass communication: Points of intersection. In T. Sebeok & J. Umiker-Sebeok (Eds.), *Semiotic Web 1990.* The Hague: Mouton Press.

Bordwell, D., & Thompson, K. (1986). *Film art.* New York: Knopf.

Bower, G. H., & Cirilo, R. K. (1985). Cognitive psychology and text processing. In T. A. van Dijk (Ed.), *Handbook of discourse analysis* (Vol. 1, pp. 71–106). New York: Academic Press.

Carroll, J. M. (1980). *Toward a structural psychology of cinema.* The Hague: Mouton.

Eco, U. (1979). *The role of the reader.* Bloomington, IN: Indiana University Press.

Hall, S. (1980). Encoding/decoding. In D. H. A. L. and Paul Willis Stuart Hall (Ed.), *Culture, media, language* (pp. 127–138). London: Hutchison.

Haviland, S., & Clark, H. (1974). What's new. Acquiring new information as a process of comprehension. *Journal of Verbal Learning and Verbal Behavior, 13,* 512–521.

Hochberg, J. (1986). Representation of motion and space in video and cinematic displays. In W. Kaufmann (Ed.), *Handbook of perception* (Vol. 2, pp. 000). New York: Wiley.

Katz, G. (1988a, October 27). Memories made of campaign negatives. *USA TODAY,* p. 6a.

Katz, G. (1988b, October 27). Viewers like feel of positive spots. *USA TODAY,* p. 7a.

Kintsch, W., & van Dijk, T. (1978). Toward a model of text comprehension and production. *Psychological Review, 85*(5), 363–393.

Marcel, A. J. (1983). Conscious and unconscious perception: An approach to the relations between phenomenal experience and perceptual processes. *Cognitive Psychology, 15,* 238–300.

McCabe, E. (1988, December 12). The campaign you never saw. *New York,* pp. 33–48.

Metz, C. (1974). *Film language: A semiotics of cinema.* New York: Oxford.

Meyer, D., & Schvaneveldt, R. (1976). Meaning, memory structure, and mental processes. In C. Cofer (Ed.), *Structure of human memory* (pp. 000). San Francisco, CA: Freeman.

Petty, R., & Cacioppo, J. (1986). *Communication and persuasion: Central and peripheral routes to attitude change.* New York: Springer-Verlag.

Pudovkin, V. (1954). *Film technique and film acting.* London: Vision.

Rumelhart, D. (1977). Understanding and summarizing brief stories. In D. Laberge & M. Collins (Eds.), *Basic processes in reading: Perception and comprehension* (pp. 265–304). Hillsdale, NJ: Lawrence Erlbaum Associates.

Strange, J. J., & Black, J. B. (1989, May). *Imagined point of view. Causal inference and mental models of narrative events.* Paper presented to the Information Systems Division of the International Communication Association, San Francisco, CA.

van Dijk, T. (1988a). *News analysis: Case studies of international and national news in the press.* Hillsdale, NJ: Lawrence Erlbaum Associates.

van Dijk, T. (1988b). *News as discourse.* Hillsdale, NJ: Lawrence Erlbaum Associates.

II

Psychological Processing of Issues, Images, and Form

4

The Effects of Visual Structure and Content Emphasis on the Evaluation and Memory for Political Candidates

Seth F. Geiger
University of California, Santa Barbara

Byron Reeves
Stanford University

TELEVISION AND POLITICAL ADVERTISING

The role of television in political campaigns is a double-edged sword: More voters have access to more campaign information than ever before; but television, by emphasizing style over substance, may foster an electorate incapable of making informed decisions. Critics claim that the content in political advertisements, as well as inherent characteristics of the television medium, work together to highlight a candidate's image at the expense of information about political issues. This chapter examines image and issue content in political advertisements, and the interaction of content with message attributes unique to television. Two questions are posed: (a) What is the impact of an image or issue message on the evaluations and memory for political candidates? (b) Does the visual structure of political advertisements enhance or detract from the influence of image and issue messages on candidate evaluation and memory?

The first question is concerned with the influence of message content, the second with message structure. First, a definition of image and issue advertisements is presented. These two types of content are presumed to encourage different processing strategies; one primarily affective, and the other cognitive. The implications of these two processing modes on candidate evaluation are then outlined. The second section addresses the visual structure of advertisements in relation to processing and candidate evaluations. The final section discusses the interaction between content and structure in reference to evaluation and memory for candidates and their messages.

Images, Issues, and the Evaluation of Political Candidates

A candidate's image is a cluster of traits that reflect the candidate as a person and as a politician (Nimmo & Savage, 1976; Shyles, 1984). These traits accentuate personality (e.g., honest, intelligent, open-minded, sincere, trustworthy, warm), and ability and activity (e.g., capable, effective, strong, decisive, hardworking) (Kinder, Peters, and Abelson, 1980). Image political advertisements describe candidates as individuals with reference to these attributes (Garramone, 1986). Issue advertisements refer to policies advocated by a candidate or past accomplishments that indicate future behavior. Although the focus is on issues, image information may be indirectly extracted from issue advertisements. Voters treat past and promised actions as hypothetical events from which traits can be inferred (Carlston, 1980). Consequently, there is an asymmetry between image and issue advertisements; voters can derive information about a candidate from an issue advertisement, but issue information cannot be implied from an image message.

Evidence for the assumed superiority of television in conveying image versus issue information is equivocal. Ottati, Fishbein, and Middlestadt (1988) have shown that voters can and do derive issue information from political advertisements. They compared the relative importance of candidate's expressed messages with affective factors such as the syntax used to frame messages, and the political biases of the subjects. Issue information was superior to both message syntax and bias in predicting a voter's perception of issue positions. McClure and Patterson (1976) contended that political advertisements are more effective than news broadcasts in informing the electorate about issues in presidential elections, and that attempts to manipulate a candidate's image with television advertising are unsuccessful.

Contradicting these findings are studies on candidate image that indicate the following: voters focus primarily on image information (Glass, 1985), nonverbal information is an important factor in assessing a candidate (Rosenberg & McCafferty, 1987), and image characteristics do ultimately influence voting (Nygren & Jones, 1977). Comparisons between media suggest that television favors images over issues. People that use television as a primary source of campaign information are more likely to focus on image attributes (Keeter, 1987). Also, television viewers are less capable of differentiating candidates based on issues, but are more adept at discriminations based on personal attributes (Wagner, 1983).

The dichotomy between image and issue orientation focuses on the presumed differences between political advertisements and on how advertising detracts or contributes to an informed electorate. Although the distinction is rooted in political commentary, there may be an important psychological correlate to this comparison. The distinction may describe two different ways that political information on television is processed: one an affective route, and the other a cognitive one (Snyder & DeBono, 1985). The stress placed on personality and ability in image advertisements is intended to trigger an affective response from viewers that imparts a positive *feeling* about the candidate. Mitchell (1986) contended that affective responses give prominence to the visual channel. This has been supported by Burns and Beier (1973), who demonstrated a dominance for visual cues when responses are affective. Also, affective responses are characterized by less cognitive activity and depth of processing (Greenwald & Leavitt, 1985), characteristics which reinforce an emphasis on visual information.

Issue advertisements transmit semantic messages that are *comprehended* rather than felt. These messages elicit more rational responses associated with attempts to persuade voters to judge a candidate or their positions favorably (Fishbein & Ajzen, 1981). An issue appeal requires comprehension of material typically presented in the audio channel. Because information about a candidate's personal qualities is not presented directly, inferences and increased mental effort are required in order to assess the candidate. Issue advertisements, because they focus on comprehension, should be processed at a deeper level, promoting inferences about candidates even when the focus of the message is not on personal attributes (Greenwald & Leavitt, 1985).

Both affective and cognitive processes play important roles in evaluating candidates (Abelson, Kinder, Peters, & Fiske, 1982). One question in this study concerns the influence of image and issue messages on candidate *evaluations,* without respect to whether information is learned. It may be the case that mere presentation of issues causes positive evaluations, even if no issue positions are retained. Two past studies dealt with this question. Kaid and Sanders (1978) examined the effects of an advertisement's image or issue orientation on the evaluation of a political candidate. Issue advertisements produced significantly more positive evaluations than did image advertisements. Conover (1981) found that a candidate's issue position produced a greater number of inferences regarding personal attributes than did either the match between the political party of the candidate and the voter, or the candidate's incumbency. These studies indicate that issue advertisements elicit more positive evaluations, and more elaborate representations of candidates compared with image advertisements. Therefore, candidates presented in issue advertisements should be evaluated more positively than candidates in image messages.

Structure and the Evaluation of Political Candidates

Political advertisements, like all television material, contain both content (e.g., image and issue) and structure. *Structure* refers to visual syntax, or the way in which a visual sequence is pieced together. Structure includes conventions such as cuts and edits, changes in the physical location or focal length of the camera, and special effects. A dynamically structured sequence contains a number of these features as well as shifts between different scenes and locations, multiple characters, and multiple sources of audio (e.g., different voices, music, voice overs). Static sequences occur in a single location, involve little or no camera movement, no cuts, fewer characters, and a single audio source.

Film theorists view structure as an important factor in attention, in demarcating segments within a sequence, and in maintaining interest during a viewing period (Hochberg, 1986). When watching television, viewers respond to shifts in structure in predictable ways. Structural shifts within a visual sequence produce automatic attention to new information (Geiger & Reeves, 1989). Changes in structure define perceptual units, resulting in better memory for information that follows the change (Carroll & Bever, 1976). A dynamic or quickly paced visual sequence, characterized by a faster cutting rate between segments, will produce a higher level of attention over time (Hochberg & Brooks, 1978). Consequently, structure is an important determinant of how visual sequences are processed and remembered.

Political advertisements vary dramatically in their visual structure (Kaid & Davidson, 1986). Shyles (1986) analyzed the relationship between content and structure in advertisements drawn from the presidential primaries of 1980. Image advertisements were less formal, made use of unusual camera angles, had a more rapid pace of cutting, and used announcers or citizen testimonials in the audio track. Issue advertisements were more formal, and presented the candidate at a neutral camera angle, talking directly into the camera. The fact that image and issue advertisements used structure in different ways indicates the importance of structure as a factor in conveying a particular message.

Although structure and content can be treated as independent message attributes, structure can influence the meaning constructed from messages (Geiger, 1988). Kraft (1986) addressed the effects of cutting on the evaluation of filmed sequences. Subjects rated films containing cuts as more dynamic and compelling than uncut sequences. Cutting also had an effect on the evaluation of characters presented in a short film (Penn,

1971). Based on a semantic differential measure of nine personal attributes across three dimensions (evaluative, activity, and potency), characters were rated more active and potent in structurally dynamic films than in structurally static ones. In a third study (Kraft, 1987), camera angles produced a connotative effect on the evaluation of characters depicted in a film. Low camera angle shots produced attributions of strength and action to characters; shots from high camera angles elicited attributions of weakness and inactivity. These studies provide evidence for a connotative effect of structure on the evaluation of characters within a television sequence.

The relationship between structure and content is not simply additive, the two interact to influence processing and candidate evaluation. Although no single study has tested the interaction of content and structure directly, one study (Meadow & Siegelman, 1982) allows for a comparison of the four cells. They compared ratings for politicians based on exposure to a series of advertisements that varied in content and structure. Static structure advertisements contained no cuts or camera movements, and depicted candidates talking directly into the camera. Dynamic structure advertisements presented rapidly paced visuals, cuts between different scenes and settings, and the use of voice overs on the audio track. Although these results are difficult to interpret because of confounds in the experimental design, there were differences in candidate evaluation between exposure to the different cells. When a sequence of commercials included dynamic image advertisements, candidates were given higher leadership ratings. In sequences where a static issue advertisement was depicted, candidates were rated high on warmth and humaneness. The impact of structure, therefore, may vary with message content and processing style.

Structure is important within the context of political commercials because it influences how television is processed, primarily by highlighting new information. When the new information is social, an interrupt, and subsequent arousal leads to intensified judgments and greater cognitive interpretation (Fiske, 1981). As demonstrated by the connotative effect of structure on assessments of activity, dynamic structure can be transferred to social attributions. Structurally dynamic television should produce more intense candidate evaluations than structurally simple programs, especially for positive qualities associated with dynamism. Because issue advertisements require inferences to assess the personal qualities of a candidate, the increased processing demands caused by interruptions should have a greater influence on these messages.

Following are the specific predictions for the influence of structure on the evaluation of candidates:

1. Candidates will be evaluated more positively in structurally dynamic than in structurally static advertisements;
2. Structure will influence only attributes that reflect on a candidate's activity and dynamism, and not their personality;
3. Structure will influence issue advertisements more than image advertisements.

Content, Structure, and Memory

Virtually all of the psychological research in political communication has focused on candidate evaluation and voting intention as dependent variables, and memory has been all but ignored as a criterion. But memory may have an important influence on candidate evaluation, and ultimately, voting (Srull & Wyer, 1989). For example, implicit in an assessment of voting, or learning and persuasion is an accurate and facile recognition of candidates and their messages. Consequently, both accuracy and facility of recognition were criterion measures in addition to evaluations. There are three predictions about how content and message structure will affect memory. First, if the processing of image advertisements is affective, and attends primarily to the visual channel, then memory for visual features should be better for image than for issue advertisements. Second, if issue advertisements are processed cognitively, and the audio channel is primary, then there should be better memory for audio information in issue advertisements. Finally, dynamic messages should produce automatic attentional responses that interrupt processing and focus attention on novelty. These interruptions should result in poorer recognition memory compared with static sequences.

There should also be an interaction between message content and message structure. One of the most important features of structure is its capacity to elicit automatic responses. Affective processing is itself primarily automatic or stimulus-driven, because the characteristics of the stimulus determine the flow of attention. This is contrasted with cognitive processing that is primarily controlled by the viewer, and demands focal attention and limited resources (Norman & Bobrow, 1975). Because image advertisements focus on affect, they should be interrupted more by structural shifts than issue advertisements that are processed more mindfully. Therefore, memory for image advertisements that have a dynamic structure should be poorer than for issue advertisements with a comparable degree of dynamic structure.

In summary, the predictions for memory are as follows:

1. Visual recognition will be better for image advertisements than for issue advertisements;

2. Audio recognition will be better for issue advertisements than for image advertisements;
3. Static structure should produce better recognition for both visual and audio tasks than dynamic structure;
4. Dynamic structure should result in greater interference with image advertisements than will static structure.

METHOD

Subjects

Twenty-seven adults recruited from two community groups were paid $10 for their participation. They ranged in age from 21 to 74. There were 16 women and 11 men, with 13 being Democrats, 12 Republicans, and 2 Independents.

Stimulus Materials

Subjects viewed a sequence of sixteen 30-second political advertisements. The advertisements were drawn from 1986 congressional and gubernatorial campaigns. Two criteria were used to ensure that subjects had no prior knowledge of or exposure to these particular candidates: (a) the advertisements were taken from political campaigns that occurred in other parts of the country, between candidates that were not nationally prominent, and; (b) no political cues such as party affiliation or endorsements were depicted in any of the spots.

The selected advertisements differed on two dimensions: content (image/issue orientation), and structure (static/dynamic). Image advertisements focused on a quality or characteristic of the candidate as a person. Issue advertisements concentrated on a specific policy advocated by the candidate or a past accomplishment that reflected a policy stand. Spots with a static structure took place in one scene or location with the candidate talking directly into the camera, and were composed from a head-on camera angle without cuts or other shifts. In static spots, there was no use of voice overs, music, or other pacing conventions common to television. Advertisements with a dynamic structure presented candidates in a number of settings, were quickly paced with cuts and camera movement, used voice overs and music, and employed special effects.

To determine the messages that were used in the study, a sample of 26 advertisements drawn from the campaigns of 18 candidates were rated by seven judges. Each 30-second spot was rated on two scales: degree of image orientation, and degree of issue orientation. Coders were given definitions for both of the scales. Each advertisement was rated immediately after viewing. The advertisements selected for the final study were those that maximized the differences between image scores and issue scores. The mean difference scores for the ratings between image and issue advertisements was significant, T (14) = 22.3, $p < .001$. Sixteen political advertisements, drawn from 15 different political campaigns comprised the stimulus set for the study (see Table 4.1). There were four different messages distributed across each of four cells: static image, static issue, dynamic image, and dynamic issue. Challengers and incumbents were distributed evenly across the four cells. Of the candidates, 14 were men, and 2 were women. The two women each

Table 4.1 Political Advertisements from the 1986 Congressional and Gubernatorial Political Campaigns Used as Stimulus Materials

Candidate	Race	Content	Structure
Wayne Owens	Utah, House	Image	Dynamic
William O'Neill	Connecticut, Governor	Issue (roads)	Dynamic
Barbara Mikulski	Maryland, Senate	Image	Static
Robert Kasten	Wisconsin, Senate	Issue (environment)	Static
Winfield Dunn	Tennessee, Governor	Image	Static
Kent Conrad	North Dakota, Senate	Image	Dynamic
Dale Bumpers	Arkansas, Senate	Issue (military)	Static
Louise Slaughter	New York, House	Issue (senior citizens)	Dynamic
Jim Bilbray	Nevada, House	Issue (nuclear dump)	Static
Wyche Fowler	Georgia, Senate	Image	Static
Alfonse D'Amato	New York, Senate	Issue (crime)	Dynamic
John McKernan	Maine, Governor	Image	Dynamic
George Mickelson	South Dakota, Governor	Issue (jobs)	Dynamic
Mark Andrews	North Dakota, Senate	Issue (farm prices)	Static
John McCain	Arizona, Senate	Image	Dynamic
Henson Moore	Louisiana, Senate	Image	Static

represented one replication of two different cells (static-image, and dynamic-issue). All of the candidates were Caucasian.

Three different sequences of the 16 political advertisements were constructed, each a different randomized order. For each sequence, the 16 advertisements were separated by 70 seconds of black. This pause was inserted to allow subjects time to complete an evaluation of the candidate they had just seen. Total running time for the presentation was 29 minutes and 12 seconds.

Design and Dependent Measures

Two within-subject factors were used, each with two levels: (a) advertisement content (image or issue orientation), and (b) structure of the advertisement (static or complex). There were four replications for each of the four cells in the design. Each replication was an advertisement for a different candidate.

There was a single between-subjects factor, the three different candidate presentation orders. The presentation orders were generated using a four-level latin-square design. Each of the four types of political spots, (static-image, static-issue, dynamic-image, dynamic-issue), were located in each of the four possible presentation positions once and only once. Subjects viewed all of the four types of advertisements through a complete cycle, before the next set of advertisements began. This design controlled for serial position effects produced by viewing order, and for effects of primacy and recency in subsequent memory tests.

Subjects evaluated each candidate on 10 different attributes, using semantic differential scales with ranges of plus 3 to minus 3. The 10 attributes were:

> dishonest/honest, untrustworthy/trustworthy, incapable/capable, ineffective/effective, indecisive/decisive, unintelligent/intelligent, weak/strong, close-minded/open-minded, lazy/hardworking, and insincere/sincere.

These attributes were conceptualized as two dimensions, one that measured activity and potency (capable, effective, decisive, strong, hardworking), and the second, an evaluative dimension (honest, trustworthy, intelligent, open-minded, sincere) that captured personal qualities (Osgood, Suci, & Tannenbaum, 1957). Each subject was given 17 response sheets with all 10 of the attributes listed. All ratings were completed immediately after exposure to each political advertisement.

Memory for the advertisements was tested using a choice recognition task. After viewing all 16 of the political advertisements, 32 visual segments were presented to subjects on the same video monitor that had been used to view the advertisements. The presentation order for all visual segments was completely randomized. One second of visual material without audio was presented. Ten seconds of black separated each of the visual segments. Half of the segments were drawn from the advertisements people had just seen (targets), and half were from other political advertisements that were not seen (foils). All of the visual recognition segments presented the political candidates as their central figures and contained no cuts or other structural features. All of the segments for the foils were drawn from political candidates that would not have a high likelihood of recognition from some previous exposure. The total running time for the visual segments was 6 minutes and 58 seconds.

Subjects were instructed to decide if the visual segments were new or old material, and to make this decision as quickly as possible. Data from this task was divided into two parts: accuracy, or the proportion of correct responses, and latency to response (in msec).

After completing the memory task for the visual segments, the same procedure was repeated for audio segments. The audio probes were presented over the speaker of the television monitor, without visuals. Again, half of the audio segments were taken from the advertisements that had just been seen, and half were from different political advertisements. All of the segments used were distinct phrases, and they began and ended with the start and end of a phrase. Each audio segment lasted for approximately three seconds. The presentation order was randomized, and all of the segments were separated by 10 seconds of silence. Accuracy and latency scores were recorded for the audio segments. The total running time for the audio segments was 8 minutes and 29 seconds.

Procedure

Subjects participated in the experiment individually. Twenty-seven people were randomly assigned to the three presentation orders. The procedure was identical for all three groups. Subjects were brought into a viewing room and seated in a chair located 6 feet from a television monitor. The experimenter then stated that the study was about how people evaluate political candidates based on campaign advertisements. Subjects were told that all of the advertisements they were about to see were used in real political campaigns that were conducted in other regions of the country. A rating sheet was distributed and the 10 attributes used in the evaluation were explained. Viewers were encouraged to make their judgments based on first impressions according to whatever criteria they felt was important to them.

Finally, it was explained that each candidate would be evaluated immediately following the advertisement, and that there would be "just over a minute" to complete the evaluation. They would be alerted by a tone from the television monitor about 10 seconds before the next advertisement was to begin. After answering questions, the experimenter instructed the subjects to pay careful attention to the advertisements, because they would be asked questions about them later. The experimenter then started the videotape and left the room.

The stimulus tape began with 10 seconds of black, followed by a series of instructions that were presented in text on the video monitor. There were 8 different screens of instructions presented in succession for 10 seconds each. These instructions were followed by 10 seconds of black, and a practice political advertisement that was used to acclimate the subjects to the length of the spots, and to the evaluation task. This first practice advertisement was rated "neutral" on the image/issue dimension, and contained aspects of both static and dynamic structure. All of the advertisements were followed by 70 seconds of video black to allow time for evaluations. After 60 seconds a tone alerted the subject to the start of the next advertisement.

Immediately after the viewing and evaluation portion of the study, the experimenter returned to the room, and stated that the second part of the study would be a test of their memory for the advertisements they had just seen. The experimenter said that they were about to see a series of short video segments, half of which were taken from the political advertisements they had just seen, and half from different political advertisements. Their task was to decide if the segment was from a new or an old advertisement, and to make this decision as quickly as possible by pressing one of two buttons located on a game paddle connected to a computer. The same basic instructions were repeated for the audio segments. After answering any questions, the experimenter inserted a second tape into the video deck, and left the room.

The recognition memory tape began with 10 seconds of black, followed by six pages of instructions presented in text on the video monitor. The text was followed by 10 seconds of black, and then 33 visual probes, the first a practice probe, followed by a random ordering of 16 targets (old material) and 16 foils (new material).

Ten seconds after the end of the visual segment task, four pages of text instructions appeared on the television monitor. These instructions were followed by 10 sec of silence, and then 33 audio probes, the first a practice probe, and the following 32 a random ordering of 16 targets and 16 foils.

At the completion of the recognition tests, the experimenter returned, subjects completed a questionnaire that included demographic, media use, and political items. People were then debriefed.

Apparatus

Stimuli were presented on one-half inch VHS videotapes over a 19 inch Sony PVM-1910 color monitor. During the recognition tasks, the stimulus sequence was interfaced with an IBM AT computer via a longitudinal time code signal that was recorded on the second audio channel of the videotape, and read by a digital time code reader board installed in the computer. At the first video frame of each of the probes, the time code signal started a clock in the computer. Responses to these probes were made on a CH game paddle, and stored in the computer with the corresponding time code number.

RESULTS

Evaluation of candidates

A 2 (image/issue) × 2 (static/dynamic) repeated measures ANOVA was computed to assess the influence of advertisement content and structure on the evaluation of candidates. The dependent measure was a single index of all evaluation items. A factor analysis did not confirm two dimensions for the evaluative scales. The index was constructed using the factor scores from a single-factor solution.

There was a main effect for advertisement content (image, issue) $[F (1,428) = 61.5, p < .001]$. As predicted, candidates were rated more positively in issue advertisements than in image advertisements (Fig. 4.1). Dynamic structure produced more positive candidate evaluations than static structure $[F (1,428) = 26.1, p; < .001]$. The prediction that dynamic structure would have a greater influence on issue advertisements was also supported $[F (1,428) = 15.8, p < .001]$. Dynamic structure produced significantly more positive evaluations in issue advertisements than in image messages.

Visual memory for candidates

Analyses for visual recognition latency and accuracy were conducted separately. To test for visual recognition latency, a separate 2 (image/ issue) × 2 (static/dynamic) repeated measures ANOVA was computed using reaction times for recognition to previously viewed political candidates as the dependent variable.

A significant main effect was found for the content of advertisements $[F (1,428) = 8.2, p < .01]$. As predicted, pictures drawn from image advertisements were recognized significantly faster (Fig. 4.2). The pre-

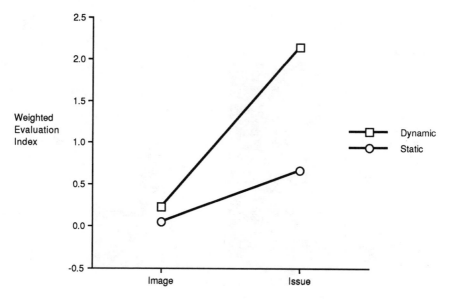

FIGURE 4.1.   Evaluation of political candidates.

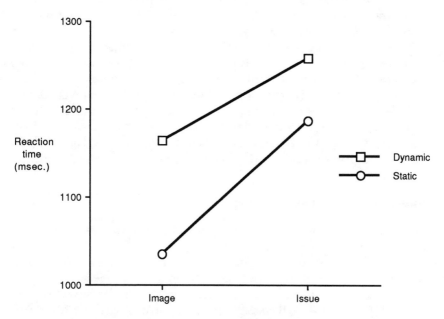

FIGURE 4.2.   Recognition time to visual probes.

137

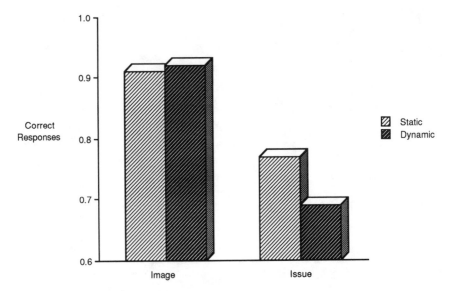

FIGURE 4.3.   Proportion of correct responses to visual probes.

dicted interference effect for structure was also found [$F(1,428) = 5.4$, $p < .05$]. Structurally simple advertisements were recognized faster than structurally dynamic ones. There were no significant interactions between content and structure for visual recognition.

To assess the accuracy of visual recognition for old (target) and new (foil) candidates, another 2 (image/issue) × 2 (static/dynamic) repeated measures ANOVA was computed. The dependent variable in this case was the proportion of correctly identified visual probes that were drawn from advertisements that had just been viewed. There was a significant main effect of image-issue orientation on accuracy [$F(1,428) = 25.3$, $p < .001$], with greater accuracy for image advertisements (Fig. 4.3). The main effect for structure and the interaction with content were not significant.

Audio Memory for Candidates

The analysis for audio response latency and accuracy were also conducted separately. To test for recognition of candidates' stated messages, a 2 (image/issue) × 2 (static/dynamic) repeated measures ANOVA was computed, with response latency to an audio probe as the dependent variable. Significant main effects were found for advertisement content [$F(1,428) = 22.1, p < .001$], and for structure [$F(1,428) = 6.5$, $p < .02$]. A significant content by structure interaction was also found [$F(1,428) = 27.9, p < .001$].

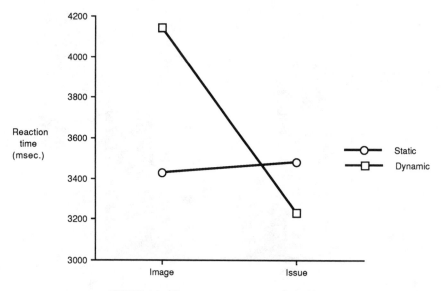

FIGURE 4.4.   Recognition time to audio probes.

Figure 4.4 illustrates the relationship between content, structure, and audio recognition. As predicted, issue advertisements were recognized faster than image advertisements. Static visual structure resulted in faster recognition of audio material than dynamic structure. Structure had a greater impact on image than on issue advertisements; dynamic-image advertisements were recognized significantly slower than static-image advertisements. Structure had no influence on response latency to issue advertisements.

The accuracy of responses to audio probes was calculated in another 2 (image/issue) × 2 static/dynamic) repeated measures ANOVA, using the proportion of correct responses to targets as the dependent variable. Neither of the main effects were significant. There was a significant interaction [$F (1,428) = 14.9, p < .001$]. Dynamic structure interfered with the correct identification of image advertisements, but contributed to the identification of issue advertisements (Fig. 4.5).

DISCUSSION

All of the predicted main effects for candidate evaluation were confirmed. Candidates in issue advertisements were evaluated more positively than candidates in image advertisements. Also, dynamic structure produced more positive evaluations. The predicted interaction was also

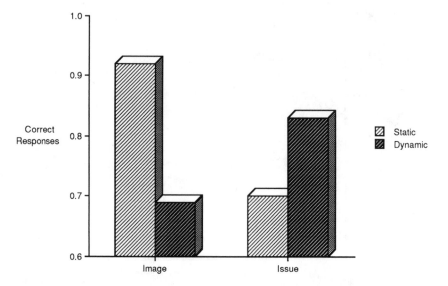

FIGURE 4.5. Proportion of correct responses to audio probes.

confirmed. Issue advertisements were more affected by dynamic structure than were image advertisements, and dynamic issue advertisements produced the most positive candidate evaluations.

Some support was also found for the distinction between affective and cognitive processing. Image advertisements displayed superior recognition for visual information, whereas issue advertisements were better for the recognition of spoken messages. Dynamic structure interfered with memory for both image and issue advertisements.

The predicted interaction for the audio recognition task did occur; dynamic structure interfered with recognition for image advertisements, but had no effect on issue advertisements. The powerful influence of visual structure on the recognition of audio material indicates that interference can occur between modalities. One explanation is that affective processing, which is stimulus-driven, is more susceptible to interference from dynamic structure. An alternative explanation is that different audio information was presented in dynamic image and issue advertisements. Dynamic-image advertisements made greater use of secondary sources of audio material such as music and special effects. The addition of these other sources may explain the greater difficulty in recognizing audio messages.

The relationship between evaluation and memory was not straightforward. For visual recognition, candidates were evaluated more positively in issue advertisements, but were remembered better within image content. Dynamic structure contributed positively to the evaluation of a candidate, but inhibited memory for both visual and audio information. Finally, structure interacts with issue advertisements in evaluation, and with image advertisements in audio recognition. These results provided some support to conclude that structure produces greater elaboration during cognitive processing, and greater interference during affective processing.

The results of this study have a number of practical implications for political campaigns. Image advertising is inferior to issue advertising in imparting a positive candidate evaluation, and for memory to a spoken message, but superior in memory for a candidate. In cases where positive candidate images are important, issue advertisements are more effective, although there is a trade off in visual memory. The introduction of structure as a factor contributes an important feature. The use of more dynamic message features associated with television is actually counterproductive when the goal is to make a candidate memorable, but is successful in producing positive evaluations.

Memory for a candidate, as well as the evaluation of a candidate, are not synonymous with voting. But this study does indicate how candidates are initially assessed, and ultimately remembered, critical processes at the inception of a campaign, and for uninvolved voters throughout a campaign. If a large proportion of the electorate relies on television for campaign information, then initial impressions and memory could be powerful influences on voting.

REFERENCES

Abelson, R. P., Kinder, D. R., Peters, M. D., & Fiske, S. T. (1982). Affective and semantic components in political person perception. *Journal of Personality and Social Psychology, 42,* 619–630.

Atkin, C. & Heald, G. (1976). Effects of political advertising. *Public Opinion Quarterly, 40,* 216–228.

Bolland, J. M. (1985). The structure of political cognition: A new approach to its meaning and measurement. *Political Behavior, 7,* 248–265.

Brent, E. & Granberg, D. (1982). Subjective agreement with the presidential candidates of 1976 and 1980. *Journal of Personality and Social Psychology, 42,* 393–403.

Burns, K. & Beier, E. G. (1973). Significance of vocal and visual channels in the decoding of emotional meaning. *Journal of Communication, 23,* 118–130.

Carlston, D. (1980). Events, inferences, and impression formation. In R. Hastie, T. M. Ostrom, E. B. Ebbesen, R. S. Wyer, D. L. Hamilton, & D. E. Carlston, (Eds.), *Person memory: The cognitive basis of social perception.* (pp. 89–119). Hillsdale, NJ: Lawrence Erlbaum Associates.

Carroll, J. M. & Bever, T. G. (1976). Segmentation in cinema perception. *Science, 191,* 1053–1055.

Conover, P. J. (1981). Political cues and the perception of candidates. *American Politics Quarterly, 9,* 427–448.

Fishbein, M. & Ajzen, I. (1981). Attitudes and voting behavior: An application of the theory of reasoned action. In G. M. Stephenson & J. M. Davis (Eds.), *Progress in applied social psychology.* (pp. 253–313). New York: John Wiley.

Fisk, A. D. & Schneider, W. (1984). Memory as a function of attention, level of processing, and automatization. *Journal of Experimental Psychology: Learning, Memory, and Cognition, 10,* 181–197.

Fiske, S. T. (1981). Social cognition and affect. In J. H. Harvey, (Ed.), *Cognition, social, behavior and the environment.* (pp. 227–264). Hillsdale, NJ: Lawrence Erlbaum Associates.

Garramone, G. (1986). Candidate image formation: The role of information processing. In L. L. Kaid, D. Nimmo, & K. R. Sanders, (Eds.), *New perspectives on political advertising.* (pp. 235–247). Carbondale, IL: Southern Illinois University Press.

Geiger, S. F. (1988, May) *Stimulus characteristics, processing strategies, and television viewing: A levels of processing approach.* Paper presented to the Information Systems Division, at the Meeting of the International Communication Association, New Orleans, LA.

Geiger, S. F. & Reeves, B. (1989, May) *The effects of scene changes and semantic relatedness on attention to television.* Paper presented to the Mass Communication Division, at the Meeting of the International Communication Association, San Francisco, CA.

Glass, D. P. (1985). Evaluating presidential candidates: Who focuses on their personal attributes? *Public Opinion Quarterly, 49,* 517–534.

Greenwald, A. G. & Leavitt, C. (1985). Cognitive theory and audience involvement. In L. F. Alwitt & A. A. Mitchell, (Eds.), *Psychological processes and advertising effects.* (pp. 221–240). Hillsdale, NJ: Lawrence Erlbaum Associates.

Hochberg, J. (1986). Representation of motion and space in video and cinematic displays. In K. R. Boff, L. Kaufman, & J. P. Thomas (Eds.), *Handbook of perception and human performance,* Volume II. (pp. 22-1–22-64). New York: John Wiley.

Hochberg, J. & Brooks, V. (1978). Film cutting and visual momentum. In J. W. Senders, D. F. Fisher, & R. A. Monty (Eds.), *Eye movements and the higher psychological functions.* (pp. 293–314). Hillsdale, NJ: Lawrence Erlbaum Associates.

Kaid, L. L. & Davidson, D. K. (1986). Elements of videostyle: Candidate presentation through television advertising. In L. L. Kaid, D. Nimmo & K. R. Sanders, (Eds.), *New perspectives on political advertising.* (pp. 184–209). Carbondale, IL: Southern Illinois University Press.

Kaid, L. L. & Sanders, K. R. (1978). Political Television Commercials: An experimental study of type and length. *Communication Research, 5,* 57–70.

Keeter, S. (1987). The illusion of intimacy: Television and the role of candidate personal qualities in voter choice. *Public Opinion Quarterly, 51,* 344–358.

Kinder, D. R., Peters, M. D., Abelson, R. P., Fiske, S. T. (1980). Presidential prototypes. *Political Behavior, 2,* 315–337.

Klatzky, R. L. (1980). Human Memory, New York: W. H. Freeman.

Kraft, R. N. (1986). The role of cutting in the evaluation and retention of film. *Journal of Experimental Psychology: Learning, Memory, and Cognition, 12,* 153–163.

Kraft, R. N. (1987). The influence of camera angle on comprehension and retention of pictorial events. *Memory & Cognition, 15,* 291–307.

McClure, R. D. & Patterson, T. E. (1974). Television news and political advertising. *Communication Research, 1,* 3–31.

Meadow, R. G. & Sigelman, L. (1982). Some effects and noneffects of campaign commercials: An experimental study. *Political Behavior, 4,* 163–175.

Mitchell, A. A. (1986). The effect of verbal and visual components of advertisements on brand attitudes and attitude toward the advertisement. *Journal of Consumer Research, 13,* 12–24.

Nimmo, D. & Savage, R. L. (1976). *Candidates and their images.* Pacific Palisades, CA: Goodyear.

Norman, D. A. & Bobrow, D. G. (1975). On data-limited and resource-limited processes. *Cognitive Psychology, 7,* 44–64.

Nygren, T. E. & Jones, L. E. (1977). Individual differences in perceptions and preferences for political candidates. *Journal of Experimental Social Psychology, 13,* 182–197.

Osgood, C., Suci, G. J., & Tannenbaum, P. H. (1957). *The measurement of meaning.* Urbana: University of Illinois.

Ottati, V., Fishbein, M., & Middlestadt, S. E. (1988). Determinants of voters' beliefs about the candidates' stands on the issues: The role of evaluative bias heuristics and the candidates' expressed message. *Journal of Personality and Social Psychology, 55,* 517–529.

Penn, R. (1971). Effects of motion and cutting rate in motion pictures. *Audio-Visual Communication Review, 19,* 29–50.

Rosenberg, S. W. & McCafferty, P. (1987). The image and the vote: Manipulating voters' preferences. *Public Opinion Quarterly, 51,* 31–47.

Shyles, L. (1984). Defining "images" of presidential candidates from televised political spot advertisements. *Political Behavior, 6,* 171–181.

Shyles, L. (1986). The televised political spot advertisement: Its structure, content, and role in the political system. In L. L. Kaid, D. Nimmo, & K. R. Sanders, (Eds.), *New perspectives on political advertising.* (pp. 107–138). Carbondale, IL: Southern Illinois University Press.

Snyder, M. & DeBono, K. G. (1985). Appeals to image and claims about quality: Understanding the psychology of advertising. *Journal of Personality and Social Psychology, 49,* 586–597.

Srull, T. K. & Wyer, R. S. (1989). Person memory and judgement. *Psychological Review, 96,* 58–83.

Wagner, J. (1983). Media do make a difference: The differential impact of mass media in the 1976 presidential race. *American Journal of Political Science, 27,* 407–430.

5

Selling Candidates Like Tubes of Toothpaste: Is the Comparison Apt?

Esther Thorson
University of Wisconsin-Madison

William G. Christ
Trinity University

Clarke Caywood
Northwestern University

The first political television commercials were used in the 1952 Presidential race pitting Adlai Stevenson against Dwight Eisenhower. One of the most famous executions of that campaign was an animated musical cartoon showing circus animals parading with a banner for Eisenhower, and singing "We like Ike." After the election, journalist Harlan Cleveland reported a conversation with the famous advertising copywriter, Rosser Reeves, who had directed Eisenhower's television commercials. Mass media historian Martin Mayer (1958) quoted Cleveland as saying to Reeves that his objection to the TV spots was that their real role "was selling the President like toothpaste" (p. 302).

From these early days of televised political spots through the infamous "Little Girl and the Daisy" spot for Lyndon Johnson in 1964 and the more recently controversial Willie Horton and Boston Harbor commercials that the Bush campaign produced in 1988, the dominant assumption in the popular media as well as the academic literature has been that people do process political commercials in the same way they process brand commercials. As with so many aspects of political advertising, this assumption is not based on research findings but primarily on speculation.

A 30-second execution for a political candidate may indeed have many attributes in common with an execution for a branded product or service, but candidates are not brands. And voting behavior is certainly not the same as buying behavior, although their equivalence is also often assumed in theorizing about the impact of political advertising. Thus, the assumption of "selling candidates like toothpaste," might be a misrepresentation of how people process political commercials. Because considerable information about how people do process brand ads has emerged in the last decade, it seemed possible to ask quite specifically, "Do viewers process political commercials as they process commercials for products and services, or is a different kind of processing system indicated?"

It should be noted that in this chapter the focus of the comparison between brand and political advertising is on the formation of attitudinal responses to political commercials, rather than memorial responses. This is because in the brand-processing literature, memory and attitudinal models have developed quite separately, and comparison of both sets of models is beyond the scope of a single chapter.

THE PROCESSING OF BRAND COMMERCIALS

To compare processing of political and brand commercials, the first task is to summarize the role of variables that have proved themselves important determinants of the impact of brand commercials. In fact, the 1980s have seen considerable focus on how TV commercials affect the attitudes and purchase intentions of viewers. This research has focused on three primary areas of mediating concepts in the processing: judgments about the brand, attitudes toward the advertising itself, and affect or emotion elicited by the advertising. The first concept concerns product beliefs or judgments that people develop (or have reinforced) as a function of watching a commercial. The second concept concerns the extent to which liking commercials (Aad) influences attitudes toward brands (Abr). And the third concept concerns the impact of emotional feelings experienced by viewers during a commercial. We next summarize the findings regarding the measurement and impact of these three concepts in the literature on product advertising so that they can then be applied to questions about how political commercials are processed.

Judgments About the Brand (or Candidate)

The term *judgment* is referred to in the advertising literature as beliefs and decisions made on the basis of thinking. A number of psychologists, including Zajonc (1980), argue that thinking and feeling are two different and independent evaluation systems. This differentiation has been applied in political science by Abelson, Kinder, Peters, and Fiske (1982), who provided evidence that semantic and affective responses to political candidates operated differently. For affect, or feelings, good and bad responses were virtually independent of each other, that is, people reported feeling both negative and positive feelings toward a single candidate. But good and bad semantic judgments about candidates loaded together. For example, if someone thought a candidate dishonest, he or she would likely think that candidate selfish.

Judgments are measured in many different ways, both within and across the fields of psychology, political science, and communication. In advertising, one of the most common measurements of judgments is "cognitive responding" (Wright, 1973), a method in which people are asked to list thoughts they have while watching an ad. These protocols are then content analyzed into positive, negative, or neutral judgments, or in terms of a more complex set of categories such as support arguments, counterarguments, and source derogations.

In a more close-ended approach to the measurement of judgment, Edell and Burke (1987) developed three judgment scales and demonstrated their usefulness in predicting attitudes toward brands. Their judgment scales included evaluation (believable, convincing, important, interesting, meaningful, valuable), activity (energetic, enthusiastic, exciting, imaginative, novel, original), and gentleness (gentle, lovely, serene, soothing, and tender).

In this study we chose to index beliefs about the candidates in our commercials by asking subjects to decide, for each pair of polar adjectives, where the candidate's characteristics most likely lay. These adjective pairs included such terms as stimulating–boring, articulate–inarticulate, strong–weak, smart–stupid, persuasive–unpersuasive, experienced–inexperienced, active–passive, believable–unbelievable, and so on. We assumed that there were two dimensions to a candidate's characteristics: his or her ability and his or her personality. These two dimensions are described in more detail later in the chapter.

Attitude Toward the Commercial (Aad)

A second important concept in the brand processing literature is Aad (MacKenzie, Lutz, & Belch, 1985; Mitchell & Olson, 1981; Shimp, 1981). Aad is usually measured by asking viewers to rate on three or more semantic differential scales (e.g., like–dislike, good–bad, positive–negative) how much they liked a particular commercial. Although Aad is a simple and straightforward measure, and although it does not seem particularly rational for commercial liking to affect attitude toward a brand or its purchase, it has proved to be a very important variable in the processing of commercials.

What has been particularly impressive about Aad research is that Aad effects on Abr are virtually ubiquitous. Gardner (1985, see her Table 1) summarized the studies that examined the effect of Aad as always showing a significant effect on Abr when there was a "nonbrand" set. The two studies in her Table 1 that used "brand" sets showed mixed or limited effects of Aad. In Gardner's own study, she specifically manipulated brand–nonbrand processing. Her results showed that Aad effects were less strong under brand processing than under nonbrand, but they remained significant even under brand processing. MacKenzie et al. (1985) showed in two experiments with an unfamiliar brand of toothpaste, that Aad had dual effects. Aad influenced Abr and it also influenced self-reported cognitions about the brand.

In this study, Aad was measured in a way consistent with the brand-processing literature. We used eight bipolar adjective scales: like–dislike, good–bad, pleasant–unpleasant, persuasive–unpersuasive, believable–unbelievable, truthful–deceptive, accurate–inaccurate, ethical–unethical.

Emotion Elicited by Commercials

The third important concept in the processing of commercials is affect or emotion. Advertising research has defined and measured the emotional impact of commercials in many different ways (e.g., Batra & Ray, 1985, 1986; Edell & Burke, 1986, 1987; Holbrook & Batra, 1987; Holbrook & Westwood, 1989; Stayman & Aaker, 1988; Thorson & Friestad, 1989). In psychology, systematic research on emotion dates back at least to the last century (James, 1884). Based on work by Osgood, Suci, and Tannenbaum (1957), one of many highly regarded approaches was developed by Mehrabian and Russell (1974), whose original theory suggests that emotional response can be parsimoniously described in terms of three orthogonal dimensions: pleasure–displeasure, arousal, and dominance–submissiveness. Pleasure–displeasure is conceptualized as a continuum ranging from extreme unhappiness to extreme happiness. Arousal is conceptualized as a combination of activity and alertness, and ranges from sleepy through intermediate stages of drowsiness, calmness, and alertness, to frenzied excitement. Dominance–submissiveness ranges from extreme feelings of being influenced, controlled, and cared for, to feelings of being important, in control, and potent.

Although there is some significant support for the predictive usefulness of all three of the factors (Holbrook & Batra, 1987, although it should be noted they stress pleasure, arousal, and "dominant" instead of dominance), research by Russell (1978, 1980) and others (cf. Christ, 1985a, 1985b; Whissell, 1983) indicates that a two-factor approach may be equally reasonable as a way to describe emotion. Russell (1978) suggested that "multi-dimensional scaling, successive-intervals scaling, semantic differentials, and factor analysis of verbal self-report data all seem to show convergent validity for the pleasure and arousal dimensions'' (p. 1152). Indeed, given that two factors are more parsimonious than three, looking only at arousal and pleasure to index emotional impact may even be preferable.

In research on television programming (Christ & Biggers, 1984), television commercials (Christ & Thorson, 1989), and marketing (Donovan & Rossiter, 1982) the dominance dimension was shown to have little explanatory power. Even in those studies that did not directly test the Mehrabian and Russell theory, pleasure and arousal continue to be useful and important constructs. For example, Batra and Ray (1986) indicated that three categories of affective response were most identified in consumer responses to commercials. These included social affection (pleasure), surgency, elation, vigor-activation (arousal), and deactivation (nonarousal). Edell and Burke (1987) used three feelings scales: upbeat (a combination of pleasure and arousal), negative (pleasure), and warm (pleasure).

Furthermore, although other researchers have preferred to develop taxonomies of specific qualitative kinds of emotions that might be experienced while watching commercials (e.g., Allen, Machleit, & Marine, 1987; Batra, 1984; Batra & Holbrook, 1987; Holbrook & O'Shaughnessy, 1984; Thorson, 1986), in general, those who have taken a factor-analytic approach to the use of emotional words in response to commercials, have found significant verification of pleasure and arousal as underlying dimensions. Therefore, the present study included pleasure and arousal in the conceptualization of emotional response.

Mehrabian and Russell (1974) hypothesized that emotional response may predict preference, liking, and approach/avoidance responses. Specifically they suggested that: approach is positively associated with both pleasure and arousal, approach has an inverted-U relationship with arousal, and finally, that approach generally increases with arousal when pleasure is experienced, but decreases with arousal when displeasure is experienced. These predictions lead to the necessity of indexing not only Pleasure (P) and Arousal (A), but also of their interaction (Pleasure $\times$ Arousal, i.e., PA), and curvilinear relations between the two variables, specifically Arousal squared (A^2) and Pleasure $\times$ Arousal squared (PA^2).

The Role of Judgments, Aad, and Emotion in Processing of Commercials

Now that we have defined and considered the measurement of judgments (attitudes toward brands), Aad, and emotion, and looked at the literature on their impact in the processing of commercials, the next question is how the three concepts interact with each other and relate to intention to purchase (or, for political advertising, voting intent). In light of the research on processing of product ads, there seem to be three likely relationships among the three concepts. These possibilities are shown schematically in Fig. 5.1. First, emotion may drive Aad, which in turn affects voting or purchase intent. Judgment might have an independent effect on intent (Panel A) or be affected by the flow from emotion to Aad (Panel B). This would mean that both emotion and Aad only indirectly affect voting or purchase intent. Or third, it may be that Aad, emotion, and judgment each influence intent to purchase (or vote) independently (Panel C). Although there is not sufficient opportunity to develop fully the literature behind each of these models of the processing of commercials, a short summary of that literature, as applied to the processing of products, follows.

A number of advertising researchers have asked whether Aad and emotional responding to advertising both influence Abr or whether

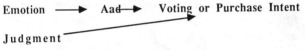

Aad mediates the effect of Emotion on Intent.   Judgment   has
an   independent   and   direct   effect   on   Intent

<u>Panel   A</u>

Emotion   → Ad →   Judgment →   Voting or Purchase Intent

Aad   and   Judgment   mediate   the   effects   of   Emotion   on   Intent.

<u>Panel   B</u>

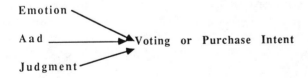

Emotion,   Aad,   and   Judgment   have   independent   effects   on   Intent.

<u>Panel   C</u>

FIGURE 5.1.   Possible relations among emotion, Aad, Acand, and voting intention.

emotional responding drives Aad and only indirectly affects Abr. Edell and Burke (1987) showed (Experiment 2) that the effect of feelings engendered by commercials directly affected Aad and were mediated by Aad onto Abr. They also showed (Experiment 1) that the effects of feelings on Aad were greater than the effects of judgments on Aad when ads were high in transformation and low in information. But when commercials were high in both transformation and information, judgments were bigger contributers than feelings. (It should be noted that Edell and Burke did not ask whether the lack of direct emotional effects on Abr held for all the four categories of transformation/information combinations.) Consistent with Edell and Burke (1987), Holbrook and Batra (1987) also showed that Aad mediates the relation between emotions and Abr.

Edell and Burke (1986), in another study, compared the relative effects of prior brand attitude and Aad on Abr for familiar and unfamiliar brands and for low and high product usage. Regardless of the level of brand familiarity, Aad had a significant impact on Abr, although prior Abr was more important when brand familiarity was high.

The one study inconsistent with the finding that emotions affect Abr only through Aad (Stayman & Aaker, 1988), asked whether once prior Abr and Aad were entered to predict Abr, emotional responding would still account for significant additions to the variance accounted for. In fact, they found that approximately 3% or 4% additional variance was accounted for by simple indices of emotion, even after Aad was taken into account, and that these additions to R^2 were significant.

Thus, most studies that have measured Aad have shown it to significantly affect Abr. This has been demonstrated for different kinds of ads and situations, including transformational and informational commercials (Edell & Burke, 1987), brand- and nonbrand-processing instructions (Gardner, 1985), and familiar and unfamiliar brands (Edell & Burke, 1986).

One of the few exceptions to the ubiquitous effects of Aad was in a study by Machleit and Wilson (1988). They hypothesized that the effect of Aad on Abr would disappear when very familiar brands were tested. They tested this hypothesis by comparing the path analyses for responses to commercials for Lee jeans and Pepsi (very familiar brands) and commercials for Lois and Mr. Christie (very unfamiliar brands). Indeed, they found no path from Aad to Ab when prior brand attitude was considered for Lee and Pepsi. There was a significant path from Aad to Ab, however, for the two commercials for unfamiliar brands. This study, then, was virtually the only one that was able to show disappearance of the effects of Aad on Abr under certain conditions (i.e., brand familiarity).

There is significant evidence then, that Aad is an important determinant of the impact of commercials. As noted earlier, however, having an attitude toward a commercial influencing one's attitude toward a brand does not indicate particularly rational processing. Nevertheless, people are not completely irrational, because judgments made about the brand are also important.

How can we decide among the various possible patterns of processing? The most popular solution in marketing and advertising research is the idea is that the processing of commercials takes one or another of the two routes. The judgment route is thoughtful, cognitive, logical, systematic, and has the goal of determining correct attitudes. This route has variously been referred to as *brand processing* (Gardner, Mitchell, & Russo, 1985); systematic processing (Chaiken, 1980); central processing (Petty, Cacioppo, & Schumann, 1983); and so on. The Aad route is not cognitive, but rather may involve short-hand decision rules (heuristic processing, Chaiken, 1980); conditioning processes (MacKenzie et al., 1985), processing information other than that relevant to the brand (nonbrand processing, posited by Gardner et al., 1985), or the use of cues other than the issue material itself (peripheral processing, Petty & Cacioppo, 1979).

It would seem that political theorists would prefer to think that central processing is the route by which people process political commercials. But there is a third possibility. It may be that the rational and the irrational go on simultaneously. That is, both Aad and emotional processing occur continually, regardless of whether judgments are being formed while people watch political commercials. If so, Aad, emotions, and judgment would all predict voting preference after viewing commercials for political candidates.

That the system works like this has been hinted at by a number of advertising researchers. For example, Gardner (1985) said in the study referred to earlier:

> the observed importance of Aad under a brand set, . . . , provides support
> for the idea that the central route to persuasion supplements rather than
> replaces the peripheral route when consumers carefully evaluate advertised brands. This notion is consistent with the growing awareness in
> psychology of the almost automatic nature of basic affective processing
> (cf. Zajonc, 1980). (p. 197)

In a similar vein, Edell and Burke (1987) suggested that "Researchers such as Mitchell (1986) and Petty and Cacioppo (1981) have suggested that the belief formation process is a central process that is cognitive in nature. Yet, Study 2 indicates that the feelings elicited by the ad contribute to belief formation. This suggests that the various elements of the persuasion process may be much more interconnected than existing models propose" (p. 430).

Consistent with the notion that emotion and Aad kinds of processing are continuous, Thorson and Page (1990) showed that when involvement in advertised product categories is high, judgments about product attributes account for the largest percentage of the variance in intent to purchase. Aad and emotional response are still significant predictors, but their importance is small. On the other hand, when product involvement is low, Aad and emotional measures account for the greatest variance, and the impact of judgment, although significant, is much lower.

Findings such as these hint at the idea that the two routes of processing may not be an "either–or" situation. The model that seems to emerge from these data suggests that (a) impressionistic processing in which Aad and emotional responding is important always occurs; and (b) analytical processing, in which judgment is paramount, may or may not kick in, depending on variables such as how involved viewers are in the situation or the product, what kind of viewing they have been instructed to do, and their own ability to handle analytical processing. The model also suggests that (c) the results of impressionistic processing may be overridden by analytical processes to one degree or another; and (d) the stronger the emotional impact of commercials, the more impact impressionistic processing will have, regardless of what other variables may be affecting the likelihood of analytical processing.

We have now taken a fairly indepth look at the processing of brand commercials. The question that we now return to is whether the role of and relations among Aad, beliefs, and emotional response are replicated when commercials are for political candidates rather than brands. We turn now to more explicit comparison of the two domains of processing.

PROCESSING POLITICAL COMMERCIALS

To articulate a test of whether the processing of political commercials is similar to that of processing brand and service ads, a prior question must first be raised. That question revolves around what constitutes a political commercial. Another way to say this is that to determine whether responses to political commercials match the processing characteristics seen in responses to brand advertising, it is important to obtain a reasonably representative sample of political commercials (see Jackson and Jacobs, 1983, for a discussion of the issue of sampling messages). Of course, the answer to whether political and brand commercials are processed alike is only good if our commercials do represent those really being used by politicians.

After viewing many commercials for many different offices, we decided that there were so many dimensions of difference as a function purely of the political office the candidate sought (e.g., presidential, national and state legislature, gubernatorial, and then local offices), that we would only sample one such level. We chose Senate races.

Based on the rather sparse literature (Kaid & Davidson, 1986) concerning kinds of political commercials, and our own evaluation of these messages, it seemed that there were four important dimensions of variation across the senators' commercials. These dimensions included whether the focus in the ad was an issue or an image emphasis; whether the focus was positive toward the candidate or negative/attacking toward his opponent; whether there was presence or absence of music; and whether the visuals of the commercial showed personal glimpses of the candidate and his family (Family), or showed the candidate in the professional world (Professional) of campaigning (e.g., talking with voters, getting on and off airplanes, visiting factories, and so on).

To increase the generalizability of the results and to assure that the dimensions of the commercials were not confounded with idiosyncracies of the candidates themselves, we then produced commercials for each of the four candidates based on combining the values on each of the four dimensions. For two of the candidates, we created all possible combinations of the four variables, resulting in 16 separate commercials for each candidate. For two of the candidates, the commercials we had available prevented production of all 16 possible executions. We therefore produced as many combinations possible (described in detail later). The creation of the commercials in this way allowed us to present subjects with a fairly wide array of commercial execution types, as well as to look at the impact of the four dimensions on processing. In this chapter, we do not, however, concentrate on the effects of the dimensions, but rather simply ask whether the models that best apply to the processing of brands also satisfactorily predict responses to our sample of political commercials.

Four Dimensions of Political Commercials

To provide a rational for choosing the four message dimensions examined here, we look first at the handful of studies that have indexed the processing impact of issue versus image commercials, and of attack and positive copy strategies. We know of no political studies related to our professional–family visuals variable, nor to the impact of presence of music. There are, however, four important studies concerned with issue–image and attack–positive appeals.

In the earliest of these studies, Kaid and Sanders (1978) defined issue commercials as those that "were concerned with specific policy issues (such as jobs or roads)" (p. 60). Image commercials were defined as those that "were concerned with related personal characteristics of the candidate without advocating any specific issue positions" (p. 60). Kaid and Sanders used four commercials to test the comparative impact of issue and image approaches: a 60-second image and a 60-second issue commercial, and a 5-minute issue and 5-minute image commercial for a gubernatorial campaign. (We ignore the impact of commercial length for present purposes.) One of the four political commercials was presented to different groups of college students in a 30-minute television program that also included other product commercials. After viewing the 30 minutes of programming, the students were asked, among other things, to evaluate the candidate (using 12 semantic differential items anchored by the terms unqualified–qualified, unsophisticated–sophisticated, honest–dishonest, humorous–serious, insincere–sincere, old-fashioned–modern, successful–unsuccessful, handsome–ugly, unfriendly–friendly, liberal–conservative, excitable–calm, and spender–saver.)

In the Kaid and Sanders study it was not reported whether the 12 scales were either factor analyzed or subjected to an internal reliability test. Instead, the combination of 12 items was treated as a single factor. Looking at the items, it seems likely that more than one dimension may have been assessed. For example, factors may have emerged along both personality (i.e., insincere–sincere, unfriendly–friendly, etc.) and professional (i.e., liberal–conservative, spender–saver, etc.) dimensions.

The issue ads produced significantly more positive attitude scores than did the image commercials. It should be noted that the test administered to the students also asked for free recall of the content of the commercials. For memory, the image commercials were stronger, with the mean number of items recalled for the image commercials significantly higher than for the issue group.

In a second relevant experimental study, Roddy and Garramone (1988) examined the effect of issue versus image strategies in commercials where a candidate attacked his opponent. The study also looked at what kind of response the commercials of the target of the attack took, but we ignore that particular issue here. It should be noted that both the issue and image commercials used in the study were attack, or in the nomenclature used here, negative commercials. The results showed that people preferred issue attack commercials to image attack commercials, and that the attacking candidates' character was rated as more positive with issue attack commercials. There were, however, no significant differences found between issue and image attack commercials on likelihood of voting for the attacking candidate.

There have been no direct comparisons of positive and attack appeals in commercials. Surlin and Gordon (1977) showed that people considered attack commercials unethical, but that they nevertheless perceived these commercials to be informative. Merritt (1984) carried out a survey examining attitudes in a campaign (California State Assembly) in which both candidates used attack appeals. Merritt's results indicated that the attack advertising evoked negative affect toward both candidates.

As noted above, there is no literature on the role of visuals and music on the impact of televised political commercials. There is, however, analogous research for the visuals and music in the literature on product advertising. It is that literature that is used to generate hypotheses in the present study.

Gorn (1982) and Stout and Leckenby (1988) have shown that the presence of liked music is associated with enhanced attitudes toward brands and with both actual choice of, or intention to choose a brand. Similarly, Rossiter and Percy (1980) and Percy and Rossiter (1983) showed that print advertisements with predominant illustrations had more positive effects on attitudes than did ads that deemphasized illustrations. Mitchell (1983) showed clear evidence that the presence of pictures or visuals that represented warm, human, or generally pleasant emotions were associated with enhanced brand attitude and greater intention to purchase.

The Tests

We are now ready to articulate a test of whether the processing of political commercials is similar to that of processing product and service commercials. This question boils down to the relative roles played by beliefs about the candidate, attitudes toward the political commercials themselves, and emotional responding to commercials. As we have seen, these three variables are critically important to the processing of brand commercials. For political commercials, it might be that only judgments are important. This would indicate a highly rational form of advertising and be very different from brand processing.

But if processing in the political commercial domain is like processing in the product domain, then all three variables will be important. Their relations to each other might take one of several forms. First, emotions might be the antecedent variables leading to Aad and judgments are developed based on those variables. Or, it might be that emotion, Aad, and judgment are each part of the ongoing flow of processing and that no one of these variables plays the role of antecedent variable.

To test the role of Aad, emotion, and judgments, as well as the flow of causality through the causal variables to the dependent variable (i.e., voting intention), the analysis will depend on the work of Rosenberg (1968). He suggested three statistical requirements that must be satisfied if an antecedent, independent, and dependent variable flow of causality is to be identified. (It should be kept in mind that his notation included the testing of two variables, whereas the present analysis tests three.) The first requirement is that all three variables must be related. Second, when the antecedent variable is controlled, the relationship between the independent and the dependent variable should not vanish. And third, when the independent variable is controlled, the relationship between the antecedent variable and dependent variable should disappear.

To test these relationships in the present study, we simply take each of the three independent variables (emotion, Aad, and beliefs) and test the influence at every level of entry into a regression equation predicting voting intention. For example, if emotion is antecedent to Aad, then (a) both variables will be correlated with voting intention. (b) When emotion is controlled there will still be a relation between Aad and intention. But when (c) Aad is controlled, the relationship between emotion and voting intention will disappear.

A secondary question of this research concerns whether the dimensions of variations of the commercials would affect the causal flow. For example, both music and the family visuals in the background might be expected to produce stronger emotional responses in the viewer. If so, then emotion (pleasure or arousal or both) as an independent variable might play a greater role in accounting for variance in voting intention. Or, arousal might itself be expected to play a greater predictive role when the scripts are in attack format, or when the family visuals are used in the background. Thus, we also examine the form of regressions predicting voting intention for each of the two values on each of the four dimensions of commercial manipulation: positive–attack; issue–image, music–no music; and professional–family.

METHOD

Subjects

The subjects were 161 students in introductory undergraduate communication courses at a large, midwestern university. Students received extra credits toward their class grade in exchange for their participation.

Design

The stimulus commercials used in the study involved a balanced manipulation of four factors: (a) image versus issue commercials; (b) negative versus positive commercials; (c) commercials with and without music; and (d) commercials that featured candidates with their families and those that featured candidates in more neutral settings (i.e., shaking hands with, listening to, or visiting constituents.) Nearly all of the manipulations were repeated for each of four real but unfamiliar Senatorial candidates. Each subject saw one commercial for each candidate, but that commercial may have been any one of the 16 combinations of the four factors.

Stimuli

Scripts. Four "generic" scripts were created (see Appendix A). These scripts were balanced in terms of number of words, number of issues/images, number of mentions of senator, congressman (some of the candidates were current congressmen, but all were seeking the U.S. Senate), and candidate's name. The same scripts were read for each candidate with the appropriate candidate's name being used. The only changes in the script occurred at the end of the commercials, with each candidate having his own tagline, that is, Phil Gramm ("Common Sense . . . Uncommon Courage"), Gordon Humphrey ("Keep Him in the United States Senate"), Ray Shamie ("A Senator for All Seasons"), and John Warner ("Leadership for Virginia in the United States Senate").

The first of the scripts was called *issue-positive.* This script featured four issues the candidate was said to support. Each of the four issues was deemed not to be highly controversial during the time the study was run in Fall 1988. The issues included: favors family security by supporting broad-based family programs, programs to ensure job security, state water rights, and comprehensive health care for all ages.

The second of the scripts was called *issue-negative.* This script featured three issues the candidate supported that his opponent did not support. The issues included: rights for the elderly, state economic growth, and greater school funding.

The third category of script was called *image-positive.* This script related four positive image attributes of the candidate. These attributes included: working hard for the great people of this state, a dedicated family man, a law-abiding citizen, and someone you can believe/trust because he reflects our values.

The fourth kind of script was called *image-negative.* This script related four positive attributes of the candidate (intelligent, compassionate, family man, trustworthy), and three negative attributes of the candidate's opponent: has cheated the people of this state, tells lies to the constituency, and uses deception.

Music. Upbeat, patriotic instrumental music was used. Two selections were randomly rotated to alleviate the concern that there would be specific responses to one example of music. The two musical selections came from national anthems of third-world countries. Half of each candidate's commercials had a musical background and half were without music. The music was professionally mixed onto the commercials.

Visual Backgrounds. Two types of film footage were used as visual backgrounds in the commercials. Family backgrounds showed the candidate with his family and professional backgrounds showed the candidate shaking hands with his constituents; visiting sites such as factories, deboarding planes, and doing other political candidate kinds of activities. For Gramm and Humphrey, each background was integrated with each of the four scripts. This led to eight background-script combinations for these two candidates. The Shamie and Warner commercials each yielded only one kind of background. Shamie's background featured family visuals, and Warner's background featured him engaged in professional activities. For these two candidates there were only four background-script combinations.

Candidates. The raw material for production of each of the sets of commercials came from real commercials for four candidates who had run for the U.S. Senate in the last 10 years (Phil Gramm, Gordon Humphrey, Ray Shamie, and John Warner). To summarize the use of the variables listed here, each of the four candidates was shown in two types of background settings, with or without music, being promoted with one of four different scripts. For Gramm and Humphrey there were 16 different commercials produced. For Shamie and Warner there were 8 different commercials produced.

Procedure

Subjects, tested in groups of six to eight, sat around a horseshoe table configuration about 8 to 10 feet from a 19-inch television. Each group was shown one of 16 orders of 13 videotaped ads. Included in the 13 ads were 5 political ads and 8 brand ads. Each group of political ads contained four target commercials with one execution for each of the four candidates. The individual executions for each candidate, as well as the commercials for brands were rotated among the 16 orders. The order of target and nontarget commercials, although the individual commercials were rotated, was as follows:

1. brand commercial
2. political commercial (questionnaire was administered)
3. brand
4. brand (questionnaire was administered)
5. political (questionnaire was administered)
6. brand
7. brand
8. political (no questionnaire—fifth candidate)
9. brand
10. political (questionnaire was administered)
11. brand
12. brand
13. political (questionnaire was administered)

A final questionnaire dealing with memory for all the commercials as well as some general political orientations was administered at the completion of viewing of all 13 commercials.

Dependent Measures

Attitudes and feelings toward the commercials and the candidates were assessed with a variety of measures. Attitude toward the ad (Aad) and the candidate (Acand) were assessed with a series of bipolar adjective scales.

Ad attitude (Aad) was assessed with 9, nine-point, bipolar adjective pairs: believable–unbelievable; persuasive–unpersuasive; like–dislike; pleasant–unpleasant; truthful–deceptive; accurate–inaccurate; ethical–unethical; good–bad.

Candidate attitude (Acand) was assessed with 19 nine-point, bipolar adjective pairs: warm–cold; emotional–unemotional; friendly–unfriendly; concerned–unconcerned; compassionate–uncompassionate; kind–unkind; honest–dishonest; sincere–insincere; believable–unbelievable; rational–irrational; appealing–unappealing; attractive–unattractive; stimulating–boring; articulate–inarticulate; weak–strong; smart–stupid; persuasive–unpersuasive; experienced–inexperienced; active–passive.

Feelings were assessed along the two dimensions hypothesized by Mehrabian and Russell (1974) and Russell (1978). Pleasure was indexed with the 6 nine-point bipolar adjective pairs: hopeful–despairing;

pleased–annoyed; happy–unhappy; relaxed–bored; satisfied–unsatisfied; contented–melancholic.

Arousal was assessed with 6 nine-point bipolar adjective pairs: stimulated–relaxed; wide awake–sleepy; excited–calm; frenzied–sluggish; jittery–dull; aroused–unaroused.

Familiarity was also assessed with a nine-point bipolar adjective scale: "familiar" to "unfamiliar"

RESULTS

Reliability of the Dependent Variable Scales

Using Cronbach's alpha, average reliability of the scales was assessed: Aad (.88), Acand (.94), pleasure (.88), and arousal (.88). Aad's reliability would be increased to .91 by eliminating the ethical–unethical subscale. Before the ethical–unethical subscale was eliminated from the analysis, it was decided to perform a factor analysis on Aad, Acand, and pleasure and arousal to see if, indeed, the scales were consistently tapping one construct.

Factor Analysis of the Scales

Principal factor analysis with varimax rotation was used to analyze the Aad, Acand, and emotion (pleasure and arousal) scales.

Aad. The analysis produced two factors with eigenvalues greater than 1.0. Factor 1, which contained all subscales except ethical–unethical, had an eigenvalue of 4.97. Factor 2, which contained the ethical—unethical subscale had an eigenvalue of 1.04. Based on the reliability scores and the factor analysis, the ethical–unethical subscale was eliminated from any further analysis.

Acand. A factor analysis produced two factors with eigenvalues greater than 1.0. By eliminating subscales that did not load at least .20 higher on one factor than another factor, we were left with two factors with seven subscales each.

Factor 1, with an eigenvalue of 9.91, included: warm–cold; emotional–unemotional; friendly–unfriendly; compassionate–uncompassionate; kind–unkind; honest–dishonest; sincere–insincere.

Factor 2, with an eigenvalue of 2.64, included: stimulating–boring; articulate–inarticulate; weak–strong; stupid–smart; persuasive–unpersuasive; experienced–inexperienced; active–passive.

Factor 1 seemed associated with a candidate's character. Factor 2 seemed associated with a candidate's abilities. Factor 1 might be considered reflecting more general, human qualities, whereas Factor 2 reflects the more specific qualities associated with a public figure.

It is clear from the reliability score that the 19 items that make up Acand hold together as a "global" measure of attitude toward candidates. This factor is called *Acand* in subsequent analyses. What is equally clear from the factor analysis is that two subconstructs emerge within the global construct. The first, which is comprised of seven subscales and refers to a candidate's character, is called *Achar* ($\alpha = .93$) and refers to a candidate's ability, is called *Aabil.* ($\alpha = .90$).

Emotion (Pleasure and Arousal). As would be expected, two factors with eigenvalues of more than 1.0 were formed. Factor 1, which corresponded to "arousal," had an eigenvalue of 5.51, with all arousal subscales loading on this factor. Factor 2, which corresponded to "pleasure," had an eigenvalue of 2.25, with all pleasure subscales loading on this factor. All subscales loaded more than .20 higher on one factor than the other with the lowest loading being .64 for boring–relaxed on the pleasure factor.

This analysis, along with the reliability scores, helped confirm the internal validity of the pleasure and arousal scales.

Research Questions Concerning the Relations of Emotion, Aad, Beliefs, and Voting Intention (Whole Sample)

The first test to determine the interrelationships of the three independent variables and voting intention hinged on the interrcorrelations among the three kinds of variables. Table 5.1 shows these correlations.

Table 5.1 Intercorrelations Among Voting Intent, Aad, Acand, Aabil, and the Measures of Emotion

	Voting intent	*Aad*	*Achar*	*Aabil*
Aad	.59	—	—	—
Achar	.43	.58	—	—
Aabil	.57	.68	.46	—
Pleasure	.58	.80	.60	.64
Arousal	.35	.43	.12	.46
PA	−.14	−.26	−.19	−.15
A^2	−.18	−.32	no	−.32
PA^2	.31	.52	.35	.43

Note: One-tailed tests were used for all comparisons. All correlations were significant at $p < .001$.

As can be seen, all the variables were significantly correlated with each other except that Achar was not significantly correlated with one emotional variable, A2. This means that the first requirement for antecedent relations specified by Rosenberg was fulfilled.

The second Rosenberg requirement is that when antecedents are controlled, the relationship between the independent and the dependent variable should *not* go to zero. Table 5.2 shows the result of a test in which every possible order of emotion, Aad, and beliefs was entered in a hierarchical regression to predict voting intention. As can be

Table 5.2 Voting Intent as a Function of Aad, Aabil, Achar, and the Measures of Emotion

*Run 1:	$AdjR^2$	$Adj R^2$ Change	Run 2:	$AdjR^2$	$Adj R^2$ Change
D**	.1307		D	.1307	
A	.4400	.3093	A	.4400	.3093
C	.5410	.1010	E	.4921	.0521
E	.5590	.0180	C	.5590	.0669
Run 3:			Run 4:		
D	.1307		D	.1307	
C	.5243	.3936	C	.5243	.3936
A	.5410	.0167	E	.5561	.0318
E	.5590	.0180	A	.5590	.0029
Run 5:			Run 6:		
D	.1307		D	.1307	
E	.4654	.3347	E	.4654	.3347
A	.4921	.0267	C	.5561	.0907
C	.5590	.0669	A	.5590	.0029

*Note: Six regression were run using a forced hierarchical approach entering each of the main variables in different orders. The dummy variables that take into account the repeat measures design were always entered first.

Run 1: Aad, then Achar and Aabil, then Emotional response
Run 2: Aad, then Emotional response, then Achar and Aabil
Run 3: Achar and Aabil, then Aad, then Emotional response
Run 4: Achar and Aabil, then Emotional response, then Aad
Run 5: Emotional response, then Aad, then Achar and Aabil
Run 6: Emotional response, then Achar and Aabil, then Aad

Emotional response was always entered with pleasure and arousal first, then PA and A^2, then PA^2 (see Cohen & Cohen, 1975, p. 98).

**D = Dummy variables
  A = Attitude toward the advertisement
  C = Judgments of the Candidates' Character and Ability
  E = Emotion-Eliciting Qualities of the Advertisement (Pleasure, Arousal, PA, A^2, and PA^2).
**All reported adjR² and R²changes are significant at the $p < .05$ level.

seen,no matter which class of the independent variables was allowed to enter first, the impact of the other remained significant. Thus, Rosenberg's second requirement is met.

The third Rosenberg requirement is that when the independent variable is controlled, the relationship between the antecedent variable and the dependent variable does drop to zero. This can also be tested by the analyses shown in Table 5.2. Here, however, we have already seen that no matter which class of the independent variables is entered first in the regression, the other variables, although the magnitude of their effect is diminished, still remain significant predictors of voting intention. Based on the third Rosenberg requirement, therefore, we reject the notion that any of the independent variables (i.e., emotion, Aad, or beliefs) serve as antecedents to the other variables. Instead, it is clear that these three variables share considerable overlap in the variance they account for in voting intention. It is for this reason that whichever variables are entered first lessen the R^2s for the other variables. But no matter which of the variables are entered first or second, the third one still remains significant. This means that each of the three independent variables accounts for some unique variance in voting intention. This in turn means that each of the three variables have a small, unique direct effect on voting intention. So, we conclude that emotion, Aad, and beliefs about candidates engendered by a political commercial may occur in an integrated, perhaps simultaneous way and that each class of variable has a small direct effect on voting intention.

Flow of Effect Among the Independent Variables for Particular Kinds of Commercials

A second area of research question concerned whether the impact of emotion, Aad, and beliefs on voting intention would vary as a function of the type of commercial people saw. To test this, we made a series of bisections of the data. First, we grouped all data from commercials with positive scripts separately from those with attack scripts. Second, we grouped all issue separately from image commercials. The third cut groups music versus no-music commercials, and the fourth cut differentiated professional and family background commercials. This meant that each analysis involved all the pertinent commercials, and except for the grouping of interest, all other differentiations were ignored.

The results are shown in Table 5.3. One expectation was that commercials with music and family visuals would show greater effects of the emotional response. As expected, emotion has an impact for music vs. no-music commercials. Unexpectedly, emotional response played a part in professional rather than family backgrounds. Emotional response was also important in issue and image commercials.

Table 5.3 Voting Intent as a Function of Aad, Aabil, Achar, and Emotion

Commercial type	Statistically Significant Variables within the Equation Used to Account for Voting Intent	AdjR2 of the final equation
Positive scripts*	Aabil**	.57
Negative scripts	Achar and Aabil	
	Arousal, Pleasure, PA^2	.68
Issue scripts	Achar and Aabil	
	Pleasure, PA^2	.58
Image scripts	Aad	
	Achar and Aabil	
	Arousal, Arousal^2	.49
Music used	Achar and Aabil	
	Arousal and Pleasure, PA^2	.63
No music used	Achar and Aabil	.61
Professional background	Achar and Aabil	
	Arousal, Pleasure, and PA^2	.57
Family background	Achar and Aabil	.60
All	Aad	
	Achar and Aabil	
	Arousal, Pleasure, PA^2	.56

*All manipulations were collapsed across the other dimensions. A hierarchial, repeat measures design was used forcing in the dummy variables, then Aad, then Achar and Aabil, then Pleasure and Arousal, then PA and A^2, and finally PA^2.

**Aad = Attitude toward the advertisement; Achar = Judgment of the candidates' character; Aabil = Judgment of the candidates' abilities; PA and PA^2 = interactions of Pleasure and Arousal

Also of interest was the fact that attack, professional visuals, image, and music commercials each showed a significant effect of arousal. As when other emotional variables are significant within a regression equation, this means that the arousal elicited by the commercial made a significant contribution to explaining the variance in voting intent.

Another strong pattern exhibited in Table 5.3 is that Aabil and Achar were strong predictors of voting intent with Aabil being a significant predictor for all catagories of commercials. This suggests that people responded strongly to the candidates in general and specifically to the candidate's perceived ability. The combination of emotional response and attitudes toward the candidates being in most of the eight equations supports the idea that both are important to people when determining voting intent.

A surprising finding was that Aad entered only the image equation. This suggests that people's emotional response to the ads and particularly their attitude toward the candidate accounts for most of the voting intent variance. However, when all the dimensions are combined it should be noted that Aad remains significant in the equation.

Finally, it is interesting to note that the curvilinear variable PA2 appeared in attack, issue, music, and professional background equations. This would indicate that for those kinds of commercials the more pleasurable or unpleasurable the commercial, the greater the impact of high- or low-arousing material on voting intent. In addition, the more moderate the pleasure elicited by the commercial, the relatively less the impact was of high- or low-arousing material on voting intent.

DISCUSSION

In several important ways, this study took a somewhat different approach to looking at political commercials. First, the study sampled four candidates rather than using just one. Second, the study also manipulated the kinds of commercials that were produced for each candidate. We looked at positive–attack scripts, issue–image scripts, and two kinds of visual background information, family scenes and politicking scenes. Third, we presented each of these formats either with or without music. The one way in which the sample was limited to one dimension was that each of the candidates was running for U.S. Senate. This limitation seemed necessary in that there is evidence that the various levels of political office, local, state, and national, produce very different levels of consumer involvement (Rothschild, 1978), and it was important not to allow involvement to become confounded with the variables manipulated in the design.

Another way in which the present study was different was that it attempted to ask processing questions via regression analyses rather than using analysis of variance to indicate the effects of various dimensions of messages. The goal was to ask whether emotion, Aad, and beliefs about candidates would affect voting intention responses in a way analogous to how emotion, Aad, and brand beliefs affect purchase intention. Whereas there appears to be an antecedent–consequent relation among emotion, Aad, and brand beliefs, a similar relationship did not occur for the processing flow in response to the political commercials. Here it appeared that all three independent variables shared variance accounted for in voting intention, but that each variable also had a small but significant direct effect on voting intention. This seems the most important finding of the study.

Insofar as the question of "rationality" is concerned, beliefs about the candidates, particularly about ability kinds of beliefs were clearly important. These beliefs, as noted earlier, directly affected voting intention. This result indicates that at least for a first and single message about a candidate, people are forming impressions of his abilities as a political leader and that these impressions partially influence voting intention. In addition, there was no indication that beliefs about the candidate's ability were themselves influenced by the antecedent effects of emotional response to the message or by Aad. Viewers of political commercials can therefore be said to be partially rational decision makers.

On the other hand, the effects of emotional response to the commercials and to liking for the commercials were equally important. This would be considered a less rational approach to decision making in response to televised political commercials. Interestingly, however, emotion did not serve as an antecedent to Aad, nor did Aad serve as an antecedent to emotion. It appears that for these political commercials people experienced emotion and indicators of that emotion (pleasure and arousal) influenced voting intention. The viewers also liked the commercials to various degrees, and this also influenced their voting intention. The final outcome of all this processing was a voting intention to a small degree but significantly influenced by direct effects of beliefs, emotions, and Aad.

So, the present study was different from others in that it sampled politicians, manipulated four important dimensions of political commercials across those politicians, and it examined the results in terms of the relative influence of three processing variables, emotion, Aad, and beliefs, about the candidates. At least for the Senate races sampled here, there is strong and consistent indication that beliefs about candidates play as important a role as the emotional responses to the messages themselves and to liking for the messages.

The study also looked at the comparative processing of fairly common dimensions of political commercials. Overall, the processing of each of the four pairs of types, positive–attack, issue–image, music–no music, and family–professional visual backgrounds, was similar in that emotion, Aad, and beliefs all played a role in determining voting intention. The only exceptions were that Aad did not significantly affect the professional or the attack ads. Beliefs about candidate abilities were always significant predictors, but beliefs about candidate personality characteristics were significant only for attack ads. Arousal generally played a lesser role than pleasure. Pleasure was a significant predictor in each of the eight equations, but arousal was significant only for attack, issue, and family background commercials.

Therefore, this study makes some interesting contributions to our understanding of political commercials. As all studies, it leaves many related questions unanswered and raises additional questions. First, it may be that Senate races are intrinsically higher involving, at least higher than local elections (Rothschild, 1978). On the other hand, the subjects in this study had mostly never heard of any of our candidates, nor were they candidates that our subjects would ever really have the opportunity to vote for. We suspect therefore that processing involvement was lower than would be seen in the real world for real senatorial candidates. This would mean the present results would only apply when processing involvement is low, and not when it is high.

Second, the study involved forced viewing, clearly a higher involving activity than what is usually involved with natural television viewing—certainly higher than for commercials when they are embedded in program material.

Third, there is the question of the extent to which our attack, positive, issue, image, and family and professional background manipulations were representative of real world commercials of these categories. For example, the Willie Horton and Boston Harbor commercials of the Bush–Dukakis Presidential race of 1988 were attack commercials, but clearly of much greater emotional and visual impact than the executions developed here. We expect that the ads developed for this study are most representative of lower budget commercials developed in non-Presidential races where money for high-impact, highly creative executions is usually much tighter. We would not want to claim, then, that our attack, or positive, or image, or whichever types of ads are representative of all ads that might be placed in those categories. And, of course, the results of a studies such as this one can be generalized only so far as the commercials are representative of the population existent in the real world of political commercials.

Nevertheless, the results of the present study would seem to encourage those interested in political advertising to adopt either the ad sampling approach or the processing analysis using regression or both. As our sampling of political commercials grows in sophistication and our understanding of the psychological processing in response to those commercials improves, we should gradually come closer to a real understanding of the impact of individual commercials that seem to play so important a role in political campaigns.

ACKNOWLEDGMENTS

The authors thank the National Political Advertising Research Project and the Gannett Foundation for funding the research reported here.

REFERENCES

Abelson, R. P., Kinder, D., Peters, M. D., & Fiske, S. T. (1982). Affective and semantic components in political person perception. *Journal of Personality and Social Psychology, 42,* 619–630.

Allen, C. T., Machleit, K. A., & Marine, S. S. (1987, October). *On assessing the emotion-*

ality of advertising via Izard's Differential Emotions Scale. Paper presented at the Association for Consumer Research, Boston, MA.

Batra, R. (1984). Affective advertising: Role, processes, and measurement. In R. A. Peterson, W. D. Hoyer, & W. R. Wilson (Eds.), *The role of affect in consumer behavior: Emerging theories and applications* (pp. 53–85). Lexington, MA: D. C. Heath.

Batra, R., & Holbrook, M. B. (1987). Development of a set of scales to measure affective responses to advertising. *Journal of Consumer Research, 14*(3), 404–420.

Batra, R., & Ray, M. L. (1985). How advertising works at contact. In L. Alwitt & A. A. Mitchell (Eds.), *Psychological processes and advertising effects* (pp. 13–44). Hillsdale, NJ: Lawrence Erlbaum Associates.

Batra, R., & Ray, M. L. (1986). Affective responses mediating acceptance of advertising. *Journal of Consumer Research, 13*(2), 234–249.

Chaiken, S. (1980). Heuristic versus systematic information processing and the use of source versus message cues in persuasion. *Journal of Personality and Social Psychology, 39*(5), 752–756.

Christ, W. G. (1985a). The construct of arousal in communication research. *Human Communication Research, 11*(4), 575–592.

Christ, W. G. (1985b). Voter preference and emotion: Using emotional response to classify decided and undecided voters. *Journal of Applied Social Psychology, 15*(3), 237–254.

Christ, W. G., & Biggers, J. T. (1984). An exploratory investigation into the relationship between television program preference and emotion-eliciting qualities—A new theoretical perspective. *Western Journal of Speech Communication, 48,* 293–307.

Christ, W. G., & Thorson, E. (1989). *Liking ads and being activated toward brands: Effects of pleasure, arousal, and category of emotional commercial.* Unpublished manuscript, School of Journalism and Mass Communication, University of Wisconsin, Madison, WI.

Cohen, J., & Cohen, P. (1975). *Applied multiple regression/correlation analysis for the behavioral sciences.* New York: Wiley.

Donovan, R. J., & Rossiter, J. R. (1982). Store atmosphere: An environmental approach. *Journal of Retail, 58,* 34–57.

Edell, J. A., & Burke, M. C. (1986). The relative impact of prior brand attitude and attitude toward the ad on brand attitude after ad exposure. In J. Olson & K. Sentis (Eds.), *Advertising and consumer psychology* (Vol. 3, pp. 93–107). New York: Praeger.

Edell, J. A., & Burke, M. C. (1987). The power of feelings in understanding advertising effects. *Journal of Consumer Research, 14*(3), 421–433.

Gardner, M. P. (1985). Does attitude toward the ad affect brand attitude under a brand evaluation set? *Journal of Marketing Research, 22,* 192–198.

Gardner, M. P., Mitchell, A., & Russo, J. E. (1985). Low involvement strategies for processing advertisements. *Journal of Advertising, 14*(2), 4–12.

Garramone, G. M. (1984). Voter responses to negative political ads. *Journalism Quarterly, 61,* 250–259.

Gorn, G. J. (1982). The effects of music in advertising on choice behavior: A classical conditioning approach. *Journal of Marketing, 46,* 94–101.

Holbrook, M. B., & Batra, R. (1987). Assessing the role of emotions as mediators of consumer responses to advertising. *Journal of Consumer Research, 14,* 404–420.

Holbrook, M. B., & O'Shaughnessy, J. (1984). The role of emotion in advertising. *Psychology and Marketing, 1*(2), 45–64.

Holbrook, M. B. & Westwood, R. A. (1989). The role of emotion in advertising revisited: Testing a typology of emotional responses. In P. Cafferata & A. Tybout (Eds.), *Cognitive and affective responses to advertising* (pp. 353–372). Lexington, MA: Lexington Books.

Jackson, S., & Jacobs, S. (1983). Generalizing about messages: Suggestions for design and analysis of experiments. *Human Communication Research, 9*(2), 169–191.

James, W. (1884). What is an emotion? *Mind, 9,* 188–205.

Kaid, L. L., & Davidson, D. K. (1986). Elements of videostyle. In L. L. Kaid, D. Nimmo, & K. R. Sanders (Eds.), *New perspectives on political advertising* (pp. 000). Carbondale, IL: Southern Illinois University Press.

Kaid, L. L., & Sanders, K. R. (1978). Political television commercials: An experimental study of type and length. *Communication Research, 5*(1), 57–70.

Machleit, K. A., & Wilson, R. D. (1988). Emotional feelings and attitude toward the advertisement: The roles of brand familiarity and repetition. *Journal of Advertising, 17*(3), 27–35.

MacKenzie, S. B., Lutz, R. J., & Belch, G. E. (1985). The role of attitude toward the ad as a mediator of advertising effectiveness: A test of competing explanations. *Journal of Marketing Research, 13,* 130–143.

Mayer, M. (1958). *Madison Avenue, U.S.A.* New York: Harper & Brothers.

Mehrabian, A., & Russell, J. A. (1974). *An approach to environmental psychology.* Cambridge, MA: MIT Press.

Merritt, S. (1984). Negative political advertising: Some empirical findings. *Journal of Advertising, 13*(3), 27–38.

Mitchell, A. A. (1983). The effects of visual and emotional advertising: An information-processing approach. In L. Percy & A. G. Woodside (Eds.), *Advertising and consumer psychology* (pp. 000). Lexington, MA: Lexington Books.

Mitchell, A. A., & Olson, J. C. (1981). Are product attribute beliefs the only mediator of advertising effects on brand attitudes? *Journal of Marketing Research, 18,* 318–332.

Osgood, C. E., Suci, G. J., & Tannenbaum, P. H. (1957). *The measurement of meaning.* Urbana, IL: University of Illinois Press.

Percy, L., & Rossiter, J. R. (1983). Mediating effects of visual and verbal elements in print advertising upon belief, attitude, and intention responses. In L. Percy & A. G. Woodside (Eds.), *Advertising and consumer psychology* (pp. 000). Lexington, MA: Lexington Books.

Petty, R. E., & Cacioppo, J. T. (1979). Issue involvement can increase or decrease persuasion by enhancing message-relevant cognitive responses. *Journal of Personality and Social Psychology, 37,* 1915–1926.

Petty, R. E., Cacioppo, J. T., & Schumann, D. W. (1983). Central and peripheral routes to advertising effectiveness: The moderating role of involvement. *Journal of Consumer Research, 10,* 135–146.

Roddy, B. L., & Garramone, G. M. (1988). Appeals and strategies of negative political advertising. *Journal of Broadcasting & Electronic Media, 32*(4), 415–427.

Rossiter, J., & Percy, L. (1980). Attitude change through visual imagery in advertising. *Journal of Advertising, 9,* 10–16.

Rothschild, M. L. (1978). Political advertising: A neglected policy issue in marketing. *Journal of Marketing Research, 15,* 58–70.

Rosenberg, M. (1968). *The logic of survey analysis.* New York: Basic.

Russell, J. A. (1978). Evidence of convergent validity on the dimensions of affect. *Journal of Personality and Social Psychology, 36,* 1152–1168.

Russell, J. A. (1980). A circumplex model of affect. *Journal of Personality and Social Psychology, 39,* 1161–1178.

Shimp, T. A. (1981). Attitude toward the ad as a mediator of consumer brand choice. *Journal of Advertising, 10*(2), 9–15.

Stayman, D. M., & Aaker, D. A. (1988). Are all the effects of ad-induced feelings mediated by Aad? *Journal of Consumer Research, 15,* 368–373.

Stout, P., A., & Leckenby, J. D. (1988). Let the music play: Music as a nonverbal element in television commercials. In S. Hecker & D. W. Stewart (Eds.), *Nonverbal communication in advertising* (pp. 000). Lexington, MA: Lexington Books.

Surlin, S. H., & Gordon, T. F. (1977). How values affect attitude toward direct reference political advertising. *Journalism Quarterly, 54,* 89–98.

Thorson, E. (1986). *The role of emotion in advertising.* Technical report for Ogilvy and Mather Research & Development Center, San Francisco, CA.

Thorson, E., & Friestad, M. (1989). The effects of emotion on episodic memory for TV commercials. In P. Cafferata & A. Tybout (Eds.), *Advertising and consumer psychology* (pp. 000). Lexington, MA: Lexington Books.

Thorson, E., & Page, T. J., Jr. (1990). *On the ubiquity of Aad—>Abr effects.* Paper presented at the annual meeting of the American Academy of Advertising, Orlando, FL, March.

Whissell, C. M. (1983). Perceived bodily correlates of emotion in relation to a two-dimensional model of affect space. *Perceptual and Motor Skills, 57,* 135–138.

Wright, P. (1973). The cognitive processes mediating acceptance of advertising. *Journal of Marketing Research, 10,* 53–62.

Zajonc, R. B. (1980). Feeling and thinking: Preferences need no inferences. *American Psychologist, 35,* 151–75.

APPENDIX A: AN EXAMPLE OF THE SCRIPTS USED IN THE STUDY

Script 1: Phil Gramm Issue/Support (Positive)

Congressman Phil Gramm wants to be your Senator

Because your issues are his issues, Phil Gramm will work hard for family security by supporting broad-based family programs and programs to ensure job security.

He supports state water rights.

He will work to increase comprehensive health care for all ages.

We need Phil Gramm because he takes positive stands on these important issues.

Common Sense

Uncommon Courage

Phil Gramm for United States Senate.

Script 2: Phil Gramm Issue/Attack (Negative)

Congressman Phil Gramm wants to be your Senator.

A leader on tough issues, Phil Gramm is not afraid to take stands for the people of this state.

While he votes yes, his opponent Bob Edwards votes "no."

No to rights for the elderly!

No to state economic growth!

No to greater school funding!

Let Phil Gramm vote yes for you on these issues.
Common Sense
Uncommon Courage
Phil Gramm for United States Senate.

Script 3: Phil Gramm Image/Support (Positive)

As your Senator, Congressman Phil Gramm will work hard for the great
people of this state.
Like you, he is a dedicated family man, a law-abiding citizen.
He is someone you can believe in.
Because Phil Gramm reflects our values, values that have helped make
our country great, he deserves our trust.
Vote yes for Phil Gramm . . . a man of the people
Common Sense.
Uncommon Courage.
Phil Gramm for United States Senate.

Script 4: Phil Gramm Image/Attack (Negative)

Congressman Phil Gramm for United States Senator
Intelligent, compassionate, family man.
This election, you do have a choice.
As this Sunday's editions of the newspapers disclosed, Phil Gramm's
opponent, Jim Roberts, has cheated the people of this state.
Telling lies and using deception in one's personal life doesn't work . . .
it doesn't work in public life either.
Vote for Phil Gramm, someone you can trust.
Common Sense
Uncommon Courage
Phil Gramm for United States Senate.

6

The Impact of Presentation Techniques: Theoretical Aspects and Empirical Findings

Hans Mathias Kepplinger

Television is both a visual and person-oriented medium, and these characteristics are prerequisites for most of its reporting. For example, themes that can be pictured are given preference in reporting. As a rule this happens by depicting people who are either participating in the reported event or doing the reporting. The pictorial reporting of the press also consists, to a large degree, of photographs of people. It therefore appears compelling to regard the presentation of persons as a cause, and the way they are perceived by viewers as an effect of television reporting and print media's pictorial reporting.

Throughout this chapter I call this effect *presentation impact*. It addresses all effects—viewer's perceptions of TV, advertising, radio and press content—caused by the nonverbal and paraverbal behavior of persons. It also addresses the effects of their depiction by photographers, camera operators, lighting technicians, sound technicians, film editors, and journalists. In the main, these are the impressions viewers and listeners gain of the characteristics of the depicted person, and the conclusions they draw from them.

Presentation impacts are the result of a process with a number of phases. At its outset there is the *authentic behavior,* a person's way of speaking and his or her body language that can be influenced by the recording situation. Then follows the *presented behavior,* which occurs almost simultaneously but must be differentiated from the authentic behavior. The third phase is the *perceived behavior,* which must be distinguished from the authentic and presented behaviors because it can be modified by characteristics of the audience, including their attitude to the person presented and their sensitivity to nonverbal behavior, and journalistic presentation techniques. The perceived behavior encompasses the way of speaking, the body language, and the overall impression created by persons or their media representation. The fourth phase is the *attributed behavior*. This concerns credibility as well as the intentions and possible behaviors audiences attribute or deny to a person because of audience perceptions of that person in press photographs, radio reports or TV presentations. This includes the credibility of statements made about a person, which may be influenced by optical and acoustical impressions. Attributions represent conscious or unconscious conclusions drawn from what the recipients have received. Hence, presentation impacts go far beyond mere reproduction by the recipients of the authentic and presented behavior.

Figure 6.1 shows the multiphase effects process as a model. It explains how recording techniques and editing techniques place a filter between authentic and presented behavior. A similar filter is formed between presented and perceived behavior by the recipient characteristics, and the depicted image.

Without claiming completeness, the model of presentation impacts organizes several influential factors into eight bundles: the real and the presented, the perceived and the attributed behavior, the recording and editing techniques, and the recipient characteristics and depicted image. The first four bundles of factors concern the behavior and the way it is perceived, the second set of bundles concerns the modifications by producers and recipients. Beyond this, one can differentiate between the situation and its presentation, and between the reactions of the recipients, to each of which belong four bundles. The various bundles of factors interact as shown in simplified form in the model. Also, the individual factors within the larger eight factor bundles interact. This is demonstrated in three examples.

A person's way of speaking and body language are not independent entities. Rather, they form a more or less integrated unit. Moreover, a person's way of speaking and body language depend on the same features in other persons, for example, the person being talked to or an audience. Authentic behavior is therefore not really an independent factor. Rather, it results from various interactions. Nor are light, camera angle, and shot size independent of each other. Instead, certain light conditions demand certain shot sizes and certain camera angles demand certain lighting. In other words, the recording techniques are interdependent. These interactions become clearest in the bundle of perceived behavior. The perception of body language influences the perception of speech, and both are clearly linked to the overall impression a presented

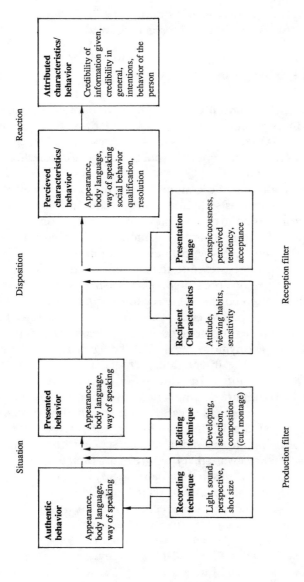

FIGURE 6.1.   Presentation impacts as a model.

Situation   Disposition   Reaction

Authentic behavior

Appearance, body language, way of speaking

Presented behavior

Appearance, body language, way of speaking

Percieved characteristics/ behavior

Appearance, body language, way of speaking social behavior qualification, resolution

Attributed characteristics/ behavior

Credibility of information given, credibility in general, intentions, behavior of the person

Recording technique

Light, sound, perspective, shot size

Editing technique

Developing, selection, composition (cut, montage)

Recipient Characteristics

Attitude, viewing habits, sensitivity

Presentation image

Conspicuousness, perceived tendency, acceptance

Production filter   Reception filter

175

person creates. Each of the eight factor bundles can be broken down into a causal model of its own. Theoretically, it would be possible to integrate all such causal models into an all-encompassing model of presentation impacts. In practice, however, this would produce an incomprehensible complexity of relationships. This is why a complex outline of all effects and interactions is eschewed.

INFLUENCES ON BEHAVIOR

The behavior of persons presented in press photos, in radio news stories, and in television news is influenced by several factors. The self-presentation is therefore both a cause of presentation impacts, and a consequence of interaction-specific and media-specific conditions of the presentation or action.

Among the media-specific conditions are the presence of reporting personnel (e.g., journalists, lighting technicians, photographers, and camera operators), and the equipment needed for reporting (e.g., microphones, lamps, still cameras, and TV cameras). Reporting personnel and equipment influence the nonverbal behavior of presenters in two ways. For one thing, by their presence they often create unfamiliar action situations for the persons presented. This is especially so for television shooting with its often considerable technical input. Also, the presence of personnel and equipment creates an awareness of at least potential publicity, the idea of acting for an anonymous mass and being observed and judged by an anonymous mass. This brings a new quality to the relationship between the interaction partners, such as journalists and politicians. The behavior of the interaction partners is addressed not only to the person they are dealing with at that moment, but much more to the public. The consequences can include so-called *reciprocal effects* (Lang & Lang, 1953), that is, the conscious or unconscious reorientation of behavior to the public, caused by the presence of the media.

People who become aware that they are being filmed in public react to this by spontaneous changes in their behavior. For example, they change the direction of their gaze, change their body deportment, and accelerate or slow down their walking pace. As a rule, however, these effects occur only if the shots are taken from a relatively short distance (Smith, McPhail, & Pickens, 1975). Participants in neutral TV interviews who know that they are being filmed display a nonverbal behavior different from interviewees who are filmed covertly. The former may make more partner-oriented gestures, nod more frequently in approval, and play less frequently with objects. At the same time, they display fewer nonverbal behaviors indicating fear. In the first minute of the interview, however, the number of fear-induced nonverbal signs is very high. These signs decrease considerably in the second minute and then more gradually from there. Beginning with the fourth minute, they hardly change (Wieman, 1981). People speaking on controversial issues and knowing they are being filmed speak longer and answer faster than people who do not know that they are being recorded. Moreover, they are more selective in the language they use to answer (Hoyt, 1976).

Among the interaction-specific action conditions are the preceding behavior of those presented as well as the preceding and simultaneous behavior of their interaction partners and observers. The preceding behavior of someone depicted (e.g., the behavior of a speaker at the beginning of his or her delivery) influences their later behavior, such as at the end of their speech. The same applies to the behavior of participants in interviews and discussion rounds. Also among the interaction-specific conditions are the preceding and simultaneous behaviors of the other presenters or participants, such as the interviewer, and of third parties attending the event. Their behavior also influences the behavior of the persons presented. Neither the preceding behavior of the presented person, nor the preceding and simultaneous behavior of the interaction partners and third parties is completely discernable in many television reports and press photographs. Hence, the audience in most cases has only rudimentary information about the causes of the behavior depicted. Although interviews, press conferences, debates, talk shows, and so forth, are major elements in radio and television reporting, these influences have rarely been examined in communication studies. This is why one has to fall back on psychological and methodological studies that do not address the media-specific elements of interviews.

Persons who are asked embarrassing questions look their interlocutor in the face less frequently than persons being asked neutral questions. The reduction of eye contact happens only, however, when the interviewees are speaking, not when they are listening or when both partners are silent. There is also less eye contact when the interviewees are called on to hide their feelings. It can be deduced from this that this form of behavior is relatively difficult to control. Individuals who are asked embarrassing questions answer more briefly compared to those being interviewed with neutral questions. However, the time in which they listen or remain silent with the interviewer stays the same (Exline, Gray, & Schuette, 1965).

Interviewers who acquaint their interlocutors with pleasant information are perceived by them as more pleasant if they look at them often. Interviewers who confront their interlocutors with unpleasant information are, by contrast, perceived by them as more pleasant if they look at them infrequently. Thus, frequent eye contact generates positive reactions among interviewees if the conversation is proceeding pleasantly, and negative reactions if the subject of conversation is unpleasant. In the first case, the interviewees tend to perceive the entire conversation as positive, in the second as negative (Ellsworth & Carlsmith, 1968). Interviewers who systematically raise their voices at the end of their questions receive affirmative answers more often than interviewers who systematically lower their voices at the end of their questions. At the same time, the discussions are found to be more interesting by the interviewees if interviewers systematically raise their voices at the end of their questions (Barath & Cannell, 1976). Studies on the so-called experimenter effect have also documented an influence of verbal and nonverbal behaviors on the recipients of conversation (Rosenthal, 1966).

EFFECTS OF NONVERBAL BEHAVIOR

The nonverbal and paraverbal behavior of persons influences the perception of viewers. Job applicants who frequently see eye contact, smile frequently, and turn toward their interlocutors in hiring interviews are assessed by independent jurors as more qualified, more motivated, and more successful than applicants who seldom seek eye contact, smile, and turn away from their interlocutor. The successful applicants also tend to more readily create the impression that they can cope with the work offered. In this, it makes no difference whether the jurors assess the behavior directly or from television recordings (Imada & Hakel, 1977). Journalists and politicians who behave defensively in television interviews create a more positive impression of their social behavior, but a more negative impression of their qualifications and resolution than politicians and journalists who are aggressive (Kepplinger, Brosius, & Heine, 1987). Interlocutors sitting close together create the impression of greater familiarity and harmony than interlocutors sitting far apart. Seeking frequent eye contact adds to this impression. By contrast, the relationships between interlocutors sitting far apart, leaning their upper bodies back, and showing serious facial expressions appears to be alien and disharmonious. The combination of behaviors with similar effects raises the overall effect up to a certain degree. Conversely, the combination of behaviors with contrasting effects tends more to lead to a re-interpretation of the discussion situation than to an average assessment of the familiarity and harmony between the interlocutors (Burgoon, Buller, Hale, & deTurck, 1984).

The social behavior of politicians and journalists who are defensive in two versions of the same television interview is received more positively when their interlocutor is aggressive rather than defensive. Conversely, the social behavior of journalists and politicians who are aggressive in two versions of the same television interview appears more negative if their interlocutor is defensive rather than aggressive (contrast effects). Similar contrast effects appear in the perception of qualification and resolution. From a theoretical point of view this means that one cannot regard the nonverbal behavior of an interview partner as a quantity of well-defined stimuli that become effective independently of the behavior of the interlocutor. Rather, one must assume that the same behaviors will have different effects in different discussion situations. It follows then that the effects caused by behavior cannot compellingly be traced back to the behavior itself. From a practical standpoint this means that in television interviews the nonverbal behavior of an interlocutor can influence the perception of the other interlocutor, which intensifies or weakens positive or negative impact (Kepplinger, Brosius, & Heine, 1987).

EFFECTS OF RECORDING TECHNIQUES

The characteristics of press photographs, radio reports, and TV reports are influenced by recording techniques. These techniques extend to lighting, sound recording, and the use of cameras. The use of various techniques is constrained by the given situation. These limitations may be dictated by space, technical facilities, organizational necessities, and professional conventions. But within these constraints there is usually great leeway for variation and this is reflected in topical reporting. On the influence of lighting, the findings of an experiment suggest people lighted from a source on one side from medium height create a better impression in photographs than people lighted from below or above. However, lighting from below also creates positive impressions of some persons, so that one can speak of interaction between type of person and type of lighting (Tannenbaum & Fosdick, 1960). Another study demonstrates the influence of the reproduction technique on the way people are perceived, showing that various types of prints from the same negative create varying assessments (Shoemaker & Fosdick, 1982). An experiment was also made of the influence of shot size of photographs on how people are perceived. This shows that head shots create a more empathic impression than shots also showing shoulders and arms. However, the depicted persons in this also appear to be less dynamic (Brosius, Holicki, & Hartmann, 1987).

There have been several studies on the effects of cameras. Here, distinctions have to be made between experiments on the effects of focus sizes, vertical camera angles, and horizontal camera perspectives (Tuchman, 1973; Zettl, 1977). Close-up and face shots impart more favorable impressions than full-length shots. This applies independently of the duration of the shots (Schulz, van Lessen, Schlede, & Waldmann, 1976). Head shots showing the full face make the person depicted appear more positive than shots that include the upper body and hands. This applies both to shots at eye level and to shots from a clear bottom view. It does not matter whether the person depicted is friendly and relaxed, or angry and tense (Baggaley, 1980; Kepplinger & Donsbach, 1987c). But perspectives from the clear bottom view, and mid-shots, in which the lower body or a speaker's rostrum are shown, create a more favorable impression than face and close-up shots. This still holds even if microphones hide some of the speaker's face (Kepplinger & Donsbach, 1987c). Shots from a camera placed to the side, showing a person in half profile, make the depicted person appear more positive than direct shots from the front. The side shots make the subject appear above all more reliable and more knowledgeable (Baggaley, 1980).

Vertical camera perspectives greatly influence the way depicted persons are perceived but have practically no influence on how well their statements are remembered. Camera perspectives influence the person's perception with regard to the tendency of perception, in the sense of a more positive or a more negative overall impression, and with regard to the homogeneity of perception, in the sense of a more or less discrepant personality image. The more extreme vertical camera perspectives are, the more conspicuous and negative they appear to the television viewers. This holds especially for top views.

Lower camera angles are the least conspicuous, are most readily perceived as neutral, and impart the best overall impression. In addition, they enhance somewhat the retention of the statements of the depicted person. Shots from a clear top view, on the other hand, are very conspicuous, are rarely perceived as neutral, and tend to make the depicted persons appear less favorable (Beverly & Young, 1978; Kepplinger & Donsbach, 1987a, 1990; Mandell & Shaw, 1973; McCain, Chilberg, & Wakshlag, 1977; Tiemens, 1970).

Top views have a greater influence on perception than bottom views, given equal perspective deviations from the eye level of the depicted person. Consequently, equally great variations in the camera angles have effects of different extent. Every camera angle influences the perception of two types of personal characteristics in opposite directions. A positive depiction of the characteristics of Type A is linked with a negative depiction of the characteristics of Type B, with the contrasting effects being greater, the more extreme the shot angles become (low homogeneity). Counted under Type A are the characteristics friendly–

aggressive; under Type B are the characteristics relaxed–tense (Kepplinger & Donsbach, 1987a, 1990). The influences of the camera angles and the influences of characteristics of the depicted persons may possibly be interacting. However, the findings show that the behavior of the depicted persons modifies the influence of the camera angles only weakly, if at all (McCain, et al., 1977; Tiemens, 1970).

Vertical camera angles influence the followers of the depicted person much more than his or her opponents. This applies to the perception of both positive and negative characteristics. Shots from clear bottom and clear top views level out the perception of followers and opponents, thus both perceive the depicted persons similarly (Kepplinger & Donsbach, 1986). The supporters' stronger capacity to respond is also shown in the reaction to presentation of positive and negative emotions. Supporters empathize with them much more intensively than do opponents (McHugo, Lanzetta, Sullivan, Masters, & Englis, 1985).

EFFECTS OF EDITING TECHNIQUES

The way press pictures and radio and TV presentations are edited has a substantial influence on their impact on recipients. Here we discuss the selection of what is to be published from the available picture and sound material, and the way it is processed for publication. Processing involves the spatial and temporal placement of the recordings (slot, sequence), the combination of pictures and text (subheadings, texts), and the composition of various items or individual elements of items (editing, montage). Use of the various possibilities depends on the picture and/or sound recordings available. But within those constraints there is wide scope for variety, which determines topical reporting. When topical reporting is analyzed it is usually impossible to tell whether differences in presentation are due to differences in recording or in editing. Hence, both possibilities have to be investigated.

There are typical pictures of every person that almost perfectly impart the same impression created generally by many photographs of that person. On the other hand, contrast series can be culled from any larger quantity of photos of a person that convey very different impressions of their social behavior, their resolution, and their moods. We are looking here at character portrayals, fictional depictions, and impressions within the bounds of given personal characteristics, which permit no conclusions to be drawn about actual characteristics (Kepplinger & Hartmann, 1987a). Contrast series that produce character portrayals can be composed of unknown or known persons (van Tubergen & Mahsman, 1974), and can be pointed out in topical press reporting (Kepplinger,

Hartmann, Schindler, & Nies, 1987). Repeated presentation of similar pictures of one person generates, within a few weeks, very stable person stereotypes. The presentation of contrast series to different audiences creates different person stereotypes. But when the observers are confronted with the depicted person these differences collapse. Although optically induced stereotypes possess great persistence, they have very little resistance against the real impression (Kepplinger & Hartmann, 1987b).

The combination of photos or films with texts can influence the way recipients perceive the persons depicted, the imparting of factual information, and the opinions about persons and issues. Most studies of the combination of photos and text have focused on how persons are perceived, suggesting the influence of the photos and texts depends on their relative weight in the given report. This is why a distinction has to be made between the combination of photos with picture captions, and the illustration of articles with photos (Wallbott, 1986). The illustration of articles with one photo of each person whose behavior is being described changes the way persons are perceived. The same articles impart different impressions with and without photos, whereby the kind of impressions always depend on the type of person photographed (Warr & Knapper, 1966).

Combining photos of more or less attractive people with tendentious captions creates different impressions than photos and texts on their own. Herein, the verbal statements influence primarily the evaluation of the persons, whereas the pictorial depictions influence the impression of potency and activity they convey. If the verbal and visual characterizations point in the same direction, they bolster each other; if they conflict, medium impressions tend to be created (Kerrick, 1959). The influence of photos on judgments of the attractiveness of people, compared with verbal characterization, increases as more negative depictions of people appear. This is why photos of unattractive people, or photos showing people unattractively, when compared to verbal characterizations, have a greater influence on judgments of attractiveness than photos of attractive persons or those showing people attractively (Lampel & Anderson, 1968). In the combination of very favorable or very unfavorable photos of well-known politicians with positive and negative texts about the persons, the tendencies of the texts are assessed in varied ways, but the photos are assessed similarly. Reports of unfavorable photos more readily tend to be taken for realistic depictions than pictured reports with negative texts. This is probably due to the negative effects attributed to the author rather than the subject of the report (Kepplinger, Holicki, Hartmann, & Winning, 1987).

Most studies on the visualization of television news have focused on how information is imparted. The main questions here is how that can be improved (Huth, 1979). Here we must distinguish between two procedures: the use of news films and the summarized repetition of reports (recaps). As a rule, news films are better remembered than news items that are only spoken about. However, the influence of visualization on retention is not very great. It is, moreover, dependent on the subject and shows more readily in foreign news. This is probably due to the fact that the films stimulate the normally low interest in news from abroad (Edwardson, Grooms, & Pringle, 1976; Gunter, 1980a,b; Hazard, 1963; Katz, Adoni, & Parness, 1977; Renckstorf, 1976; Renckstorf & Rohland, 1980). Effects similar to those created by news films are created in television news by still photographs (Findahl & Höijer, 1981), although they can cause misunderstandings by generating wrong interpretations (Findahl & Höijer, 1985). News films improve knowledge transfers especially when picture and text are redundant, that is, contain the same or similar information (Drew & Grimes, 1987; Findahl, 1981; Reese, 1984; Son, Reese, & Davie, 1987; Winterhoff-Spurk, 1983). Recaps of news generally improve retention. It makes no difference in this whether the verbal summaries are supported by graphics (Bernard & Coldevin, 1985; Coldevin, 1975).

As a rule, opinions about persons and issues are relatively stable once they are established. Consequently, direction and intensity of opinions are harder to change than the type and extent of knowledge (Klapper, 1960). There are indications, however, that visual depictions have greater influence on opinion change than verbal depictions. This holds true for both press and television reports. Pictured reports on tendentious statements by politicians on controversial matters that show the authors in each case, change the opinions about politicians and issues more than mere spoken reports. Pictured reports about positive remarks by positively perceived politicians on negatively perceived issues cause readers' judgments of politicians and issues to move closer together. After reading, the politicians appear less positive and the issues less negative (Mehling, 1959). There are similar differences in the effect of variously processed television news. Television items in which two persons represent opposing positions tend to generate polarization of viewer opinions; television items in which one person puts forward the same arguments tend to bring their views closer together (Göhring, Pfeiffenberger, & Schneider, 1981). The differences are probably due to the presence of opponents that raises the persuasiveness of their arguments, whereas presentation by journalists tends to level it out. The illustration of accusations by film shots that optically document what is being said strengthens negative judgments created by the spoken word. Personal responses of those attacked in the newscasts substantially weaken these negative assessments. Negative assessments that have resulted from the illustration of accusations remain stable for a long time if they are not challenged immediately by personal responses (Weinberger, Allen, & Dillon, 1984).

Film editing and montage are major elements in shaping radio and television items. Here formal and content variations have to be distinguished. The formal variations include the sequence of items within broadcasts, the order of individual sequences within contributions and the sequencing of various shots. The content variations include the visual and auditory commentary on the event by inserted shots (Kepplinger, 1980, 1982). In both cases, influences on the way people are perceived and on the way information is conveyed are possible. However, research findings address only some aspects. Theoretically, the succession of shots of a person from various camera angles can influence viewers' perception in three ways. First, the individual shots could be perceived as if they were separate and unconnected. Second, the preceding shots, as reference perspectives, could modify the influences of the following shots. Third, the influences of the individual shots could fuse into an overall impression. The research findings are contradictory. It is therefore not possible to state which assumption is valid (Kepplinger & Donsbach, 1987a, b, 1990; McCain et al., 1977).

The speed of cuts in a film has influence on the perceived potency and activity of the persons or issues depicted. The faster the cutting, the more readily an impression of potency and activity grows. The speed of cut is irrelevant, however, to the evaluative dimension of persons and issues. Slowing down or speeding up the cutting can create differing impressions, depending on the persons or issues the scenes are showing. An important part is played in this by the speed at which the depicted persons and objects themselves are moving (Penn, 1971). Television films that show an event in chronological sequence are generally judged more informative, clearer, and more original than television films presenting events in achronological sequence. This holds especially for television films with lengthy shots from short distances (close-ups). Television films that are chronologically sequenced generally convey clearly more information than achronological sequenced films. This applies to both pictorial and textual information, with the pictorial information in particular being better retained. However, conveying of information by achronological films with brief shots and short distances is similarly good. Chronologically sequenced television films may possibly also have a greater influence on the opinions about the persons shown, but the differences with achronological films are small (Schulz et al., 1976; Schulz & Waldmann, 1985).

In the presentation of opposing viewpoints, the impact of the arguments depends on their sequence. The available findings do not, however, permit a general statement as to whether the first argument (primacy) or the last argument (recency) has greater impact. The reason is that different effects can occur under different conditions (Allen, 1973; Hovland & Mandell, 1957; Luchins, 1957; Lund, 1925; Miller & Campbell, 1959). The studies on sequence effects were carried out using information on controversial issues. Another result is shown by studies on contrasting presentations of persons. Positive information about a person creates favorable impressions and negative information creates unfavorable impressions, with the effects of positive and negative information being roughly equal. The favorable impressions are weakened more by subsequent negative information than the unfavorable impressions by subsequent positive information. Over and above this, in the long term the impressions improved by subsequent positive information worsen again, while the impressions worsened by subsequent negative information remain in the long term (Briscoe, Woodyard, & Shaw, 1967; Richey, McClelland, & Shimkunas, 1967). On the basis of these findings, it is to be assumed that media-induced negative images of persons are more persistent than corresponding positive images.

Speakers appear to be more unpopular, less interesting, less knowledgeable, and more confused on television if shots of a bored rather than interested audience are edited into what the speaker is saying (Duck & Baggaley, 1975). If speakers are explicitly introduced as knowledgeable and experienced, but then shown with a bored audience, they appear less interesting and less popular than if they are explicitly introduced as lacking knowledge and experience about the subject, but are shown with an interested audience. The visual presentation of negative and positive reactions from the audience overlays the contradictory verbal presentation (Baggaley, 1980). Speakers who speak with vigor on the radio on a controversial topic get poorer marks from the listeners if disagreement rather than applause is to be heard at several points. The disagreement influences the ratings of the speaker clearly more than the applause. In the case of an audience perceived as attractive by the listener, the effects are stronger than with an unattractive audience. This also applies to the impact of the content of a speech. Speakers influence the opinions of their listeners much more if applause is to be heard at several points, than if no audience response is recognizable. Speakers' impact on listener opinion is smallest if disapproval is heard. Audience reactions here, too, have greater impact if in the view of the listeners the audience is attractive (Landy, 1972). Similar effects occur if the listeners hear positive and negative audience reactions and believe that the audience has the same convictions as themselves (Kelley & Woodruff, 1956).

The placement of reports within radio and television newscasts has an independent influence on the retention of contents. Radio listeners remember items at the beginning and at the end of newscasts much better than items in the middle. Retention of the last items is even better than of the first (Tannenbaum, 1954). Television viewers are less likely to remember individual items concerning a single subject, the further toward the end the items are placed. If reports on other themes are inserted in the news no comparable memory losses occur (Gunter, 1979; Gunter, Berry, & Clifford, 1981). Television viewers best remember ad spots in feature films if they are run at places where things are not particularly exciting. Retention is less good if the placement is after conflict climaxes and conflict resolutions. It is worst when placed between both parts (Bryant & Comisky, 1978).

The opinion or affect influencing content of TV items placed before and after a news item influences the emotional reactions to the news item. A negative context increases the positive emotional responses to the positive reports. The same occurs analogously for a positive context (contrast effects), although a negative context makes more impact than a positive one. The impact of the following item is greater than that of the preceding one (Mundorf, 1987).

GENERALIZATION OF PERCEPTIONS

People generally tend to seek adequate explanations for the behavior of others because this is a prerequisite to their comprehending, predicting, and controlling that behavior. One can, theoretically, impute two classes of reasons: dispositions of persons and aspects of situations. In the first case, the observers put the behavior down to characteristics of the actors; in the second, to the circumstances of their actions. Dispositions of persons are their abilities and their motives. Motivation encompasses their intention and their efforts to achieve aims. Aspects of the situation are the difficulty of tasks and the part played by coincidence in coping with them. From these theoretical assumptions a great many assumptions can be derived. For example, if all persons succeed in an activity, this tends to be put down to aspects of the situation (difficulty, coincidence); if only two persons succeed this tends to be attributed to dispositions of the persons (abilities, motivation); if one of the two put less effort into it, this is explained by greater ability. In all cases we are dealing with the interpretations of the observers, who put the observed behavior down to unobserved causes and thereby causally explain the situation. The attribution of the behavior to dispositions of persons (personal causality) prompts predictions about their behavior in comparable situations. These are interpretations by the observers in which future behavior is anticipated with the aid of identified causes. The observers have an interest in properly explaining and forecasting the behavior of others. But because of lack of information, wrong information, and flaws in processing, there are wrong interpretations (misattributions). In these cases the past behavior is wrongly explained and the future behavior wrongly forecast (Heider, 1958).

To the observers, listeners, and viewers of press photos, radio reports, and television items, the interaction-specific and media-specific conditions of action remain more or less hidden because the presentations given are only excerpts of a larger action context. The excerpts are defined by temporal and spatial limitations that are more or less arbitrarily drawn. Because of the temporal limitations of the excerpts—fractions of a second in the case of photos—the preceding occurrence, which can be a cause of the behavior, remains unknown unless it is specifically mentioned. Thus, the depictions of aggressive gestures may not contain any indications of whether it was provoked by aggressive behavior of others or not. Because of the spatial limitation of the excerpt, the environment of the occurrence, which could likewise be a cause of the behavior depicted, remains unknown unless specifically mentioned. Thus, the depictions of nervous gestures may contain no indications of whether it was caused by the behavior of others, such as with the audience of talk shows. To the extent that information about the interaction-specific and media-specific action contexts of the depicted actors is missing, their behavior is probably attributed to their personal dispositions. The impression is created of personal causality and responsibility, which could be right or wrong.

Acting persons as a rule possess more and different information about the action context than passive observers. Hence, they lean theoretically to different interpretations of behavior. Whereas acting persons attribute their behavior primarily to aspects of the situation, passive observers tend to explain it in terms of the actor's dispositions (Jones & Nisbett, 1971). Viewers of television shots of a discussion tend to attribute the behavior presented to aspects of the situation, rather than to the dispositions of the persons involved if they have taken part in the discussion as participant rather than as observers. If the participants see a recording from their own point of view (shots of the discussion partner), they more strongly explain their own behavior by the aspects of the situation than if they see a recording from the perspective of their interlocutors (shots of themselves; Storms, 1973). Viewers of television shots who are asked to put themselves in the position of the persons depicted are more likely to attribute the behavior of these persons to aspects of the situation than do naive observers (Regan & Totten, 1975).

The variation of the context of persons by editing techniques can, for the reasons outlined, exert considerable influence on the perception of emotions and the attribution of dispositions. The best known examples of this were provided in the 1930s by filmmaker and theoretician Lev Kuleshov (Kuleshov effects), whose systematic proofs are provided by a series of experimental studies.

The observers of press photos interpret the emotions of depicted persons very differently, depending on whether the given picture excerpt shows only head and shoulders or includes body and environment (Munn, 1940). The complete removal of the action context can lead observers of press photos to think they see exactly the opposite to what the depicted persons actually felt—pain rather than joy, revulsion rather than attraction, and so on (Spignesi & Shor, 1981). The presentation of positive or negative audience responses makes a speaker appear more competent or more incompetent (Baggaley, 1980; Kelley & Woodruff, 1956; Landy, 1972).

There is a strong convergence between the characteristics of photographed persons that observers perceive and the types of motives they attribute to the depicted persons or the actions they impute to them. This holds, above all, for the perceptions of the social behavior and the resolve of the presented persons. Observers who perceive a person as trust-inspiring or hesitant consequently attribute to him or her those motives and actions judged to be trust-inspiring or hesitant by independent jurors. Similarly, observers perceiving a person as deceptive or energetic attribute to them the corresponding motives and actions. If various observers perceive photos depicting the same individual differently, they attribute to this person, in part, differing motives and actions. At the same time, positive and negative statements about the depicted persons appear to them to be more or less credible, with negative imputations especially gaining credibility by negative depictions (Kepplinger & Hartmann, 1987c).

The observers of persons attribute the behavior of actors to their intentions, especially when, from the point of view of the observers, it is unusual and happens voluntarily (Jones & Davis, 1965). This also applies to formal and aesthetic peculiarities of the behavior of persons. For example, observers tend more to attribute the behavior of those who are conspicuously dressed in television interviews or are put in the center by lighting effects to the disposition of the actors, than the behavior of persons who are inconspicuously dressed and do not hold center positions (McArthur & Post, 1980). Because of the general differences in the interpretations of behavior by actors and observers, and the specific differences in the conceptions of unusual and voluntary behaviors, actors and observers can develop different perceptions of the causes of the same behavior. The differences between observers and actors in this are presumably greater as the distance between them increases. The closer the observers are to the actors, the more readily they are likely to attribute their behavior to aspects of the situation; the more distant they are, the more likely they will attribute it to the dispositions of the actors. For the same reason different observers with different attitudes would probably attribute the behavior of the same person to different causes. Such influences have only been demonstrated, however, for the reception of entertainment programs (Girodo, 1973; Leckenby, 1977, 1981).

CONCLUSIONS

Looking over the findings at hand, one recognizes two structural qualities of the effects that can be called asymmetry and contrast. Asymmetrical effects are produced by negative photos of persons and negative statements about them; combinations of negative photos with positive statements and positive photos with negative statements; equally great changes of camera angles upward and downward; negative and positive audience reactions in radio and TV items; and negative and positive reports within the context of individual TV news items. There is also asymmetry in the responsiveness of the followers and opponents of persons whose behavior is visually presented. Contrast effects occur from the depiction of persons from extreme camera angles, through the defensive or aggressive behavior of a person in a television interview, through the behavior of interlocutors in a television interview, and through the imbedding of behavioral sequences in positive and negative contexts. In all cases a strong accentuation of positive qualities is linked with accentuation of negative qualities and vice versa. The essential questions in this are whether strong accentuations appear desirable from the point of view of the actors, and which qualities should be strongly accentuated under which conditions. In this, the point of view of the actor can differ extremely from the points of view of the reporters or a filming crew and that of the audience.

REFERENCES

Allen, R. (1973). Primacy or recency: The order of presentation. *Journalism Quarterly, 50,* 135–138.
Baggaley, J. (1980). Psychology of the TV image. Westmead, Farnborough: Gower.
Barath, A., & Cannell, C. F. (1976). Effect of interviewer's voice intonation. *Public Opinion Quarterly, 40,* 370–373.

Bernard, R. M., & Coldevin, G. O. (1985). Effects of recap strategies on television news recall and retention. *Journal of Broadcasting & Electronic Media, 29*, 407–419.

Beverly, R. E., & Young, T. J. (1978). *The effect of mediated camera angle on receiver evaluations of source credibility, dominance, attraction and homophily.* Paper presented at the International Communication Association Convention. Chicago.

Briscoe, M. E., Woodyard, H. D., & Shaw, M. E. (1967). Personality impression change as a function of the favorableness of first impressions. *Journal of Personality, 35*, 343–357.

Brosius, H.-B., Holicki, S., & Hartmann, T. (1987). Einfluß der Gestaltungsmerkmale von Wahlplakaten auf Personenwahrnehmung und Kompetenzzuschreibung [The influence of election poster lay-out on person perception and the attribution of competence]. *Publizistik, 32*, 338–353.

Bryant, J., & Comisky, P. W. (1978). The effect of positioning a message within differentially cognitively involving portions of a television segment on recall of the message. *Human Communication Research, 5*, 63–75.

Burgoon, J. K., Buller, D. B., Hale, J. L., & deTurck, M. A. (1984). Relational messages associated with nonverbal behaviors. *Human Communication Research, 10*, 351–378.

Coldevin, G. O. (1975). Spaced, massed, and summary treatments as review strategies for ITV production. *AV Communication Review, 23*, 289–303.

Drew, D. G., & Grimes, T. (1987). Audio-visual redundancy and TV news recall. *Communication Research, 14*, 452–461.

Duck, S. W., & Baggaley, J. (1975). Audience reaction and its effect on perceived expertise. *Communication Research, 2*, 79–85.

Edwardson, M., Grooms, D., & Pringle, P. (1976). Visualization and TV news information gain. *Journal of Broadcasting, 20*, 373–380.

Ellsworth, P. C., & Carlsmith, J. M. (1968). Effects of eye contact and verbal content on affective response to a dyadic interaction. *Journal of Personality and Social Psychology, 10*, 15–20.

Exline, R., Gray, D., & Schuette, D. (1965). Visual behavior in a dyad as affected by interview content and sex of respondent. *Journal of Personality and Social Psychology, 1*, 201–209.

Findahl, O. (1981). The effect of visual illustration upon perception and retention of news programmes. *Communications, 7*, 151–167.

Findahl, O., & Höijer, B. (1981). Studies of news from the perspective of human comprehension. In G. C. Wilhoit & H. de Bock (Eds.), *Mass communication review yearbook* (Vol. 2, pp. 393–403). Beverly Hills: Sage.

Findahl, O., & Höijer, B. (1985). Some characteristics of news memory and comprehension. *Journal of Broadcasting & Electronic Media, 29*, 379–396.

Girodo, M. (1973). Film-induced arousal, information search, and the attribution process. *Journal of Personality and Social Psychology, 25*, 357–360.

Göhring, W., Pfeifenberger, W., & Schneider, F. (1981). Proporzkommunikation und Vermittlerkommunikation: Eine Studie zur Wirkungsforschung [Balanced communication and mediating communication: A study in media effects]. *Media Perspektiven, 12*, 838–848.

Gunter, B. (1979). Recall of television news items: Effects of presentation mode, picture content and serial position. *Journal of Educational Television and Other Media, 5*, 57–61.

Gunter, B. (1980a). Remembering televised news: effects of visual format on information gain. *Journal of Educational Television, 6*, 8–11.

Gunter, B. (1980b). Remembering television news: effects of picture content. *Journal of General Psychology, 102*, 127–133.

Gunter, B., Berry, C., & Clifford, B. R. (1981). Proactive interference effects with television news items: further evidence. *Journal of Experimental Psychology, 7*, 480–487.

Hazard, W. R. (1963). On the impact of television's pictured news. *Journal of Broadcasting, 7*, 43–51.

Heider, F. (1958). *The psychology of interpersonal relations*. New York: Wiley.

Hovland, C. I., & Mandell, W. (1957). Is there a "law of primacy in persuasion"? In C. I. Hovland (Ed.), *The order of presentation in persuasion* (pp. 13–22). New Haven: Yale University Press.

Hoyt, J. L. (August 1976). *The effects of being televised: An experimental test*. Paper presented at the annual meeting of the Association for Education in Journalism. College Park, Md.

Huth, Silvia (1979). Verstehen und Behalten von Nachrichtensendungen: Eine ausgewählte Darstellung empirischer Befunde [Understanding and remembering news shows: A discussion of selected results]. *Fernsehen und Bildung, 13*, 115–165.

Imada, A. S., & Hakel, M. D. (1977). Influence of nonverbal communication and rater proximity on impressions and decisions in simulated employment interviews. *Journal of Applied Psychology, 62*, 295–300.

Jones, E. E., & Davis, K. E. (1965). From acts to dispositions: The attribution process in person perception. In L. Berkowitz (Ed.), *Advances in experimental social psychology* (Vol. 2, pp. 219–266). New York: Academic Press.

Jones, E. E., & Nisbett, R. E. (1971). *The actor and the observer: Divergent perceptions of the causes of behavior*. Morristown, NJ: General Learning Press.

Katz, E., Adoni, H., & Parness, P. (1977). Remembering the news: What the picture adds to recall. *Journalism Quarterly, 54*, 231–239.

Kelley, H. H., & Woodruff, C. L. (1956). Members' reactions to apparent group approval of a counternorm communication. *Journal of Abnormal and Social Psychology, 52*, 67–74.

Kepplinger, H. M. (1980). Optische Kommentierung in der Fernsehberichterstattung über den Bundestagswahlkampf 1976 [Visual comments in television coverage of the election campaign 1976]. In T. Ellwein (Ed.), *Politikfeld-Analysen 1979* (pp. 163–179). Opladen: Westdeutscher Verlag.

Kepplinger, H. M. (1982). Visual biases in television campaign coverage. *Communication Research, 9*, 432–466. Reprint: E. Wartella, D. C. Whitney, & S. Windahl (Eds.), *Mass communication review yearbook* (Vol. 4, pp. 391–405). Beverly Hills, CA: Sage.

Kepplinger, H. M. (1987). *Darstellungseffekte. Experimentelle Untersuchungen zur Wirkung von Pressefotos und Fernsehfilmen* [Presentation effects: Experimental studies on the effects of press photographs and TV news films]. Freiburg: Alber.

Kepplinger, H. M., Brosius, H.-B., & Heine, N. (1987). Der Einfluß nonverbaler Verhaltensweisen auf die Personenwahrnehmung in Fernsehinterviews [The influence of nonverbal behavior on person perception in television interviews]. In H. M. Kepplinger: *Darstellungseffekte. Experimentelle Untersuchungen zur Wirkung von Pressefotos und Fernsehfilmen* (pp. 57–91). Freiburg: Alber.

Kepplinger, H. M., & Donsbach, W. (1986). The influence of camera perspectives on the perception of a politician by supporters, opponents, and neutral viewers. In D. Paletz (Ed.), *Political Communication ?esearch* (pp. 63–71). Norwood, NJ: Ablex.

Kepplinger, H. M., & Donsbach, W. (1987a). Der Einfluß von Kameraperspektiven auf die Auffälligkeit und wahrgenommene Tendenz sowie die Informationsvermittlung und die Personenwahrnehmung [The influence of camera perspectives on the conspicuousness, the perceived tendency, learning, and person perception]. In H. M. Kepplinger: *Darstellungseffekte. Experimentelle Untersuchungen zur Wirkung von Pressefotos und Fernsehfilmen* (pp. 92–124). Freiburg: Alber.

Kepplinger, H. M., & Donsbach, W. (1987b). Der Einfluß von Perspektivwechseln auf die

Wahrnehmung eines Redners [The influence of changes in camera perspectives on the perception of a speaker]. In H. M. Kepplinger: *Darstellungseffekte. Experimentelle Untersuchungen zur Wirkung von Pressefotos und Fernsehfilmen* (pp. 125–135). Freiburg: Alber.

Kepplinger, H. M., & Donsbach, W. (1987c). Der Einfluß von Einstellungsgrößen und Mikrophonstellungen auf die Wahrnehmung eines Redners [The influence of shot size and microphone position on the perception of a speaker]. In H. M. Kepplinger: *Darstellungseffekte. Experimentelle Untersuchungen zur Wirkung von Pressefotos und Fernsehfilmen* (pp. 136–146). Freiburg: Alber.

Kepplinger, H. M., & Donsbach, W. (1990). The impact of camera perspectives on the perception of a speaker. *Studies in Educational Evaluation, 16,* 133–156.

Kepplinger, H. M., & Hartmann, T. (1987a). Das Identitätsproblem der Personenwahrnehmung anhand von Fotos [The problem of character identity in the perception of persons on photographs]. In H. M. Kepplinger: *Darstellungseffekte. Experimentelle Untersuchungen zur Wirkung von Pressefotos und Fernsehfilmen* (pp. 165–203). Freiburg: Alber.

Kepplinger, H. M., & Hartmann, T. (1987b). Die Stabilität der Personenwahrnehmung anhand von Fotos [The stability of the perception of persons on photographs]. In H. M. Kepplinger: *Darstellungseffekte. Experimentelle Untersuchungen zur Wirkung von Pressefotos und Fernsehfilmen* (pp. 204–229). Freiburg: Alber.

Kepplinger, H. M., & Hartmann, T. (1987c). Die Generalisierung der Personenwahrnehmung anhand von Fotos [The generalization of the perception of persons on photographs]. In H. M. Kepplinger: *Darstellungseffekte. Experimentelle Untersuchungen zur Wirkung von Pressefotos und Fernsehfilmen* (pp. 230–265). Freiburg: Alber.

Kepplinger, H. M., Hartmann, T., Schindler, W., & Nies, U. (1987). Charakterfiktionen von Reagan, Breschnew, Schmidt und Genscher in Stern und Time [Character fictions of Reagan, Breshnew, Schmidt and Genscher in Stern and Time]. In H. M. Kepplinger: *Darstellungseffekte. Experimentelle Untersuchungen zur Wirkung von Pressefotos und Fernsehfilmen* (pp. 304–334). Freiburg: Alber.

Kepplinger, H. M., Holicki, S., Hartmann, T., & Winning, K. (1987). Asymmetrien der Foto- und Textrezeption anhand bebilderter Meldungen über Strauß, Schmidt, Beckenbauer und Jürgens [Asymmetrical reception of photos and texts in illustrated news stories on Strauß, Schmidt, Beckenbauer and Jürgens]. In H. M. Kepplinger: *Darstellungseffekte. Experimentelle Untersuchungen zur Wirkung von Pressefotos und Fernsehfilmen* (pp. 266–303). Freiburg: Alber.

Kerrick, J. S. (1959). News pictures, captions and the point of resolution. *Journalism Quarterly, 36,* 183–188.

Klapper, J. T. (1960). *The effects of mass communication.* New York: The Free Press.

Lampel, A. K., & Anderson, N. H. (1968). Combining visual and verbal information in an impression-formation task. *Journal of Personality and Social Psychology, 9,* 1–6.

Landy, D. (1972). The effects of an overheard audience's reaction and attractiveness on opinion change. *Journal of Experimental Social Psychology, 8,* 276–288.

Lang, K., & Lang, G. E. (1953). The unique perspective of television and its effect: A pilot study. *American Sociological Review, 18,* 3–12.

Leckenby, J. D. (1977). Attribution of dogmatism to TV characters. *Journalism Quarterly, 54,* 14–19.

Leckenby, J. D. (1981). Attributions to TV characters and opinion change. *Journalism Quarterly, 58,* 241–247.

Luchins, A. S. (1957). Primacy-recency in impression formation. In C. I. Hovland (Ed.), *The order of presentation in persuasion* (pp. 33–61). New Haven: Yale University Press.

Lund, F. H. (1925). The psychology of belief: The law of primacy in persuasion. *Journal of Abnormal and Social Psychology, 20,* 183–191.

Mandell, L. M., & Shaw, D. L. (1973). Judging people in the news—unconsciously: Effect of camera angle and bodily activity. *Journal of Broadcasting, 17,* 353–362.

McArthur, L. Z., & Post, D. L. (1980). Figurale Betonung und Personenwahrnehmung [Figural emphasis and person perception]. In W. Herkner (Ed.), *Attribution—Psychologie der Kausalität* (pp. 137–156). Bern: Verlag Hans Huber.

McCain, T. A., Chilberg, J., & Wakshlag, J. (1977). The effect of camera angle on source credibility and attraction. *Journal of Broadcasting, 21,* 35–46.

McHugo, G. J., Lanzetta, J. T., Sullivan, D. G., Masters, R. D., & Englis, B. G. (1985). Emotional reactions to a political leader's expressive displays. *Journal of Personality and Social Psychology, 49,* 1513–1529.

Mehling, R. (1959). Attitude changing effect of news and photo combinations. *Journalism Quarterly, 36,* 189–198.

Miller, N., & Campbell, D. (1959). Recency and primacy in persuasion as a function of the timing of speeches and measurements. *Journal of Abnormal and Social Psychology, 59,* 1–9.

Mundorf, N. (1987). Affect bias in the response to news-story sequences (Doctoral dissertation, Indiana University).

Munn, N. L. (1940). The effect of knowledge of the situation upon the judgement of emotion from facial expression. *Journal of Abnormal and Social Psychology, 35,* 324–338.

Penn, R. (1971). Effects of motion and cutting-rate in motion pictures. *AV Communication Review, 19,* 29–51.

Reese, S. D. (1984). Visual-verbal redundancy effects on television news learning. *Journal of Broadcasting, 28,* 79–87.

Regan, D. T., & Totten, J. (1975). Empathy and attribution: turning observers into actors. *Journal of Personality and Social Psychology, 32,* 850–856.

Renckstorf, K. (1976). Zur Wirkung von Darstellungsformen in Fernsehnachrichten [On the effects of presentation forms in TV news]. *Rundfunk und Fernsehen, 24,* 379–385.

Renckstorf, K., & Rohland, L. (1980). *Nachrichtensendungen im Fernsehen: Band 2. Absichten, Interessen und Muster der Medienzuwendung—Konturen des "aktiven" Publikums* [News shows in television: Vol. 2. Intentions, interests and patterns of media reception—outlines of the "active" public]. Berlin: Spiess.

Richey, M. H., McClelland, L., & Shimkunas, A. M. (1967). Relative influence of positive and negative information in impression formation and persistence. *Journal of Personality and Social Psychology, 6,* 322–327.

Rosenthal, R. (1966). *Experimenter effects in behavioral research.* New York: Appleton Century Crofts.

Schulz, W., van Lessen, R., Schlede, C., & Waldmann, N. (1976). Die Bedeutung audiovisueller Gestaltungsmittel für die Vermittlung politischer Einstellungen: Medienanalytische und experimentelle Untersuchungen am Beispiel sozialkundlicher Filme [The role of audio-visual means in the communication of political attitudes: Media analyses and experimental studies of political education films]. *AV Forschung, 15,* 49–209.

Schulz, W., & Waldmann, N. (1985). Effekte der Film-Montage: Experimentelle Überprüfung der Wechselwirkung einiger Gestaltungsmittel von AV-Medien [Effects of film montage: Experimental testing of the interaction between some audio-visual means]. In G. Bentele & E. W. B. Hess-Lüttich (Eds.), *Zeichengebrauch in Massenmedien. Zum Verhältnis von sprachlicher und nichtsprachlicher Information in Hörfunk, Film und Fernsehen* (pp. 332–348). Tübingen: Niemeyer.

Shoemaker, P. J., & Fosdick, J. A. (1982). How varying reproduction methods affects response to photographs. *Journalism Quarterly, 59,* 13–20, 65.

Smith, R. L., McPhail, C., & Pickens, R. G. (1975). Reactivity to systematic observation with film: A field experiment. *Sociometry, 38,* 536–550.

Son, J., Reese, S. D., & Davie, W. R. (1987). Effects of visual—verbal redundancy and recaps on television news learning. *Journal of Broadcasting, 31,* 207–216.

Spignesi, A., & Shor, R. E. (1981). The judgement of emotion from facial expressions, contexts, and their combination. *The Journal of General Psychology, 104,* 41–58.

Storms, M. D. (1973). Videotape and the attribution process: reversing actors' and observers' points of view. *Journal of Personality and Social Psychology, 27,* 165–175.

Tannenbaum, P. H. (1954). Effect of serial position on recall of radio news stories. *Journalism Quarterly, 31,* 319–323.

Tannenbaum, P. H., & Fosdick, J. A. (1960). The effect of lighting angle on the judgment of photographed subjects. *AV Communication Review, 8,* 253–262.

Tiemens, R. K. (1970). Some relationships of camera angle to communicator credibility. *Journal of Broadcasting, 14,* 483–490.

Tuchman, G. (1973). The technology of objectivity: Doing "objective" TV news film. *Urban Life and Culture, 2,* 3–26.

Van Tubergen, G. N., & Mahsman, D. L. (1974). Unflattering photos: How people respond. *Journalism Quarterly, 51,* 317–320.

Wallbott, H. G. (1986). Person und Kontext: Zur relativen Bedeutung von mimischem Verhalten und Situationsinformationen im Erkennen von Emotionen [Person and context: The relative importance of mimic behavior and situational information in the recognition of emotions]. *Archiv für Psychologie, 138,* 211–231.

Warr, P. B., & Knapper, C. (1966). The relative importance of verbal and visual information in indirect person perception. *British Journal of Social and Clinical Psychology, 5,* 118–127.

Weinberger, M. G., Allen, C. T., & Dillon, W. R. (1984). The impact of negative network news. *Journalism Quarterly, 61,* 287–294.

Wieman, J. M. (1981). Effects of laboratory videotaping procedures on selected conversation behaviors. *Human Communication Research, 7,* 302–311.

Winterhoff-Spurk, P. (1983). Fiktionen in der Fernsehnachrichtenforschung: Von der Text-Bild-Schere, der Überlegenheit des Fernsehens und vom ungestörten Zuschauer [Fictions in television news research: On the gap between text and picture, the superiority of television, and the undisturbed viewer]. *Media Perspektiven, 10,* 722–727.

Zettl, H. (1977). Toward a multi-screen television aesthetic: some structural considerations. *Journal of Broadcasting, 21,* 5–19.

III

Differential Processing of Positive and Negative Advertising

7

Emotion and Memory Responses for Negative Political Advertising: A Study of Television Commercials Used in the 1988 Presidential Election

John E. Newhagen
University of Maryland

Byron Reeves
Stanford University

If negative advertising does not work, its increasing use across the American political landscape would be difficult to explain (see Guskind & Hagstrom, 1988; Nugent, 1987). During the 1988 Presidential campaign, for instance, viewers saw 30-second spots charging that Michael Dukakis was soft on criminals, allowed pollution to go unchecked, and was weak on national defense. There were images of criminals walking to freedom through penitentiary gates, disgusting pools of industrial pollution, and Dukakis smiling from the turret of an Army tank as it drove in circles around an open field. Late in the campaign, Dukakis countered with his own negative attacks on George Bush, and at one point tried to make the negative tone of the Bush campaign an issue itself.

Yet a review of research results casts doubt on the effectiveness of negative political advertising. Negative commercials can boomerang on the sponsor (Garramone, 1985; Shapiro & Rieger, 1989) and can produce unstable attitudes (Krugman, 1981). And correlations between attitude shift and memory are weak at best (see Petty, Cacioppo, & Kasmer, 1988; Rothschild, 1974).

Much of the work in negative political advertising is based on persuasion models using attitude as the independent variable and behavior change as the dependent variable (see Fishbein & Ajzen, 1981, for a description of attitude-behavior persuasion models; and Berry, 1983, for a discussion of their limitations in communication research). Negativity has been defined in the jargon of media consultants as a production technique or as an example of a particular genre of commercial advertising (Nugent, 1987). This chapter looks within that genre and examines the advertisements themselves as the source of different emotions in the viewer, rather than as a characteristic of the sponsor's verbal message.

The dependent variable of interest for a candidate is election day behavior, the vote. But no single exposure to a 30-second political television spot per se was likely ever intended to sway many viewer's votes. Complex attitude structures associated with such behaviors as purchasing or voting are based on hundreds, if not thousands, of exposures to persuasive messages (Fazio, Sanbonmatsu, Powell, & Kardes, 1986). This study investigated the relationship between emotion and memory for the ads as a first step to better understand the complex attitude structures associated with the behavior of interest in politics—the vote.

Negativity and Political Advertising

An election can be thought of as a marketing campaign in which there are only two products, the candidates, with advertising categorized according to the relationship between ad sponsor and opponent (Merritt, 1984). Three categories of negative advertising spring from this perspective:

- *True negative,* or attack ads, where an effort is made to diminish the image of the opponent through an outright attack, while the sponsor's image is not mentioned. Roddy and Garramone (1988), for instance, defined negative political advertising as attacks on opponents using a variety of accusations and innuendos about issue positions or personal character.
- *Comparative* ads, where an attempt is made to lessen the image of the opponent and promote a positive image of the sponsor as an alternative.
- *Hope,* or *positive* ads in which the sponsor is promoted as the solution to some problem or issue, such as drug abuse or inflation, without explicitly attacking the opponent.

A consequence of defining negativity in these terms, a tradition rooted in both the practice of American politics and the social psychology of attitudes, is that little attempt has been made to describe theoretically the specific qualities of negative messages that distinguish their effects from other similar messages. An untested assumption implicit in this perspective is that somehow negativity gives messages power. A Democratic pollster reflected an intuitive understanding of the effectiveness of negative advertising when he commented about cost effectiveness in expensive urban television markets: people process negative information faster, with one or two exposures to a negative appeal as memorable as 5 to 10 exposures to a positive appeal (Guskind & Hagstrom, 1988). Another professional consultant stated that negative advertising draws the viewer's attention, is easier to understand, and more memorable than its positive counterpart (Nugent, 1987).

These observations are quite consistent with evidence from recent experiments about the effects of emotional television messages on memory. Srull (1983, 1984) found positive emotion in commercials lead to elaborated semantic encoding of information, whereas negative affect corresponded to computational episodic encoding. Friestad and Thorson (1984) found "poignant" ads, ads with both a positive and negative component, to be better remembered than neutral commercials. Reeves, Newhagen, Maibach, Basil, and Kurz (1989) found negative public service announcements to be more memorable than positive announcements in a study similar in design to this one.

But what qualities of negativity empowers political television advertising? A clearer understanding of negativity can be found in an examination of the concept's cognitive and affective components.

TWO-LEVEL INFORMATION PROCESSING AND POLITICAL ADVERTISEMENTS

Much of the work on political advertising focuses on candidate images and learning about campaign issues (Kaid, 1981; Patterson & McClure, 1976), rather than memory or other cognitive responses that are *specific to the advertisements*. Mitchell (1983) categorized the processing of such high-level message features such as a candidate's issue stands as "Level 1," or controlled verbal processing. Mitchell suggested that a viewer's attitude toward the ad (Aad or Att_a in the parlance of consumer research; see Lutz, 1985) was a mediating variable. Attitude toward the ad is defined as an affective feeling about the advertisement, with affect processed in the "Level 2," or nonverbal channel.

Cacioppo and Petty (1985) called these two levels the central and peripheral routes to the processing of persuasive messages. The central route is employed by highly involved message receivers, and includes a high degree of information elaboration and comparisons with prior knowledge. In the context of a persuasive television appeal, viewers employing the central route also manifest stable attitude structures about the attitude object promoted by the message (this corresponds to attitude toward the brand, or Att_b; see Hill & Mazis, 1986). In the case of political advertising, the attitude object, or brand, is the candidate.

Peripheral processing corresponds to the psychological heuristics used by low-involvement message receivers. It involves reliance on secondary message features, such as affective cues in the speaker's facial expression, that are not intrinsic to the topic of the appeal. Also attitude structures for viewers employing peripheral processing are typically volatile.

Much work in political advertising casts the definition of negativity at the level of an attribute associated with the topic of the candidates verbal appeal (Att_b). This by definition limits investigation to central cues, and excludes consideration of peripheral commercial-related cues (Att_a). Viewing at a central level implies high attention, high involvement, and thoughtful consideration of the message topic (Krugman, 1986). It overlooks other attributes of the commercial on the viewer, such as color, music, pacing, cuts, facial expressions, or other formal nonverbal features of the television image (Donohew, Finn, & Christ, 1988). Lanzetta, Sullivan, Masters, and McHugo (1986) reported, for instance, that exposure to images of then-President Reagan's smiling face increased subject's positive assessment for him, regardless of their prior political disposition. They maintained that repeated exposures to attractive facial displays conditioned viewers to make positive emotional responses.

It is important to emphasize that, after a review of research in both political science and television effects, the idea of a highly motivated, highly knowledgeable, and attentive message receiver implicitly suggested by topic-oriented definitions of negativity in political advertising is precisely what is *not* anticipated. Quite the contrary, these literatures suggest most people employ a second, lower level of processing similar to the one just described by the consumer advertising and social psychological models just reviewed.

Processing Level and Political Science

A topic of concern in political science during the last several decades has been how the vast majority of citizens choose candidates based on scanty, poorly organized information. Converse (1964) described a "minimalist" view of political beliefs and identified two groups of citizens. Members of the first group are typically part of a highly involved and well-educated elite, employing logic and ideology to organize their political attitudes. The second larger group represents average citizens whose knowledge of abstract ideas and political details is limited (Sniderman & Tetlock, 1986). Brady and Sniderman (1985) said that the less involved people in the second group use affect to guide attitude formation rather than logic guided by ideology. Fiske and Kinder (1981) described political schema, or memory structures used to organize complex information. They see political elites as highly involved experts, organizing declarative and procedural knowledge into abstract schema. Low-involvement people, on the other hand, use more consensual, simple schema that emphasize affect.

Processing Level and Television Viewing

Television viewing per se is a form of effortless vigilance, or low-involvement monitoring, that does not include conscious, selective, or effortful attention (Krugman, 1986). Zillmann (1984) also depicted most people as low-involvement viewers who watch television to relax and to achieve a state of mild arousal. Thus, political science and communication research suggest a powerful match between television as a vehicle for emotional persuasion, and the levels of low information and involvement typical of people most likely to be watching. For these people, the potential for television to influence political decisions is large, because television is the major and often the sole source of political information (Chaffee, 1981).

EMOTIONAL RESPONSES WITHIN NEGATIVE MESSAGES

When the label *negative* is used to categorize the relationship between sponsor and opponent, it describes a Level 1 feature of the message. What such labeling fails to capture are other Level 2 features of the message that might elicit emotions in the viewer.

Labels for political ads, like other television messages, are typically assigned with reference to an entire message. Most negative political commercials are 30 seconds long, regardless of the quality or sequencing of information *within* the message. Emotional responses, or even Level 1 responses, however, may occur in time periods that do not exactly overlap the boundaries of messages (Reeves, 1989). If *emotion* is defined as an action state residing in the organism, produced by a mismatch between its current goals and the environment (see Frijda, 1988; Oatley & Johnson-Laird, 1987), the traditional 30-second stimulus boundaries represented by the beginning and end of the spot are arbitrary. This could be the case for two of the three categories of negative political commercials previously discussed, comparative and positive, and could include message features that evoke both positive and negative emotions.

Emotional responses, including psychological, physiological, and subjective changes, have been observed to cycle from activation to extinction in less than 15 seconds (Zajonc, 1984). Significant differences in the on-line measurement of warmth in product advertising, for instance, were recorded across 7-second intervals (Aaker, Stayman, & Hagerty, 1986). Kern (1988) described how producers construct emotion sequences in so-called "get them sick, get them well" ads. The first half of the message is used to establish a negative emotion in association with some threat to the viewer. During the second half, the problem is resolved in conjunction with the activation of a positive emotion associated with the candidate.

These studies suggest a more detailed view of emotional complexity *within* a 30-second "spot." There are two consequences for research: (a) message *segments* should be categorized as to emotional content rather than categorizing entire messages; and (b) responses from individuals that are used to define messages should be assessed "on-line," so that responses that change *during* a single ad can be matched with corresponding message segments.

PERIPHERAL MESSAGE CUES, EMOTION OF THE VIEWER, AND MEMORY

The psychophysiological emotional state of the viewer of a political advertisement, then, may be in large part determined by features such as music, the use of color, or cuts and pacing in the message that have little or nothing to do with its topic. The relationship between such emotion-eliciting features and memory have come to be the source of a good deal of research during the last decade (for reviews of research into the relation between emotion, mood, and memory in cognitive psychology see Blaney, 1986; Bower, 1987; Bower & Mayer, 1989).

All emotions are potentially relevant to encoding of television images by low-involvement viewers, but negative ones are the most psychologically compelling. Negative emotions are elicited by circumstances that demand action in the face of a threat (Frijda, 1988). Frijda described what he called "hedonic asymmetry," a constant negative emotional pull interrupted only sporadically by extinguishable positive emotions. Positive emotional states are more ephemeral, tending to decay rapidly with their strength measured compared to previous states.

An important issue in the relationship between emotion and memory is the conceptualization of negativity. Is "negative" a single category or does it describe several different emotions? The relationship between cognition and emotion remains controversial (see Lazarus, 1984; Zajonc, 1984), but there is general agreement that there are about five to seven primary affective states, the majority of which are negative (see Ellis, Thomas, & Rodriguez, 1984; Lang, 1985; Lazarus, 1984; Muncy, 1986; Zajonc, 1984). Associated with each of these emotions is a unique affective "program," that includes psychological and physiological changes in the organism (Lang, 1985). They include changes in cognitive capacity and information-processing strategy, both of which could affect memory (Izard, Kagan, & Zajonc, 1984).

Conover and Feldman (1986) used a similar categorization to group political appeals into three negative emotions (fear, anger, disgust), and one positive emotion (hope). It is often the case, however, that these appeals are combined in a single message. Thus, messages whose central topic is negative can have at least three sets of peripheral emotion sequences embedded in them: (a) the true negative, or attack ads would be expected to have negative peripheral cues, represented by fear, disgust, or anger, embedded throughout the commercial; (b) comparative ads can be expected to begin with an attack on the sponsor's opponent in the context of one of the three negative emotions, and then suggest a resolution on a positive, hopeful note in favor of the sponsor; and (c) positive hope ads, represented by generally positive appeals, where the sponsor is promoted as the solution to some background problem, such as inflation.

This leads to the prediction that memory will be enhanced for true negative, or attack advertising, to the degree they contain emotion-laden cues, such as dark colors and static camera techniques. From the point of view of commercial advertising, true negative commercials evoke negative attitudes toward the competition's brand (Att_b), in this case the sponsor's opponent, as well as evoking negative emotions resulting from peripheral message features (Att_a) that would enhance memory. The enhancement should be apparent both in the certainty about whether information was present, and for the immediacy of response.

This study examined memory for political advertisements used in the 1989 presidential campaign in terms of three negative emotions, and their combination with the positive emotion of hope. The previous discussion suggests two predictions about the relationship between these emotions and memory:

1. Negative messages should elicit psychological states that enhance encoding and information processing. This should be reflected in a *negative* correlation between response latency and memory (the more

negative the message, the quicker the recognition of information from the message), and a *positive* correlation with accuracy (the more negative the message, the more accurate the response).

2. The boundaries of emotional content in advertisements will not necessarily correspond to the beginning and end of 30-second segments. This should be reflected by on-line rating scores for "liking" or "not liking" that change significantly within a message according to their emotional content.

METHOD

The experiment included two within-subject factors: (a) type of ad (true negative, comparative, and positive); and (b) time in ad (first half, second half). In addition, there was a continuous measure of "liking" (generated by a hand-held dial connected to a computer during stimulus viewing) that was averaged in 3-second segments for each viewer and each ad.

The dependent variables were accuracy of recognition (percentage of pictures and words from the target messages that could be identified), and latency to recognition (reaction time to identification of material from target messages). Recognition measures were repeated for visual and audio information.

Pretest Subjects

A pretest was conducted to categorize ads into the three groups. Participating were 31 undergraduate students. They ranged from 19 to 22 years old, and were balanced for gender and political participation. Groups of about 10 subjects in classrooms were shown 34 different political advertisements, 29 from the Bush–Dukakis campaign and 5 from other recent Senatorial races. To the knowledge of the experimenters, the commercials from the Bush–Dukakis campaign represented a census of ads used during the campaign.

Prior to the screening, the subjects were given forms to fill out after viewing each commercial. The forms were made up of four 6-point scales, each representing a different positive or negative emotion. The extremes of each scale were labeled "Weak" and "Strong." The four emotions were hope, disgust, anger, and fear. The order of the four emotions was randomized across commercials. At the beginning of the session an experimenter explained that he wanted the subjects to rate what emotions they thought the commercials evoked. After each commercial the tape was stopped long enough for all subjects to make the ratings.

Mean values were assigned for each message on anger, disgust, fear, and hope. A separate score was calculated for the first and second half of each commercial. The commercials receiving negative ratings throughout were categorized as true negative. Likewise, the ads receiving positive ratings throughout were categorized positive. Finally, the commercials with negative ratings during the first half and positive ratings for the second half were categorized as comparative.

Experimental Subjects

The subjects in the experiment were 30 adults from the local community. They ranged in age from 19 to 69 years old, and were approximately equally divided by gender and political affiliation. Subjects individually viewed one of three 25-minute stimulus tapes that contained 28 advertisements that were each 30 seconds long, each followed by 5 seconds of video black. A brief description of the advertisements is in Table 7.1. The order of presentation of the 28 advertisements was rotated in blocks across three different stimulus tapes.

Subjects first read and signed a consent form and were then seated 6 feet from a television monitor. An experimenter briefly described the session and began a videotape. Instructions for the experiment appeared on the screen. People were told to pay attention to the program, and to move the handle on a game paddle according to their liking for the material they viewed; left was for "like," right was for "don't like." They were instructed to give a general rating to what they watched, and not focus on any particular feature, such as the candidate or the issues discussed. A 1-minute practice program followed. The instructions were then repeated, and viewing and data recording began.

At the end of the tape, an experimenter re-entered the room and administered a questionnaire. People were asked to write down information about their political party affiliation, how much attention they paid to the 1989 presidential election, who they preferred, and if they voted. They also were asked their age, gender, and education. They were given 5 minutes to finish the questionnaire.[1]

A second videotape was then shown that contained pictures and sound bites from the advertisements. Subjects were asked to press a "yes" or a "no" button to indicate whether the material was from the messages they had viewed. There were three practice presentations and

---

[1]The questionnaire was meant as a distractor task and the data from it were not analyzed.

Table 7.1 Political Advertisements from the 1988 Preidential Campaign Used as Stimulus Material

Title	Sponsor	Emotions	Content
California environment	Bush	− −	Attack on Dukakis environmental record
Promises	Bush	− −	Don't trust Dukakis record on crime
Dead wrong	Dukakis	− +	Dukakis talks tough on drugs
Truth	Bush	− −	Bush talks about Democratic failures
Harbor	Bush	− −	Attack on Dukakis failure to clean Boston harbor
Keeping Amer. working	Bush	+ +	Bush talking head on good economy
Remember	Bush	− −	Dramatization of Bush's backroom handlers plotting
His mistakes	Dukakis	− −	Boston street corner interviews on Dukakis failures
Jimmy	Bush	+ +	Dramatization of youth working in a pizza parlor rather than attending college
Bay	Bush	− −	Response to Bush environmental charges
Tax blizzard	Dukakis	− −	Dramatization of couple receiving tax bills due to Dukakis increases
Failed	Dukakis	− −	Dukakis attack on Bush environmental record
Gorbachev	Bush	+ +	Pictures of Bush with world leaders
Crunch	Dukakis	− −	Attack on Bush Social Secuirty Policy
Oval office	Dukakis	− −	Zoom on the Oval Office with warning Quayle might be President
Tank	Bush	− −	Attack on Dukakis defense record, showing Dukakis on top of a tank
In charge	Dukakis	+ +	Speech on trade and other issues
Blackboard	Dukakis	− +	Attack on Bush education policy, pitch for Dukakis
The quiz	Bush	− −	Attack on Dukakis crime record
Chairman	Dukakis	− −	Attack on Bush record as drug chairman
Two paychecks	Dukakis	+ +	Dramatization of a young couple struggling to pay the bill at a checkout stand
America workmanship	Dukakis	+ +	Shows American factory workers with promise for strong eonomy
Your own mind	Bush	− −	Bush attack on Dukakis crime record
Furlough from the truth	Dukakis	− −	Dukakis charge that Bush also had a past with a prison furlough program
Elderly care	Dukakis	− −	Elderly couple at a bus stop with Dukakis promise not to cut Social Sec.
Revolving door	Bush	− −	Prisoners walk from prison gates while Dukakis furlough of a murderer is attacked
Effort	Dukakis	− −	Attack on Reagan-Bush failure to control drugs
Drugs	Dukakis	+ +	Pictures of kids playing while drug control is discussed

then a repeat of the instructions. There were 112 one-second video segments shown without audio. Fifty-six of the segments were from the stimulus tape, one from the first half of each advertisement, and one from the second half. The remaining 56 were foils selected from other Bush–Dukakis advertisements not used in the stimulus tapes. There were 28 two-second sound segments for the audio-recognition task. They were played without video over the television monitor speaker. The other 28 segments also were from other material.

At the end of the experiment, people were debriefed about the intent of the experiment and thanked.

Experimental Procedure

All video presentations were played from one-half inch VHS tapes on a 19-inch color monitor. The stimulus sequence was connected to an IBM AT computer via a longitudinal time code output recorded on audio Channel 2. The time code was read by a time code reader board in the computer. A preset time code selected to correspond to the beginning of each advertisement triggered a computer program that sampled liking scores at 11 three-second epochs. The last epoch ended 3 seconds after the end of the commercial. The data were generated by movement of the handle on the game paddle, and ranged from 5 for the extreme right hand position, 82 in the center, to 169 at the extreme left.

For the recognition tape, data time codes were preselected and stored in a computer file to correspond to the onset of the video or audio segments. The file also included a code to indicate whether the material was in the stimulus tape or a foil. When the computer matched the time code on the videotape with the time code stored in the preset file, an internal clock in the computer started and ran until the subject depressed one of two buttons on the game paddle indicating the material was in the stimulus material or not. Reaction time (+ or − 1 msec) was recorded with the time code number that corresponded to the video frame that appeared when the tone began, along with a code to indicate if the selection was correct. Visual latency in milliseconds was computed for recognition of two 1-second video presentations, one sampled from the first half of each message, and the other sampled from the second half of the commercial. Audio recognition in milliseconds was recorded for one 2-second audio presentation from each commercial. Accuracy was measured for both audio and visual recognition using responses to the same presentations used in the latency tests. In the case of visual latency and accuracy, totals were computed by summing the values from the first and second presentations.

RESULTS

The dependent variable for this study was recognition memory, separated into accuracy and latency for both visual and audio information. Independent variables included message emotion, liking, and time. The analyses were divided into three parts: (a) the relationship between message type and memory; (b) changes in "liking" as a function of message type and time; and (c) the relationship between liking and memory.

Commercial Type and Memory

Repeated measures analysis of variance was used to examine the relationship between commercial type and memory. There were 6 commercials classified as positive, 12 as true negative, and 7 as comparative. To achieve a balanced design of 6 commercials per type, 6 true negative ads and 1 comparative ad were eliminated from the analysis. This was accomplished by eliminating the commercials with the lowest emotion ratings in their particular category.

Recognition Memory

There were four results concerning emotional strength and memory: (a) the four emotions were highly collinear and could not be examined independently; (b) visual and audio information from true negative messages was recognized faster and with more accuracy than information from comparative or positive messages; (c) for visual information, this relationship increased during the second half of the commercials; and (d) results for comparative and positive commercials were similar.

Visual Recognition Latency and Accuracy

As predicted, there was a main effect for message type and latency to visual recognition [$F(2,58) = 21.51$, $p < .001$].[2] Although no main effect was detected for the position of material in the commercial and recognition, position did interact with ad type [$F(2,58) = 6.25$ $p < .004$]. These effects are shown in Fig. 7.1a.

Visual material from the beginning of true negative ads was recognized at least 64 msec faster than either positive or comparative ads, and 266

---

[2]All analysis of variance probabilities are adjusted according to the Greenhouse Geisser procedure.

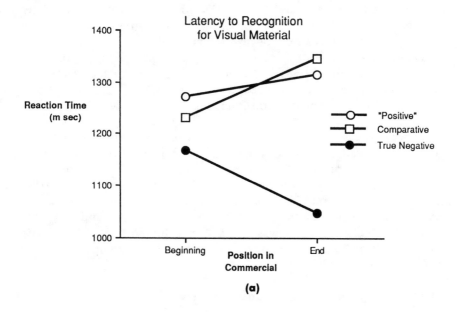

(a)

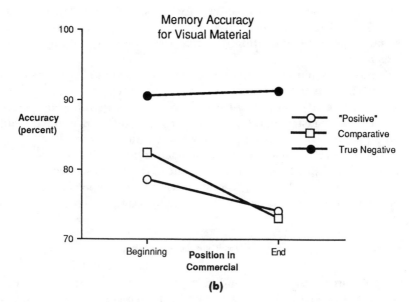

(b)

FIGURE 7.1. Memory for visual material in emotion-laden political commercials.

msec faster for material at the end of the ads. The similarity of recognition for positive and comparative ads is also evident, with times for these two commercial types differing by only 41 msec for material at the beginning and 31 msec for material at the end.

Figure 7.1b shows the main effect for message type on accuracy of visual recognition [$F(2,58) = 18.56 \, p < .001$] and for the position of material in either the first or second half of the ads [$F(1,29) = 4.61 \, p < .04$]. The message type-position interaction was not statistically significant.

As was the case for recognition, accuracy in identifying material from true negative ads was better than either comparative or positive messages. Results for true negative messages changed little over time, with 90% accuracy for material from the beginning of the ads, and 91% accuracy for material from the end. Material from the first half of comparative messages was identified accurately 83% and 79% for positive ads. Recognition was less accurate for both of these in the second half of the messages, with 73% accuracy for comparatives and 74% for positive ads.

Audio-Recognition Latency and Accuracy

For audio recognition, main effects for message type [$F(2,58) = 10.64 \, p < .001$] and accuracy [$F(2,58) = 15.87 \, p < .001$] were detected. These results were similar to those for visual recognition, although position was not varied.

Figure 7.2a shows the largest difference for audio recognition were between true negative messages, and the other two types. Material from true negative ads was recognized 142 msec faster than for comparatives and 189 msec faster than for positive ads. The difference in recognition time for positive and comparative ads was only 47 msec.

A similar relation for accuracy in identifying audio material can be seen in Fig. 7.2b. Material from true negative messages was accurately identified 84% of the time, whereas it was identified 68% of the time for positive messages, and 64% of the time for comparatives.

LIKING FOR ADVERTISEMENTS BY MESSAGE TYPE

Liking scores provide a second assessment of the emotional content of the messages. Figure 7.3 shows a significant main effect for message type [$F = 41.2; \, df \, 10; \, p < .001$], epoch [$F = 2.9; \, df \, 2; \, p < .001$], and on liking for the commercials.

There were two more detailed results. First, the epoch-message type

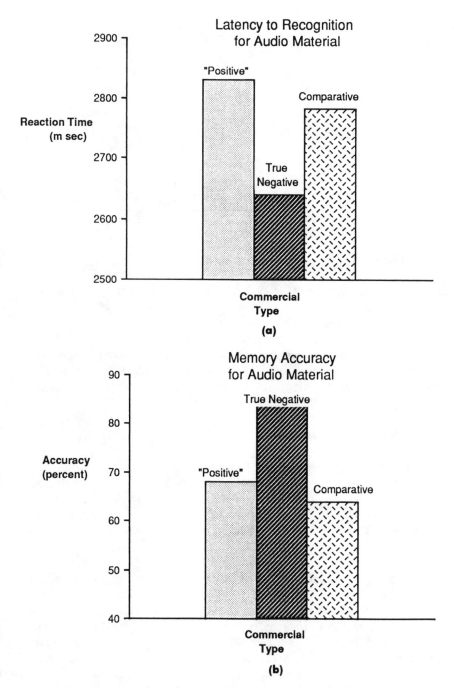

FIGURE 7.2. Memory for audio material in emotion-laden political commercials.

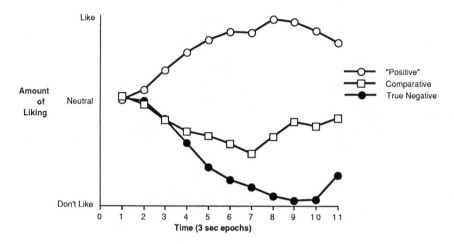

FIGURE 7.3.   Amount of liking for three types of commercials over time.

interaction was significant [$F = 18.05$; $df\ 20$; $p < .001$]. Liking ratings for positive and true negative advertisements were mirror images, with liking scores steadily increasing for the first 20 seconds, where they peaked, and then fell. Subjects rated comparative commercials as expected, responding to negative material in the first half, and then moving in a positive direction during the second half. However, neither the rating for the negative material nor the positive material achieved the intensity of the other two commercial types.

Liking for the Advertisements and Memory

The zero-order correlation between liking for the entire commercial, and accuracy and latency was not significant. However, examining the correlations at each of the 11 three-second epochs within the commercials did reveal a pattern.

Figure 7.4a shows that the correlation between visual recognition for the second picture and liking steadily increased over time, becoming statistically significant at epoch 7 ($r = .33$; $p < .01$), and epoch 8 ($r = .33$; $p < .01$). The relationship showed that greater liking resulted in poorer (i.e., slower) memory.

Figure 7.4b shows that the negative correlation between visual accuracy and liking for the second picture became statistically significant during epoch 6 ($r = -.33$; $p < .01$), epoch 7 ($r = -.36$; $p < .01$), epoch 8 ($r = -.37$; $p < .01$), and epoch 9 ($r = -.32$; $p < .01$). This means that greater liking resulted in poorer (i.e., less) accuracy.

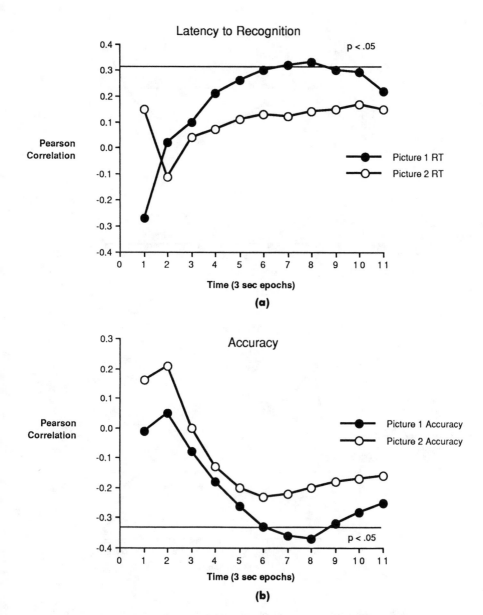

FIGURE 7.4. Zero-order correlations between liking for advertisements and memory for visual material over time.

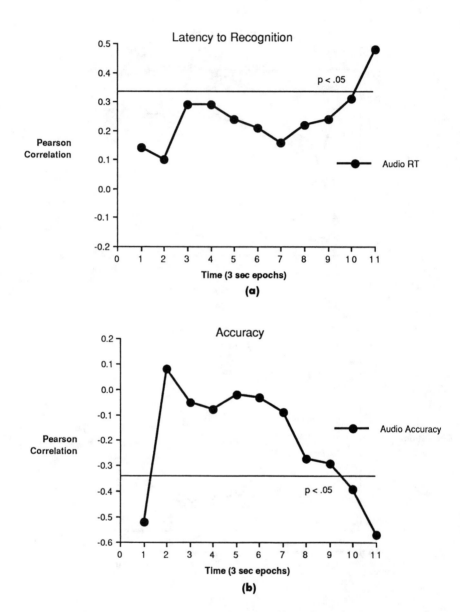

FIGURE 7.5. Zero-order correlations between liking for advertisements and memory for audio material over time.

Figure 7.5a shows that the correlation between latency to respond to audio material and liking was statistically significant during only epoch 11 ($r = .49$; $p < .01$). As was the case with visual recognition, greater liking resulted in poorer memory and slower response times.

Figure 7.5b shows a negative correlation between accuracy in identifying material from the commercials and liking. Correlations steadily decreased and became statistically significant during epoch 10 ($r = -.39$; $p < .01$) and epoch 11 ($r = -.58$; $p < .01$). The negative correlation indicates that as liking increased, accuracy decreased.

DISCUSSION

The primary research question in this study was whether negative advertising "worked." If success is defined as recognition memory, then negative advertising does increase both the accuracy and speed of visual recognition. However, if success is defined as "liking," negative advertising is judged less favorably than ads with at least some positive material. Given an additional speculation about the endurance of these effects—namely, that the degree of "liking" may be forgotten while information is not—negative advertising, in a practical sense, is probably a good bet. Kaid and Sanders (1978) reported just such a "sleeper effect" in their study of political advertising, where memory for a message persisted despite initial negative ratings for its source. This suggests that, in large part, people's response that they do not like negative advertising is based on a Level 1 assessment of the nature of the topic-related features of the commercials. Such Level 1 processing is associated with cues central to the sponsor's message and generally associated with the "rational" or "thoughtful" component of a candidate's appeal. On the other hand, memory differences for the advertisements appear to be related to Level 2 features of the ads themselves and lead to differential encoding of information in the messages. These second-level cues are associated with peripheral features of the message such as color, pacing, or the facial expressions on the television screen, and may have little or nothing to do directly with the topic of the ad.

One example of the difference between Level 1 and Level 2 cues can be found in a commercial that featured an unseen narrator's ominous voice warning that a spreading plague of drug abuse threatened America's youth, and suggested a vote for Michael Dukakis as the only solution to stop it. The video portion of the commercial, however, showed soft colorful images of small children at play on a grassy playground. While experimenters initially classified this commercial as a fear appeal, due to the strength of the topic, both groups of viewers rated it as the most positive of the 28 commercials, apparently because of the strength of the nonverbal, peripheral cues.

Noting the distinction that positive and negative affect are not symmetric (see Diener & Emmons, 1985) is an important distinction in marketing political or consumer products. Consumer appeals that laud a product as the solution to some social problem (such as mouthwash and bad breath respectively) correspond closely to positive political commercials that offer hope in the face of adversity or praise past achievements. Comparative advertising also is employed by both, but rarely (especially in the 1988 Presidential campaign) do political ads use sentimental themes as positive as many product and service ads might be. Conversely, Level 1 negative advertising is virtually absent from product campaigns, although there are similarities between negative political ads and PSAs that depend on fear to motivate changes in consumption or other health practices.

One of the goals of the present study was to differentiate *forms* of negative messages in relation to psychological evidence about emotions. To this end, the pretest used three different negative categories (fear, anger, disgust) in addition to one positive (hope). Although the categories could be distinguished conceptually, they cannot be separated empirically using subjective responses. All four of the emotions reduced to a single negative–positive continuum. However, a more differentiated line of study ought not be abandoned. There is strong evidence that each of these emotions corresponds to unique psychological and physiological states that in turn affect not just the quantity of information but also the quality. Those differences might be reflected by the formation of more or less complex memory structures. It may be that further pursuit of these fine differences will lead to a deeper understanding of the link between emotion and different processing strategies.

Another theoretical premise of the study was that analysis of television commercials would benefit from examination of message *segments,* defined theoretically, rather than analysis of intact messages that are defined by traditional industry boundaries. Correlations between liking for the commercials and memory suggest that complex processing takes place in brief periods of time. During the first 20 seconds of the commercials the steady increase in the negative relationship between memory and liking suggests increased arousal and biased associative encoding as a response to primitive features of the messages. Then, during the last 10 seconds, the decrease in the relationship between memory and liking indicate the stimulus appears to have lost novelty, with psychophysiological adjustments having been successful in reducing the mismatch between the internal state of the viewer and the environment.

This also is true for visual memory for positive, comparative, and true negative ad types, where differences were detected only in the second half of the ads. This is consistent with research that suggests that emotions, as opposed to moods, are short, in the range of 8 to 10 seconds, and that their influence cannot be detected until after the emotion is activated (Zajonc, 1984). Consequently, the effects of emotion in traditional messages should be specific to a portion of the messages, and attributed to material sufficiently prior to the target portion, or to segments in other prior messages. This resulted in obtaining emotion values for two halves of each message, and examining one variable, liking, over 11 three-second epochs. Analyses that segmented messages in each case showed results that would not have been apparent if data were collapsed to conform with traditional message boundaries.

In summary, the fact that the relationship between exposure to political television advertising and voting behavior is complex should not in itself be sufficient reason to abandon its study. The formation of attitudes that lead up to political behavior are surely the result of hundreds, if not thousands, of exposures to persuasive appeals such as political television advertisements. We believe we have shown that defining political advertising solely in terms of the so-called "rational" or "thoughtful" aspects of the sponsor's topic, as is the case for what has come to be known as "negative" television spots, overlooks the impact on memory of other important message features. We further believe that the literatures of communication research, social psychology, and political science all suggest the importance of such lower level features on memory and attitude formation, and ultimately on political behavior.

A final practical consideration has to do with the impact of negative political advertising on the American political system. The political consultant might take heart from the fact that the results of this study indicate that negative political advertising "works" in the sense that viewers remember it better. But the democratic theorist might focus on the result that people do not like negative political advertising. Those results show negative advertising does not work in the sense they may be increasing disillusionment with American politics, a suggestion supported by record low voter turnout.

REFERENCES

Aaker, D., Stayman, D., & Hagerty, M. (1986). Warmth in advertising: Measurement, impact, and sequence effects. *Journal of Consumer Research, 12,* 365–381.

Berry, C. (1983). Learning from television news: A critique of the research. *Journal of Broadcasting, 24*(4), 359–370.

Blaney, P. (1986). Affect and memory: A review. *Psychological Bulletin, 99*(2), 229–246.

Bower, G. (1987). Commentary on mood and memory. *Behavioral Research Theory,* 25(6), 443–455.

Bower, G., & Mayer, J. (1989). In search of mood-dependent retrieval. *Journal of Social Behavior and Personality,* 4(2), 121–156.

Brady, H., & Sniderman, P. (1985). Attitude attribution: A group basis for political reasoning. *American Political Science Review, 79,* 1061–1078.

Cacioppo, J., & Petty, R. (1985). Central and peripheral routes to persuasion: The role of message repetition. In L. Alwitt & A. Mitchell (Eds.), *Psychological processes and advertising effects* (pp. 91–111). Hillsdale, NJ: Lawrence Erlbaum Associates.

Chaffee, S. (1981). Mass media in political campaigns: An expanding role. In D. Rice & W. Paisley (Eds.), *Public communication campaigns* (pp. 181–198). Sage Pub., Beverly Hills.

Conover, P., & Feldman, S. (1986). The role of inference in the perception of political candidates. In R. Lau & D. Sears (Eds.), *The 19th annual Carnegie Symposium on Cognition: Political cognition* (pp. 127–155). Hillsdale, NJ: Lawrence Erlbaum Associates.

Converse, P. (1964). The nature of belief systems in mass publics. In D. Apter (Ed.), *Ideology and discontent* (pp. 207–261). New York: The Free Press.

Diener, E., & Emmons, R. (1985). The independence of positive and negative affect. *Journal of Personality and Social Psychology, 47*(5), 1105–1117.

Donohew, L., Finn, S., & Christ, W. (1988). "The nature of news" revisited: The roles of affect, schema, and cognition. In L. Donohew, H. Sypher, & C. T. Higgins (Eds.), *Communication, social cognition, and affect* (pp. 195–218). Hillsdale, NJ: Lawrence Erlbaum Associates.

Ellis, D., Thomas, R., & Rodriguez, I. (1984). Emotional mood states and memory: Elaborative encoding, semantic processing, and cognitive effort. *Journal of Experimental Psychology: Learning, Memory, and Cognition, 10*(3), 470–482.

Fazio, R., Sanbonmatsu, D., Powell, M., & Kardes, F. (1986). On the automatic activation of attitudes. *Journal of Personality and Social Psychology, 50*(2), 229–238.

Fishbein, M., & Ajzen, I. (1981). Acceptance, yielding, and impact: Cognitive processes in persuasion. In R. Petty, T. Ostrom, & T. Brock (Eds.), *Cognitive responses in persuasion* (pp. 339–360). Hillsdale, NJ: Lawrence Erlbaum Associates.

Fiske, S., & Kinder, D. (1981). Involvement, expertise, and schema use: Evidence from political cognition. In N. Cantor & J. Kihlstrom (Eds.), *Personality, cognition, and social interaction* (pp. 171–187). Hillsdale, NJ: Lawrence Erlbaum Associates.

Friestad, M., & Thorson, E. (1984, May). *The role of emotion in memory for television commercials.* Paper presented to the Mass Communication Division of the International Communication Association, Honolulu, Hawaii.

Frijda, N. (1988). The laws of emotion. *American Psychologist, 43*(5), 349–358.

Garramone, G. (1985). Effects of negative political advertising: The roles of sponsor and rebuttal. *Journal of Broadcasting and Electronics Media, 29*(2), 147–159.

Guskind, R., & Hagstrom, J. (1988). In the gutter. *National Journal,* Vol. 20, 2782–2790.

Hill, R., & Mazis, M. (1986). Measuring emotional responses to advertising. In R. Lutz (Ed.), *Advances in consumer research* (Vol. 13, pp. 164–169). Provo, UT: Association for Consumer Research.

Izard, C., Kagan, J., & Zajonc, R. (1984). *Emotions, cognition and behavior.* Cambridge: Cambridge University Press.

Kaid, L. (1981). Political advertising. In D. Nimmo & K. Sanders (Eds.), *Handbook of political communication* (pp. 249–271). Beverly Hill, CA: Sage.

Kaid, L., & Sanders, K. (1978). Political television commercials: An experimental study of type and length. *Communication Research, 5*(1), 57–70.

Kern, M, (1988, May). *Schools of media consulting: Emotional, new informational and quick response thinking in the eighties: An elite study.* Paper presented to the International Communication Association Annual Convention, New Orleans, LA.

Krugman, H. (1981). The impact of television advertising: Learning without involvement. In M. Janowitz & P. Hirsch (Eds.), *Reader in public opinion and mass communication* (pp. 403–408). New York: The Free Press.

Krugman, H. (1986, February/March). Low recall and high recognition of advertising. *Journal of Advertising Research,* 79–86.

Lang, P. (1985). The cognitive psychophysiology of emotion: Fear and anxiety. In A. Tuma & J. Maser (Eds.), *Anxiety and the anxiety disorders* (pp. 151–170). Hillsdale, NJ: Lawrence Erlbaum Associates.

Lanzetta, J., Sullivan, D., Masters, R., & McHugo, G. (1985). Emotional and cognitive responses to televised images of political leaders. In S. Draus & R. Perloff (Eds.), *Mass media and political thought: An information processing approach* (pp. 85–116). Beverly Hills, CA: Sage.

Lazarus, R. (1984). On the primacy of cognition. *American Psychologist, 39*(2), 124–129.

Lutz, R. (1985). Affective and cognitive antecedents of attitude toward the ad: A conceptual framework. In L. Alwitt & A. Mitchell (Eds.), *Psychological processes and advertising effects: Theory, research, and applications* (pp. 45–63). Hillsdale, NJ: Lawrence Erlbaum Associates.

Merritt, S. (1984). Negative political advertising: Some empirical findings. *Journal of Advertising, 13*(3), 27–38.

Mitchell, A. (1983). Cognitive processes initiated by exposure to advertising. In R. Harris (Ed.), *Information processing research in advertising* (pp. 13–42). Hillsdale, NJ: Lawrence Erlbaum Associates.

Muncy, J. (1986). Affect and cognition: A closer look at two competing theories. In R. Lutz (Ed.), *Advances in consumer research* (Vol. 13, pp. 226–230). Provo, UT: Association for Consumer Research.

Nugent, J. (1987). Positively negative. *Campaigns and Elections, 7*(6), 47–49.

Oatley, K., & Johnson-Laird, P. (1987). Towards a cognitive theory of emotions. *Cognition and emotion, 1*(1), 29–50.

Patterson, T., & McClure, R. (1976). *The unseeing eye.* New York: Putnam.

Petty, R., Cacioppo, J., & Kasmer, J. (1988). The role of affect in the Elaboration Likelihood Model of persuasion. In L. Donohew, H. Sypher, & E. Tory Higgins (Eds.), *Communication, social cognition, and affect* (pp. 117–146). Hillsdale, NJ: Lawrence Erlbaum Associates.

Reeves, B. (1989). Theories about news and theories about cognition: Arguments for a more radical separation. *American Behavioral Scientist,* Vol. 33, No. 2, pp. 191–198.

Reeves, B., Newhagen, J., Maibach, E., Basil, M., & Kurz, K. (1989, May). *Negative and positive television messages: Effects of message type and message context on attention and memory.* Paper presented to the International Communication Association annual convention, San Francisco, CA.

Roddy, B., & Garramone, G. (1988, May). *Negative political advertising: Appeals and strategies.* Paper presented to the International Communication Association, New Orleans, LA.

Rothschild, M. (1974). *The effects of political advertising on the voting behavior of low involvement electorate.* Unpublished doctoral dissertation, Stanford University, Stanford, CA.

Shapiro, M., & Rieger, R. (1989, May). *Comparing positive and negative political advertising.* Paper presented to the Political Communication Division of the International Communication Association, San Francisco, CA.

Sniderman, P., & Tetlock, P. (1986). Public opinion and political ideology. In M. Hermann (Ed.), *Political Psychology* (pp. 64–72). San Francisco: Jossey-Bass.

Srull, T. (1983). Affect and memory: The impact of affective reactions in advertising on the representation of product information in memory. R. Bagozzi and A. Tybout (Eds.) *Advances in consumer research* (Vol. 10, pp. 520–525). Provo, UT: Association for Consumer Research.

Srull, T. (1984). The effects of subjective affective states on memory and judgment. In T. Kinnear (Ed.), *Advances in consumer research* (Vol. 11, pp. 530–533). Provo, UT: Association for Consumer Research.

Zajonc, R. B. (1984). On the primacy of affect. *American Psychologist, 39*(2), 117–123.

Zillmann, D. (1984). *Connections between sex and aggression.* Hillsdale, NJ: Lawrence Erlbaum Associates.

8

Emotion, Formal Features, and Memory for Televised Political Advertisements

Annie Lang
Washington State University

The study reported here investigates what is learned from political advertisements within the context of a research program designed to study how individuals process televised information. This approach is based on the idea that political commercials make up a unique subset of media content that requires study. Further, that although it is valuable to study political commercials within the social and political environment of a campaign, it is equally valid to investigate how individuals process political commercials as stimuli in a controlled environment.

This theoretical perspective makes two assumptions. First, that aspects of the medium of television, that is to say its structural features, affect how we take in the information presented on television. An attempt is made to assess television in terms of its various stimulus properties such as camera techniques, speed of presentation, luminance levels, movement, and audio–visual presentation mode. Second, it is assumed that the content of television also has an effect on how we process and learn the information presented. Aspects of television content such as emotion, style, reality, and violence must be studied concurrently with the structural aspects of the medium.

This theoretical perspective assumes that structure and content have independent and interdependent effects on how we learn from television. The purpose of this research is to investigate, within the media subset of political advertisements, how one aspect of content, in this case emotion, and one aspect of structure, in this case scene changes, affect memory for both the audio and visual information contained in the commercials. Most previous research in these areas has either looked at the effects of emotion or emotional valence on memory *or* examined the effects of formal features on attention and memory. This study tries to look at both the effects of emotion and the effects of formal features on memory *and* at the interaction of emotion and formal features.

Recent research has demonstrated fairly conclusively that emotional content has a significant impact on the processing of and memory for televised commercials (Thorson, in press). Theoretical perspectives in this literature on *how* emotion affects processing and recall vary. Good reviews of the theoretical literature on emotion and information processing can be found in Scherer and Ekman (1984) and Izard, Kagan, and Zajonc (1984).

Looking only at the results of research on commercials and public service announcements, while recognizing that these studies have varied theoretical approaches, it appears that emotional commercials are better recalled than nonemotional commercials (Friestad & Thorson, 1985; Rothschild, Thorson, Hirsch, Goldstein, & Reeves, 1983; Thorson, in press). Further, the valence of the emotion, negative or positive, also influences recall and recognition for the commercial (Friestad & Thorson, 1985; Lang, 1989; Reeves, Newhagen, Mailbach, Basil, & Kurz, 1989; Shapiro & Rieger, 1989).

Specifically, Friestad and Thorson (1985) have shown that poignant commercials, defined as commercials that contain both negative and positive emotional messages, are remembered significantly better than either negative-only or positive-only commercials. In addition, the single-emotion commercials are remembered significantly better than neutral or nonemotional commercials.

Shapiro and Rieger (1989) have shown significantly better recall for negative political commercials compared to positive political commercials. Similarly, Reeves et al. (1989) have shown better memory for negative public service announcements (PSAs) compared to positive PSAs. Lang (1989) has also shown enhanced recall for negative commercials compared to positive commercials. Based on these findings, the first hypothesis states:

Hypothesis 1: There will be a main effect for emotion such that negative commercials are remembered better than positive commercials.

In addition to overall memory differences, it has been demonstrated that emotion affects the processing of television commercials. Specifically, emotional valence of television messages has been shown to evoke lateralization of alpha activity in the EEG patterns during television viewing (Davidson, 1984; Dimmond, Farrington, & Johnson, 1976; Reeves & Lang, 1986; Reeves, Lang, Thorson, & Rothschild, 1989). Research suggests that the right-brain activity of subjects is significantly greater during viewing of negative emotional television messages than it is during viewing of positive emotional television messages. This suggests the possibility that lateralized brain activity may be evoked by the presence of emotion in television.

Lang and Friestad (1987) and Lang (1989) have theorized that this lateralization in activity caused by the emotional valence of the television message might result in differences in the processing of and memory for the audio and visual information in television commercials. They argue, based on the traditional dichotomy of the left brain as the verbal processor and the right brain as the visual processor: (a) that positive commercials will evoke greater left-brain processing and therefore more memory for verbal information, and (b) conversely, that negative commercials will evoke greater right-brain processing and therefore more memory for visual information. In a test of this theory, Lang and Friestad (1987) demonstrated that the amount of visual recall for commercials was related to emotional valence as predicted but they did not find a significant difference for positive commercials and verbal memory. The present study tests this hypothesis again:

Hypothesis 2: There will be an interaction between emotion and audio–visual information such that visual information will be remembered better in negative commercials than in positive commercials and audio information will be remembered better in positive commercials than in negative commercials.

The following hypotheses deal with the relationship between the formal features of television and viewers' attention to and memory for televised information. The theoretical perspective of this chapter is based on Ohman's (1977) model of information processing and the orienting response as reformulated for television by Lang and Thorson (1988). Basically, this perspective suggests that structural features of television (things like onsets, offsets, camera movement, edits, etc.) elicit orienting responses in viewers. Orienting responses are involuntary physiological "calls" for attention and processing. Thus, the orienting response is theorized to be the mechanism responsible for moment-to-moment variation in attention to a televised message. Further, this variation in attention seems to be related to memory for specific information contained in the television messages. Findings from various streams of research support this approach to the information processing of television.

First, previous research, using a variety of techniques to measure attention, has shown that the formal features of television do influence viewers' attention to television.

Two groups of researchers, Anderson (1985; Anderson & Levin, 1976; Anderson & Lorch, 1983) and Calvert, Huston, Watkins, and Wright (1982) have repeatedly demonstrated correlations between salient perceptual features of television (things like camera techniques, funny voices, movement, and music) and children's attention (measured as eyes on screen) to television. They find that some formal features of television reliably elicit attention from nonattentive viewers and maintain attention in inattentive viewers. Lang (1990) suggested that this eyes-on-screen measure of attention may be measuring the behavioral component of an orienting response.

Reeves et al. (1985) have shown that adult television viewers' attention, measured as the blocking of the alpha frequency in the EEG, another component of the orienting response, is greater immediately following on-screen cuts, scene changes, and movement, regardless of content. They have also provided some evidence that viewers are better able to recall and recognize information immediately following these attention eliciting formal features.

Lang (1990), using EKG to measure cardiac-orienting responses in attentive adult subjects, has shown that commercial onsets, cuts, and movement do elicit orienting responses.

Thorson and Lang (1988; Lang & Thorson, 1989) have also shown cardiac-orienting responses to videographics in television messages and have demonstrated differences in recall and recognition related to the interaction of the formal features and the complexity of the message. Specifically, they found that when the informational content of a television message was familiar to subjects, videographic special effects enhanced learning of content during and after the videographic event, but that when content was unfamiliar, the use of videographic special effects inhibited learning both during and after the videographic event. This result, they suggest, is due to the attentional capacity of the viewer. If a viewer is expending a great deal of processing capacity to process the information content in the message, then a call for additional attentional resources (i.e., an orienting response) momentarily overloads the processing system resulting in some loss of information. Conversely, if the viewer is not expending much processing capacity to process the information content in the message, then a call for additional attentional resources momentarily increases attention to the message resulting in increased retention of information. This leads to the third hypothesis:

Hypothesis 3: Information removed in time from a formal feature (in this study, commercial onsets and scene changes) will be remembered better than information occurring concurrently with a formal feature.

The theory further suggests that in addition to their independent effects on attention and memory, emotion and formal feature complexity should interact with one another. Formal features imbedded in emotional messages should result in increased attention to the stimulus and, perhaps, increased memory for the content of the stimulus.

Reeves, Newhagen et al. (1989) discussed two possible explanations for the effects of emotional valence on cognitive processing. One was that negative emotions are more primary than positive emotions. As a result the processing of negative emotional material is automatic, whereas the processing of positive emotional material requires controlled processing resources. As a result, cognitive load is higher during positive emotional messages leaving less spare attentional capacity available to respond to the formal features call for central processing resources. Meanwhile, during the processing of negative emotional messages, the processing load is lighter, leaving more spare attentional capacity available to respond to the call for central processing.

The other possibility was based on Kahneman's (1973) capacity theory of attention. Kahneman suggested that the amount of attention available at any given moment is partially determined by the arousal level of the organism. When people are more aroused they have greater attentional capacity. Several researchers (Greenwald, Cook, & Lang, in preparation; Reeves, Newhagen, et al., 1989) have demonstrated that negative material is simply more arousing than positive material. As a result, the viewer may have greater attentional capacity during negative emotional commercials than during positive emotional commercials. It follows, then, that memory should be better for negative commercials because attention is greater.

Empirical evidence exists to support the latter position. Using heart rate to measure orienting responses, Lang (1990) compared positive emotional commercials with rational (nonemotional) commercials and found, first, that the emotional commercials were more arousing than the neutral commercials and, second, that there was a significant interaction between orienting and emotion such that the orienting responses evoked by formal features embedded in positive emotional commercials were larger and longer than those evoked by formal features embedded in rational commercials. However, the effects of increased arousal and larger orienting responses on recall and recognition are not known because no performance measures were conducted in her study.

Bradley, Petry, Greenwald, and Lang P. (in preparation), using emotional slides as opposed to video, have shown effects of arousal and emotion on recall and recognition. They found that emotional slides increase arousal, that memory is better for more arousing material, and that emotional slides are remembered better than neutral slides.

Although the design of this study does not allow us to distinguish between these competing theoretical explanations, both of them make the same prediction for the direction of the effects of the interaction between emotion and formal features on memory. This prediction is the fourth hypothesis:

Hypothesis 4: There will be an interaction between emotion and formal features such that memory for information presented concurrently with a formal feature will be better in negative commercials than in positive commercials.

In addition, the attention literature shows that many performance deficits may be caused by overloading a specific response or perception system rather than a result of overloading attention or general processing resources (Schneider, Dumais, & Shiffrin, 1984). Thus, for example, people may be able to perform multiple tasks simultaneously without impairment as long as the tasks do not require the same response or perceptual system. It follows then, that because the formal features defined in this study are visual they will have a more detrimental effect on the processing of visual information than they will on the processing of verbal information because both the formal feature and the visual content of the message require the visual perception system. This leads to the fifth hypothesis:

Hypothesis 5: There will be an interaction between the visual formal feature and memory for audio–visual material such that memory for visual information presented concurrently with a visual formal feature will be worse than memory for verbal information presented concurrently with a visual formal feature.

Finally, because emotion grows and changes over time, time was included as a factor in the design. It seemed plausible to suggest that as the commercial proceeded, emotion would increase. Based on this intuitive notion, it seemed likely that as emotion increased over time memory would increase over time and that any other effects of emotion should also increase over time. Thus, the sixth and seventh hypotheses were formulated:

Hypothesis 6: There will be a main effect for time such that memory will increase over the course of the commercial.

Hypothesis 7: All the emotional effects will interact with time such that the effect of the emotion is magnified over time.

METHODS

Subjects

Subjects were 67 undergraduates at a western university. Their participation in the study satisfied a course requirement. There were 35 females and 32 males.

Materials

Four orders of the stimulus tapes were prepared. Subjects viewed eight political commercials, four positives and four negatives, embedded in nine distractor segments. The distractor segments were always presented in the same order; the commercials appeared in four different orders. Table 8.1 shows the four commercial orders and the distractor segments.

The commercials were chosen from a pool of 172 political advertisements. Each ad was rated independently by two coders. The coders

Table 8.1 Stimulus Tape Orders

Item	Order 1	Order 2	Order 3	Order 4
Distractor 1		Wheel of Fortune		
Commercial 1	Pos. 1	Pos. 2	Neg. 1	Neg. 2
Distractor 2		World Series		
Commercial 2	Neg. 3	Neg. 4	Pos. 3	Pos. 4
Distractor 3		MacNeil/Lehrer		
Commercial 3	Pos. 3	Pos. 4	Neg. 3	Neg. 1
Distractor 4		USA Today		
Commercial 4	Neg. 4	Neg. 2	Pos. 2	Pos. 1
Distractor 5		Newton's Apple		
Commercial 5	Pos. 4	Pos. 3	Neg. 2	Neg. 4
Distractor 6		SCTV		
Commercial 6	Neg. 1	Neg. 3	Pos. 1	Pos. 2
Distractor 7		Marbles		
Commercial 7	Pos. 2	Pos. 1	Neg. 4	Neg. 3
Distractor 8		Johnny Carson		
Commercial 8	Neg. 2	Neg. 1	Pos. 4	Pos. 3
Distractor 9		Rocky and Bullwinkle		

judged whether the ads were intended to be emotional and how emotional the ads made them feel. In addition, they coded the presence or absence of certain structural features theorized to convey emotion (such as music, soft focus, emotional words, and symbols) and the number of scene changes per commercial. Using these ratings the four most negative and the four most positive ads were chosen for use in the study.

All commercials were 30 seconds in length (or edited to be so) and were judged to be of broadcast quality. The tapes were played on a Sharp videocassette recorder connected to a Sharp 19-inch color television set.

Memory was assessed using three different measures, a free-recall test, a cued-recall test, and a multiple-choice test. For the free-recall test subjects were given paper and pencil and asked to write down everything they could remember about the commercials they had seen. When they were finished these pages were collected.

For the cued-recall test subjects were given, as a recall cue, a list of the candidates in the commercials. They were told that if this list caused them to remember any commercials they had not previously recalled they should now write everything they could remember about those commercials. They were instructed not to write any more about commercials they had already described.

The multiple-choice test consisted of 12 questions about each commercial. The 12 questions were made up of 6 questions about information available only in the audio track of the commercial and 6 questions about information available only in the video portion (i.e., on screen) of the commercial. Within these two groups, 3 of the questions were about information that occurred (on screen or in the audio track) at the same time (or very nearly the same time) as a scene change. The other 3 questions were about information that was removed in time from the scene changes. In addition, the questions were also designed so that there were 4 questions (2 visual and 2 audio) about information appearing in each 10-second period of the commercial. Table 8.2 shows a breakdown of the questionnaire design.

Procedure

Subjects viewed the stimulus tapes in groups of four. They were seated in a small room about 8 feet from the television screen. Subjects were instructed simply to watch television. They were told that they would be asked questions about what they had seen afterward. The viewing lasted about 40 minutes.

Immediately following the viewing, subjects were given, sequentially, the free-recall test, the cued-recall test, and the multiple-choice test.

Table 8.2 Questionnaire Design

Question	Audio–Visual	Immediate–Delayed	Time Period
1	A	I	1
2	A	D	1
3	A	I	2
4	A	D	2
5	A	I	3
6	A	D	3
7	V	I	1
8	V	D	1
9	V	I	2
10	V	D	2
11	V	I	3
12	V	D	3

After finishing the multiple-choice test subjects were thanked and dismissed.

Data Analysis

The free- and cued-recall data were coded independently by two coders. A coding scheme was devised in which the coders read the recall protocol for each commercial and then counted the number of visual ideas and the number of verbal ideas recalled. Visual ideas were defined as any single image recalled from the commercial or any global visual description of the commercial. Verbal ideas were defined as any single thought including names, states, office the candidate was running for, or global audio descriptions. Two training sessions were held to discuss and practice implementation of the coding rules. Final correlations between the two coders ranged from $r = .85$ to $r = .99$.

These visual and verbal recall scores were then analyzed in a mixed model 4 (Order) × 2 (Emotion) × 2 (Audio–Visual) × 4 (Repetitions) ANOVA. Order was the between subjects factor. The four levels of the order factor represent the four orders of presentation of the commercials.

The within-subject factors were emotion, audio–visual, and repetitions. The two levels of the emotion factor were positive and negative emotions. The two levels of the Audio–Visual factor were audio and visual. The four levels of the Repetitions factor represent the four different negative and positive commercials.

The multiple choice data were analyzed with a mixed model 4 (Order) × 2 (Emotion) × 2 (Audio–Visual) × 2 (Immediate–Delayed) × 3 (Time) ANOVA. Again the order factor is the between subjects factor and represents the four orders of presentation.

The within factors are emotion, audio–visual, immediate/delayed, and time. The levels of the emotion and audio–visual factors are the same as for the free-recall analysis. The levels of the immediate–delayed factor are immediate (information occurring at the same point in time as a scene change) and delayed (information occurring removed in time from a scene change). The levels of the time factor are the three 10-second periods making up each 30-second commercial, called beginning, middle, and end.

RESULTS

Hypothesis 1

This hypothesis predicted that negative commercials would be remembered better than positive commercials. The main effect for emotion was significant, and in the predicted direction, in both the free-recall and multiple-choice analyses.

The result of the free-recall analysis is shown in Fig. 8.1. More information is remembered from the negative ads than is remembered from the positive ads $[F(1,65) = 6.74, p < .012]$.

The multiple-choice results are shown in Fig. 8.2. In this case, the negative commercials generate significantly more accurate memory than the positive commercials $[F(1,65) = 13.96, p < .0004]$.

Hypothesis 2

This hypothesis predicted an interaction between emotion and audio–visual memory. The interaction was significant in both the multiple-choice and the free-recall analysis.

The results of the multiple-choice analysis $[F(1,65) = 53.46, p < .0001]$ are shown in Fig. 8.3. As was predicted and has been found previously (Lang & Friestad, 1987), visual memory was better for negative commercials than for positive commercials. However, the expected difference between negative and positive commercials for audio (verbal) memory again did not appear.

The same pattern of results appeared in the free-recall analysis. The emotion × audio–visual interaction was significant $[F(1,65) = 14.87, p < .003]$ and is shown in Fig. 8.4.

Hypothesis 3

This hypothesis predicted that information removed in time from a scene change or commercial onset would be better remembered than

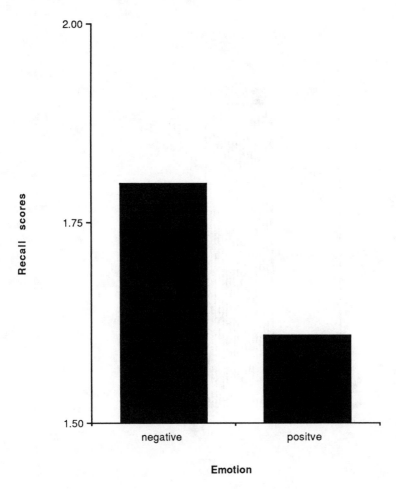

FIGURE 8.1. Main effect of emotion-free recall.

information that occurred simultaneously with the scene change or commercial onset. This hypothesis was supported [$F(1,65) = 23.7, p < .0001$] and is shown in Fig. 8.5.

Hypothesis 4

This hypothesis predicted an interaction between emotion and the immediate–delayed factor. The interaction was significant [$F(1,65) = 6.2, p < .0154$] and is shown in Fig. 8.6. As predicted, the scene changes and commercial onsets damage memory more during negative commercials than they do during positive commercials.

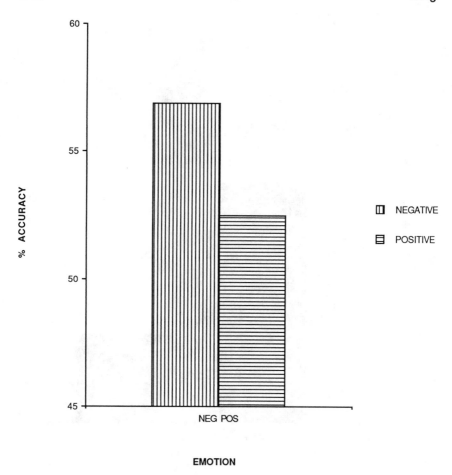

FIGURE 8.2. Main effect for emotion—multiple choice.

Hypothesis 5

This hypothesis predicted an interaction between the immediate/ delayed factor and the audio–visual factor. The interaction was significant [$F(1,65) = 5.68, p < .02$] and is shown in Fig. 8.7. As predicted there is more interference from the scene changes and commercial onsets with visual memory than there is with audio memory.

Hypothesis 6

This hypothesis predicted that memory would improve over the time course of the commercial. The main effect for time was significant

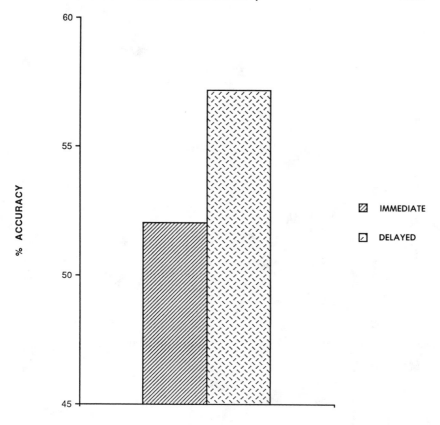

FIGURE 8.3.   Emotion ¼ audio–video interaction.

$[F(1,65) = 5.7, p < .0043]$ and is shown in Fig. 8.8. Although the prediction was that memory would improve linearally over the course of the commercial, what this figure shows is a marked superiority for memory of the information in the middle of the commercial.

Hypothesis 7

This hypothesis predicted that all of the emotional effects would be magnified by the passage of time. Hence, the prediction was for significant emotion × time, emotion × audio–visual × time, and

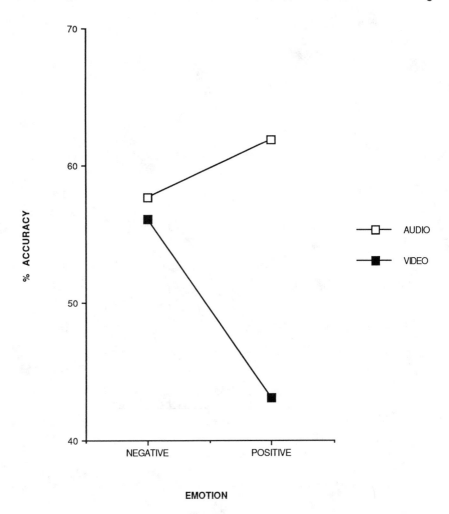

FIGURE 8.4. Emotion ¼ A/V interaction—free recall.

emotion × immediate–delayed × time interactions. The emotion × time interaction and the emotion × audio–visual × time interaction were not significant.

The emotion × immediate–delayed × time interaction [$F(1,65)$ = 7.43, $p < .0009$] is shown in Fig. 8.9. The prediction is that the effects of the emotion should be magnified over time. Although this is partially true for the positive emotions, the reverse appears to be the case for the negative emotions.

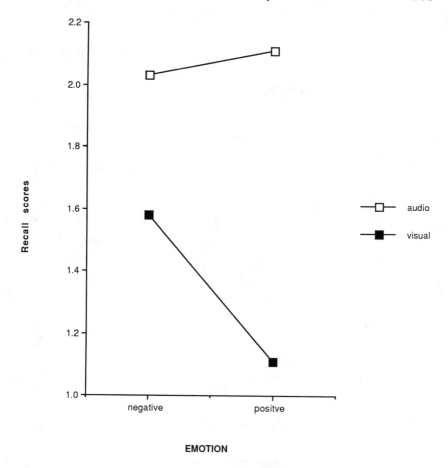

FIGURE 8.5.   Main effect imed–delayed.

DISCUSSION

Implications for Future Research

The results of the study provide several insights into how we process emotional political advertisements, and indeed, how we process emotional television.

First, this study clearly replicates several previous findings. As has been demonstrated frequently (Bradley et al., in preparation); Friestad & Thorson, 1985; Reeves, Newhagen et al., 1989; Shapiro & Rieger, 1989), this study shows better memory for negative emotional stimuli (in this case political advertisements) than for positive emotional stimuli.

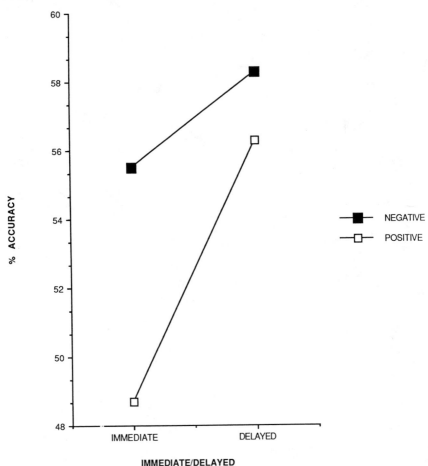

FIGURE 8.6.   Emotion ¼ Immediate–delayed interaction.

Second, this study replicates the finding of Lang and Friestad (1987) of greater visual memory for negative commercials than for positive commercials. Also, as was found in that study, there is very little evidence for the prediction that positive emotion improves verbal memory.

It is interesting to note that for these first two findings, the results were identical for both the free-recall and the multiple-choice data providing some construct validity for the visual and audio memory measures (see Fig. 8.1, 8.2, 8.4, and 8.5).

Third, this study adds more information to the debate over whether formal features (such as scene changes and commercial onsets) aid

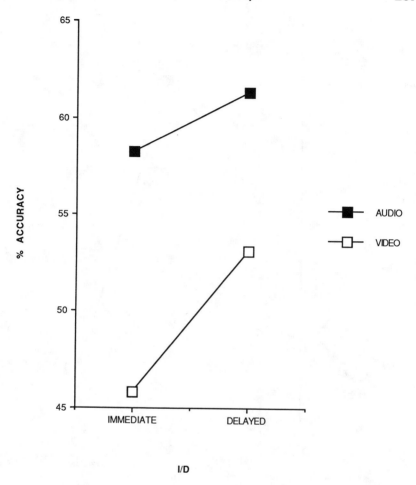

FIGURE 8.7. Audio–video ¼ Immediate–delayed interaction.

memory for the information in the commercial by drawing attention to it through the mechanism of an orienting response, or damage memory for the information in the commercial by interrupting ongoing processing, also through the mechanism of an orienting response.

The significant main effect for the immediate–delayed factor supports the position that there is at least some damage associated with a formal feature. However, it also suggests that memory for information following the formal feature, but not occurring simultaneously with it, may be improved. Future research should test memory for information presented concurrently with the formal feature and at varying lengths of time following the formal feature.

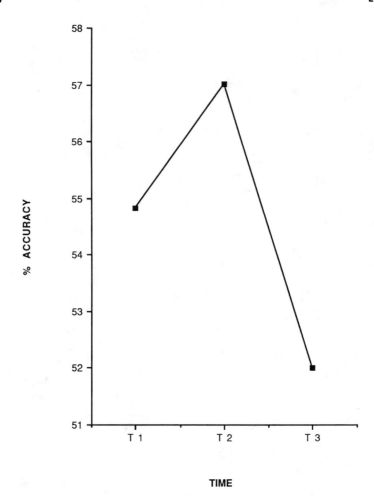

FIGURE 8.8. Main effect time.

Fourth, there is evidence that the effects of the formal feature are to some extent system specific. In other words, this study used visual formal features only and found that they interfered primarily with visual memory, suggesting that the visual system might be somewhat overloaded. The damage to audio memory was much less. Future research should look at the effects of audio formal features on audio and visual memory respectively.

Fifth, the negative effects of the formal features are mitigated during negative emotional commercials, compared to positive emotional commercials. As discussed previously, there are several possible theoretical explanations for this finding.

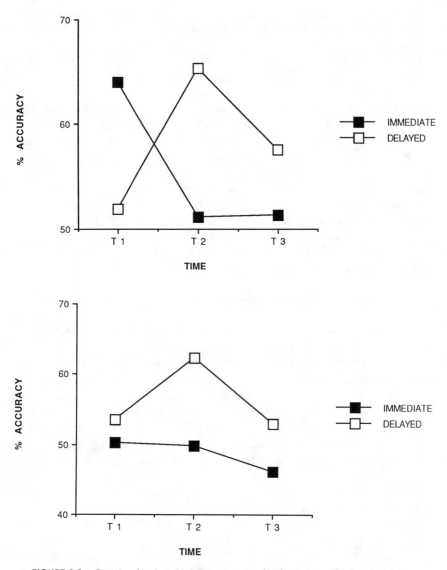

FIGURE 8.9. Emotion ¼ time ¼ I/D interaction (top) negative; (bottom) positive.

One possibility is that positive emotion requires controlled processing resources, whereas negative emotion is automatic. Accordingly, a call for attention (such as a scene change or commercial onset) would increase the controlled processing load and damage memory for positive commercials. The other possibility is that negative commercials are more arousing than positive commercials. From that it would follow that attentional capacity would be greater during negative commercials than during positive commercials and memory would be less damaged. Further research should be designed to decide between these two possibilities. To that end, a measure of arousal, such as heart rate, and a measure of attention capacity, such as secondary task reaction time could be included in the data collection.

Sixth, the main effect for time suggests the interesting possibility that emotion may to some extent nullify the serial position effect. If this finding were further explored and replicated it might suggest that emotion improves memory for commercials by increasing memory for information in the middle of the commercials.

Finally, the interaction with time, although confusing and difficult to interpret, serves to underscore the fact that the processing of television is an ongoing activity. One-shot studies cannot adequately reflect or investigate the processing that occurs during viewing. Greater effort must be made to include time as a factor in research on the cognitive processing of television.

Implications for Political Advertising

In general, this study and other research that approaches learning from the media in an information-processing context does suggest that both structure and content play a role in determining what we remember from television and, in this study, what we remember from a political advertisement. Understanding the complex interaction of content and structure may suggest ways to use aspects of each, such as emotion and scene changes, to ensure better memory for a political advertisement.

For example, the use of emotion, both positive and negative, in political advertisements is a hotly debated issue (Garramone, 1984; Shapiro & Rieger, 1989). In general, the debate has focused on whether voters like or dislike emotional ads, whether they are persuasive, and whether they are informative.

The approach to political advertisements taken in this research suggests a different way to look at emotion in political advertisements. It argues that emotional content not only affects the conscious preferences and thoughts of television viewers but that it also acts to modulate what they remember from a political advertisement. In other words, emotion may actually act to focus attention on certain aspects of the commercial and it may directly affect the way that information is encoded. This study, for example, supports the notion that negative commercials may lead to greater visual memory which suggests that important information be placed in the video portion of the commercial.

Work by Peter Lang and his colleagues (Bradley et al., in preparation) suggests that emotion increases memory for the emotional material itself but not for nonemotional information presented concurrently. This would argue for incorporating the message-to-be-remembered directly in the emotional material rather than having, for example, an emotional scene with the message contained in a nonrelated voice-over.

Still other research (Bradley et al., in preparation; Friestad & Thorson, 1985; Lang, 1989) suggests that emotion affects immediate recall and delayed recall differently. Generally, the effects of emotional valence (whether a commercial is negative or positive) are most apparent immediately after viewing. Delayed recall, however, is clearly better for emotional material than it is for neutral material. This might suggest different strategies for the use of emotion in commercials at different points in the campaign.

Even more striking are the possible implications for the findings on cuts and scene changes presented in this chapter. It is fairly common practice to use structural aspects of television, such as cuts and edits, to maintain visual interest. This research along with other research by Lang and Thorson (1989) argues against this practice. Although it is fairly apparent that the scene change does elicit attention (Lang & Thorson, 1989) that call for attention may actually damage processing and memory for the information being presented concurrently. This suggests that if visual structural aspects of television are used to call attention, care must be made to separate them in time from any audio message that you want viewers to remember.

Of course many of the results reported here are preliminary and not entirely understood, but it seems clear that research on political advertisements from the perspective of how we process television can have many practical implications for the political advertiser and researcher. It may, one day, in conjunction with other theoretical perspectives, help to explain how political advertisements function in the political arena as well as the psychological one.

ACKNOWLEDGMENT

This research partially supported by a grant from the Gannett Foundation.

REFERENCES

Anderson, D. R. (1985). Online cognitive processing of television. In L. F. Alwitt & A. A. Mitchell (Eds.), *Psychological processes and advertising effects: Theory, research, and application* (pp. 177–200). Erlbaum, New Jersey.

Anderson, D. R., & Levin, S. R. (1976). Young children's attention to *Sesame Street*. *Child Development, 47,* 806–811.

Anderson, D. R., & Lorch, E. P. (1983). Looking at television: action or reaction. In J. Bryant & D. R. Anderson (Eds.), *Children's understanding of television* (pp. 1–34). Hillsdale, NJ: Lawrence Erlbaum Associates.

Bradley, M., Petry, M., Greenwald, M., & Lang, P. (in preparation). *Memory for emotional slides.* Gainesville, FL: University of Florida.

Calvert, S. L., Huston, A. C., Watkins, B. A., & Wright, J. C. (1982). The relation between selective attention to television forms and children's comprehension of content. *Child Development, 53,* 601–612.

Davidson, R. J. (1984). Hemispheric asymmetry and emotion. In K. Scherer & P. Ekman (Eds.), *Approaches to emotion* (pp. 39–59). Hillsdale, NJ: Lawrence Erlbaum Associates.

Dimmond, S., Farrington, L., & Johnson, P. (1976). Differing emotional response from right and left hemispheres. *Nature, 261,* 690–692.

Friestad, M., & Thorson, E. T. (1985, May). *Effects of four types of emotion-eliciting TV messages on memory and judgment.* Paper presented at the International Communication Association Annual Meeting, Honolulu, HI.

Garramone, G. (1984). Voter responses to negative political ads. *Journalism Quarterly, 61*(2), 250–259.

Greenwald, M., Cook, E., & Lang, P. (in preparation). *Affective judgment and psychophysiological response: Dimensional covariation in the evaluation of pictorial stimuli.*

Izard, C., Kagan, J., & Zajonc, R. (1984). *Emotions, cognition, and behavior.* Cambridge: Cambridge University Press.

Kahneman, D. (1973). *Attention and effort.* Englewood Cliffs, NJ: Prentice-Hall.

Lang, A. (1989, May). *The effects of over-time emotion on visual and verbal memory for television messages.* Paper presented to the Information Systems Division of the International Communication Association, San Francisco, CA.

Lang, A., & Friestad, M. (1987, May). *Differences in memory for emotional television messages and hemispheric specialization.* Paper presented to the International Communications Association, Montreal, Canada.

Lang, A., & Thorson, E. (1989). *The effects of television videographics and lecture familiarity on adult cardiac orienting responses and memory.* Paper presented to the Information Systems Division of the International Communication Association, San Francisco, CA.

Lang, A. (1990). Involuntary attention and physiological arousal evoked by structural features and mild emotion in TV commercials. *Communication Research, 17,* 3, pp. 275–299.

Ohman, A. (1977). The orientation response, attention and learning: An information-processing perspective. In H. D. Kimmel, E. H. Van Olst, & J. F. Orlebeke (Eds.), *The orientation reflex in humans* (pp. 443–472). Hillsdale, NJ: Lawrence Erlbaum Associates.

Reeves, B., & Lang, A. (1986, May). *Emotional television scenes and hemispheric specialization.* Paper presented to the International Communication Association. Chicago, IL.

Reeves, B., Lang, A., Thorson, E., & Rothschild, M. (1989). Emotional television scenes and hemispheric specialization. *Human Communication Research, 15*(4), 494–508.

Reeves, B., Newhagen, J., Mailbach, E., Basil, M., & Kurz, K. (1989). *Negative and positive television messages: Effects of message type and message context on attention and memory.* Paper presented to the Mass Communication division of the International Communication Association, San Francisco, CA.

Reeves, B., Thorson, E., Rothschild, M., McDonald, D., Hirsch, J., & Goldstein, R. (1985). Attention to television: Intrastimulus effects of movement and scene changes on alpha variation over time. International Journal of Neuroscience, 25, pp. 241–255.

Rothschild, M., Thorson, E., Hirsch, J., Goldstein, R., & Reeves, B. (1983). EEG activity and the processing of television commercials. Graduate School of Business.

Shapiro, M., & Rieger, R. (1989, 000). *Comparing positive and negative political advertising*. Paper presented to the political advertising division of the International Communication Association, San Francisco, CA.

Scherer, K., & Ekman, P. (1984). *Approaches to emotion*. Hillsdale, NJ: Lawrence Erlbaum Associates.

Schneider, W., Dumais, S., & Shiffrin, R. (1984). Automatic and Control Processing and Attention. In R. Parasuraman (Ed.), *Varieties of attention* (pp. 1–27). New York: Academic Press.

Thorson, E. (1990). Processing television commercials. In Brenda Dervin, Lawrence Grossberg, & Ellen Wartella, Eds. *Paradigm dialogues in communication, Vol. II: Exemplars*. Newbury Pk, CA: Sage.

Thorson, E., & Lang, A. (1988, May). *The effects of videographic complexity on memory for televised information*. Paper presented to the International Communication Association, New Orleans, LA.

9

Positive and Negative Political Advertising: Effectiveness of Ads and Perceptions of Candidates

Michael Basil
Caroline Schooler
Byron Reeves
Stanford University

Political candidates attach increasing importance to negative television advertising. In recent campaigns, the number of negative ads has increased dramatically (Merritt, 1984). During the 1988 presidential campaign, the popular press asserted that negative political advertising had reached an all-time high (McLeod, 1989; Shapiro & White, 1988; Stengel, 1988; Taylor & Broder, 1988). The press also felt that Dukakis' failure to respond to Bush's attacks in the 1988 presidential campaign affected the election (Beatty, 1988; Colford, 1988). That is, negative ads appeared to tip the balance in the election.

The increase in negative ads is partially attributable to proprietary research that shows negative messages have powerful effects (Sabato, 1981). Candidates hope that attacking ads will lead voters to dislike or fear opponents, and consequently, negative ads are seen as more damaging to the attacked candidate than the attacker (Kaid & Boydston, 1987). This may be a good political strategy because feelings about candidates have been shown to be important determinants of voting decisions (Abelson, Kinder, Peters, & Fiske, 1982; Brody & Page, 1973; Foti & Lord, 1982; Lau, 1986; Markus & Converse, 1979).

An important factor in political advertising is the context or sequencing of advertisements. Two important decisions that political strategists face are whether to initiate attacks, and whether to respond to attacks from other candidates. Another context effect is whether running a collection of negative ads provides a cumulative advantage or a backlash against the candidate who sponsors them.

Before investigating whether the effects of negative and positive advertising are different, it is important to distinguish the ways in which advertising effects are measured. Research suggests that advertisements may have different effects for different dependent variables (Batra & Ray, 1985; Beattie & Mitchell, 1985). Previous studies have found that messages may differentially affect memory, judgment, and behavior (Hastie & Park, 1986; McGuire, 1964; Roberts & Maccoby, 1974). Studying these outcomes independently does not allow the effects on one variable to be related to other variables of interest. When variables are studied simultaneously, however, one can explore how ads may be well remembered, yet have no real influence on behavior.

Consumer research suggests that a distinction should be made between effects attributable to responses to an ad, and those caused by evaluations of the product. Research that has separated these attitudes finds different effects (Batra & Ray, 1985; Lutz, 1985; Lutz, MacKenzie, & Belch, 1983; Shrimp, 1981; Srull, 1983). Advertisements have been found to affect both the formation of product attribute beliefs, and attitudes toward the advertisements. Both of these components can then affect brand attitudes (Mitchell, 1986).

Studies of political advertising also examine effects in at least two domains: memory for ads and attitudes toward candidates. Studies focusing on ads often find negative ads to be effective (Merritt, 1984; Newhagen & Reeves, this volume); that is, well remembered. However, studies of candidate perception find negative ads to be counterproductive (Garramone, 1984; Shapiro & Rieger, 1989); that is, the ads harm the attacking candidate. The conflict may arise from the fact that negative advertisements are rated as "effective" because the *message* itself is remembered, but "ineffective" because the *candidate* sponsoring the ad is harmed. Thus, the distinction between memory for ads and evaluation of candidates offers an explanation as to why research does not agree on the general effectiveness of negative political advertising.

This chapter examines the effects of positive and negative political advertising on both criteria: influence of ads and perceptions of candidates. The first part of the chapter concentrates on reactions to political advertisements, whereas the second part examines perceptions of candidates. The effects of negative and positive political commercials were measured in a laboratory experiment using two unfamiliar campaigns. There were five considerations in the choice of design. First, the use of unfamiliar campaigns removed the influence of prior knowledge of the candidates. Although previous knowledge would not necessarily change ad effects, it would probably weaken them, and make them less observable. Second, an experiment ensured that all people, regardless of motivation, received the same information. Because equal information does not occur naturally, this was an opportunity to hold information constant, but let involvement vary naturally. Third, there was control over frequency of exposure; a necessary condition to study ad memorability. Fourth, the design allowed measurement of backlash effects without the confounding influence of election results. Backlash effects, or unfavorable perceptions of candidates who sponsor negative ads, seem especially likely for people who support losing candidates. Supporters of winning candidates are probably less likely to be bothered by negative ads. Finally, demonstrating backlash effects in a lab setting would suggest that backlash is a real and powerful phenomenon, not an artifact of a particular research method.

Although experiments have tested differences between positive and negative advertising, stimuli created especially for the research were used (Beattie & Mitchell, 1985; Shapiro & Rieger, 1989). These ads create problems because limited budgets do not allow for the quality of production that occurs in real ads, and therefore the created ads may appear artificial. In addition these studies often make use of a single ad per candidate or product (e.g., Shapiro & Rieger, 1989). This not only makes generalizations about ads difficult, but further entangles the ad and product domains.

EFFECTIVENESS OF ADS: INFLUENCE AND RECALL

The first part of this discussion focuses on reactions to individual ads, specifically how the emotional valence of single ads, and the valence of preceding ads affects influence ("leaning" toward candidates) and recall of the ads themselves.

Emotional Valence

Researchers have classified *positive* advertising as bolstering messages, and *negative* ads as attack or refutation messages (Kaid & Davidson, 1986). Positive ads promote a candidate's favorable personal attributes or issue positions. Negative advertising identifies the opponent and explicitly refers to either the candidate's general image or his or her specific policies with the goal of creating a negative impression (Merritt, 1984). Attack ads call attention to failings in the opponent's character or issue positions (Pfau & Burgoon, 1988). Refutation ads, also called rebuttal ads, charge as false the claims of another commercial (Garramone, 1985a). Although refutation ads could be neutral in tone, in practice they are almost always negative.

Four studies demonstrate better memory for negative than for positive television commercials (Lang & Friestad, 1987; Newhagen & Reeves, this volume; Reeves, Newhagen, Maibach, Basil, & Kurz, 1989; Thorson & Friestad, 1985). Although not the explanation usually offered, these differences may exist because negative television messages elicit different physiological changes and greater arousal (Lang, 1985). Responses to potentially dangerous stimuli may be "hard-wired" in the brain, bypassing the elaborate processing associated with higher order mental activities (Zajonc, 1984). According to Lang (1985), this makes sense from an evolutionary perspective since it is more important for survival to know when to withdraw or flee than it is to know when to approach.

In fact, research indicates that people may automatically discriminate, and use more quickly, information that is uncertain or negative, compared with positive information (Reeves, Thorson, & Schleuder, 1986). Messages with negative emotion have also been shown to elicit more attention, and they are better recognized (Reeves et al., 1989). Furthermore, negative stimuli have been found to enhance performance because of greater arousal (Lang, 1985). However, actual behavior based on negative information may depend on conscious thought about appropriateness, necessity, or other constraints (Reeves et al., 1989).

Context Effects

Research usually focuses on how the valence of the advertisements themselves (positive vs. negative) predicts influence and memorability. One shortcoming of this research is that the stimulus ads are often imbedded in typical television programs and advertising, most of which is positive (Kennedy, 1971; Soldow & Principe, 1981). When the valence of the surrounding material is manipulated, however, an interaction between message valence and context valence emerges (Reeves et al., 1989). Therefore, this study examined how message sequences that present similar or contrasting valences affect peoples' perceptions of political candidates.

Two theories make partially conflicting predictions about the effects of ad context and order. Theories of semantic networks and spreading activation have led to a *mood congruency* prediction (Bower, 1981): People will attend to and remember more from an emotional message if the tone of the incoming message agrees with their current mood. This is because stimuli that match an individual's current emotions are thought to receive greater attention and processing effort (Srull, 1984). Mood congruency suggests the following hypothesis:

Hypothesis 1a: Advertisements will be better remembered when their valence agrees with that of the surrounding context.

A single political study showed an effect similar to mood congruency: heightened effects for messages that elicit similar emotions in a sequence (Roseman, Abelson, & Ewing, 1986). In these cases, a positive ad, within a series of positive ads, should have a stronger effect than if it were surrounded by negative ads. Conversely, a negative ad should be more effective within a sequence of negative ads. The dependent variable here is influence rather than memory, but the explanation is similar. The hypothesis is as follows:

Hypothesis 1b: Advertisements will be more influential when their valence agrees with the surrounding context.

Assimilation-contrast theory (Sherif & Hovland, 1961) makes an opposite prediction with regard to the effects of message context on ad influence. This theory posits that contextual effects change the meaning of reward and value for the individual. Experiments on person perception found that the existence of a prior negative state increased the response to a positive statement due to contrast (Aronson & Linder, 1965; Wyer & Carlston, 1979). After a negative message, a positive statement will be evaluated more positively, and may have a more powerful effect than the same statement preceded by another positive message. Similarly, a negative message following a positive statement will appear more negative than the second of two negative statements. Assimilation-contrast effects have also been demonstrated using warm and humorous ads for consumer products (Aaker, Stayman, & Hagerty, 1986). For context effects of negative and positive political ads, the following hypothesis is suggested:

Hypothesis 2a: Advertisements will be more influential when their valence contrasts with that of prior messages.

Contrast effects also seem to render messages more memorable, both for recall (Srull, 1983) and for recognition (Reeves et al., 1989). This leads to the next hypothesis:

Hypothesis 2b: Ads will be better remembered when their valence contrasts with the surrounding context.

Position Effects

Examination of message order has demonstrated that relative location within a sequence will moderate the effect of a message (McGuire, 1985). Asch (1952) determined that early items have more powerful effects on impression formation than do later items. Furthermore, when the information presented is inconsistent, early items are more influential (Chalmers, 1969; Wyer & Schwartz, 1969). Research suggests that early messages in a competitive persuasive campaign are more powerful because they are viewed with less suspicion (Lana, 1964; Schultz, 1963), and they form the guidelines against which later messages are judged (Asch, 1956; Sherif, 1936). It appears that primacy may dominate impression formation, leading to Hypothesis 3a:

Hypothesis 3a: Early messages will be more influential on candidate preference than later messages.

For memory, both primacy and recency effects operate. Information presented at the beginning and the end of a sequence is remembered better than that presented in the middle (Anderson & Farkas, 1973; Crano, 1977; Hovland, 1951; Miller & Campbell, 1959; Murdock, 1962). Memory for early items (primacy) may benefit from additional processing and elaboration (Miller & Campbell, 1959). Improved memory for late items (recency), however, appears to be due to forgetting. Investigations of order effects on recall for television advertisements have found that early ads are remembered best, followed by late ads, whereas those presented in the middle are the most likely to be forgotten (Webb & Ray, 1979). Therefore, according to primacy–recency findings, we suggest Hypothesis 3b:

Hypothesis 3b: Early messages and late messages will be remembered better than those in the middle.

CANDIDATES: LIKING, PERCEIVED STRENGTH, AND VOTE

The second part of the chapter focuses on how positive and negative political ads affect perceptions of candidates. Political candidates have been shown to suffer "backlash effects" for attacking opponents (Garramone, 1984; Shapiro & Rieger, 1989). In other words, negative advertising can evoke negative affect toward the ad sponsor (Garramone, 1984; Merritt, 1984; Pfau & Burgoon, 1988). As explained earlier, backlash effects are usually studied with surveys that use recall as the measure of exposure (Garramone, 1984; Merritt, 1984). However, recall may not accurately reflect exposure because respondents may not remember or be able to report on all the ads they saw during a campaign.

Assimilation-contrast theory, mentioned earlier, suggests that the context of messages influences perceptions of individuals, in this case, political candidates. Experiments on person perception found that a prior negative comment increased the effect of a positive statement, causing subjects to like a person more than when they hear two positive comments in sequence (Aronson & Linder, 1965). Similarly, a negative message following a positive statement will appear more negative than the second of two negative statements (Helson, 1964).

Other research indicates that voters do not like negative campaigns, and that this dislike leads them to evaluate the sponsoring candidates negatively (Garramone, 1984; Merritt, 1984; Shapiro & Rieger, 1989). This suggests the next hypothesis:

Hypothesis 4: Candidates who run positive campaigns will be most liked, candidates who run negative campaigns least liked.

On the other hand, inoculation theory (McGuire, 1964; Roberts & Maccoby, 1974) warns about ignoring counterarguments. This theory speaks directly to preceding refutations, asserting that "it is wise to mention rather than ignore possible counterarguments against one's position since this enhances the individual's resistance to subsequent counterarguments" (McGuire, 1981, p. 49). Research using inoculation theory has also examined rebuttals to attacks in political campaigns. Studies have found that following an attack, rebuttal by the targeted candidate works to foster negative perceptions of the attacker, but does not make audience members more likely to vote for the target (Garramone, 1985a; Pfau & Burgoon, 1988). Thus, it seems that candidates should respond to an opponent's negative advertising, although it is not clear whether such rebuttals help. Based on this evidence, we hypothesize that:

Hypothesis 5: Candidates who do not respond to attacks will be perceived as lower in *strength* than those who respond.

Method

Overview. This experiment examined the influence of ad valence (positive or negative), and surrounding context (positive or negative) on reactions to the candidates portrayed in the messages. Message-domain effects were leaning toward candidates and recall of the ads. Candidate-domain effects were liking, perceived strength, and voting preference.

Subjects. The experiment was run in April and May 1989 with 24 paid participants from the local community in Palo Alto, California. There were 15 women and 9 men between 23 and 72 years of age.

Political party affiliations were 50% Democratic, 33% Republican, and 17% Independent.

Stimuli. Ads were taken from two different 1986 Senatorial campaigns: Breaux versus Moore in Louisiana, and Andrews versus Conrad in North Dakota. Two judges designated ads as positive or negative on two objective criteria—whether the ad named the opponent, and whether the ad attacked the opponent on position, lying, or running an unfair campaign.

These ads were assembled into six different tapes. Each tape contained ads for both "campaigns"—Andrews/Conrad and Breaux/Moore. A campaign consisted of a total of six ads—three for each of the candidates. All three ads for each candidate were the same valence—positive or negative. Ads alternated between the two candidates; the first ad was for Candidate A, the second for Candidate B, the third for Candidate A, and so on. This resulted in all subjects seeing both positive and negative ads, and ads in both positive and negative contexts, although the specific messages varied across subjects. Ads were separated with 5 seconds of blank material (video black). The two campaigns, the order of candidates, and the ads themselves were presented in counterbalanced order in a Latin-square design. In summary, each subject saw 12 of the 24 experimental ads.

Procedure. Subjects were seated in front of a Sony 20-inch television monitor and given a short practice session with the experimental procedure. This consisted of viewing a Dukakis ad from the 1988 U.S. presidential campaign. After the ad, subjects were asked to indicate "Who the ad makes you lean toward." There was a continuous preference scale with Dukakis' name on one end, and Bush's name on the other. They could mark anywhere along the scale. After marking the scale, subjects were shown a 1988 Bush ad and again asked to mark "Who the ad makes you lean toward."

Subjects were then told that one of the two experimental "campaigns" would be next. They were given a new form with the names of the candidates they would be seeing, and they were asked to mark the scale after each ad. The experimenter then started the tape and left the room. In the 5-second breaks between ads, subjects marked the scales according to whom the ad made them favor. After seeing the complete "campaign" (i.e., six ads), the experimenter re-entered the room, and asked subjects to fill out a questionnaire. The questionnaire asked subjects to recall as much as they could about each commercial, and to indicate the order in which they saw them. Subjects were also asked to rate candidates on liking, and perceived strength (9-point scales). The procedure was then repeated for a second "campaign." At the end of the experiment (i.e., two "campaigns"), subjects filled out a form asking for their party affiliation and which candidate they would vote for in the two elections.

Design: Effectiveness of Ads

Message effectiveness was assessed in two ways: ad influence, measured as the candidate people "leaned" toward after each ad; and memory for ads, measured as free recall after each "campaign."

The analysis of the "leaning" measure was broken into two parts: (a) the direction of leaning and (b) the strength of the preference. *Direction* of preference was indicated by which side of the neutral point on the continuous preference scale the subject marked. *Strength* of ad influence was the distance between the subject's mark on the candidate preference scale and the neutral point.

Recall of the ad, the other dependent measure, was measured as a dichotomous variable: The ad was either remembered or not. Ad recall was coded by two coders, one aware of the actual ads that were seen, the other not. The agreement between raters was 90%, resolved in favor of the former.

The three independent variables were: valence of the ad (positive, negative); valence of the preceding ad (positive, negative); and location of ad (beginning, middle, end). In addition, two covariates were used: candidate's party (Democratic, Republican); and subject's party (Democratic, Independent, Republican).

Design: Perceptions of Candidates

During the experiment, data were also gathered on subjects' perceptions of the *candidates* after watching an entire six-ad "campaign." Instead of measuring influence and recall for individual ads, the effects of different campaigns on subjects' evaluations of the four *candidates* were assessed. Each subject saw two "campaigns," each comprised of six ads. Three of these ads were for each candidate. All of one candidates' ads were of the same valence. That is, a candidate could present a series of either positive or negative ads while his or her opponent presented a series of either positive or negative ads. Ads were edited together and presented on videotape. Campaigns, candidates, and the ads within each campaign were presented in a counterbalanced order.

Procedure.   After each "campaign" was over, the experimenter entered the room and gave subjects a questionnaire that asked their perceptions of each candidate. This included two separate 9-point rating scales: the first was, "How much do you like this candidate?" (NOT AT ALL to VERY MUCH) and the second, "How effective do you think this candidate would be as a leader?" (NOT STRONG to VERY STRONG). This procedure was then repeated for the second campaign.

Three *dependent measures* were used to assess advertising effects on candidate perception and potential backlash effects: *liking*, perceived *strength* of candidates, and a simulated *vote*.

Independent variables measured across the four candidates were: valence of the candidate's sequence of ads (positive, negative); valence of the opponent's sequence of ads (positive, negative). The valence judgments were the same ones used for the individual ads. Again, candidate's party (Democratic, Republican) and subject's party (Democratic, Independent, Republican) were used as covariates.

Results

Effectiveness of Ads

For *direction* of preference, a dichotomous variable, a logistic regression was performed. This is a probability analysis of which candidate an ad makes subjects favor. The results show that the ads caused viewers to support the sponsoring candidate ($\beta = .834$, $df = 238$, $p < .001$), regardless of whether these ads were negative or positive. Valence of the opponent's ads did not affect the direction of preference. This finding suggests that ad valence alone did not determine whom subjects leaned toward.

There were no significant main effects of ad valence or context valence on strength of preference. There was, however, an interaction between ad valence and preceeding valence [$F(1,238) = 4.5, p < .05$]. Positive ads were more effective when preceded by negative ads. Negative ads were equally effective when preceded by negative or positive ads. This effect is shown in Fig. 9.1, and partially supports Hypothesis 1b—mood congruency theory.

Position of the ad was not significantly related to strength or direction of candidate preference, so primacy–recency effects were not found as predicted in Hypothesis 3a.

Recall. A logistic regression analysis indicated that positive ads were recalled better ($\beta = .434$, $df = 219$, $p < .05$). There was also an interaction between ad valence and context ($\beta = -1.81$, $df = 219, p < .01$). Recall for ads in a negative context showed contrast effects, but all ads were recalled equally well when shown in a positive context. This

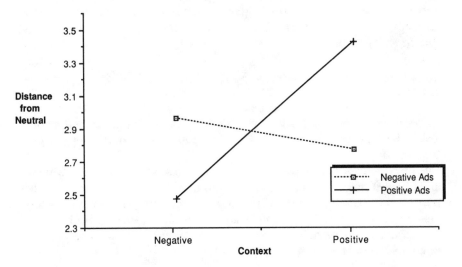

FIGURE 9.1.   Ad influence—distance from neutral.

demonstrates partial support for assimilation-contrast effects on recall (Hypothesis 2b). These effects are shown in Fig. 9.2.

Later ads in the sequence were remembered better than middle ads ($\beta = .299$, $df = 219$, $p < .05$). However, early ads were not remembered better than middle ads. Overall, 75% of late ads were remembered, versus 65% of early ads and 63% of middle ads. This finding conflicts

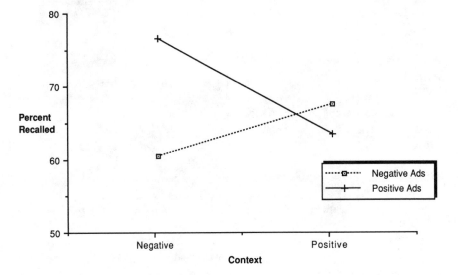

FIGURE 9.2.   Ad recall—percent correct.

with Hypothesis 3b, which predicted that early and late ads would be remembered better than ads in the middle of the sequence. The effect is shown in Fig. 9.3.

Perceptions of Candidates

Candidates who presented positive ads were *liked* more than those who presented negative ads (Fig. 9.4), but this only approached significance [$F(1,119) = 2.76, p < .10$]. Consequently, Hypothesis 4 is not supported.

However, candidates whose *opponents* presented positive ads were liked better than candidates whose opponents presented negative ads [$F(1,119) = 6.2, p < .05$]. Although not predicted, these data suggest that candidates who run negative ads "turn voters off" to both candidates. Subjects were no more likely to favor candidates who responded to attacks than those who did not respond.

Strength. Candidates were perceived as stronger when they presented positive ads [$F(1,101) = 10.2, p < .01$] and when their opponents presented positive ads [$F(1,101) = 6.36, p < .05$] (see Fig. 9.5). As predicted, candidates who responded to attacks were perceived as stron-

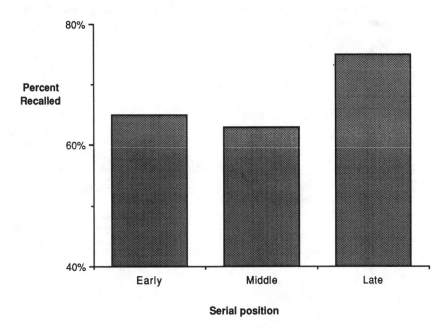

FIGURE 9.3. Ad recall by serial position.

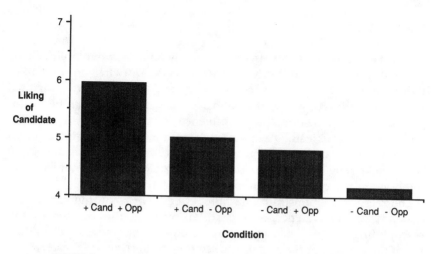

FIGURE 9.4. Candidate liking by valence of own and opponents' ads.

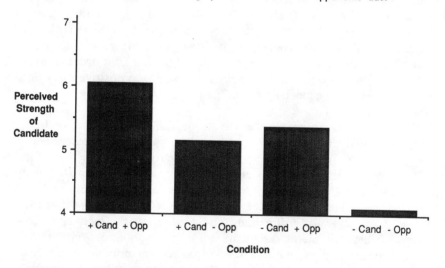

FIGURE 9.5. Candidate perceived strength by valence of own and opponents' ads.

ger than those who did not respond, but this contrast only approached significance (Tukey's $p < .10$), so Hypothesis 5 is not supported.

Vote was studied using a logistic regression to determine whether it was affected by valence of the candidate's ads or valence of opponent's ads. No differences were found. However, vote was affected by candidate liking and perceived strength. Subjects were most likely to vote for the candidate whom they liked the most ($\beta = .673$, $df = 41$, $p < .01$). Perceptions of how strong the candidates would be as leaders only approached significance in determining vote ($\beta = .522$, $df = 41$, $p < .10$).

CONCLUSIONS

These data show that the effects of negative and positive political ads differ depending on the criterion for effects. Drawing on models of "attitude-toward-the-ad" in consumer research, the effects of individual messages and perceptions of candidates across messages can be distinguished. These two domains of influence led to five definitions of ad effectiveness: (a) "leaning" toward a candidate based on a single ad; (b) recall of an ad; (c) liking for a candidate after seeing a "campaign;" (d) perceived strength of a candidate after seeing a "campaign;" and (e) vote intention at the end of a "campaign."

Our results demonstrate that the effectiveness of individual ads depends on the valence of the ads as well as the valence of the surrounding ads. Ads had more impact on leaning toward a candidate when the valence of the ad was the same as the surrounding material. In this case, the match between an ad's valence and surrounding material make the ad *influential*. This finding is in partial accord with spreading activation theories, such as the mood congruency effect, that posit greater attention and processing effort for messages agreeing with an individual's current mood. These results suggest that in order to maximize influence, it is preferable to run positive ads in positive campaigns and contexts, and especially to run negative ads in negative campaigns and contexts.

The results for memory, however, indicate that ads were better *recalled* when they contrasted with the surrounding context. Specifically, this occurred most markedly in negative contexts. Therefore, assimilation-contrast effects seems to partially determine an ad's memorability. Why the context effect was larger in negative contexts than positive is not clear. But contexts that promote recall of ads differ from those that make ads influential. The finding that effectiveness and memorability are distinct concurs with Thorson and Wells' (1987) conclusion that presentations rendering ads memorable differ from presentations enhancing purchase intention. In a political campaign, however, ad influence is probably more important than memory for ads. The candidate is trying to persuade voters, not enhance memory, and consequently, placing ads in congruent contexts may be more effective. Because most television programming and advertising is positive, using positive ads would ensure similar valence with surrounding material.

These results suggest that message valence, independent of context, influences candidate *liking*. Message valence also affected the perceived *strength* of candidates. Overall, positive ads were more effective in promoting candidate liking, and leading people to think a candidate would be a strong leader. People disliked candidates whether they or their opponent presented negative ads. Negative campaigns for either candidate creates negative perceptions of *both* candidates in a race. These findings were in accord with results reported by Shapiro and Rieger (1989), and provide a further demonstration of backlash effects (Garramone, 1984; Merritt, 1984).

Because vote intention was related to liking, it appears that negative ads may indeed alienate voters. This may have important implications for voting. Voter turnout in 1988 was the lowest since 1964 when the federal government began surveying voters (McLeod, 1989). Commentary in the popular press has implicated the highly negative advertising that characterized the 1988 campaign as a cause of low turnout (McLeod, 1989). Many formal models of the electoral process state that a cause of nonvoting is disgust with the alternatives prorfered by the parties (Converse, 1966). Research has determined that "while neither indifference nor alienation is characteristic of the American public, when they are present they affect political participation" (Brody & Page, 1973, p. 7). Under theories of democratic policymaking, nonvoting has serious consequences for social choice to the extent that segments of the population are alienated from the candidates and do not vote.

In conclusion, the differences observed across these five dependent variables demonstrates that a determination of ad effectiveness depends on where you look. The separation of attitudes-toward-ads and attitudes-toward-candidates was important in this study. People, even those who are not highly involved with a political campaign, make such differentiations. Research should follow suit. As the number of negative ads grows, questions regarding the strategy of "going negative" become increasingly germane.

ACKNOWLEDGMENTS

Thanks to Steve Chaffee, Ed Maibach, and Mike Shapiro for their time, interest, and insight on earlier drafts, and to Frank Biocca for his patience.

REFERENCES

Aaker, D. A., Staymen, D. M., & Hagerty, M. R. (1986). Warmth in advertising: Measurement, impact, and sequence effects. *Journal of Consumer Research, 12,* 365–381.

Abelson, R. P., Kinder, D. R., Peters, M. D., & Fiske, S. T. (1982). Affective and semantic components in political person perception. *Journal of Personality and Social Psychology, 4,* 619–630.

Anderson, N. H., & Farkas, A. J. (1973). New light on order effects in attitude change. *Journal of Personality and Social Psychology, 28,* 88–93.

Aronson, E., & Linder, D. (1965). Gain and loss of self esteem as determinants of interpersonal attractiveness. *Journal of Experimental Social Psychology, 1,* 156–171.

Asch, S. E. (1952). *Social psychology*. Englewood Cliffs, NJ: Prentice-Hall.

Asch, S. E. (1956). Studies of independence and conformity: A minority of one against a unanimous majority. *Psychological Monographs, 70* (9, Whole No. 416).

Batra, R., & Ray, M. L. (1985). How advertising works at contact. In L. F. Alwitt & A. A. Mitchell (Eds.), *Psychological processes and advertising effects* (pp. 13–43). Hillsdale, NJ: Lawrence Erlbaum Associates.

Beattie, A., & Mitchell, A. (1985). The relationship between advertising recall and persuasion: An experimental investigation. In L. Alwitt & A. Mitchell (Eds.), *Psychological processes and advertising effects theory, research, and applications* (pp. 129–155). Hillsdale, NJ: Lawrence Erlbaum Associates.

Beatty, J. (1988, November 2). Dukakis agonizes: The can-do candidate comes out fighting. *Los Angeles Times,* Sect. II, Col 1, p. 17.

Bower, G. (1981). Mood and memory. *American Psychologist, 74,* 51–61.

Brody, R., & Page, B. (1973). Indifference, alienation and rational decisions: The effects of candidate evaluations on turnout and the vote. *Public Choice, 15,* 1–17.

Chalmers, D. K. (1969). Meanings, impressions, and attitudes: A model for the evaluation process. *Psychological Review, 76,* 450–460.

Colford, S. W. (1988). Campaign flak flies: Polls ads have negative charge. *Advertising Age, 59,* 4.

Converse, P. E. (1966). The concept of the normal vote. In A. Campbell, P. E. Converse, W. E. Miller, & D. E. Stokes, (Eds.), *Elections and the political order* (pp. 9–39). New York: Wiley.

Crano, W. D. (1977). Primacy versus recency in retention of information and opinion change. *Journal of Social Psychology, 101,* 87–96.

Foti, R. S., & Lord, R. (1982). Effects of leadership labels and prototypes on perceptions of political leaders. *Journal of Applied Psychology, 67,* 326–333.

Garramone, G. M. (1984). Voter responses to negative political ads: Clarifying sponsor effects. *Journalism Quarterly, 61,* 250–259.

Garramone, G. M. (1985a). Effects of negative political advertising: The role of sponsors and rebuttal. *Journal of Broadcasting and Electronic Media, 29,* 147–159.

Garramone, G. M. (1985b). Candidate image formation: The role of information processing. In L. L. Kaid, D. Nimmo, & K. R. Sanders (Eds.), *New perspectives on political advertising* (pp. 237–247). Carbondale, IL: Southern Illinois Press.

Hastie, R., & Park, B. (1986). The relationship between memory and judgement depends on whether the judgement task is memory-based or on-line. *Psychological Review, 93,* 258–268.

Helson, H. (1964). Current trends and issues in adaptation-level theory. *American Psychologist, 19,* 26–38.

Hovland, C. I. (1951). Human learning and retention. In S. S. Stevens (Ed.), *Handbook of experimental psychology* (pp. 619–659). New York: Academic Press.

Hovland, C. I. (1957). *The order of presentation in persuasion.* New Haven, CT: Yale University Press.

Kaid, L. L., & Boydston, J. (1987). An experimental study of the effectiveness of negative political advertisements. *Communication Quarterly, 35,* 193–201.

Kaid, L. L., & Davidson, D. K. (1986). Elements of videostyle: Candidate presentation through television advertising. In L. L. Kaid, D. Nimmo, & K. R. Sanders (Eds.), *New perspectives on political advertising* (pp. 184–209). Carbondale, IL: Southern Illinois University Press.

Kennedy, J. R. (1971). How program environment affects TV commercials. *Journal of Advertising Research, 11,* 33–38.

Lana, R. E. (1964). Existing familiarity and order of presentation of persuasive communications. *Psychological Reports, 15,* 607–610.

Lang, P. J. (1985). The cognitive psychophysiology of emotion: Fear and anxiety. In R. S. Rosenzweig & L. W. Porter (Eds.), *Annual Review of Psychology, 37,* 565–610.

Lang, A. (1989, May). *Effects on memory of emotion over-time within TV messages on visual and verbal memory.* Paper presented at the annual meeting of the International Communication Association, San Francisco.

Lang, A., & Friestad, M. (1987, May). *Hemispheric specialization and memory for emotional television messages.* Paper presented at the annual meeting of the International Communication Association, Montreal, Canada.

Lau, R. R. (1986). Political schemata, candidate evaluations and voting behavior. In R. R. Lau & D. Sears (Eds.), *Political cognition* (pp. 95–126). Hillsdale, NJ: Lawrence Erlbaum Associates.

Lutz, R. J. (1985). Affective and cognitive antecedents of attitude toward the ad: A conceptual framework. In L. F. Alwitt & A. A. Mitchell (Eds.), *Psychological processes and advertising effects* (pp. 85–114). Hillsdale, NJ: Lawrence Erlbaum Associates.

Lutz, R. J., MacKenzie, S. B., & Belch, G. E. (1983). Attitude toward the ad as a mediator of advertising effectiveness: Determinants and consequences. In R. M. Bagozzi & A. M. Tybout (Eds.), *Advances in consumer research* (Vol. 10, pp. 532–539). Ann Arbor, MI: Association for Consumer Research.

Markus, G. B., & Converse, P. E. (1979). A dynamic simultaneous equation model of electoral choice. *American Political Science Review, 73,* 1055–1070.

McLeod, R. G. (1989, March 8). Fewer Americans are voting. *San Francisco Chronicle,* p. A 16.

McGuire, W. J. (1964). Inducing resistance to persuasion: Some contemporary approaches. In L. Berkowitz (Ed.), *Advances in Experimental Social Psychology* (Vol., pp. 191–229). New York: Academic Press.

McGuire, W. J. (1981). Theoretical foundations of campaigns. In R. Rice & W. Paisley (Eds.), *Public communication campaigns* (pp. 67–83). Beverly Hills, CA: Sage.

McGuire, W. J. (1985). Inducing resistance to persuasion: Some contemporary approaches. In E. Aronson & L. Berkowitz (Eds.), *Handbook of social psychology* (Vol. 1, pp. 233–346). New York: Random House.

Merritt, S. (1984). Negative political advertising: Some empirical findings. *Journal of Advertising, 13,* 27–38.

Miller, N., & Campbell, D. T. (1959). Recency and primacy in persuasion as a function of the timing of speeches and measurement. *Journal of Abnormal Social Psychology, 59,* 1–9.

Mitchell, A. A. (1986). The effect of verbal and visual components of advertisements on brand attitudes and attitude toward the advertisement. *Journal of Consumer Research, 13,* 12–24.

Murdock, B. B., Jr. (1962). The serial position effect in free recall. *Journal of Experimental Psychology, 64,* 482–488.

Nass, C., & Reeves, B. (1989, May). *Levels of analysis in communication research: Theoretical and operational considerations.* Paper presented at the International Communication Association, San Francisco.

Pfau, M., & Burgoon, M. (1988). Inoculation in political campaign communication. *Human Communication Research, 15,* 91–111.

Reeves, B., Biocca, F., Pan, Z., Oshagan, H., Neuwirther, K., & Richards, J. (1988). *Unconscious processing and priming with pictures: Effects on emotional attributions about people on television.* Unpublished manuscript.

Reeves, B., & Garramone, G. (1983). Television's influence on children's encoding of person information. *Human Communication Research, 10,* 257–268.

Reeves, B., Newhagen, J., Maibach, E., Basil, M., & Kurz, K. (1989, May). *Negative and positive messages: Effects of message type and message context on attention and memory.* Paper presented at the annual meeting of the International Communication Association, San Francisco.

Reeves, B., & Thorson, E. (1986). Watching television: Experiments on the viewing process. *Communication Research, 13,* 343–361.

Reeves, B., Thorson, E., & Schleuder, J. (1986). Attention to television: Psychological theories and chronometric measures. In J. Bryant & D. Zillmann (Eds.), *Perspectives on media effects* (pp. 251–280). Hillsdale, NJ: Lawrence Erlbaum Associates.

Roberts, D., & Maccoby, N. (1974). Information processing and persuasion: Counterarguing and behavior. In P. Clarke (Ed.), *New models for communication research* (pp. 269–302). Beverly Hills, CA: Sage.

Roseman, I., Abelson, R., & Ewing, M. (1986). Emotion and political cognition: Emotional appeals in political communication. In R. Lau & D. Sears (Eds.), *Political cognition* (pp. 279–294). Hillsdale, NJ: Lawrence Erlbaum Associates.

Sabato, L. J. (1981). *The rise of political consultants: New ways of winning elections.* New York: Basic Books.

Schultz, D. P. (1963). Primacy-recency with a sensory variation framework. *Psychological Record, 13,* 129–139.

Shapiro, M. A., & Rieger, R. H. (1989, May). *Comparing positive and negative political advertising.* Paper presented to the International Communication Association, San Francisco.

Shapiro, W., & White, J. E. (1988, November 14). Why it was so sour. *Time,* p. 18–21.

Sherif, M. (1936). *The psychology of social norms.* New York: Harper & Row.

Sherif, M., & Hovland, C. I. (1961). *Social judgement: Assimilation and contrast effect in communication and attitude change.* New Haven, CT: Yale University Press.

Shrimp, T. A. (1981). Attitude toward the ad as a mediator of advertising effects on brand attitude? *Journal of Marketing Research, 18,* 318–332.

Soldow, G. F., & Principe, V. (1981). Responses to commercials as a function of program context. *Journal of Audience Research, 21,* 59–65.

Srull, T. (1983). Affect and memory: The impact of affective reactions in advertising on the representation of product information in memory. *Advances in Consumer Research, 11,* 520–525.

Srull, T. (1984). The effects of subjective affective states on memory and judgement. *Advances in Consumer Research, 11,* 530–533.

Stengel, R. (1988, February 29). Accentuating the negative. *Time,* pp. 46.

Taylor, P., & Broder, D. S. (1988, October 28). Evolution of the TV era's nastiest Presidential race: Bush team test-marketed negative themes. *Washington Post,* Col. 1, p. A1.

Tetlock, P. E. (1983). Accountability and the perseverance of first impressions. *Social Psychological Quarterly, 46,* 285–292.

Thorson, E., & Friestad, M. (1985). The effects of emotion on episodic memory for television commercials. In P. Cafferata & A. Tybout (Eds.), *Advances in Consumer Psychology,* (pp. 131–136). Lexington, MA: Lexington.

Thorson, E., & Wells, W. D. (1987). How message order affects responses. *In Research Quality: Back to Basics* (pp. 71–80). New York: Advertising Research Foundation.

Webb, P. H., & Ray, M. L. (1979). Effects of TV clutter. *Journal of Advertising Research, 19,* 7–12.

Wyer, R. S., & Carlston, D. (1979). *Social cognition, inference and attribution.* Hillsdale, NJ: Lawrence Erlbaum Associates.

Wyer, R. S., & Schwartz, S. (1969). Some contingencies in the effects of the source of a communication upon the evaluation of the communication. *Journal of Personality and Social Psychology, 82,* 467–471.

Zajonc, R. B. (1984). On the primacy of affect. *American Psychologist, 39,* 117–123.

IV

The Psychological Contexts of Processing

10

Inside the Agenda-Setting Process: How Political Advertising and TV News Prime Viewers to Think about Issues and Candidates

Joan Schleuder
Maxwell McCombs
Wayne Wanta
Southern Illinois University at Carbondale

Describing the agenda-setting function of the media has been the focus of one of the most enduring lines of research in the mass communication field. Walter Lippmann (1920, 1922, 1925) described the media's ability to determine what the public considers to be important, and Bernard Cohen (1963) is often remembered for telling us that the media are not very successful in telling us what to think, but stunningly successful in telling us what to think about. Empirical work on agenda setting has a much briefer history. McCombs and Shaw (1972) tested the agenda-setting effect during the 1968 presidential campaign using surveys and content analysis. Since this time many facets of agenda setting have been explored empirically including the time lag involved (Stone & McCombs, 1981; Winter & Eyal, 1981) and issue versus image agenda setting in presidential campaigns (Weaver, Graber, McCombs, & Eyal, 1981). Recently, Iyengar, Peters, and Kinder (1982) and Iyengar and Kinder (1987) provided experimental (cause–effect) evidence for the agenda-setting function of television news.

Understanding the agenda-setting function is important because very few people who vote for president of the United States will have personal contact of any kind with any of the candidates, nor will they have much direct, personal interaction with major campaign issues. Instead of traveling to Nicaragua, analyzing U.S. trade agreements with other nations or delving into any political issue in depth, voters tend to rely on the media to present information that they can use on Election

Day. This reliance on the media gives the media the power to determine political reality, or to set the political agenda (Iyengar & Kinder, 1987).

Studies to date have provided both field and experimental evidence for the basic idea of agenda setting. In addition, these studies have explored the contingent conditions that enhance or constrain the agenda-setting influence of the mass media. One of these contingent conditions, stated in terms of an individual's level of need for orientation (Shaw & McCombs, 1977), begins the task of explaining how the media affects the public agenda. This study continues the quest for turning inward and seeking explanations for the agenda-setting phenomenon by looking at the memory retrieval process that individuals must experience in order for agenda setting to occur.

Exposure to mediated information about political issues does not automatically result in the setting of the public's agenda. Individuals must first direct their attention to the information and then store that information in memory. They must match new information with old and retrieve the resulting representation from memory to make a decision about issue salience. Consequently, understanding how the media set the public agenda ultimately rests on understanding how attributes of media messages interact with the cognitive processing of the individuals who make up the public.

In this chapter we focus on how political knowledge stored in long-term memory can be activated by the media and assume that understanding this process will inform our understanding of how decisions about issue salience are made. The more micro-cognitive processes of attention to and the encoding of political information into memory are examined in related studies (Schleuder, 1988, 1989b, 1989c). We look at the retrieval of stored information from memory because it is the cognitive process that occurs just prior to decisions (such as determining the salience of an issue) and behaviors (such as reporting the salience determination when asked to do so by an interviewer). Thus, it seems the logical first inward step to take in the study of the agenda-setting process within individuals. Although our goal is to obtain a better understanding of the agenda-setting process, we do not draw on traditional agenda-setting theory. Instead, we use spreading-activation theory as a guide and draw heavily on the ideas about priming effects presented in recent mass communication research (Berkowitz & Rogers, 1986; Schleuder, Cameron, & Thorson, 1989, 1990; Schleuder & White, 1989).

Priming and the Spreading Activation Memory Model

Berkowitz and Rogers (1986) described the mental structure into which televised information enters as a network of thoughts, feelings, and prior memories interconnected by associative pathways. The nodes in this network are activated by information picked up by our ears and eyes or by other internal nodes based on semantic relatedness, structural relatedness (e.g., words that sound similar) and contiguity. This model of how information is stored in memory matches what is currently known about neurophysiology (Squire, 1987). Neurons correspond to nodes for some researchers (Anderson, 1978). Others argue that a node represents a set of neurons (McClelland & Rumelhart, 1981; Rumelhart & McClelland, 1986). The rate of neuronal firing, which some researchers believe to be the way information is encoded in the brain (Hinton & Anderson, 1981; Squire, 1987) can be thought of as the activation described by Berkowitz and Rogers (1986). A complete history and review of spreading-activation theory can be found in Anderson and Bower (1973).

The method used to test spreading-activation memory models is called *priming* (Anderson & Bower, 1973; Collins & Loftus, 1975; Collins & Quillian, 1969, 1972; Meyer & Schvaneveldt, 1971). An everyday example of how priming works would be a person's natural tendency to interpret an ambiguous word, such as "bank," in terms of the most recent encounter with the concept. So, if a person watches a television news story about savings and loan foreclosures and an ambiguous conversational reference to "bank" occurs about 30 minutes later, the person is likely to think of bank as an institution rather than as one side of a river. Berkowitz and Rogers (1986) used priming to investigate television programming effects on children's thoughts and actions. According to Berkowitz and Rogers (1986):

> When a thought element is activated, or brought into focal awareness, the activation radiates out from this particular node along the associative pathways to other nodes. As a consequence, for some time after a concept is activated, there is an increased probability that it and associated thought elements will come to mind again, creating what has been termed a *priming effect*. It is as if some residual excitation has remained at the activated node for a while, making it easier for this and other related thoughts and feelings to be reactivated. (pp. 58–59)

Priming is used in this study to examine the structure of memory. Iyengar and Kinder (1987), in *News that Matters: Television and American Opinion,* reported a series of experiments that use priming to provide cause–effect support for the idea that television news can affect individuals' issue agendas. They referred to priming as the changes in the standards people use to make political evaluations that occur because issues become more readily accessible in people's minds shortly after they encounter them in the news. Iyengar and Kinder use priming to answer the question: Does the agenda-setting effect exist? This chapter begins with the assumption that under certain circumstances, described in an extensive literature, the media have an agenda-setting effect. It then precedes to use a cognitive processing definition of priming and an associative network model of memory to ask the question: How does the agenda-setting process occur within individuals' minds?

Figure 10.1 shows how activation of knowledge nodes within the minds of television viewers might look. This illustration assumes that

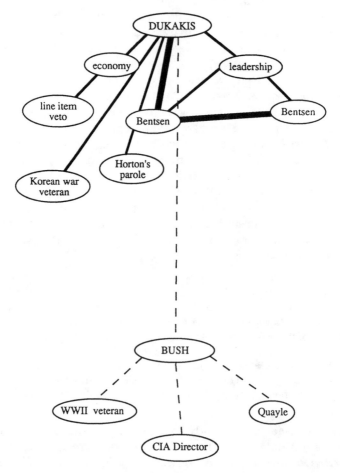

FIGURE 10.1. This illustration of a spreading activation pattern assumes that viewers have just seen information about 1988 Presidential Candidate Michael Dukakis' leadership abilities and stands on economic issues. These viewers have not watched programming that deals with the other presidential candidate, George Bush. The pattern of activation shown is one that would be suggested by spreading activation theory for a situation in which people were primed to think about Dukakis.

viewers have just seen information about 1988 presidential candidate Michael Dukakis' leadership abilities and stands on economic issues. These viewers have not watched programming that deals with the other presidential candidate, George Bush. The pattern of activation shown is one that would be suggested by spreading-activation theory for a situation in which people were primed to think about Dukakis.

Research Question and Hypotheses

Cognitive processing studies in mass communication often concentrate on how the formal features of television messages affect memory and attention (Alwitt, Anderson, Lorch, & Levin, 1980; Bryant & Anderson, 1983; Reeves, Thorson, & Schleuder, 1986; Schleuder, Thorson, & Reeves, 1987, 1988; Thorson, Reeves, & Schleuder, 1985, 1987). Although studying the effects of pacing and complexity are common, and several researchers examine the effects of presenting the same information via different media (Baggett, 1979; Salomon, 1979), few studies have addressed how presenting the same information in different forms within the same media would affect the memory process. We compare how the same political information presented as an advertisement or as a news story affects memory retrieval in this study because the question has practical implications that address agenda-setting concerns. Prior to a presidential election, viewers receive information about candidates and issues from political advertisements as well as from news stories. Some research has suggested that people learn more from watching political advertisements than from watching the news (Atkin & Heald, 1976; Patterson & McClure, 1976). If people expend more mental effort with advertisements than with the news, ads may turn out to have the stronger agenda-setting effect. If advertisements are more effective in conveying information (or in setting agendas), understanding why would be an important goal for communication research. Determining whether advertisements lead to better learning simply because they are advertisements (their form) is one logical step in exploring their agenda-setting function. Consequently, we designed an experiment that would isolate presentation form as the reason why people seemed to learn more from ads than from news.

An analysis of viewer visual and verbal recognition memory for the political information presented in this experiment showed that memory was better for advertisements than for news stories (Schleuder, 1989a). The mean for visual recognition was 3.7 out of 6 for advertisements and 3.0 for news stories [$F(1,172) = 72.04, p < .001$]. The mean for verbal recognition was 3.2 for advertisements and 2.8 for news [$F(1,172) = 25.33, p < .001$]. Viewers also paid more moment-to-moment attention to advertisements than to the same information presented in news form

[$F(1,50) = 4.30$, p < .05]. Attention was measured using a secondary task reaction time indicator (see Schleuder & Meadowcroft, in press; Thorson et al., 1985). Rather than assess viewer attention or ability to remember exactly what was seen and heard while watching television, this study examines whether political advertising is better able to activate semantically related political information than political news when the visual and verbal information presented is held constant.

Form Question: Will political information presented in the form of advertisements be a more effective prime than information presented in the form of news stories? In other words, will one presentation form result in better retrieval of information from long-term memory as indicated by higher knowledge and salience scores?

This study's four hypotheses address whether different content features of televised political messages activate semantically related information in long-term memory as predicted by the spreading-activation model's description of priming effects (Anderson & Bower, 1973; Berkowitz & Rogers, 1986). The content features include two campaign issues (leadership and the economy) and the two 1988 presidential candidates (Michael Dukakis and George Bush). The strongest support for the model would be found if the results show that subjects retrieve more prime-related information from memory than nonprimed information.

Hypothesis 1: Dukakis Prime. Subjects who see ads or news stories about Dukakis' leadership potential and his stands on economic issues (Dukakis-prime group) will retrieve more information about Dukakis than people in a no-prime control group, as indicated by higher Dukakis knowledge scores. But for Bush knowledge scores, there will be no difference between the Dukakis-prime and no-prime groups. Dukakis-primed subjects will also retrieve more information about leadership and about the economy than the no-prime group as indicated by salience and knowledge scores that are higher than those for the no-prime group.

Hypothesis 2: Bush Prime. Subjects who see ads or news stories about Bush's leadership potential and his stands on economic issues (Bush-prime group) will retrieve more information about Bush than people in a no-prime control group, as indicated by higher Bush knowledge scores. But for Dukakis knowledge scores, there will be no difference between the Bush-prime and no-prime groups. Bush-primed subjects will also retrieve more information about leadership and about the economy than the no-prime group as indicated by salience and knowledge scores that are higher than those for the no-prime group.

Hypothesis 3: Leadership Prime. Subjects who see ads or news stories about leadership potential for Bush and Dukakis (leadership-prime group) will retrieve more information about leadership than people in a no-prime control group, as indicated by higher leadership salience and knowledge scores. But for economy salience and knowledge scores, there will be no difference between the leadership-prime and no-prime groups. Leadership-primed subjects will also retrieve more information about Dukakis and Bush than the no-prime group as indicated by salience and knowledge scores that are higher than those for the no-prime group.

Hypothesis 4: Economy Prime. Subjects who see ads or news stories about Bush and Dukakis stands on the economy (economy-prime group) will retrieve more information about the economy than people in a no-prime control group, as indicated by higher economy salience and knowledge scores. But for leadership salience and knowledge scores, there will be no difference between the economy-prime and no-prime groups. Economy-primed subjects will also retrieve more information about Dukakis and Bush than the no-prime group as indicated by salience and knowledge scores that are higher than those for the no-prime group.

EXPERIMENT 1: FORM

The question of whether political information presented in the form of advertisements is a more effective prime than information presented in the form of news stories is addressed in this experiment.

Method

Subjects. There were 176 people who participated in this study. Forty-two individuals were recruited from churches and social groups in Travis County, Texas and their organizations were paid $5 for their participation. The 134 undergraduate communication students participated for course credit.

Stimuli. Eight 30-second political advertisements that aired during the 1988 presidential campaign and eight news stories produced by Channel 24 in Austin, Texas were experimental stimuli for this study. Advertisements were embedded in an episode of "Cheers" along with product advertisements. The news stories were embedded in the local evening news. The eight news stories were introduced by a news anchor and were presented as realistic news stories. They were created to resemble the eight advertisements as closely as possible. The eight news stories were taped at Channel 24 just prior to the regular newscast in which they were embedded. The news anchors wore the same clothes and introduced the stories so that the flow of the news program was uninterrupted. In addition, stories about the presidential candidates and issues under study were removed from the newscast.

Eight advertisements and eight news stories were used to enhance generalizability of the effects to other political advertisements and news stories. Generalizations about television message effects should never be based on one message per condition because idiosyncratic characteristics of individual messages could account for the results (Jackson & Jacobs, 1983). In order to keep the viewing experience as natural as possible, each subject saw only four advertisements or four news stories during their 30-minute viewing session. There were four 90-second commercial pods in the newscast and four in "Cheers." One political commercial was placed in each commercial pod in "Cheers." Twelve product advertisements were presented in the newscast. Eight of these were shown in "Cheers." The order in which the political commercial fell in the pod (first, second, or third) and the pod order (four orders) were counterbalanced to control for practice and fatigue effects. The order in which the news stories were presented was also counterbalanced (four orders). Which four ads or news stories each group of subjects saw was also counterbalanced (four viewing groups).

Because it was important that the newscast look as natural as possible, 12 pretest subjects viewed the local newscast. They were told that the newscast had been altered and it was their job to detect the alterations. Eight of the 12 said nothing about the newscast had been altered. None of the remaining 4 people was able to detect the experimental manipulation.

Experimental Procedure.   Subjects were run one at a time after being randomly assigned to view either political advertisements embedded in "Cheers" or the local newscast containing four political stories. Before the experiment began, each subject was told that he or she had signed up to participate in two entirely separate studies: one involved watching television and a second study involved answering a questionnaire. The experimenters told the subjects that they did not know what the survey-type questions would be about because it was not their study. Subjects were then told that the purpose of the television viewing study was to see how much they could remember from watching television. Those in the advertisement treatment groups viewed part of an episode of "Cheers" and a product commercial on a practice tape. They were then given visual and verbal recognition tests about information in the program and in the commercial. Those in the news treatment groups saw a portion of a newscast and a product commercial on their practice tape. They were also tested on information contained in the news and in the commercial. Subjects in all groups then viewed 30 minutes of programming and commercials. They were given visual and verbal recognition tests following the viewing period. The tests given to those viewing the advertisements focused on "Cheers," but included questions about product and political advertisements. The tests given to those viewing the news asked questions about each of the news stories, but also included questions about the product commercials present in the newscast.

All subjects were then escorted by a different experimenter to another area of the building. They were told that this study had to do with the upcoming presidential election. All 176 subjects were then interviewed in person.

Apparatus.   The subjects watched the treatments on a 19-inch Panasonic 2010 video monitor. The advertisements and programming were played on a Panasonic 6500 videotape recorder.

Design and Dependent Measures.   Form was a between-subjects factor with two levels: political advertisement and political news story.

Two salience and four knowledge measures assessed priming effects for this study (Appendix A lists the items and indexes).

Measures of salience apply only to the two issues included in the study. The leadership-salience index was created by combining the percentage of respondents who ranked the importance of presidential leadership as an issue as 1 or 2 with the percentage of respondents who ranked presidential leadership 1 or 2 as an attribute that presidents should have. These two ranking questions were combined with questions about how the respondent's choice for president was evaluated on a 7-point scale for "leadership ability, political experience, and communication skills." The economic-salience index was comprised of the percentage of respondents who ranked the importance of the national economy as the first or second most important issue facing the nation today and questions about how the respondent's choice for president was expected to perform on a 7-point scale in "strengthening our nation's economy and balancing the federal budget."

The Dukakis-knowledge index was comprised of four general questions about Dukakis, such as "Who is Mike Dukakis' runningmate?" None of these questions, or any of the knowledge questions used in the study, were answered in the commercials/news stories. The Bush-knowledge index was also comprised of four general questions about Bush, such as "Who is George Bush's runningmate?"

Leadership knowledge was assessed by asking about candidates' past leadership roles and for their stands on abortion. Economic knowledge was assessed using the question: "Can the president veto specific items of the federal budget prepared by Congress or must he approve/veto the budget in its entirety?" Asking questions about the national debt or unemployment was precluded because these issues were discussed in the commercial/news stories. (Descriptive statistics and Cronbach's alpha coefficients are listed in Table 10.1 for each dependent measure.)

It is important to note that the use of these knowledge indexes assumes that subjects had previously encountered the general political information about the candidates and issues addressed by the items. It also assumes that they stored the information in long-term memory.

Results

Salience and knowledge scores for subjects who saw advertisement primes before completing the questionnaire were compared to those who saw news story primes. A one-way, between-subjects analysis of variance produced no differences between the groups viewing advertisements and the groups viewing the news on any of the dependent measures.

Discussion

The form in which political information is presented does not appear to affect the message's ability to prime viewers to think about related information. There were no significant differences between the two groups on any of the dependent measures. This is a surprising finding because viewers paid more attention to political information presented in advertisement form than to information presented in news story

Table 10.1 Descriptive Statistics for Dependent Measures

Index	Mean	S.D.	Range	N	Alpha
Leadership salience	2.34	.99	.00–4.00	436	—
Economy salience	3.92	1.08	.00–6.25	391	.85
Dukakis knowledge	.69	.27	.00–1.0	436	.62
Bush knowledge	.75	.25	.00–1.0	437	.64
Leadership knowledge	.72	.29	.00–1.0	437	.59
Economy knowledge	.66	.47	.00–1.0	438	—

form, and they also remembered more of the information when it was presented in advertising form (Schleuder, 1989a). This suggests that pathways between semantically related pieces of information in memory are not necessarily facilitated by the presence of more or better memories acquired from intensely attending to political advertisements on television. If political advertisements and political news stories have a priming effect, these results do not provide any evidence that the priming effect derives from the message's form. The next four experiments explore whether a priming effect exists for political messages and whether the patterns produced by priming effects resemble those predicted by the spreading-activation model.

CANDIDATE AND ISSUE PRIMING

Experiments 2 through 5 compare the salience and knowledge scores produced by subjects who were primed by viewing political information about specific issues with scores produced by a group of people who did not participate in the television viewing experiments. These nonprimed control group people were part of a probability sample interviewed by telephone during the same time that the experiments were run. The experiments were conducted during the 20 days that preceded the 1988 presidential election day. No-prime control group respondents answered the same questions as subjects in the primed groups.

Because the number of subjects in each primed group was so small ($n = 44$ for Experiment 2; $n = 22$ for Experiments 3–5), and because there were no differences between the two groups on any of our measures, we collapsed across the presentation form factor so that each primed group now had either 88 or 44 subjects—half from the advertising condition and half from the news story condition.

In order to compare the experimental group to the no-prime control group, it was important to determine whether the two groups were similar on attributes that would affect the results of this study. For example, it is likely that better educated people would think more about the candidates or issues whether they had been primed to do so or not. It is also likely that people who pay a lot of attention to political news in the newspaper and on television would be more likely to think more about candidates or issues even without an immediate prime. To determine if the two groups were roughly equivalent samples, the random sample of registered voters (no-prime control group) and the primed groups were compared on all questionnaire items. Chi-square tests were used for all nominal variables and analyses of variance were computed for all other variables. Only a few differences were found.

There was no difference between the groups on education level, but, respondents in the control group had higher incomes and were older. This was expected given the high concentration of college students in the experimental group. There were no differences in the amount of attention paid to political advertising on television. However, individuals in the no-prime control group read newspapers more often, including stories about international affairs, national government, local politics, features about ordinary people, and editorials and opinion columns. People in the control group also said they paid more attention to these stories than did the subjects in the primed groups.

The no-prime control group watched more national and local news on television and paid more attention to national and local news. The no-prime control group also responded correctly more often on questions about political knowledge and general knowledge.

Individuals in the primed groups scored higher on only two items: They tended to read entertainment and sports stories more often and paid more attention to situation comedies than respondents in the no-prime control group.

Because differences between the groups existed on media use and general knowledge, indexes for these two variables were constructed to be used as covariates so that the two samples could be equated on these factors before the analyses of variance were conducted.

The media-use index was comprised of five items, such as "How many days in the last 7 did you read a newspaper?"; and the knowledge index was comprised of five items that asked respondents to name their senators and state representative, for example. Table 10.2 lists the descriptive statistics for these two control variables and their Cronbach's alpha coefficients.

It is important to note that even though these two groups were similar on many factors that might affect political knowledge and salience scores and equated on others, there may be other relevant factors on which the two groups vary.

EXPERIMENT 2: DUKAKIS PRIME

Subjects. Of the subjects described in Experiment 1, 88 participated in the prime condition. There were 220 individuals who participated in the no-prime condition.

Table 10.2 Descriptive Statistics for Control Measures

Index	Mean	S.D.	Range	N	Alpha
Media exposure	3.36	.80	.80–4.80	414	.65
General knowledge	.58	.29	.00–1.0	436	.59

Telephone
Survey Design.   The telephone survey of 220 registered
voters was conducted by 22 graduate students in an introductory
research methods course. The names selected for interviewing were a
systematic random sample of Travis County, Texas voters. Because the
Travis County voting list is compiled by precincts, use of a systematic
random sample insured proportional geographic spread of the sample
across the entire county.

Stimuli.   Four of the eight political advertisements described in
Experiment 1 and their corresponding news stories were used in this
experiment because they presented information about Dukakis, but not
about Bush. Two of these political messages described Dukakis' leadership ability, two presented Dukakis' stands on economic issues.

These four advertisements were selected from a population of 34 political advertisements that aired during the 1988 presidential campaign.
The 34 ads were collected from the respective parties, from the Political
Advertising Archive at The University of Oklahoma and by recording
them off-air. The advertisements used were judged by four coders to be
the Dukakis ads that were the most prototypical examples of commercials
about the economy and leadership. There was no variation in the rating
scores assigned to the advertisements used in this study. They were all
ranked either first or second by the coders. The coders were graduate
students in an introductory research methods course.

News stories were created to correspond with the advertisements in
the manner described in Experiment 1.

Experimental Procedure, Apparatus, and Dependent Measures.
Subjects followed the same procedure as in Experiment 1. The apparatus
and dependent measures used in Experiment 1 were also used in this
experiment.

Design.   Priming is a between-subjects factor with two levels: Dukakis-primed and no-prime.

Results

Hypothesis 1 predicted that people who saw four advertisements or news
stories for Dukakis prior to completing the questionnaire would produce
higher Dukakis-knowledge scores than the respondents who were not
primed. One-way, between-subjects analysis of covariance (controlling
for media use and general knowledge) produced the predicted differences
between priming groups. As shown in Fig. 10.2, Dukakis subjects had
higher Dukakis-knowledge scores than nonprimed respondents [$F(1,244)$
$= 8.39, p < .01$]. Also as predicted, Dukakis-primed subjects scored
higher on economic knowledge than no-prime subjects [$F(1,244) = 4.94$,

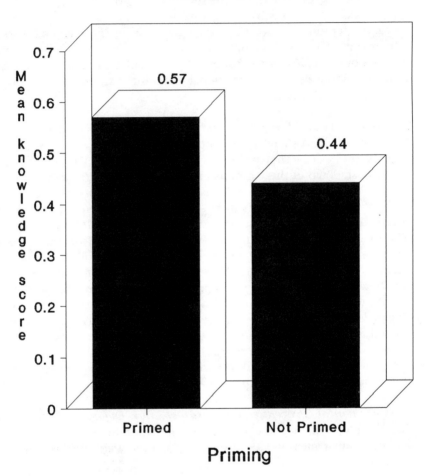

$\underline{F}$ (1,244) = 8.39, $\underline{p}$ < .01

FIGURE 10.2.   Mean Dukakis-knowledge scores as a function of priming.

p < .05]. Primed subjects also had higher leadership-knowledge scores [$F(1,244) = 4.49, p < .05$]. These results are shown in Fig. 10.3 and 10.4. As predicted, there was no effect for Bush knowledge. There were also no effects for leadership and economy salience.

Discussion

Subjects who watched four political messages that described Dukakis' leadership ability and stands on economic issues were better able to

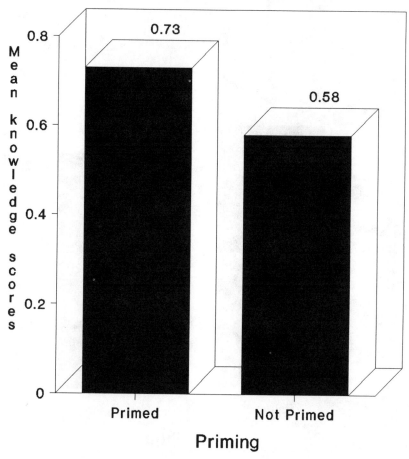

FIGURE 10.3.   Mean economy-knowledge scores as a function of priming.

retrieve political knowledge stored in memory about Dukakis, the economy, and leadership. Priming worked well for political knowledge. More importantly, for political knowledge, the pattern of results fit the spreading-activation's conceptualization of memory structure perfectly (see Fig. 10.1). Dukakis-primed subjects experienced enhanced recall for political information related to the information they had watched on television but were no better at recalling information about Bush than nonprimed subjects. Salience scores, however, were not affected by Dukakis priming.

Dukakis Primed

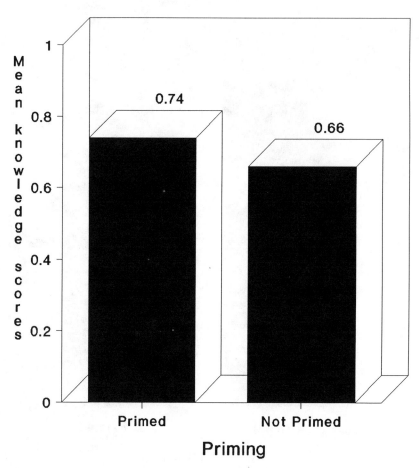

$(1,244) = 4.49, \underline{p} < .05$

FIGURE 10.4. Mean leadership-knowledge scores as a function of priming.

EXPERIMENT 3: BUSH PRIME

Subjects. Of the subjects described in Experiment 1, 44 participated in the prime condition. Participating in the no-prime condition were 220 individuals.

Survey Design, Procedure, Apparatus, and Dependent Measures. The survey design, experimental procedure, apparatus used, and dependent measures were identical to those in Experiment 2.

Stimuli. Four of the eight political advertisements described in Experiment 1 and their corresponding news stories were used in this experiment because they presented information about Bush, but not about Dukakis. The four advertisements were selected in the manner described in Experiment 2 such that two of these political messages described Bush's leadership ability, two presented Bush's stands on economic issues. News stories were created to correspond with the advertisements in the manner described in Experiment 1.

Design. Bush priming was a between-subjects factor with two levels: Bush primed and no-prime.

Results

Hypothesis 2 predicted that people who saw four advertisements or news stories for Bush prior to completing the questionnaire would produce higher Bush-knowledge scores than control group respondents. Analysis of covariance produced no differences between the primed and the no-prime groups for Bush knowledge. However, as shown in Fig. 10.5 and 10.6, subjects who were primed with Bush commercials or news stories did have higher scores on economic knowledge [$F(1,247) = 4.01$, $p < .05$] and leadership knowledge [$F(1,247) = 17.65$, $p < .001$]. Subjects in the primed groups scored higher on Dukakis knowledge [$F(1,247) = 8.99$, $p < .01$] (shown in Fig. 10.7). This finding was not predicted. There were no effects for economic and leadership salience.

Discussion

We expected subjects who watched political messages about Bush to produce higher Bush-, leadership-, and economy-knowledge scores than those produced by people who were not primed. The results indicate that messages about Bush-activated knowledge stored in long-term memory related to leadership and the economy. However, instead of enhancing recall for information about Bush, Bush priming enhanced recall for information about Dukakis. These results may indicate that the spreading-activation model is not the best heuristic to use in trying to understand how the viewers of political messages retrieve political information from memory. They may also indicate that the closest semantic links in memory to Bush have to do with Dukakis rather than with other bits of information about Bush.

Collins and Loftus (1975) found that "isnota" links between concepts stored in memory could lead to facilitated activation and faster and

Bush Primed

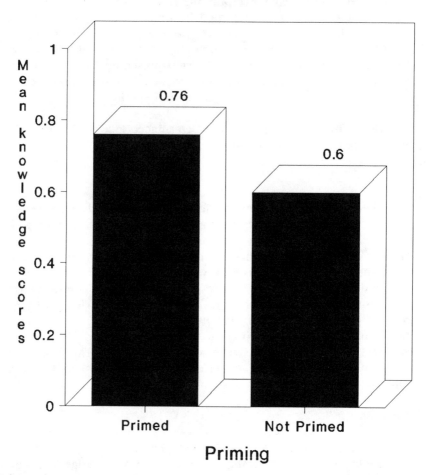

F (1,247) = 4.01, p < .05

FIGURE 10.5 Mean economy-knowledge scores as a function of priming.

better retrieval of information than "islikea" links. Perhaps the type of political campaign Bush ran emphasized the differences between the candidates such that people primed to think about Bush were better able to think of ways in which Bush was not like Dukakis. It is possible that this type of thought process resulted in better recall for information about Dukakis.

As in Experiment 2, salience scores did not differentiate between priming conditions.

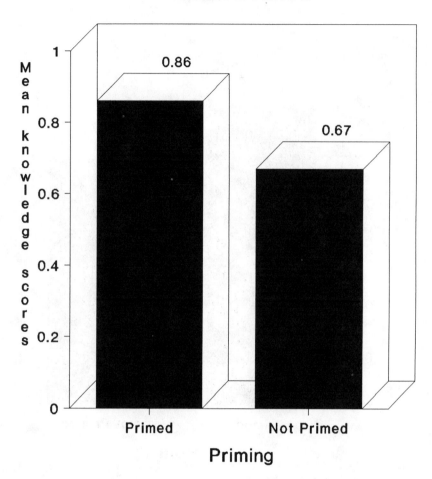

Bush Primed

F (1,247) = 17.65, p < .001

FIGURE 10.6 Mean leadership-knowledge scores as a function of priming.

EXPERIMENT 4: LEADERSHIP PRIME

Subjects. Forty-four of the subjects described in Experiment 1 participated in the prime condition. There were 220 individuals participating in the no-prime condition.

Stimuli. Four of the eight political advertisements described in Experiment 1 and their corresponding news stories were used in this experiment because they presented information about leadership for

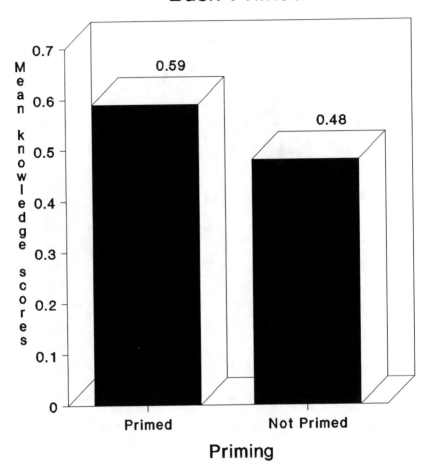

Bush Primed

Priming

$\underline{F}$ (1,247) ▪ 8.99, $\underline{p}$ ‹ .01

FIGURE 10.7   Mean Dukakis-knowledge scores as a function of priming.

both Bush and Dukakis, but did not discuss economic issues. The four advertisements were selected in the manner described in Experiment 2. News stories were created to correspond with the advertisements in the manner described in Experiment 1.

Survey Design, Procedure, Apparatus, and Dependent Measures. The survey design, experimental procedure, apparatus used, and dependent measures were identical to those in Experiment 2.

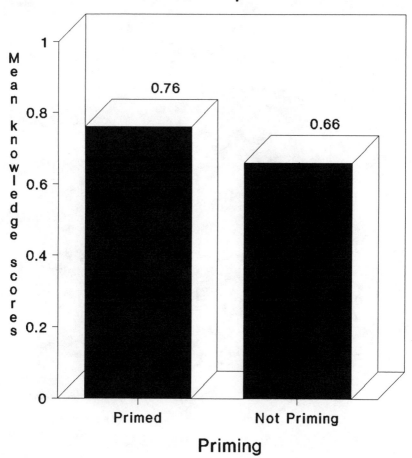

$\underline{F}$ (1,250) ▪ 4.71, $\underline{p}$ ‹ .05

FIGURE 10.8 Mean leadership-knowledge scores as a function of priming.

Design.   Priming is a between-subjects factor with two levels: leadership primed and no-prime.

Results

Hypothesis 3 predicted that people who saw four advertisements or news stories about presidential leadership would produce higher leadership-knowledge and salience scores than no-prime respondents.

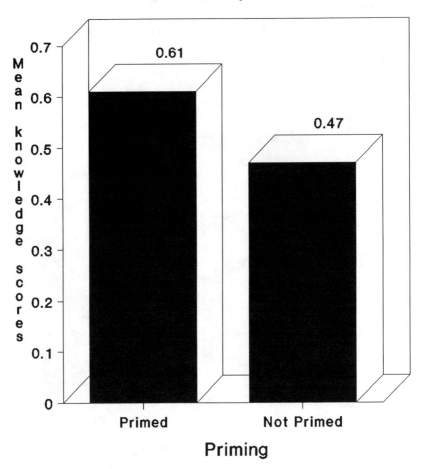

FIGURE 10.9   Mean Dukakis-knowledge scores as a function of priming.

Figure 10.8 shows that primed subjects scored higher on leadership knowledge than control respondents [$F(1,250) = 4.71, p < .05$]. As shown in Fig. 10.9, primed subjects also scored higher on Dukakis knowledge than the control group [$F(1,250) = 18.89, p < .001$]. As predicted, no differences between the priming conditions was found for economic salience. Counter to the predictions, people in the primed group scored higher on economic knowledge [$F(1,250) = 4.44, p < .05$]

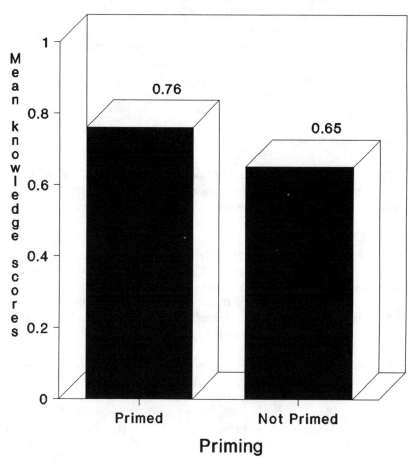

F (1,250) = 4.44, p < .05

FIGURE 10.10 Mean economy-knowledge scores as a function of priming.

(shown in Fig. 10.10). The predicted effects were not found for leadership salience or Bush knowledge.

Discussion

Watching political messages about the leadership ability of both presidential candidates resulted in better retrieval of information about related leadership issues. It also produced the predicted priming effect for Dukakis knowledge. Again, as in Experiment 3, Bush-knowledge scores did not differ as a function of priming although a priming effect was predicted for Bush knowledge. As in Experiments 2 and 3, priming did not affect salience scores. Knowledge results again provide a fairly good fit to the spreading-activation model, although messages about Bush do not seem to enhance viewer ability to retrieve Bush-related information from memory.

EXPERIMENT 5: ECONOMY PRIME

Subjects. Of the subjects described in Experiment 1, 44 participated in the prime condition. Two hundred and twenty individuals participated in the no-prime condition.

Stimuli. Four of the eight political advertisements described in Experiment 1 and their corresponding news stories were used in this experiment because they presented information about the economy for both Bush and Dukakis, but did not discuss leadership. The four advertisements were selected in the manner described in Experiment 2. News stories were created to correspond with the advertisements in the manner described in Experiment 1.

Survey Design, Procedure, Apparatus, and Dependent Measures. The survey design, experimental procedure, apparatus used, and dependent measures were identical to those in Experiment 2.

Design. Priming is a between-subjects factor with two levels: economy primed and no-prime.

Results

Hypothesis 4 predicted that people who saw four advertisements or news stories about the economy would produce higher economy salience and knowledge scores than respondents who were not primed. As shown in Fig. 10.11, analysis of covariance produced the predicted main effect for economic knowledge [$F(1,249) = 4.13, p < .05$]. The primed group also scored higher on Dukakis knowledge [$F(1,249) = 9.56, p < .01$] (shown in Fig. 10.12), providing partial support for the prediction that people in the primed group would score higher on items about Dukakis and Bush. No effects for economic salience or Bush knowledge were found, although they were predicted.

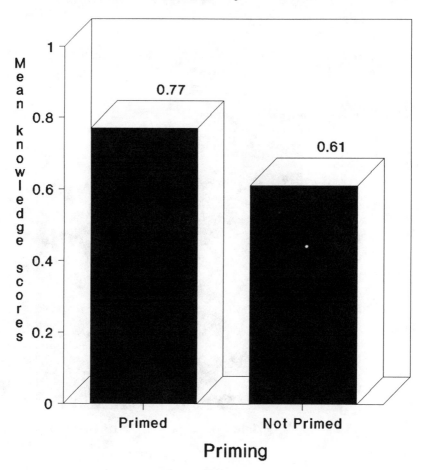

F (1,249) = p < .05

FIGURE 10.11   Mean economy-knowledge scores as a function of priming.

Table 10.3 summarizes the primary and secondary priming predictions and shows the pattern of results.

Discussion

Like the results produced by the Dukakis-priming experiment, these results provide a good fit for the spreading-activation model of memory for political information. Subjects who watched political messages about

Economy Primed

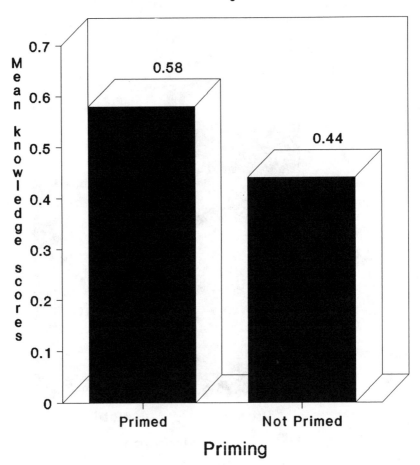

F (1,249) ▪ 9.56, p ˂ .01

FIGURE 10.12   Mean Dukakis-knowledge scores as a function of priming.

the economy produced higher economy-knowledge scores than people who were not economy primed. Priming facilitated information retrieval for Dukakis-knowledge scores, as predicted. Also as predicted, there was no difference between priming conditions for leadership-knowledge scores. The model predicted that priming would enhance Bush knowledge scores. As in Experiments 3 and 4, this enhancement was not found in the data. As in all four content-feature priming studies, issue-salience effects were not found.

Table 10.3 Spreading-Activation Theory Predictions for Each of the Dependent Measures (Leadership and Economy Salience; Dukakis, Bush, Leadership and Economy Knowledge) by Priming Experiments (Experiment 2: Dukakis Primed, Experiment 3: Bush Primed, Experiment 4: Leadership Primed, and Experiment 5: Economy Primed)

Experiment	Salience		Knowledge			
	Leadership	Economy	Dukakis	Bush	Leadership	Economy
2	+	+	+(*)		+(*)	+(*)
3	+	+	(*)	+	+(*)	+(*)
4	+		+(*)	+	+(*)	(*)
5		+	+(*)	+		+(*)

+ Priming effect predicted
(*) ANCOVA produced a statistically significant difference between the control and primed groups in the predicted direction

GENERAL DISCUSSION

Four obvious patterns emerge when the results of the four political message priming experiments are examined together (see Table 10.3). First, the knowledge results tend to support the spreading-activation model conceptualization of memory, but salience scores do not. The major exception to finding a good fit for the model in the knowledge data is provided by the Bush-priming conditions. Viewing information about Bush just prior to being asked to retrieve related information about Bush from memory never results in superior Bush-knowledge scores. On the other hand, viewing any political message at all enhances memory retrieval for information about Dukakis and the economy. It's interesting to note that although all four priming groups had higher Dukakis-knowledge scores than the nonprimed group, the knowledge score in the Dukakis-primed condition was considerably higher than the knowledge scores in the other three experimental conditions. This finding offers further support for the spreading-activation model.

If memory is structured as described by spreading-activation theorists, then a historical explanation might account for the distinct priming patterns produced by the two 1988 presidential candidates. As mentioned earlier, the type of campaigns run by the candidates may have contributed to the dramatic differences found in priming effects between Bush and Dukakis. Or, what may be at work here is a situation in which people have close links in memory between many 1988 presidential campaign issues and Dukakis, but have distant, weak links between general political information and Bush. After all, as vice president, Bush was a major supporting player on the political stage for 8 years prior to the 1988 campaign, and he quickly emerged from the primary pack to be the Republican nominee. In contrast, Dukakis was a new player on the national political stage, who only emerged from the primary pack late in the season. Novelty has a very strong enhancing effect on information processing (Reeves, Thorson, & Schleuder, 1986). Perhaps people formed a stronger general association between the 1988 election and Dukakis than between the 1988 election and Bush because Dukakis was a novel political figure.

Even if a historical reason exists for the Dukakis- and Bush-priming results that fail to meet the model, their failure-of-fit suggests a minor modification of the spreading-activation model outlined in Fig. 10.1. This set of experiments was designed to observe the results of priming on very specific points, the pattern of results suggests that exposure to any of a rather wide variety of campaign information resulted in activation of the pathways between many nodes in a larger network that could roughly be labeled "the 1988 presidential campaign network." The existence of such distinct networks is suggested by findings from an earlier field study. Williams, Shapiro, and Cutbirth (1983) found that voters discriminate between issues explicitly framed as campaign issues and other mentions of issues in forming their agenda during a presidential campaign. The results presented here illustrate the diffusion of television effects far beyond the objects and attributes emphasized in the immediate message. Exposure to televised political information in these experiments resulted in an enriched, activated network of information about the 1988 presidential campaign, as well as, in some cases—most notably the leadership-priming condition—enhanced knowledge about a specific topic.

There is a methodological weakness in the design of this study that must be considered when drawing conclusions from its results. First, the no-prime control group was not randomly assigned to that treatment. Efforts were made to make sure that the groups either were naturally-matched on variables other than priming that could affect the study results, and the two groups were statistically equated on media use and general political knowledge. However, it is still possible that the two groups vary in a systematic way that could confound any cause–effect inference drawn from the findings.

A tentative picture of how the memory retrieval process for political information may operate within individuals emerges from this study and we hope that picture can be used to better understand how agenda setting occurs. In this picture we see activation within the memory network favored pathways between knowledge nodes rather than between salience nodes. Information presented in television messages about Dukakis serving as governor of Massachusetts, for example, may have activated all semantically related pieces of "Campaign 1988" information in memory. One of those activated pieces of information may have been about Dukakis' role in paroling prisoners in his home state (one of the knowledge questions in this study). Because this information had recently been (indirectly) activated for primed subjects, they were better able to answer knowledge questions than control respondents. Evidently, nodes containing salience information about the issues were either not activated at all or not strongly activated.

Understanding more about how members of the public combine the political news presented on television with the old information they already have stored in memory will add much to our understanding of the agenda-setting process. More can be learned by looking even further inside the agenda-setting process by focusing on other mental processes, such as memory for the visual and verbal political information presented and at the moment-to-moment attention paid to messages. These processes must occur before individuals convert the information presented by the media into a statement about the most important issues or problems facing the world.

Attention and Memory: One More Step Inside the Agenda-Setting Process

The media set the public agenda by influencing individual readers and viewers one at a time. In fact, individuals must first pay attention to media messages and then remember what they have seen. Only then can they call up information about different issues and political candidates when they are asked to make salience decisions about a series of topics. Consequently, the media's ability to set the public's agenda ultimately rests on understanding how attributes of media messages interact with the cognitive processing of the individuals who make up the public.

The moment-to-moment attention allocated to political messages was collected during the 30-minute viewing period from each of the four primed groups in this study. Visual and verbal recognition memory scores were also collected after the 30-minute viewing of either "Cheers" or the news was complete (see Schleuder, in press, 1989a, 1989b). Because complexity is an attribute of television messages that has been found to have rigorous effects on attention and memory (Schleuder et al., 1987, 1988; Thorson et al., 1985, 1987), each political message was coded for complexity (see Schleuder, 1989b), in addition to being categorized by candidate and issue prototypicality.

The Findings

Dukakis Prime. Subjects paid more moment-to-moment attention to messages presented in the form of advertisements [$F(1,41) = 4.86$, p

< .05]. Mean reaction time was 379 msec for advertisements and 355 msec for news stories. Attention was measured using a reaction time secondary task (see Schleuder & Meadowcroft, in press). The more attention subjects paid to the television messages, the harder it was to pull away and allocate attention to the secondary button-pressing task. As a consequence, higher reaction time scores indicate higher levels of attention. Whenever between-group comparisons were made, motor skill was controlled for by collecting 36 simple reaction times from each subject prior to the beginning of the experiments. Subjects were equated on motor skill by entering the average of the simple reaction times as a covariate in the analysis. The means reported here are adjusted means.

These 44 subjects recognized the visual information presented in advertisement form better than the same message presented in news story form [$F(1,42) = 33.74, p < .001$]. The mean for advertisements was 4 out of 6 and 3.08 for news stories. Figure 10.13 shows the interaction between issue and complexity [$F(1,42) = 13.97, p < .001$] for visual memory. Subjects recognized more when messages were about economic issues and complex and when messages were about leadership and complex [$F(1,42) = 11.92, p < .005$]. For low-complexity messages, the type of issue discussed had no effect on visual memory. For political information about Dukakis presented verbally, message form and complexity interacted [$F(1,42) = 5.71, p < .05$], as shown in Fig. 10.14. Subjects recognized the verbal information presented in news story form equally well for low and high levels of message complexity. Scores were higher for high-complexity messages when they was presented in advertisement form [$F(1,21) = 5.33, p < .05$]. Complexity and the type of issue presented also interacted [$F(1,42) = 12.10, p < .005$], as shown in Fig. 10.15. When messages were complex, verbal information about leadership was better remembered than information about the economy [$F(1,42) = 11.10, p < .005$]. For low-complexity messages, the type of issue discussed had no effect on verbal recognition scores.

Bush Prime. Moment-to-moment attention was higher for messages about the economy than about leadership [$F(1,42) = 5.78, p < .05$]. Mean reaction time scores were 375 msec for economy and 342 msec for leadership.

The visual information in political advertisements was recognized better than the same information presented in news stories [$F(1,42) = 15.17, p < .001$]. Mean scores were 3.52 for advertisements and 2.95 for news stories. Visual memory was better for low-complexity messages [$F(1,42) = 150.79, p < .001$]. Mean scores were 4.20 for low and

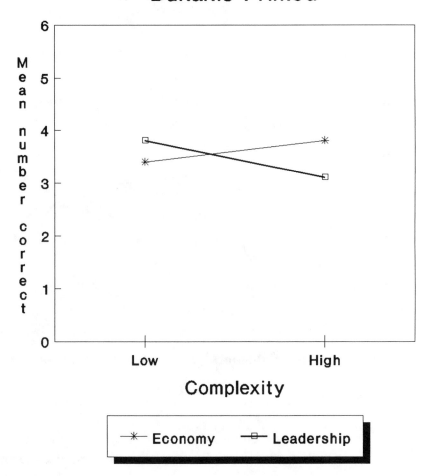

FIGURE 10.13.   Mean visual memory as a function of complexity and issue.

2.25 for high complexity. These 44 subjects scored higher on the visual recognition tests for messages about leadership [$F(1,42) = 13.82, p < .001$]. Mean scores were 3 for the economy and 3.45 for leadership. There was one interaction for visual memory [$F(1,42) = 11.74, p < .001$]. Low-complexity advertisements were better remembered than high complexity [$F(1,21) = 42.04, p < .001$] and low-complexity news stories were better remembered than high complexity [$F(1,21) =$

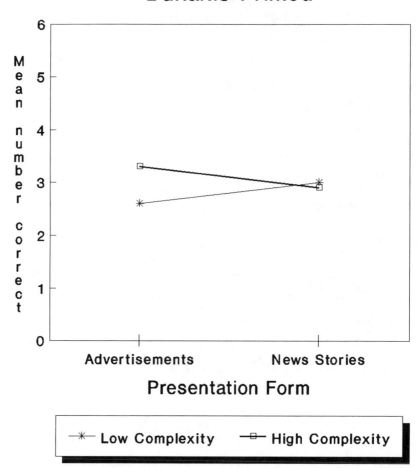

F (1,42) = 5.71, p < .05

FIGURE 10.14.   Mean verbal memory as a function of form and complexity.

115.50, $p < .001$], but high-complexity news stories produced a much greater decrement in visual recognition than high complexity advertisements (see Fig. 10.16).

Verbal recognition scores were higher for messages about leadership [$F(1,42) = 9.58, p < .005$]. Mean scores were 3.25 for the economy and 3.76 for leadership. There were two interactions for verbal recognition scores. Advertisements about leadership produced higher scores than

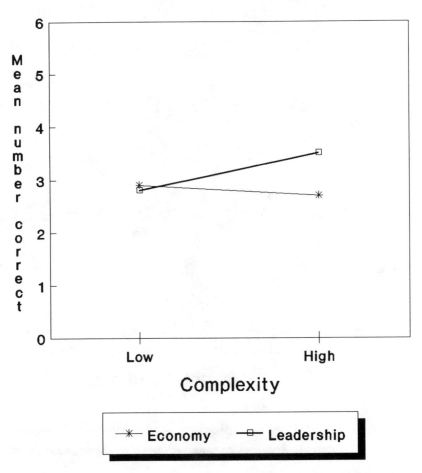

F (1,42) ▪ 12.10, p ‹ .005

FIGURE 10.15.   Mean verbal memory as a function of complexity and issue.

ads about the economy [$F(1,21) = 14.25, p < .001$], but type of issue had no effect on verbal memory for information about Bush news [$F(1,42) = 6.47, p < .05$], as shown in Fig. 10.17. For high-complexity messages, type of issue had no effect on how well low-complexity messages were remembered, but complex messages about leadership had a one-point mean memory advantage over complex economic messages [$F(1,42) = 10.08, p < .005$], as shown in Fig. 10.18.

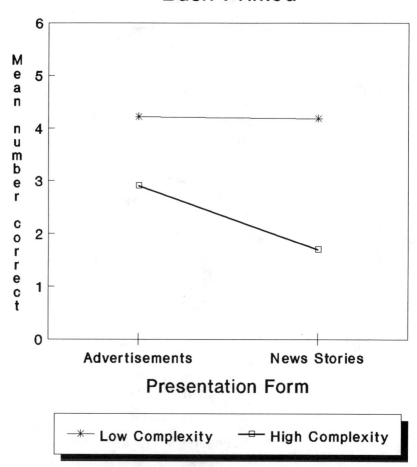

FIGURE 10.16.   Mean visual memory as a function of form and complexity.

Leadership Prime.   The 44 subjects allocated more moment-to-moment attention to advertisements [$F(1,41) = 4.63, p < .05$]. Mean reaction time scores were 386 msec for advertisements and 343 msec for news stories.

Visual recognition scores were higher when messages were presented in the form of advertisements [$F(1,42) = 10.95 \, p < .005$] with mean scores of 3.53 for advertisements and 2.93 for news stories, and for low-complexity messages [$F(1,42) = 25.04, p < .001$]. Mean scores

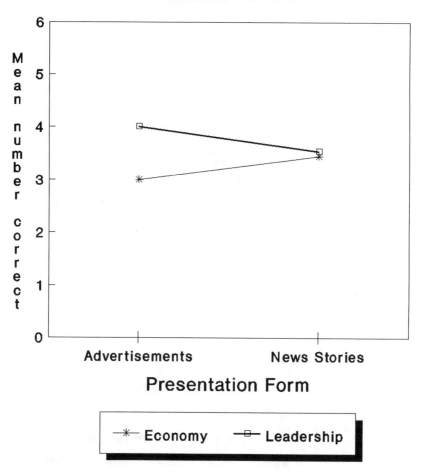

F (1,42) = 6.47, p < .05

FIGURE 10.17. Mean verbal memory as a function of form and issue.

were 3.65 for low and 2.82 for high complexity. Figure 10.19 shows the form and complexity interaction [$F(1,42) = 46.06, p < .001$]. Visual memory scores for low- and high-complexity messages presented as advertisements produced similar scores, but the visual recognition score for news stories were quite different. The mean for low-complexity news stories was 3.91 and the mean for high complexity news stories was 1.95 [$F(1,21) = 58.92, p < .001$].

Verbal recognition memory was better for complex messages [$F(1,42)$

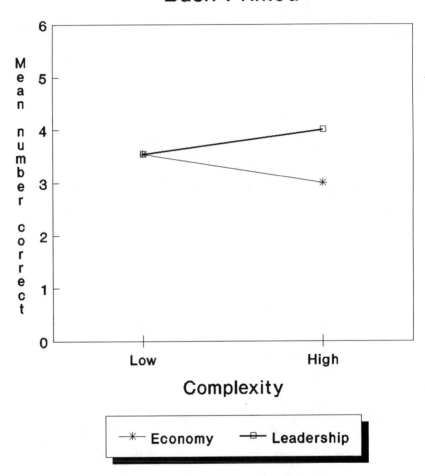

F (1,42) ▪ 10.08, p ‹ .005

FIGURE 10.18.   Mean verbal memory as a function of complexity and issue.

= 5.12, $p < .05$], with a mean score of 3.09 for low complexity and 3.50 for high complexity; and for messages about Bush [$F(1,42) = 5.71$, $p < .05$], with a mean score of 3.09 for Dukakis and 3.50 for Bush.

Economy Prime.   The 44 subjects paid more moment-to-moment attention to Bush messages than to Dukakis messages when the issue was the economy [$F(1,42) = 3.98, p < .05$]. Mean reaction times were 347 msec for Dukakis messages and 365 msec for Bush.

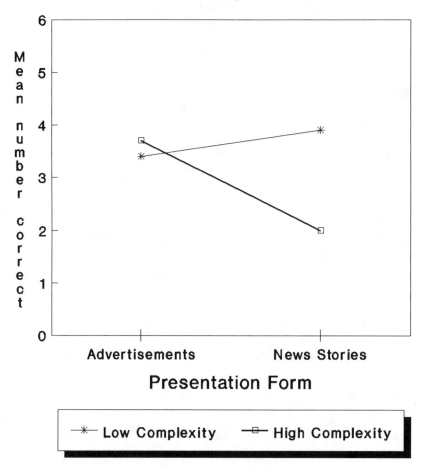

Leadership Primed

F (1,42) = 46.06, p < .001

FIGURE 10.19. Mean visual memory as a function of form and complexity.

Visual recognition was higher for advertisements [$F(1,42) = 17.73, p < .001$], with mean scores of 3.61 for advertisements and 3.03 for news stories; for low complex messages [$F(1,42) = 35.80, p < .001$] with mean scores of 3.73 for low and 2.92 for high complexity; and for Dukakis messages [$F(1,42) = 27.11, p < .001$]. Mean scores were 3.69 for Dukakis and 2.95 for Bush. Candidate and complexity interacted [$F(1,42) = 98.14, p < .001$], as shown in Fig. 10.20. Visual recognition was higher for Bush messages when complexity was low [$F(1,42) =$

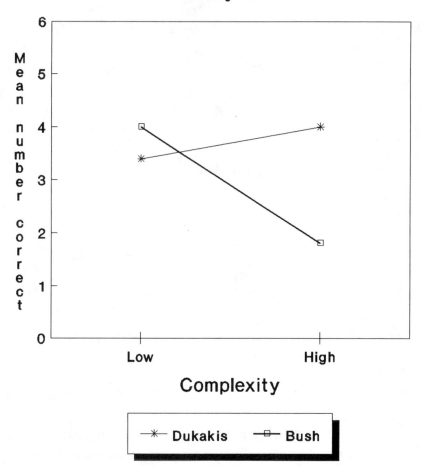

F (1,42) = 98.14, p < .001

FIGURE 10.20.   Mean visual memory as a function of complexity and candidate.

12.12, $p < .005$], and was higher for Dukakis messages when complexity was high [$F(1,42) = 98.44, p < .001$]. Complex Bush messages about the economy produced a large decrement in memory ($M = 1.86$).

There were no main effects or two-way interactions for verbal memory scores.

Implications for Agenda Setting

People in this study tended to pay more attention to political information when it was presented in advertisement form. They also tended to remember the visual information presented in advertisement form better than when the same visual footage was presented in a news story. Verbal memory was better for advertisements in only one special case: when the political message was complex and about Dukakis. Information presented as news stories never elicited more attention and was never remembered better than the same information presented in advertisement form.

Experiment 1 indicates that the ability of a political message to prime viewers to think more about a specific issue or candidate was not affected by the form in which the information was presented. The attention and memory results examined together with the priming results suggest that message form is very important at the early stages of cognitive processing. Attention and visual memory are affected by form. Viewers were more likely to pick up and store information, especially visual information, if it was presented as a political advertisement. Verbal memory can also be affected by message form. But the ability of a viewer to activate semantically related issue and candidate knowledge via the spread of activation through long-term memory does not seem to be affected by message form. If issue and candidate information is not initially stored in memory, it will not be available for activation at a later time. If the issue and candidate knowledge items used in this priming study had addressed visual aspects of the televised political messages, it would have been reasonable to expect political commercial viewers to score higher on the questions than political news watchers. This should be addressed in future research. Because all of the items used to assess priming effects addressed verbal components of political messages, it is not surprising that the political message form had little affect on priming in this study. After all, there was little difference between the effect of commercials and news stories on verbal memory, so why should form affect how activation spreads through the long-term memory system.

Whether a political message is presented in the form of an advertisement or news story, its two most basic content features are usually the issue and the candidate. Viewer attention tended not to vary as a function of the issue discussed in political messages. Viewers primed to think about Bush provided the only exception. This group allocated more attention to economic issues than to leadership issues.

The Bush-primed group provided most of the effects for visual and verbal memory based on the type of issue discussed. Bush-primed viewers had better visual memory for leadership issues than for economic issues. Bush-primed people also scored higher on verbal memory for leadership issues. This group scored particularly well on the verbal memory test when leadership issues were discussed in advertisement form or when leadership messages were highly complex. The Bush- and Dukakis-primed groups provided attention and memory scores for issues only. Experiment 3 results showed that Bush-primed people scored higher on both leadership and economic knowledge questions than nonprimed people. The verbal memory finding for this group would strongly suggest that priming for leadership would be effective. The attention and visual memory findings also suggest that information about leadership and the economy would be stored in memory and consequently accessible for later, facilitated activation. Dukakis-primed viewers scored higher on the visual memory test for complex messages about the economy. Verbal memory was better for Dukakis-primed people only for complex messages about leadership. Experiment 2 results showed that Dukakis-primed people scored higher on leadership and economic knowledge questions than nonprimed people. Priming effects do not seem related to attention for Dukakis-primed viewers, but visual and verbal memory for complex messages would suggest that some information about the economy and leadership were stored in memory and consequently accessible to have an impact on the priming study.

The economy- and leadership-primed groups provided attention and memory scores for candidates only. Attention to messages about Bush was higher for the economy-primed group. The economy-primed group also had better visual memory scores for low-complexity Bush messages. But the economy-primed people scored higher on the visual recognition test for Dukakis messages overall, and had especially high scores for complex Dukakis messages. Experiment 5 results show that only the Dukakis knowledge questions produced higher scores for the economy-primed group, but there was no priming effect for Bush-knowledge questions. Overall visual memory was better for Dukakis, which may have meant that there was more information about Dukakis stored in memory than about Bush for this group. The Dukakis-priming effect would follow logically from this conclusion. However, viewers in the economy-primed group paid more attention to Bush and yet there was no facilitation in the spread of activation through the memory system for the retrieval of information about Bush for this group.

Verbal memory was better for Bush messages for the leadership-primed group. Because Experiment 4 results show a priming effect for Dukakis-knowledge questions, but not for Bush questions, the memory results produced by the leadership-primed group seem to have no relationship to the priming results. Looking at other mental processes, such as emotional reactions to candidates and the storing of these emotional memories, might help in understanding how memories of televised political information are activated and used in the agenda-setting process.

Agenda-setting research most often deals with the media's ability to set the public's issue agenda. For the two issues examined in this study, the mental path through which televised political messages travels seems fairly logical. If an individual pays more attention to and better remembers an issue, it is more likely that the information about that issue and semantically related information will be easily activated in memory just prior to a salience decision. When the agenda-setting process for candidate salience is examined from the cognitive processing perspective, the pattern created by looking at attention, memory and priming results together is not quite so tidy. Something apart from the traditional cognitive processing variables—attention and memory—seems to account for the candidate-priming effect. Looking at the emotional responses viewers have to the candidates and considering the effects that emotional memories might have on priming would likely add much to our understanding of how the agenda-setting process operates for political candidates.

The ability of the media to set the public's agenda is rarely doubted because a long tradition of empirical agenda-setting research has provided evidence that the agenda setting effect occurs in varied situations, with varied media and for varied issues or topics. Understanding how the media set the public agenda will require at least as broad a set of investigations. Explorations of the cognitive processes of knowledge retrieval, memory, and attention should be expanded and followed by studies that look at how individuals' emotional reactions to political information presented in the media affect agenda setting. Other higher order cognitive processes, such as decision making, also provide logical exploration avenues for researchers interested in understanding the agenda-setting process. In addition, researchers will need to examine the interactions among the different mental processes that occur during the agenda-setting process and the agenda-setting effects of different situations, different media, and different issues and topics.

APPENDIX A: INDEXES USED IN THE STUDY

Dependent measures

Leadership-salience index:

1. I would like you to rate the importance of five national issues that have been raised in the campaign. On a scale of 1 to 5, with 1 being "Most Important" and 5 being "Least Important," how do you rate Presidential Leadership?

2. Now I'm going to read to you a list of five things many people feel someone must have to be a successful president—political experience,

leadership ability, intelligence, communication skills, and strong ethical values. Which of these would you consider to be the most important quality for a president to have?

Economy-salience index:
1–4. On a scale of 1 to 7, with 1 being "not at all successful" and 7 being "very successful," how successful do you feel Michael Dukakis/ George Bush (depending on respondents' professed choice for president) would be as president in the area of: strengthening our national economy, creating new jobs, balancing the federal budget, and reducing the national debt?

Dukakis-knowledge index:
1. What is Mike Dukakis' wife's first name?
2. Who is Mike Dukakis' runningmate?
3. Mike Dukakis is a veteran of which war?"

Bush-knowledge index:
1. Who is George Bush's runningmate?
2. George Bush is a legal resident of which state?
3. George Bush is a veteran of which war?

Leadership-knowledge index:
1. Is Mike Dukakis for or against legalized abortion?
2. Mike Dukakis has recently drawn criticism for his role in the Massachusetts prison parole system. Why is this?
3. Before becoming vice president, George Bush was director of what major government agency?
4. Is George Bush for or against legalized abortion?

Economy knowledge item:
1. Can the president veto specific items of the federal budget prepared by Congress or must he approve/veto the budget in its entirety?

Control Measures

Media-exposure index
1. How many days in the last 7 did you read a newspaper?
2. How often do you read the following kinds of stories? Tell me whether you read them never, rarely, sometimes, frequently, or almost always: national government and politics?
3. When you read the following kinds of stories how much attention do you pay to them? Would you say you pay them no attention, little

attention, some attention, a lot of attention, or very close attention: national government and politics?

4. How often do you watch the following kinds of television programs? Would you say you watch these programs never, rarely, sometimes, frequently, or almost always: national news?

5. When you are watching TV and the following kinds of programs appear, how much attention do you pay to them? Would you say that you pay no attention, little attention, some attention, a lot of attention, or very close attention: national news?

General-knowledge index

1. For some time now the Russians have been urging the United States to give up a new defense program as part of their negotiations for nuclear arms reduction. What is the program the Russians are asking the United States to give up?

2. South Africa has been in the news lately because of the violence directed against the government's policy of racial segregation. What is the term used to define this policy of racial segregation?

3. Can you name one of Texas' U.S. senators?

4. Can you name Texas' other senator?

5. Can you name the U.S. Representative for Travis County?''

ACKNOWLEDGMENTS

The authors wish to thank the National Political Advertising Research Project funded by the Gannett Foundation for their financial assistance. We also wish to thank Sandra Gaiser, Mark Bongiorno, Jinok Son, and the members of the Fall 1988 University of Texas, Journalism Research Methods class for their help in preparing stimulus materials, running subjects, and cleaning data. Thanks also go to Frank Biocca and two anonymous reviewers for their helpful comments.

REFERENCES

Alwitt, L., Andesson, D., Lorch, E., & Levin, S. (1980). Preschool children's visual attention to attributes of television. *Human Communication Research, 7*, 52–67.

Anderson, J. R. (1978). Arguments concerning representations for mental imagery. *Psychological Review, 85*, 249–277.

Anderson, J. R., & Bower, G. (1973). *Human associative memory.* Washington, DC: Winston.

Atkin, C., & Heald, G. (1976). Effects of political advertising. *Public Opinion Quarterly, 40*, 216–218.

Baggett, P. (1979). Structurally equivalent stories in movie and text and the effect of medium on recall. *Journal of Verbal Learning and Verbal Behavior, 18*, 333–356.

Berkowitz, L., & Rogers, K. H. (1986). A priming effect analysis of media influences. In J. Bryant & D. Zillmann (Eds.), *Perspectives on media effects* (pp. 57–81). Hillsdale, NJ: Lawrence Erlbaum Associates.

Cohen, B. C. (1963). *The press and foreign policy.* Westport, CT: Greenwood Press.

Collins, A. M., & Loftus, E. F. (1975). A spreading activation theory of semantic processing. *Psychological Review, 82* 407–428.

Collins, A. M., & Quillian, M. R. (1969). Retrieval time from semantic memory. *Journal of Verbal Learning and Verbal Behavior, 8,* 240–247.

Collins, A. M., & Quillian, M. R. (1972). Experiments on semantic memory and language comprehension. In L. Gregg (Ed.), *Cognition and learning* (pp. 240–247). New York: Wiley.

Hinton, G. E. (1981). Implementing semantic networks in parallel hardware. In Hinton, G. E., & Anderson, J. A. (Eds.). *Parallel models of associative memory* (pp. 161–188). Hillsdale, NJ: Lawrence Erlbaum Associates.

Iyengar, S., & Kinder, D. R. (1986a). Psychological accounts of agenda-setting. In S. Kraus & R. Perloff (Eds.), *Mass media and political thought* (pp. 117–140). Beverly Hills: Sage.

Iyengar, S., & Kinder, D. R. (1987). *News that matters: Television and American opinion.* Chicago: University of Chicago Press.

Iyengar, S., Kinder, D. R., Peters, M. D., & Krosnick, J. A. (1984). The evening news and presidential evaluations. *Journal of Personality and Social Psychology, 46,* 778–787.

Iyengar, S., Peters, M. D., & Kinder, D. R. (1982). Experimental demonstrations of the "not-so-minimal" consequences of TV news programs. *American Political Science Review, 76,* 848–858.

Jackson, S., & Jacobs, S. (1983). Generalizing about messages: Suggestions for design and analysis of experiments. *Human Communication Research, 9,* 169–181.

Lippmann, W. (1920). *Liberty and the news.* New York: Harcourt, Brace, & Howe.

Lippmann, W. (1922). *Public opinion.* New York: The Free Press.

Lippmann, W. (1925). *The phantom public.* New York: Harcourt Brace Janovich.

McClelland, J., & Rumelhart, D. (1981). An interactive activation model of the effect of context in perception. Part I. An account of basic findings. *Psychological Review, 88,* 159–188.

McCombs, M. E., & Shaw, D. (1972). The agenda-setting function of mass media. *Public Opinion Quarterly, 36,* 176–187.

Meyer, D. E., & Schvaneveldt, R. W. (1971). Facilitation in recognizing pairs of words: evidence of a dependence between retrieval operations. *Journal of Experimental Psychology: General, 106,* 226–254.

Patterson, M., & McClure, R. (1976). *The unseeing eye: The myth of television power in national elections.* New York: Putnam.

Reeves, B., Thorson, E., & Schleuder, J. (1986). Attention to television: Psychological theories and chronometric measures. In J. Bryant & D. Zillmann (Eds.), *Perspectives on media effects* (pp. 251–279). Hillsdale, NJ: Lawrence Erlbaum Associates.

Rumelhart, D., & McClelland, J. (1986). *Parallel distributed processing* (Vol. 1). Cambridge, MA: MIT Press.

Salomon, G. (1979). Media and symbol systems as related to cognition and learning. *Journal of Educational Psychology, 71,* 131–148.

Schleuder, J. (1990). Effects of commercial complexity, party affiliation and issue vs image strategies in political ads. *Advances in Consumer Research, 17,* 159–168.

Schleuder, J. (1989a). *The effect of political message form on cognitive processing: TV commercials vs. news stories.* Unpublished manuscript, University of Texas, College of Communication Cognitive Research Laboratory, Austin, TX.

Schleuder, J. (1989b). *How complexity interacts with content features of televised political messages to affect cognitive processing.* Unpublished manuscript. University of Texas, College of Communication Cognitive Research Laboratory, Austin, TX.

Schleuder, J., Cameron, G., & Thorson, E. (1989). Priming effects of television news teasers on attention to and memory for emotion-eliciting commercials. *1989 American Academy of Advertising Proceedings.*

Schleuder, J., & Meadowcroft, J. Reaction time measures of attention. In J. Schleuder (Ed.), *Measuring psychological responses to media messages.* Hillsdale, NJ: Lawrence Erlbaum Associates.

Schleuder, J., Thorson, E., & Reeves, B. (1987, May). *Effects of complexity and scene reordering on attention to television messages.* Paper presented to the Mass Communication Division of the International Communication Association, Montreal, Canada.

Schleuder, J., Thorson, E., & Reeves, B. (1988, May). *Effects of time compression and complexity on attention to television commercials.* Paper presented to the Mass Communication Division of the International Communication Association, New Orleans, LA.

Schleuder, J., & White, A. (1989, May). *Priming effects of television news bumpers and teasers on attention and memory.* Paper presented to the Information Systems Division of the International Communication Association, San Francisco, CA.

Schleuder, J., Cameron, G., & Thorson, E. (1990, June). *How viewers use news teasers to process TV news and commercial information more efficiently.* Paper presented to the Mass Communication Division of the International Communication Association, Dublin.

Schleuder, J., & Meadowcroft, J. (1988, August). *Time and television viewing: Chronometric measures of cognitive processes.* Paper presented to the Theory & Methodology Division of The Association of Education in Journalism and Mass Communication, Portland, Ore.

Shaw, D. L., & McCombs, M. E. (1977). *The emergence of American political issues: The agenda-setting function of the press.* St. Paul, MN: West.

Squire, L. R. (1987). *Memory and brain.* New York: Oxford University Press.

Stone, G. C., & McCombs, M. E. (1981). Tracing the time lag in agenda setting. *Journalism Quarterly, 58,* 51–55.

Thorson, E., Reeves, B., & Schleuder, J. (1985). Message complexity and attention to television. *Communication Research, 12,* 427–435.

Thorson, E., Reeves, B., & Schleuder, J. (1987). Attention to local and global complexity in television messages. In M. McLaughlin (Ed.), *Communication yearbook 10* (pp. 366–383). Beverly Hills: Sage.

Weaver, D. H., Graber, D. A., McCombs, M. E., & Eyal, C. H. (1981). *Media agenda-setting in a presidential election: Issues, images, and interest.* New York: Praeger.

Williams, W., Shapiro, M., & Cutbirth, C. (1983). The impact of campaign agendas on perception of issues in 1980 campaign. *Journalism Quarterly, 60,* 226–231.

Winter, J. P., & Eyal, C. H. (1981). Agenda-setting for the civil rights issue. *Journalism Quarterly, 46,* 376–383.

11

The Role of Cognitive Schemata in Determining Candidate Characteristic Effects

Gina M. Garramone
Michigan State University

Michael E. Steele
Ithaca College

Bruce Pinkleton
Michigan State University

Recent work in political communication has begun to focus on the cognitive processes by which political message effects are achieved (Garramone, 1983, 1984, 1985, 1986; Garramone, Steele, Hogan, & Rifon, 1987; Graber, 1984; Kraus & Perloff, 1985; McLeod, Kosicki, Pan, & Allen, 1987; Steele, Garramone, & Hogan, 1988). By specifying the nature of these mediating processes, researchers hope to gain a greater understanding of the nature of political media effects (Perloff & Kraus, 1985). One line of research in this area has investigated how both audience cognitive schemata and media message characteristics may affect the information processing and subsequent effects of political messages (Garramone, 1983, 1984, 1985, 1986; Garramone et al., 1987; Steele et al., 1988). This chapter further elaborates these relationships by investigating the roles of cognitive schemata and candidate characteristics in determining political advertising effects.

The Importance of Candidate Characteristics in Political Advertising

Dramatic increases in the proportion of campaign costs devoted to televised political advertising are well-documented, suggesting an increasingly important role of such messages in American politics (Shyles, 1986). Contributing to the importance of such messages is the fact that voters claim to learn from them both issue stands and candidate image information (Atkin, Bowen, Nayman, & Sheinkopf, 1973; Mendelsohn & O'Keefe, 1976). The issue information that voters learn from political commercials is likely obtained primarily from the audio channel of the commercial. Candidate image information, on the other hand, may be derived from both the audio and video channels. For example, candidate physical appearance, facial displays, gestures, body postures, and dress are all video-provided information relevant to image formation.

Image information obtained from the video channel of a political commercial may have important implications for various political criterion variables. For example, Rosenberg and his colleagues found that candidate physical appearance projected a distinct image of the candidate's personal qualities (Rosenberg, Bohan, McCafferty, & Harris, 1986). This image included both general impressions of the candidate's fitness for office and specific impressions on a number of character traits (e.g., competence and integrity). Furthermore, candidate physical appearance influenced subjects' intention to vote for the candidate. Other research indicates that candidate facial displays can influence attitudes toward the candidate (Lanzetta, Sullivan, Masters, & McHugo, 1985). Effects emerged even when the facial displays were embedded in the background of a television newscast during which the the candidate's voice was not heard.

And the impact of such video-transmitted image information may be of increasing importance, as research indicates a heightened role of candidate image in vote decision making since the 1960s (Keeter, 1987). However, the impact of such information on any particular individual may depend on that individual's information-processing behavior.

Schemata and Information Processing

Recent psychological research indicates that information processing is strongly influenced by cognitive schemata (Crocker, Fiske, & Taylor, 1984; Wyer, Srull, Gordon, & Hartwick, 1982). A schema is a cognitive structure that represents organized knowledge about a given concept. It includes both the attributes that constitute the concept and relationships among the attributes (Rumelhart & Ortony, 1977). Schemata aid information processing by determining what information is attended to, how it is encoded and stored, and how it is utilized (Crocker et al., 1984).

To illustrate the impact of schemata on information processing, consider a person schema and its potential effect on the processing of a political commercial. A person schema consists of abstract personality trait concepts and their interrelationships. A person schema for politicians may include all of the traits that politicians are believed to have in common (e.g., dishonest, ambitious, gregarious). Such a schema should be expected to direct attention toward information perceived as relevant to such concepts (Crocker et al., 1984; Tesser, 1978; Valenti & Tesser, 1981). For example, a candidate's five-o'clock-shadow and nervous gestures may be perceived as relevant to the trait "dishonest." Once noted, that information is likely to be encoded as an indicator of the trait. Schemata also may influence the use of information for such tasks as vote decision making. The influence of schemata on information utilization may be, in part, indirect; that is, attributable to their impact on attention and memory. Thus, the use of candidate-trait information may be determined by its retrievability from memory. However, schemata also may have a direct effect on information utilization. That is, although persons may encode some of the same candidate-trait information from a political commercial irrespective of schema type, a person processing with a person schema may be more likely to *use* that information in vote decision making than a person processing with an alternative schema.

If schemata direct attention to relevant stimuli, and if information channels are perceived to differ in the amount of relevant information they contain, then persons may differentially attend to channels based on their schemata. Similarly, various message characteristics within a channel may come into or out of prominence depending on their relevance to the processing schema. Finally, if information channels and message characteristics are differentially processed depending on the schema, then the relative *impact* of these same channels and characteristics is also likely to vary according to the processing schema.

Political Schemata and Visual Encoding

Individuals develop schemata for their various domains of experience, including the political domain. Based on responses to open-ended survey questions, Lau (1986) developed a typology of four primary schemata that people use when approaching political information: (a) candidate (politician) personality factors, (b) issues, (c) group relations, and (d) party identification. Research indicates that individuals are consistent over time in their use of particular political schemata (Kinder & Mebane, 1983; Lau, 1986; Lau & Erber, 1985; Sears & Citrin, 1985). For example, Johnston (1986) found that subjects consistently encoded either high image, high issue, or moderate image and issue responses to two candidate commercials and concluded that individuals possess a predisposition to process image or issue data, irrespective of commercial content.

Thus, persons may consistently attend to, encode and store, and utilize certain types of political information as a result of the political schema or schemata they use. Consequently, persons using *different* political schemata may be expected to differ in their information-processing behavior, including the information channels and message characteristics to which they attend and the information that they encode. For example, candidate personality trait information is more relevant to an image schema than it is to an issue schema, whereas issue information is more relevant to an issue schema than it is to an image schema. Therefore, one might expect that image processors would pay more attention to and encode more candidate-trait information from a political commercial than would issue processors, whereas issue processors would pay more attention to and encode more issue information from a political commercial than would image processors. Because issue information is conveyed primarily by the audio channel of a political commercial, whereas candidate personality trait information is conveyed by both the audio and video channels, one might expect that image processors would pay more attention to the video channel of the commercial and encode more visual information than would issue processors (Garramone, 1983, 1984). Thus, we predict that:

Hypothesis 1: Image processors will encode more visual information from political commercials than will issue processors.

Visual Encoding and Candidate Attractiveness Effects

The impact of any message characteristic should vary according to the prominence of that characteristic in the individual's memory. The more prominent the message characteristic, the greater its impact should be. Thus, one might predict that the more prominent in memory the visual information from a political commercial, the greater its impact should be. This proposition has interesting implications when combined with the fact that candidate physical appearance can influence voter perceptions of candidate personal qualities and voter choice (Rosenberg et al., 1986). Based on a series of experiments in which they manipulated candidate physical appearance with a photograph on a campaign flyer, Rosenberg et al. found that attractive candidates were evaluated more highly than were less attractive candidates, and that subjects were more likely to vote for a candidate with a favorable appearance than for a candidate with a less favorable appearance. If the prominence of visual information in memory is indicated by the amount of such information encoded, then one might predict that:

Hypothesis 2a: The amount of visual information encoded from political messages featuring attractive versus unattractive candidates will be positively related to the impact of candidate attractiveness on vote likelihood.

Hypothesis 2b: The amount of visual information encoded from political messages featuring attractive versus unattractive candidates will be positively related to the impact of candidate attractiveness on candidate evaluation.

Political Schemata and Candidate Attractiveness Effects

The existence of relationships between processing schema and visual encoding and between visual encoding and candidate attractiveness effects should result in a relationship between processing schema and candidate attractiveness effects. This latter relationship should be mediated by visual encoding. Thus, we predict that:

Hypothesis 3a: The impact of candidate attractiveness on vote likelihood will be greater for image processors than for issue processors.

Hypothesis 3b: The impact of candidate attractiveness on candidate evaluation will be greater for image processors than for issue processors.

Hypothesis 4a: The relationship between processing schema and candidate attractiveness effects on vote likelihood will be mediated by visual encoding.

Hypothesis 4b: The relationship between processing schema and candidate attractiveness effects on candidate evaluation will be mediated by visual encoding.

METHOD

Subjects.   Subjects were 239 communication arts undergraduate majors who participated in the experiment as either partial fulfillment of course requirements, or to obtain extra credit. Subjects who were asked to participate in the experiment as part of course requirements were given the option of an alternative, nonresearch participation assignment to fulfill the course requirements.

Design.   Subjects participated in two separate research stages that were contrived to appear to be unrelated research projects. In the first stage, subjects' postmessage cognitive responses to a series of televised political ads were obtained. The cognitive responses were content analyzed to determine each subject's information-processing schema (image vs. issue). In the second stage, subjects were randomly assigned to one of four treatment conditions. In each condition, subjects viewed two 30-second opposing-candidate commercials, one featuring an "attractive" candidate and the other featuring an "unattractive" candidate. The four treatment conditions were created by alternating the script and order in which each candidate appeared. Following exposure to the commercials, subjects indicated their evaluation and likelihood of voting for each candidate.

Stage 1

Procedure.   Subjects participated in groups of between 10 and 60 persons. For each group session, subjects were seated in full view of an videocassette recorder connected to a monitor. The experimenter passed out a booklet to each subject and then told subjects:

> We are conducting a study to learn how people process information. There are three parts to the study: First, you will view a series of political commercials. You then will complete a short questionnaire regarding the commercials. Finally, you will be debriefed regarding the study's theory, methodology, and expected findings.

The experimenter then played a 5-minute videotape stimulus. After viewing the stimulus, subjects were instructed:

> List all thoughts you had while viewing the political commercials. Please write one and only one thought in each box. Use as many boxes as you need. There are several pages provided. You will be given 3 minutes to complete this task.

After 3 minutes had passed, the experimenter collected the booklets, debriefed,[1] and then dismissed the subjects.

Stimulus.   The stimulus consisted of a series of eight actual political commercials from a 1984 Senatorial race in Mississippi. The commercials represented both candidates in the race and contained both candidate image information and issue information.

---

[1]In order to legitimately debrief subjects, yet maintain the validity of the separate experiment scenario, subjects were told "We are looking at how commercial type affects the manner in which people process the information from the commercial. This will be assessed through a content analysis of the thoughts generated."

Content Analysis of Cognitive Responses. Two trained coders were instructed to independently assign each thought listed by subjects to either an "issue," "image," or "other" category. In instances in which subjects wrote whole paragraphs rather than individual thoughts, coders were instructed to divide each paragraph into individual thoughts and then code each thought.

A thought was coded as *issue* if it contained restatements of/reactions to specific issue information within the message (e.g., "Winters put education first") or if it regarded the candidate's performance in a political role (e.g., "What is Thad's voting record and attendance record?"). *Image* thoughts were restatements of/reactions to nonissue candidate information within the message and included references to a candidate's character, personality, appearance, or behavior not associated with a political role (e.g., "Cochran is smart," or "the candidates have funny drawls"). Image thoughts included those that described or alluded to the type of person the candidate was, or implied the candidate's character, or inherent, enduring traits (e.g., "Cochran is conservative," or "Winters is a good man for pushing education").[2] Finally, thoughts were coded "image" if they referred to emotion-eliciting, symbolic features of the commercials (e.g., "Warm and touchy feelings," or "flags waving"). Thoughts coded as "other" included those not classified into either the "issue" or "image" categories (e.g., "The commercials were too long," "I've never heard of Cochran"). Assessment of intercoder agreement for the individual thoughts yielded a Scott's pi reliability coefficient of 77.5%. Disagreements were resolved by a third coder.

Subjects' processing schema was determined on the relative proportion of their image versus issue thoughts. Thoughts coded as "other" were excluded from the computation of this proportion. A subject was coded as an *issue* processor if a minimum of 60% of his or her thoughts were issue oriented ($N = 76$). Likewise, a subject was coded as an *image* processor if a minimum of 60% of his or her thoughts were image oriented ($N = 124$). Data from subjects having fewer than 60% of either issue or image thoughts ($N = 39$) were excluded from the study, thereby reducing the effective sample size to 200.

---

[2]Only a few of the thoughts included both issue and image observations. If a description of an issue stand or performance of a political role included attributions or inferences for a basic, enduring character trait (e.g., "Cochran is dangerous because he opposes nuclear disarmament"), or if a thought included both a description of an issue stand and an evaluation of the candidate based on that issue stand (e.g., "I'd vote for him because he supports education"), then the thought was coded as "image."

Stage 2

Procedure. The subjects from Stage 1 participated in groups of between 10 and 20 persons. For each group session, subjects were seated in full view of a videocassette recorder connected to a monitor. The experimenter passed out a booklet to each subject and then told subjects, "This study involves your viewing of two commercials. After viewing the commercials, you will be asked to complete a short questionnaire regarding those commercials."

The experimenter then played a stimulus videotape. After viewing the stimulus, subjects were instructed to "write down everything you remember from the political commercials" and informed that they would have 3 minutes to complete the task. After 3 minutes had passed, subjects were instructed to complete the remainder of the booklet. After 5 minutes had passed, the booklets were collected and the subjects were debriefed and dismissed.

Stimulus. The stimulus commercials were two 30-second commercials produced specifically for the study. In order to make the commercials appear realistic, commercial scripts were written to simulate a mayoral race in a city outside of the subjects' home state. The scripts for the two commercials were similar, yet different enough to be believable as two separate commercials. Both commercials featured a combination of still photographs and action shots borrowed from various newscasts, along with a professional narrator's voice-over.

Candidate attractiveness was manipulated by the particular candidate still photograph featured in the commercial. To select the particular photographs to be used in the stimulus commercials, a panel of judges evaluated the attractiveness of several potential "political candidates" (face only). Those candidates rated most attractive and least attractive were used in the commercials.

The candidate photos appeared twice in their respective commercials: within the first 10 seconds of the commercial, lasting for 5 seconds, and for the final 10 seconds of the commercial. Thus, each candidate's photo appeared for a full 15 seconds of the 30-second commercial.

Four commercials were created by having the two candidate photographs each featured in the two different commercial scripts. That is, the photograph of Candidate A appeared in Commercial A and in Commercial B; likewise for Candidate B. In each treatment condition, subjects were exposed to a stimulus videotape that included two commercials— one for each candidate. The four treatment conditions were created by alternating the script and order in which each candidate appeared.

Dependent Measures. Three dependent variables were measured: visual encoding, candidate evaluation, and vote likelihood.

Visual encoding was determined by coding each subject's free-recall protocols. The protocols were first broken down into individual thoughts. Two coders then independently coded each thought as either "visual" or "not visual." Thoughts were coded as "visual" if they contained information that subjects could receive only through the video portion of the commercial (e.g., "Stafford looked ugly"). Thoughts were coded "not visual" if they contained information that subjects could receive only through the audio portion of the commercial (e.g., "John Ferguson can work with both Democrats and Republicans"). Assessment of intercoder agreement yielded a Scott's pi reliability coefficient of 94%. Disagreements were resolved by a third judge. A visual processing index was constructed by summing the number of thoughts coded as "visual" ($M = 1.71$, $SD = 2.16$).

Candidate evaluation was assessed by asking subjects to rate each candidate on a 7-point semantic differential scale for a series of 10 attributes: decisive–indecisive, friendly–unfriendly, strong–weak, warm–cold, knowledgeable–unknowledgeable, likeable–unlikeable, consistent–inconsistent, intelligent–unintelligent, honest–dishonest, and trustworthy–untrustworthy. Although the direction of some of the scales was reversed on the test instrument to control for response bias, each scale was coded for analysis such that high numbers indicated a positive attribute evaluation.

Because Hypotheses 2b, 3b, and 4b concern the relationship between visual encoding and/or processing schema and candidate attractiveness effects on candidate evaluation, measures indicating "candidate attractiveness effects on candidate evaluation" were created. These measures were created by subtracting the rating of the unattractive candidate from the rating of the attractive for each of the ten attribute scales. Then, to determine whether these difference measures could be combined into a single index, the measures were submitted to a principal components factor analysis with varimax rotation. Criteria for factor retention were a minimum eigenvalue of 1.0 and a minimum variance accounted for of 10%. Two factors emerged. The first factor had an eigenvalue of 4.44 and accounted for 44.4% of the total variance. The second factor had an eigenvalue of 1.54 and accounted for 15.4% of the total variance.

Indices representing each factor were created in two steps. First, we summed together those items having a loading of greater than or equal to .60 on the primary factor and a loading of less than or equal to .40 on the secondary factor. Second, we divided this sum by the number of items included in the index. In this way, a *competence* index was created that included the attributes of decisive, strong, knowledgeable, consistent, and intelligent ($M = .48$, $SD = 1.40$, Cronbach's alpha reliability coefficient $= .83$). Similarly, a *character* index was created that included the attributes of friendly, warm, likeable, honest, and trustworthy ($M = .36$, $SD = 1.36$, alpha $= .82$).

Vote likelihood was measured by asking subjects to indicate on 7-point scales how likely it is that they would vote for each candidate in an election if they had the opportunity. The scales were coded such that "1" indicated "not at all likely" and "7" indicated "very likely." Because Hypotheses 2a, 3a, and 4a concern the relationship between visual encoding and/or processing schema and candidate attractiveness effects on vote likelihood, a measure indicating "candidate attractiveness effects on vote likelihood" was created. Parallel to the candidate evaluation measure, the vote likelihood measure was created by subtracting subjects' likelihood of voting for the unattractive candidate from his or her likelihood of voting for the attractive candidate ($M = .87$, $SD = 2.69$).

Finally, for the *manipulation check,* subjects were asked to indicate on 7-point scales how attractive they perceived each candidate to be. The scales were coded such that "1" indicated "unattractive" and "7" indicated "attractive."

Analysis. The hypotheses were tested with correlation analysis.

RESULTS

The results are reported as follows:

1. manipulation check,
2. effects of order and script,
3. effects of processing schema on visual encoding,
4. impact of visual encoding on candidate attractiveness effects,
5. impact of political schema on candidate attractiveness effects, and mediating role of visual encoding, and
6. additional analyses conducted for heuristic purposes.

Manipulation Check

Subjects' perception of each candidate's attractiveness was assessed on 7-point attractiveness scales. A paired t test indicated that subjects indeed perceived the attractive candidate ($M = 4.62$) to be more attractive than the unattractive candidate [$M = 3.04$; $t(199) = 9.06, p < .001$].

Effects of Order and Script

There were no main effects of order or script on vote likelihood, competence, or character. However, there was an order by script interaction on competence [$F(1,196) = 8.99$, $p < .05$]. To handle this interaction, all further analyses involving competence control for script, order and their interaction.

Effects of Processing Schema on Visual Encoding

A significant zero-order correlation between processing schema and visual encoding was obtained ($r = .18, p < .01$), indicating that image processors encoded more visual information from the political commercials than did issue processors (Table 11.1). Thus, Hypothesis 1 was supported.

Impact of Visual Encoding on Candidate Attractiveness Effects

The zero-order correlations between visual encoding and the dependent variables lent support for Hypotheses 2a and 2b (Table 11.1). Visual encoding was positively related to candidate attractiveness effects on vote likelihood ($r = .13, p < .05$) and competence evaluation ($r = .13$, $p < .05$). Although the correlation for character evaluation was not significant, it, too, was in the direction predicted.

Table 11.1 Zero-Order Correlations Between Visual Encoding and Processing Schema and Dependent Variables

	Total (N = 200)	Males (N = 70)	Females (N = 130)
Processing schema[b]	.18[a]	.04	.24[a]
Dependent variables:			
Vote likelihood	.13[a]	.07	.17[a]
Competence[c]	.13[a]	.20	.11
Character	.05	.22[a]	−.02

[a] $p < .05$.

[b] For processing schema, image processing is coded high and issue processing is coded low.

[c] All correlations for competence include controls for script, order and their interaction.

Impact of Political Schema on Candidate
Attractiveness Effects

Zero-order correlations were computed between processing schema and the three dependent variables (Table 11.2). Processing schema was significantly correlated with vote likelihood ($r = .14$, $p < .05$), indicating that the impact of candidate attractiveness on vote likelihood was greater for image processors than for issue processors. Thus, Hypothesis 3a was supported. Hypothesis 3b was not supported, as the correlations for competence and character evaluation were not significant. However, the correlation for competence evaluation was in the direction predicted.

To test Hypothesis 4a, that the relationship between processing schema and candidate attractiveness effects on vote likelihood will be mediated by visual encoding, a partial correlation was computed between processing schema and vote likelihood, controlling for visual encoding. Although the partial correlation was smaller than the zero-order correlation (.12 vs. .14, respectively), the decrease was minimal (Table 11.2). This suggests that the impact of processing schema on candidate attractiveness effects was primarily *direct,* rather than indirect via visual processing. Hypothesis 4a, therefore, was not supported.

Partial correlations controlling for visual encoding also were calculated between processing schema and the other dependent variables. The partials were slightly smaller than their zero-order counterparts and, similarly, were not significant (Table 11.2). Hypothesis 4b was not supported.

Additional Analyses

Although no specific hypotheses were proposed regarding the influence of gender on the variables in the model, an analysis of gender effects was

Table 11.2 Relationship Between Processing Schema and Dependent Variables

	Zero-Order[b] Correlation	Partial[c]
Vote likelihood	.14[a]	.12
Competence[d]	.06	.04
Character	.00	−.01

[a] $p < .05$.

[b] For processing schema, image processing is coded high and issue processing is coded low.

[c] Partial correlations control for visual encoding.

[d] Correlations for competence include controls for script, order, and their interaction.

undertaken for heuristic purposes. A chi-square analysis indicated that there was no relationship between gender and processing schema (χ^2 (1) = .37, p = .54). However, a t test revealed a gender by visual encoding relationship. This relationship indicates that females (M = 2.02) encoded more visual information from the political commercials than did males (M = 1.19), [t(196) = −2.81, p < .05]. Because of the gender differences on visual encoding, separate analyses were conducted for the male and female subgroups.

Males. Processing schema was not related to visual encoding (r = .04), and visual encoding correlated significantly only with candidate attractiveness effects on character evaluation (r = .22, p < .05; Table 11.1). However, processing schema was significantly correlated with candidate attractiveness effects on vote likelihood (r = .28, p < .05), a relationship that was not attenuated when controlling for visual encoding (Table 11.3). This indicates that for males the impact of candidate attractiveness on vote likelihood was greater for image processors than for issue processors, and that this relationship was independent of visual encoding. Thus, for males, processing schema had a significant, direct, impact on candidate attractiveness effects on vote likelihood.

Females. A very different pattern of effects emerged for females. Processing schema was significantly correlated with visual encoding (r = .24, p < .05), indicating that, for females, image processors encoded more visual information from the political commercials than did issue processors (Table 11.1). And visual encoding was significantly correlated with candidate attractiveness effects on vote likelihood (r = .17, p < .05), although not with effects on competence or character evaluation. However, no significant relationships emerged between processing

Table 11.3 Relationship Between Processing Schema and Dependent Variables for Males and Females

	Zero-Order[b] Correlation		Partial[c] Correlation	
	Males	*Females*	*Males*	*Females*
Vote likelihood	.28[a]	.06	.27[a]	.02
Competence[d]	.15	.03	.15	.00
Character	.13	−.08	.13	−.07

[a]p < .05.
[b]For processing schema, image processing is coded high and issue processing is coded low.
[c]Partial correlations control for visual encoding.
[d]Correlations for competence include controls for script, order, and their interaction.

schema and attractiveness effects on any of the three dependent variables (Table 11.3). Thus, although visual encoding was related to candidate attractiveness effects on vote likelihood, and processing schema was related to visual encoding, the relationships were not sufficiently strong to result in a significant relationship between processing schema and attractiveness effects on vote likelihood.

DISCUSSION

The purpose of this research was to investigate the roles of cognitive schemata and candidate characteristics in determining political advertising effects. More specifically, it sought to determine whether the impact of candidate attractiveness would be greater for image processors than for issue processors, and whether this difference would be mediated by the encoding of visual information from the political commercials.

The research is discussed in three phases: (a) limitations to generalizability, (b) interpretation of the findings for each hypothesis, and (c) overview of the results and their implications.

Before discussing the results and their implications, it is important to mention possible limitations to the generalizability of the findings. First, a sample composed of college students is not representative of the general public. Some research indicates that young people may be less likely than their elders to approach political information with an image schema (Garramone, 1984). Also, as voters who have grown up with the video politics of television, young people may differ from their elders in their reactions to visual political stimuli. These potential problems with generalizability suggest the need to replicate this study with a sample more representative of the electorate.

A second limitation is the artificiality inherent in the experimental setting with respect to lack of context. To control for confounding factors, subjects were presented in Stage 2 with commercials representing two fictitious candidates. In a real campaign, voters are presented with different types of information that might reduce the impact of candidate attractiveness. However, two points may be made in support of the external validity of the findings. First, subjects were led to believe that the commercials were real. Second, the commercials contained significant issue information, providing subjects with other bases on which to evaluate the candidates.

The following interpretation of the findings for each hypothesis includes an analysis of any gender differences which emerged. As proposed in Hypothesis 1, image processors encoded more visual information from the political commercials than did issue processors. However, this relationship held only for females. Females also encoded almost twice as much visual information overall than did males. Taken together, these two findings suggest that the visual information provided by political commercials may not be as important to males as to females. However, the relationship between gender and visual processing may be quite different when the political commercials feature *female* candidates.

As proposed in Hypothesis 2, the encoding of visual information from the political commercials was positively related to candidate attractiveness effects on the dependent variables. But again, the pattern of relationships depended on gender. A significant relationship between visual encoding and candidate attractiveness effects emerged for vote likelihood for females and for character evaluation for males. This finding may indicate that males and females differ with respect to the relevance of visual information for particular judgments.

Hypotheses 3 and 4 proposed that the impact of candidate attractiveness would be greater for image processors than for issue processors, and that this difference would be mediated by the encoding of visual information from the political commercials. The results indicated that attractiveness effects did vary by processing schema, but only for males, only for vote likelihood, and not via visual encoding.

At least three possible explanations may be offered for the failure of visual encoding as a mediating variable. First, the visual encoding index measured overall encoding of visual information from the stimulus, not just encoding of candidate appearance. This may have attenuated its role as a mediator. Second, perhaps it is ease or availability of memory, rather than quantity, that determines attractiveness effects (Pryor & Kriss, 1977). Thus, an index comprised of the number of visual thoughts encoded would not measure availability of memory. Finally, perhaps the impact of processing schema on candidate attractiveness effects is primarily *direct,* such that although both issue and image processors have the same information regarding candidate attractiveness in memory, image processors are more likely to use the information in their political judgments. This seems a plausable explanation, as research indicates that appearance information is readily encoded into and retained in memory (Bower, 1970).

The fact that processing schema was related to candidate attractiveness effects on vote likelihood, but not on the candidate evaluation measures, may be due to the nature of the measures. The vote likelihood measure was based on the difference between single vote likelihood scales for each candidate. The candidate evaluation measures, on the other hand, were comprised of five attribute scales each. It seems likely, therefore, that the vote likelihood measure reflected a more *global* evaluation of the candidates, whereas the candidate evaluation measures reflected more specific evaluations, evaluations on individual scales that may vary in their relationship to attractiveness, and evaluations more heavily based on information remembered from the political commer- cials. If this is so, then it seems consistent that candidate attractiveness effects would be greater for the global than for the more specific, complex, information-based judgments.

The finding that processing schema was related to attractiveness effects only for males, as well as the other gender differences evident in the results, may be attributed to differences between males' and females' political schemata. Because differences in socialization lead to differences in experience, interests, and motivation, and because experience, interest, and motivation are related to schema development, it would not be surprising if the differential socialization of males and females resulted in unidentical political schemata. Even subtle differences in the strength of linkages between concepts and attributes within a political schema might lead to the types of gender differences manifest in the present research.

Overall, the findings are consistent with the notion of cognitive schemata, and with the propositions that schemata direct attentional processes and influence information utilization. The findings also support the position that cognitive schemata have an important role in determining media effects. The conceit of the rational voter, however, suffered another blow, as the results indicated that candidate attractiveness influenced both candidate evaluation and vote likelihood. Perhaps it was not totally unreasonable to suggest that Dan Quayle's handsome face had the power to sway some voters.

Although much research shows significant stability in political schemata over time (Kinder & Mebane, 1983; Lau, 1986; Lau & Erber, 1985; Sears & Citrin, 1985), schema research also indicates that the schema applied in a particular situation may be guided by which schemata have been used recently, and/or by the individual's needs (Fiske & Taylor, 1984). Because a given schema is more likely to be used if it has been applied recently, political commercials might be created such that the first part of the commercial "primes" a particular schema to be used in processing the remainder of the commercial. The primed schema would be one likely to generate information processing effects beneficial for the candidate. For example, extremely attractive candidates might want to capitalize on their good looks by priming viewers to process their commercials with an image schema.

Because a given schema is more likely to be used if it is relevant to the individual's needs, individuals may vary in the application of their schemata over the course of a political campaign. For example, early in a campaign, there may be too many candidates for the average voter to evaluate based on issue stands. In such a situation, voters may find image schemata more expedient. At the end of the campaign, however, with fewer candidates to consider, voters may begin to engage their issue schemata. This construction is consistent with the findings of Weaver and his colleagues that voters were highly interested in the personal characteristics of candidates throughout the campaign, but appeared to become highly interested in candidate issue positions shortly before the election (Weaver, Graber, McCombs, & Eyal, 1981).

ACKNOWLEDGMENTS

This chapter is a report of research conducted as part of the National Political Advertising Research Project, funded by the Gannett Foundation. The authors are indebted to Professor Julian Kanter, curator of the Political Commercial Archive at the University of Oklahoma, for commercials used as experimental stimuli.

REFERENCES

Atkin, C. K., Bowen, L., Nayman, O. B., & Sheinkopf, K. G. (1973). Quality versus quantity in televised political ads. *Public Opinion Quarterly, 37,* 209–224.

Bower, T. G. R. (1970). Analysis of a mnemonic device. *American Scientist, 58,* 496–510.

Crocker, J., Fiske, S. T., & Taylor, S. E. (1984). Schematic bases of belief change. In J. R. Eiser (Ed.), *Attitudinal judgment* (pp. 197–218). New York: Springer-Verlag.

Fiske, S. T., & Taylor, S. E. (1984). *Social cognition.* Reading, MA: Addison-Wesley.

Garramone, G. M. (1983). Issue versus image orientation and effects of political advertising. *Communication Research, 10,* 59–76.

Garramone, G. M. (1984). Audience motivation effects: More evidence. *Communication Research, 11,* 79–96.

Garramone, G. M. (1985). Motivation and political information processing: Extending the gratifications approach. In S. Kraus & R. Perloff (Eds.), *Mass media and political thought: An information-processing approach* (pp. 201–219). Beverly Hills, CA: Sage.

Garramone, G. M. (1986). Candidate image formation: The role of information processing. In L. L. Kaid, D. Nimmo, & K. Sanders (Eds.), *New perspectives on political advertising* (pp. 235–247). Carbondale, IL: Southern Illinois University Press.

Garramone, G. M., Steele, M. E., Hogan, P., & Rifon, N. (1987, August). *Gratifications sought and the processing of print messages.* Paper presented to the Association for Education in Journalism and Mass Communication, San Antonio, TX.

Graber, D. (1984). *Processing the news: How people tame the information tide.* New York: Longman.

Johnston, D. D. (1986, May). *Image and issue political information processing.* Paper presented to the International Communication Association, Chicago.

Keeter, S. (1987). The illusion of intimacy: Television and the role of candidate personal qualities in voter choice. *Public Opinion Quarterly, 51,* 344–358.

Kinder, D. R., & Mebane, W. R. (1983). Politics and economics in everyday life. In K. Monroe (Ed.), *The political process and economic change* (pp. 141–180). New York: Agathon Press.

Kraus, S., & Perloff, R. M. (1985). *Mass media and political thought: An information-processing perspective.* Beverly Hills, CA: Sage.

Lanzetta, J. T., Sullivan, D. G., Masters, R. D., & McHugo, G. J. (1985). Emotional and cognitive responses to televised images of political leaders. In S. Kraus & R. Perloff (Eds.), *Mass media and political thought: An information-processing approach* (pp. 85–116). Beverly Hills, CA: Sage.

Lau, R. R. (1986). Political schemata, candidate evaluations, and voting behavior. In R. R. Lau & D. O. Sears (Eds.), *Political cognition* (pp. 95–126). Hillsdale, NJ: Lawrence Erlbaum Associates.

Lau, R. R., & Erber, R. (1985). Political sophistication: An information-processing perspective. In S. Kraus & R. Perloff (Eds.), *Mass media and political thought: An information-processing approach* (pp. 37–64). Beverly Hills, CA: Sage.

McLeod, J. M., Kosicki, G. M., Pan, Z., & Allen, S. G. (1987, August). *Audience perspectives on the news: Assessing their complexity and conceptual frames.* Paper presented to the Association for Education in Journalism and Mass Communication, San Antonio, TX.

Mendelsohn, H., & O'Keefe, G. L. (1976). *The people choose a president: Influences on voter decision making.* New York: Praeger.

Perloff, R. M., & Kraus, S. (1985). Introduction: Political communication processes and effects. In S. Kraus & R. Perloff (Eds.), *Mass media and political thought: An information-processing approach* (pp. 9–12). Beverly Hills, CA: Sage.

Pryor, J. B., & Kriss, N. (1977). The cognitive dynamics of salience in the attribution process. *Journal of Personality and Social Psychology, 35,* 49–55.

Rumelhart, D. E., & Ortony, A. (1977). The representation of knowledge in memory. In R. C. Anderson, R. J. Spiro, & W. E. Montague (Eds.), *Schooling and the acquisition of knowledge* (pp. 99–135). Hillsdale, NJ: Lawrence Erlbaum Associates.

Rosenberg, S. W., Bohan, L., McCafferty, P., & Harris, K. (1986). The image and the vote: The effect of candidate presentation on voter preference. *Public Opinion Quarterly, 30,* 108–127.

Sears, D. O., & Citrin, J. (1985). *Tax revolt: Something for nothing in California.* Cambridge, MA: Harvard University Press.

Shyles, L. (1986). The televised political spot: Its structure, content, and role in the political system. In L. L. Kaid, D. Nimmo, & K. Sanders (Eds.), *New perspectives on political advertising* (pp. 107–138). Carbondale, IL: Southern Illinois University Press.

Steele, M. E., Garramone, G. M., & Hogan, P. (1988, May). *Attractiveness and persuasion: The roles of processing motivation and involvement.* Paper presented to the International Communication Association, New Orleans.

Tesser, A. (1978). Self-generated attitude change. In L. Berkowitz (Ed.), *Advances in experimental social psychology* (Vol 11, pp. 289–338). New York: Academic Press.

Valenti, A. C., & Tesser, A. (1981). On the mechanism of thought-induced attitude change. *Social Behavior and Personality, 9,* 17–22.

Weaver, D. H., Graber, D. A., McCombs, M. E., & Eyal, C. H. (1981). *Media agenda setting in a presidential election: Issues, images, and interest.* New York: Praeger.

Wyer, R. S., Jr., Srull, T. K., Gordon, S. E., & Hartwick, J. (1982). Effects of processing objectives on recall of prose materials. *Journal of Personality and Social Psychology, 41,* 674–688.

12

Reactions To Political Advertising Depend on the Nature of the Voter–Candidate Bond

Linda F. Alwitt
DePaul University

John Deighton
University of Chicago

John Grimm
Multi Quest Inc., Metairie, LA.

The general hypothesis in this research is that to predict how a voter will process and respond to a persuasive message it is necessary to account for the moderating effect of an attitudinal bond or relationship between a voter and a candidate. We argue that the bond between a person and an attitude object may be multidimensional, rooted in one or more of several independent psychological processes. Recent work on attitude strength (Abelson, 1988; Raden, 1985) has conceived of the construct as multidimensional. If that is so, then it is possible that each component of a person–object attitudinal bond may moderate differentially the processing of messages that relate to an underlying attitude.

We use the dimensions of subjective verifiability, objective verifiability and performance to form a typology of bonds, each of which, we argue, plays a different mediating role in the processing of political advertising messages. These three dimensions can be thought of as parallel to affect, cognition, and behavior in the tripartite theory of attitude (McGuire, 1985).

CONCEPTS AND MEASURES

Dimensions of Person–Object Bond

We examine three bases on which an attitudinal bond between a person and an object might be strongly held: a basis in objective verifiability, a basis in subjective verifiability, and a basis in performance or the ability to use the attitude with facility. The first two bases reflect the competence of a person to hold an attitude, whereas the last reflects his or her application of the attitude in specific contexts. (The distinction between competence and performance is drawn from psycholinguistics, for example, Greene, 1972.)

Objectively Verifiable Bond. This dimension refers to the extent to which an attitude is rooted in "good reasons," so that rational or utilitarian arguments are available to support the attitude. When a person is bonded to an object by an attitude in this sense, the value of the object can be easily verbalized, and readily justified by reference to objective evidence. A person whose attitude toward a political candidate was strong on this dimension would tend to agree or disagree strongly with statements such as, "If this candidate were president, he would make progress on the drug problem." When the bonding of an attitude rests on reason, messages will tend to be processed by a central path (Petty & Cacioppo, 1981).

Subjectively Verifiable Bond. This dimension refers to the extent to which an attitude "feels right," by tapping expressive values. An indicator of a subjectively verifiable bond might be strong agreement or disagreement with a statement such as, "This candidate makes me feel secure and safe." Such a bond cannot be easily verified by reference to events or data, nor justified by recourse to facts. It can frame either central or peripheral paths of processing an attitude in that it may provide the basis for rationalization ("he will ruin the economy") or for emotionalization ("he has shifty untrustworthy eyes").

Performance-Based Bond. Another dimension of attitudinal bonding is that the attitude is used with facility. This facility is the result of two components—ability and motivation. Ability is due to past cognitive effort expended in gathering and assimilating information, in developing pro and con arguments, and in defending the point of view. It reveals itself in the tendency to assimilate rather than to accommodate to messages about the attitude object (following Piaget; see Flavell, 1963). With high ability, one can fit a message into the existing semantic network rather than change the structure of the network to match that of the message. This makes the attitude more resistant to change. The motivational component of a performance-based bond is arousal. The Yerkes–Dodson law states that the quality of performance is an inverted-U function of arousal (Kahneman, 1973). At low and at high levels of arousal, an attitude is used with less facility than at moderate levels of arousal. If ability and arousal are additive and equal in their contribution to performance, the effects of performance should be expressed by a negatively accelerated function (see Fig. 12.1a).

If we assume that attitudes can be strong or weak on each of these three dimensions, then eight kinds of relationships between a person and an attitude object may be defined. If we further anticipate interactions among these three dimensions in their effect on persuasion, then each type of bond gives rise to a different reaction to political advertising.

The goal of this research is to examine the relationship between the proposed dimensions of attitudinal bonds with a candidate and reactions to political advertising for that candidate. Specifically, we offer four hypotheses:

Hypothesis 1: When a voter has a subjectively verifiable basis to support a candidate, political advertising in favor of the candidate generates more positive or fewer negative responses to the candidate's personality, as well as more support and fewer counterarguments.

Hypothesis 2: When a voter has an objectively verifiable basis to support a candidate, political advertising in favor of the candidate generates fewer counterarguments or more support arguments than when the attitude is not objectively verifiable.

Hypothesis 3: Performance-based bonds moderate subjectively verifiable bonds. They will increase positive or decrease negative responses to the candidate's personality, and increase support or decrease counterargument in response to political advertising.

Hypothesis 4: Performance-based bonds moderate objectively verifiable attitude bonds to decrease counter argument or increase support argument in response to political advertising.

Hypotheses 1 and 2 follow from the definitions of the bonds. Hypotheses 3 and 4 are based on the assumption that the ability and arousal components of performance bonds are additive and of equal strength.

Measures

To test the hypotheses, we developed measures of the three dimensions of attitudinal bonds, and to explore the validity of our constructs we developed measures of manifestations of attitude strength, attitude direction, previous attitude, and voting intentions.

Dimensions of Attitudinal Bonds. Likert-type scales were developed for each of the three dimensions. They consist of statements to

Effect of Performance Bond

High arousal

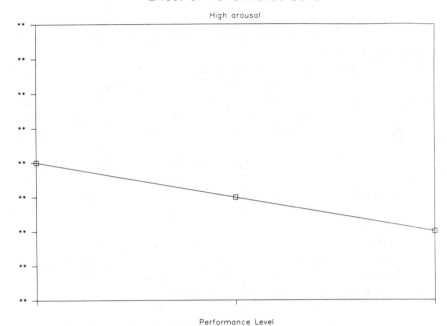

Performance Level

Effect of Performance Bond

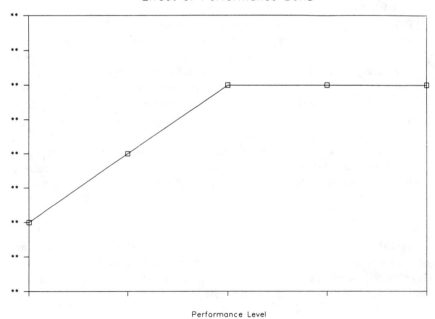

Performance Level

FIGURE 12.1. Theoretical effects of performance bond. (a) Assumes ability and arousal are additive and equal in contribution to performance. (b) Assumes high level of arousal.

which subjects rated agreement on a 5-point scale from 1 (disagree strongly) to 5 (agree strongly).

We did not attempt to separate bond dimensions from direction of attitude in wording the items, because we anticipated that self-reports of bonds would be confounded with direction. Rather, we inferred the strength of bonds by extracting direction from the item scores. We did so by subtracting voting intention from each item score. The measure of voting intention was a 5-point agree–disagree rating of the statement "I support Michael Dukakis for president." The remainder of each scale item score after subtracting the direction score is a measure of bond dimension strength over and above attitude direction for that scale item. Bond strength has directionality but the degree of directionality is incremental to attitude direction. A high value of the dimension means the basis for the bond is stronger than the direction; a low value means the basis is weaker than the direction.

The scales were pretested twice for clarity and comprehensibility. One pretest sample consisted of 40 University of Illinois–Chicago undergraduates. Nineteen received a version that referred to Michael Dukakis as the candidate and 21 received a version that referred to George Bush as the candidate for President of the United States. The other pretest sample consisted of 72 University of Chicago Graduate School of Business students. They rated items that referred to George Bush as the candidate.

The wording of the scales was clarified based on the pretesting. The scales, as finally used, referred only to Michael Dukakis. Table 12.1 shows the items for each of the measures of subjectively verifiable, objectively verifiable and performance-based bond scales. Note that a high rating on items of the former two scales indicates a favorable attitude to Dukakis, but a high rating on the performance bond scale items can be either positive or negative to Dukakis.

The objectively and subjectively verifiable bond scales are skewed positively in the sample of voters in this study. This reflects that the voters in the sample tended to agree more with specific subjectively and objectively verifiable statements about the candidate, Michael Dukakis, than their voting intention would suggest. The performance scale is approximately normally distributed. The objectively and subjectively verifiable bond scales have an adequate level of internal consistency (coefficient alpha = .93 and .74 respectively). The performance-based bond scale has a somewhat lower internal consistency (coefficient alpha = .65), which suggests that the scale may measure multiple performance-related components of attitudinal bonding.

Manifestations of Attitude Strength.   Attitude strength can be manifested in various ways, including increased resistance to attitude change

Table 12.1   Scale Items for Dimensions of Attitudinal Bonds

Subjectively Verifiable Attitudinal Bond

If Michael Dukakis were president I would feel uncomfortable about his actions at times. (negative)
I'm proud to support Michael Dukakis for president.
It makes me feel good to know Michael Dukakis would be president.

Objectively Verifiable Attitudinal Bond

As president, Michael Dukakis would help make the U.S. safer from crime.
It doesn't matter who becomes president, the country will still be the same.
As president, Michael Dukakis would give me a better standard of living.
As president, Michael Dukakis would give me a better standard of living.
As president, Michael Dukaksi would be likely to maintain good relations with other countries.
As president, Michael Dukakis would make progress on the drug problem.
As president, Michael Dukakis would keep us out of military conflicts.
As president, Michael Dukakis would make sure there were more jobs in the U.S.

Performance-Based Attitudinal Bond

I talk about Michael Dukais a lot with my friends and family.
I know more about Michael Dukakis than most people.
It's easy for me to explain my views about Michael Dukakis to other people.
I don't think about the presidential election as much as most people. (negative)
I haven't though much about why I feel the way I do about Michael Dukakis. (negative)

or attitude stability (Krosnick, 1988); certainty of the attitude (Raden, 1985); ease of access to the attitude (Fazio, Chen, McDonel, & Sherman, 1982), including "automatic" responses (Shiffrin & Schneider, 1977); greater affective–cognitive consistency (Norman, 1975); increased intensity or generalized attitude strength (Raden, 1985); and ability to rationalize the attitude.

Five measures of the manifestations of attitude strength were constructed to supply evidence of the convergent validity of our attitudinal bonding scales.

Affective–cognitive consistency was measured by the difference between 5-point agree–disagree ratings of the statements: "My decision on whether or not to vote for Michael Dukakis is based on his positions on issues important to the U.S." and "My decision about whether or not to vote for Michael Dukakis is based on my personal opinion of him."

Stability was based on the difference in likelihood ratings of two scenario statements: "Now that George Bush won the Republican Party nomination/Imagine that Ronald Reagan had won the Republican Party nomination, how likely are you to vote for Michael Dukakis."

Centrality was measured by a 6-point scale anchored at one end by Bush and the other by Dukakis. The statement was: "Thinking about

George Bush and Michael Dukakis as presidential candidates, which one do you think about more?"

Complexity was measured by a 5-point agree–disagree rating of the statement: "I have more reasons than most people to feel the way I do about Michael Dukakis as a Presidential candidate."

Certainty was measured by a 5-point agree–disagree rating of the statement: "I am very sure I will vote for Michael Dukakis."

Previous Attitudes. Because voters were interviewed in the 2 weeks prior to the 1988 presidential election, some may have acquired strong attitudes about the candidates before they were exposed to the advertising used in this study. An estimate of the strength of previous attitudes was measured by a 12-point scale of if and when the voter decided to vote for one or the other candidate. Although this variable was used as a covariate in analyses of the data, it did not alter interpretation of the results.

Demographics. Demographic information was gathered about age, education, occupation, annual household income, party registration, and party of candidates for which he or she usually votes.

Reactions to Advertising. Response protocols to political advertising were scored on the following measures:

Counterargument: Number of comments that disputed or argued with statements on issues made in the advertising.
Support argument: Number of comments that supported statements on issues made in the advertising.
Positive candidate comments: Number of positive comments about the candidate himself.
Negative candidate comments: Number of negative comments about the candidate himself.

The counterargument and support argument coding follows Wright (1973). Positive and negative candidate comments follow from the hypotheses, and are standard evaluative categories in advertising copy research.

The response protocols were rated by two of the authors. Interrater differences were not significant [$F(1,78) = .95$].

METHOD

Procedure

Subjects were interviewed individually during the 2 weeks immediately preceding the 1988 U.S. Presidential election. They were asked to complete a questionnaire that included the scales on dimensions of attitudinal bonds, voting intentions, attitude direction, attitude strength manifestations, if and when the voting decision was made, and demographics. Then the subject was shown one Dukakis television commercial. The subjects were asked: "What went through your mind as you watched this commercial"; "What was the main idea of this commercial"; "Did this commercial make you feel differently about this presidential candidate and why"; "What, if anything, did you learn from this commercial that you did not know before"; "Is there anything else you'd like to say?" Interviewers recorded the subject's responses to questions about the commercial verbatim, and probed for complete responses.

Advertisements

Two television commercials for Michael Dukakis as presidential candidate were used in this research. Both were executions of the theme, "Take charge of America's future."

The first, "Leadership," related statistics on Dukakis' performance as Governor of Massachusetts over clips showing him speaking before crowds. A voice-over reported that "America's governors voted him the most effective governor in the Nation." The second, "Miracle," had a similar structure, listing a different set of accomplishments as Governor of Massachusetts over scenes from the Democratic convention. However, it concluded with the voice of Dukakis taken from his acceptance speech, "By working together all of us are enriched."

Subjects

Two hundred and seven female voters from New Orleans, LA volunteered to be interviewed at churches and schools in exchange for donations to the host organizations. Half saw one Dukakis commercial and the rest saw the second Dukakis commercial. The number of subjects under and over the age of 35 was controlled within each of the commercial exposure groups. As can be seen in Table 12.2, the groups did not differ in demographic characteristics or voting intentions.

RESULTS

Measurement Checks

Attitude Dimensions and Attitude Strength

The three bases for an attitudinal bond between a voter and a candidate have face validity in that they are related to manifestations of

Table 12.2 Demographics, Voting Intentions and Reactions to the Two Political Commercials

	Commercial A	Commercial B
Demographics		
% over age 35	51%	51%
Income less than $30,000	23	26
Income $30,000 or more	67	64
High school graduate or less	28	30
Some college education	35	41
College graduate or more	36	29
Housewife	42	45
Blue collar	30	30
White collar	27	25
Party registrationn:		
Democrat	50	51
Republican	35	37
Voting Intention:		
George Bush	68	71
Michael Dukakis	11	13
Other candidate	2	1
Do not plan to vote	3	1
Undecided	14	10
Reactions to Advertising		
No. Support arguments (SA)	.76	.56
No. Counterarguments (CA)	.85	.82
No. Positive candidate statements (PC)	.49	.41
No. Negative candidate statements (NC)	.44	.33
Number of issues (NI)	1.67	1.52
Attitudinal bond Dimenstions (mean rating):		
Subjectively verifiable bond	.66	.54
Objectively verifiable bond	1.93	1.88
Performance-based bond	.07	.07

Note: Percentages may not total 100% because of missing responses. There were no differences between commercials for any of the demographics, voting intention, nor reactions to advertising.

attitude strength. The attitudinal bond scales were median split to create high and low levels for each scale (see Table 12.3). Analyses of variance of the several manifestations of attitude strength show significant main or interaction effects of some of the dimensions of bonds for affective–cognitive consistency, stability, centrality, certainty and complexity. Table 12.4 summarizes the ANOVA results.

Attitude Dimensions and Attitude Direction

The two aspects of attitude—bond dimensions and direction—were separated by extracting direction from scales on the three dimensions of

Table 12.3 Values of attitudinal Bond Dimensions for High and Low Levels and Interscale Correlations

	Scale Level		
	Low	*High*	
	Attitudinal Bonds		
Subjectively verifiable	− .48	1.76	
Objectively verifiable	1.43	2.50	
Performance-based	− .65	.83	
	Intercorrelations		
	S	O	P
Subjectively verifiable (S)	1.00		
Objectively verifiable (O)	0.59	1.00	
Performance-based (P)	− 0.51	− 0.40	1.00

Table 12.4 Summary of Significant Effects of Bond Dimensions in ANOVAS of Manifestations of Attitude Strength

	Affective–Cognitive Consistency	*Stability*	*Centrality*	*Complexity*	*Certinty*
Subjectively Verifiable bond (S)	—	—	—	—	a
Objectively Verifiable bond (O)	—	—	—	—	a
Performance-based bond (P)	a	—	—	—	c
S × O	—	—	—	c	a
S × P	—	c	—	—	—
O × P	—	—	—	—	—
S × O × P	—	—	b	—	—

Note: a: $p = .000$
b: $p = < .01$
c: $p = < .05$

attitudinal bonds. The degree of relationship between bonds and attitude direction is specific to this sample of voters on this election. Table 12.5 shows attitude direction for levels of the three attitude bond dimensions. Attitude direction is related to subjectively verifiable bonds $[F(1,199) = 43.90, p = .0001]$, objectively verifiable bonds $[F(1,199) = 13.07, p = .0001]$, and performance-based bonds $[F(1,199) = 4.93, p = .03]$. In addition, there is a subjectively × objectively verifiable bond interaction $[F(1,199) = 15.10, p = .0001]$.

Attitudes are favorable to Dukakis when subjectively verifiable bonds are strong, and when performance-based bonds are weak. The relation-

Table 12.5 Attitude Direction for Attitude Bond Dimensions

| | Subjectively Verifiable Bond | | |
	Low	High	
Objecively verifiable bond			
Low	1.03	1.94	1.31
High	1.00	3.00	2.41
Performance-based bond			
Low	1.03	2.85	2.31
High	1.01	1.92	1.24
	1.02	2.62	

ship of objectively verifiable bonds to attitude direction depends on the level of subjectively verifiable bonds. When subjectively verifiable bonds are strong, attitudes to Dukakis are more favorable when objectively verifiable bonds are also strong. However, when subjectively verifiable bonds are weak, attitudes toward Dukakis are unfavorable regardless of the strength of objectively verifiable bonds (see Fig. 12.2).

Intercorrelations of Bond Dimensions

The three dimensions of bonding are highly intercorrelated. Subjectively and objectively verifiable attitudinal bonds are positively related, but each of them is negatively related to performance-based bonding (see Table 12.3). This result describes the specific attitudes of voters in this sample. Most of the voters were opposed to Dukakis as a presidential candidate. Those who did support Dukakis tended to be less articulate, either because of the local social context or their personal propensities.

Attitude Direction and Reactions to Political Advertising

Attitude direction is related to reactions to advertising, as expected. Recall that positive attitudinal direction is favorable to Dukakis. The correlation of attitude direction with the number of support arguments is .50 and with counterarguments is − .31. Correlations of attitude direction with comments about the candidate are lower, but also in the expected direction, .13 for positive candidate comments and − .04 for negative candidate comments.

Verbal Reactions to Advertising as a Function of Dimensions of Attitudinal Bonds

The median-split attitudinal bond scales were entered into analyses of variance with the response protocol codes as dependent variables.

Attitude Direction

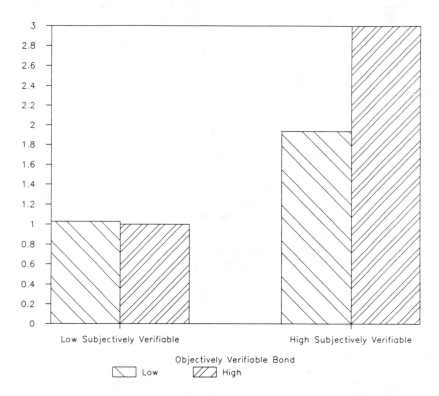

FIGURE 12.2. Effects of subjectively and objectively verifiable bonds on attitude direction.

Of the four protocol codes, three vary with dimensions of attitudinal bonds: number of support arguments, number of counterarguments, number of negative candidate comments. Table 12.6 summarizes results of the ANOVAs. Table 12.7 shows mean values for the four protocol codes for levels of the subjectively verifiable bond, the objectively verifiable bond and performance-based bond, and for the performance-based bond within each of the other two dimensions.

Hypotheses 1 and 3

The part of Hypothesis 1 that states that there are more positive or fewer negative candidate statements with a high level of subjectively verifiable bonds, is not supported. There is a three-way interaction among the attitudinal bond dimensions [$F(1,199) = 5.11, p = .03$] for the number of negative candidate statements in response to the adver-

Table 12.6 Summary of Significant Effects of Bond Dimensions in ANOVAS of Reactions to Advertising

	Reaction to Advertising			
	Support Arguments	Counter-arguments	Positive Candidate Comments	Negative Candidate Comments
Subjectively Verifiable bond (S)	a	—	—	—
Objectively Verifiable bond (O)	b	a	—	—
Performance-based bond (P)	—	c	—	—
S × O	—	—	—	—
S × P	b	—	—	—
O × P	—	—	—	—
S × O × P	—	—	—	c

Note: a: $p = .001$
b: $p = <.01$
c: $p = < .05$

tising. The mean number of negative candidate comments is shown in Table 12.8. When there is a strong objectively verifiable basis for the attitude, there is a greater difference in the number of negative personal comments about the candidate for high and low subjectively verifiable and performance bases. When there is a weak objectively verifiable basis, differences in the number of negative personal comments are smaller for levels of the other two dimensions.

The part of Hypothesis 1 that states that there are more support or fewer counter arguments with a high level of subjectively verifiable bonds is supported. Strong subjectively verifiable bonds are associated with more support arguments [$F(1,199) = 10.84, p = .001$].

With regard to Hypothesis 3, the number of support arguments associated with subjectively verifiable bonds is moderated by the strength of performance-based bonds [$F(1,199) = 7.76, p = .006$]. However, the direction is not as hypothesized. When performance-based bonds are weak, strong subjectively verifiable bonds are associated with more support arguments than when performance-based bonds are strong (see Table 12.7 and Fig. 12.3). That is, voters with the strongest subjectively verifiable bonds with Dukakis offered the most support arguments when their strength was based on little self-perceived cognitive effort.

Consistent with the support argument results, when performance-based bonds are weak, strong subjectively verifiable bonds are associated with fewer counterarguments [$t(105) = 2.38, p = .02$] (see Table 12.7).

Table 12.7 Reactions to Advertising for Attitudinal Bond Dimensions

	Reaction to Advertising			
	Support Arguments	Counter-arguments	Positive Candidate Comments	Negative Candidate Comments
Subjectively verifiable bond				
Low	.31	1.05	.40	.36
High	1.03	.61	.49	.41
Objectively verifiable bond				
Low	.41	1.10	.45	.40
High	.98	.51	.44	.37
Performance-based bond				
Low	.89	.61	.40	.37
High	.41	1.08	.49	.40
Performance-based = low Subjectively verifiable				
Low	.25a	.91e	.25	.41
High	1.16a	.48e	.47	.36
Performance-based = high Subjectively verifiable				
Low	.33b	1.11	.47	.35
High	.64b	1.00	.56	.56
Performance-based = low Objectively verifiable				
Low	.65c	.91f	.37	.41
High	.1.07c	.38f	.43	.34
Performance-based = high Objectively verifiable				
Low	.24d	1.21g	.50	.39
High	.80d	.77g	.47	.43

a $t(105) = 4.33, p = .0001$
b $t(98) = 1.93, p = .057$
c $t(105) = 2.00, p = .05$
d $t(98) = 3.92, p = .0001$
e $t(105) = 2.38, p = .02$
f $t(105) = 3.32, p = .001$
g $t(98) = 2.04, p = .04$

Because voters are likely to have a moderately high level of motivation about the candidates in the last 2 weeks prior to the election, the additive effect of moderately high arousal with ability could explain the results. The combined effects of moderately high arousal with ability could cause the performance bond to moderate the other bonds inversely (see Fig. 12.1b). This could result in a higher level of support arguments with strong subjectively verifiable bonds when performance bonds are weak, as observed.

Table 12.8 Negative Comments about Candidate Related to Attitudinal Bond Dimensions

Subjectively Verifiable	Objectively Verifiable	Performance-based Bond	Negative Comments
Low	Low	Low	.32
Low	Low	High	.39
Low	High	Low	.54
Low	High	High	.14*
High	Low	Low	.48
High	Low	High	.33
High	High	Low	.29
High	High	High	.69*

*$t(28) = 2.60$, $p = .02$

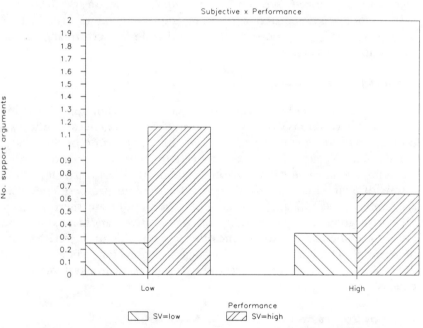

FIGURE 12.3. Effects of subjectively verifiable and performance-based bonds on support arguments.

In summary, Hypothesis 1 holds for counter- and support arguments about the advertising but is not supported with regard to the relation between subjectively verifiable attitudinal bonds and personal comments about the candidates. Hypothesis 3 is not supported but the results may be explained post hoc by a modification of Hypothesis 3.

Hypothesis 2

In support of Hypothesis 2, strong objectively verifiable bonds are associated with more support arguments. An ANOVA of the number of support arguments shows a main effect for objectively verifiable bonds [$F(1,199) = 7.38, p = .007$]. Also in support of Hypothesis 2, stronger objectively verifiable bonds with Dukakis lead to fewer counterarguments. An analysis of variance of the number of counterarguments shows a main effect for objectively verifiable bonds [$F(1,199) = 11.80, p = .001$].

Hypothesis 4

Hypothesis 4, that the effect of an objectively verifiable basis for attitudinal bonds on support and counterargument is moderated by the level of performance-based bonds, is not supported. Strong performance-based bonds are associated with more counterarguments [$F(1,199) = 5.09, p = .025$], but the objectively verifiable × performance-based interaction is not significant.

Differences Between Commercials

There are no overall differences between the two commercials for any of the voter reactions, as can be seen in Table 12.2. Because the two political advertisements are replications for the purpose of this study, we do not expect differences between them in the relationship of attitudinal bond dimensions to voter reactions to the advertising. Of 28 *F* tests of main effects and interactions for the four protocol codes, 24 are similar in significance levels. The other 4 indicate there is more support argument, counterargument, or negative candidate comment for one commercial but not for the other as a function of the relationship dimensions. Overall, these results suggest that voter–candidate bond dimensions are manifested in reactions to advertising in a systematic and relatively stable manner.

Types of Voters and Reactions to Advertising

The analysis up to this point has found that response to advertising is a function of three dimensions of voter–candidate relationships and some interactions among the dimensions. If voters are described as above or below the median on each dimension, up to eight different profiles are possible, and each profile would manifest a different response style. Some of the profiles, however, might be empirically under-represented.

We therefore elected to cluster the voters in our sample to determine which combinations of dimensions were predominant and whether their advertising responses were as predicted.

Each respondent was defined by her score on the three bond dimensions, and the resulting matrix was subjected to a hierarchical cluster analysis. An average linkage method was used with a squared Euclidean distance metric. The four cluster solution was chosen based on a scree test of the ratio of within- to between-groups variance.

Habit-Driven Democrats. This group has a strong subjectively based bond to Dukakis but a weak objectively based bond. They perceive that they expend little effort in their voting decision. They offer many support arguments in response to the advertising, more than the rationally judgmental and passionately opposed clusters, and include the strong supporters of Dukakis. This group, older than the other three clusters, include the highest proportion who usually vote as Democrats. There were fewer high income voters in this group than in the other three clusters.

Table 12.9 Reactions to Advertising by Type of Voter–Candidate Bond

	Type of Voter–Candidate Bond			
	Habit-Driven Democrats	*Rationally Judgemental*	*Uninvolved Opposition*	*Passion Opposed*
Number in group	27	82	78	20
Subjectively verifiable bond	.296a	.020b	−.239c	−1.100d
Objectively verifiable bond	.074a	1.235b	.689c	1.375bd
Performance-based bond	−.230a	.305b	−.510c	−.370ac
Support arguments	1.111a	.488b	.744ab	.400b
Counterarguments	.778ab	1.,024a	.628b	.950ab
Positive candidate comments	.519a	.427ab	.256b	.550a
Negative candidate comments	.704a	.390a	.423a	.300a
Age: 30 or less	15%	20%	21%	20%
30–40	33	59	53	60
40 or more	52	22	26	20
Education				
Some college	74	70	72	70
Household income				
$50,000 or more	22	32	41	30
Registered Democrat	48	51	53	45
Usually vote for				
Democratic Party	33	9	18	15
Attitude direction	3.48	1.17	1.53	1.03

Note: Across clusters, values with similar letters are not significantly different from each other.

Rationally Judgmental.   This group has a strong objectively verifiable bond with Dukakis and perceive that they have considered their voting decision. They have a neutral subjectively based bond with the candidate. They offer as many counterarguments as do habit-driven Democrats, but the ratio of counter to support arguments is about two to one. While including as many registered Democrats as habit-driven Democrats, only 9% usually vote for the Democratic party. They might be characterized as "rationally judgmental" about Dukakis, and generally did not support him.

Uninvolved Opposition.   This group is somewhat opposed to the candidate on a subjective basis but moderately bonded to him on an objectively verifiable basis. They perceive themselves as having expended little effort on the voting decision. In response to the Dukakis advertising they offer about the same number of support and counterarguments. Most of them are under 40 years of age and they include the highest percentage of high income subjects of all the clusters. Over half are registered Democrats but, more than the rationally judgmental cluster, they tend to vote for the Democratic party.

Passionately Opposed.   This cluster is strongly opposed to Dukakis on a subjectively verifiable basis although they bond with him on an objective level. They perceive themselves to have exerted little effort in their voting decision. Like the rationally judgmental and the uninvolved opposition clusters, most of them are under 40 years of age and a third have household incomes over $50,000. About half are registered Democrats and 15% voted for that party in the last election. In response to the advertising, they are similar to the rationally judgemental cluster in making twice as many counter arguments as support arguments.

One issue of importance to the sample of voters in this study was not included in the survey but is mentioned in voter reactions to the advertising. This issue is Dukakis' stand on abortion. Many among the voters in this study, although they may approve of Dukakis' stands on many issues, disagree with his stand on abortion. Their voting decision may be based on this one issue. For this reason, the voters in the passionately opposed cluster may be characterized instead as "one-issue" voters.

DISCUSSION

Reactions to political advertising are not only related to the direction of a voter's attitude about the candidate but also to the dimensions of his or her bond with the candidate. In particular, support and counterarguments to political advertising are related to objectively verifiable as well as to subjectively verifiable and performance-based dimensions of attitudinal bonds.

Both strong objectively and subjectively verifiable bases for a bond with the candidate result in expression of more support arguments and fewer counterarguments in reaction to political advertising for that candidate, in support of Hypotheses 1 and 2. These results are consistent with the idea that either subjectively or objectively verifiable bonds can facilitate a central path to processing an attitude (Petty & Cacioppo, 1981). That is, a subjectively verifiable base for the attitude may prepare the voter to attend to the issues in political advertising for a candidate. We found little evidence that subjectively verifiable bonds between a voter and the candidate are reflected in reactions to peripheral aspects of a political commercial such as the candidate's personal characteristics.

In this study, strong performance-based attitudinal bonds are associated with weak subjectively and objectively verifiable bonds with the candidate. Consistent with this tendency among the voters sampled in this study, strong performance bonds are associated with high levels of counterargument and low levels of support argument in response to the advertising. There can be several reasons for these results.

First, the results may be specific to this sample of voters. Although positive scores on the subjectively and objectively verifiable scales indicate support for the candidate, a positive score on the performance bond scale could be either favorable or unfavorable toward the candidate. Thus, highly involved voters might not support Michael Dukakis for president. Given the political atmosphere in Louisiana and the outcome of the election, this is not unreasonable.

Second, many Dukakis supporters may never have been highly involved with the election. Dukakis supporters may include many diehard Democrats who would vote for their party regardless of specific characteristics of the candidate that, if considered, might cause them to change their voting intention. This is an example of mindlessness (Langer, 1989; Langer, Blank, & Chanowitz, 1978). That is, one relies on distinctions one has used in the past to guide one's behavior. In this case, one votes for the candidate of the Democratic party without considering his stands on specific issues or his personal characteristics. There is an attitudinal inertia associated with mindlessness so that the voter may not react to situational changes that might call for a reassessment of attitudinal bonds. For example, the voter may mindlessly accept all candidates of one political party rather than generate an attitude about the candidate himself. The Habit-driven Democrat voters may demonstrate mindlessness in that they are older than the other voters and firmly

Democratic in a part of the country that traditionally has supported that party.

Third, in the 2 weeks before the election, Dukakis supporters may no longer expend much effort in thinking about or discussing the election or the candidates because they have already made their decision. They would have a low score on the performance-bond scale but high scores on the subjectively and objectively verifiable bond scales. Their attitudes would be over-rehearsed or automatized.

Another characteristic of performance bonds in this study is that they moderate subjectively verifiable bond effects on the number of support and counterarguments. With weak performance bonds, there are greater differences in subjectively verifiable bond levels for the number of support and counterarguments, than with strong performance bonds. This result may be due to the moderately high level of arousal generated by the election when these voters were interviewed, in the 2 weeks before the election. Evidence from diverse sources suggests that people perform more poorly at a high than at a moderate level of arousal (Kahneman, 1973). Their poor performance may be due to a narrowed range of attention in conditions of high arousal (Easterbrook, 1959; Kahneman, 1973). In the current study, voters who are highly involved during the final days of the election may have a narrowed range of attention that causes them to be less influenced by the advertising than less involved voters. For highly involved voters, the strength of subjectively or objectively verifiable bonds with the candidate may not influence their reactions to advertising.

We have identified four types of bonds between voters and the candidate based on the three dimensions of attitudinal bonds: habit-driven Democrats; rationally judgmental; uninvolved opposed; passionately opposed. These four types are similar to the four types of consumers identified on the basis of brand loyalty by Cushing and Douglas-Tate (1985): routine brand buyers, involved information seekers, uninvolved brand switchers, and involved brand loyalists. Although the attitudinal direction of the four bond types in the present research differs from that of Cushing and Douglas-Tate, the types are similar. Just as this study finds that the four bond types differ in their reactions to advertising, so did Cushing and Douglas-Tate find that their four groups also differed in their reactions to commercials for products.

Manifestations of attitude strength and attitude direction clearly differ in how they are influenced by attitudinal bond dimensions. The dimensions examined in this research, subjectively and objectively verifiable bonds and performance-based bonds, all influence attitudinal direction. Although not orthogonal, the three dimensions have different effects on manifestations of attitude strength. This initial exploration of attitudinal bond dimensions suggests they are worthy of further study to tease apart their structure and relationships with attitude direction and behavior.

Attitudinal bond dimensions were measured indirectly in this study. Other approaches to measurement are needed to provide converging evidence of the role they play in attitudes and their effects on behavior. One approach would be to separate attitudinal direction from bonding dimensions in the way scale items are presented to subjects. Another would be to expand the scale points in order to "fold" the scale and still have enough variance to be analyzable.

A number of structural and methodological questions about attitude strength dimensions remain. Among them are:

1. Is the relationship among the dimensions specific to this sample and issue, or generalizable?
2. Exactly how are the bond dimensions related to manifestations of attitude strength?
3. What is the relationship between attitude direction and dimensions of attitude bonds, and is it consistent across samples and issues?

Future research also must address other issues such as how attitudinal bond dimensions develop, and what is the relationship of those dimensions to distinctly different types of advertising such as lecture versus drama (Wells, 1987).

CONCLUSIONS

Dimensions of attitudinal bonding differentially influence how voters react to political advertising. In particular, support and counterarguments are influenced by objectively and subjectively verifiable dimensions of attitudinal bonds. In this study, the effect of subjectively verifiable bonds on support and counter arguments is moderated by performance-based bonding so that strong subjectively verifiable bonds are associated with more support and fewer counter arguments when the voter perceives him or herself to exert little cognitive effort. We offer several explanations for the effects of the performance bond: the specific sample of voters in this study, mindlessness, automatization, and a narrowed range of attention in high levels of arousal.

Four voter types, based on the three relationship dimensions, react differently to political advertising for the candidate. Their support of the candidate is characterized on the basis of habit, rational judgment, passionate opposition, or uninvolved opposition. These types are similar to those found in consumer research.

REFERENCES

Abelson, R. P. (1988). Conviction. *American Psychologist, 43,* 267–275.

Cushing, P., & Douglas-Tate, M. (1985). The effect of people/product relationships on advertising processing. In L. F. Alwitt & A. A. Mitchell (Eds.), *Psychological processes and advertising effects* (pp. 241–259). Hillsdale, NJ: Lawrence Erlbaum Associates.

Easterbrook, J. A. (1959). The effect of emotion on cue utilization and the organization of behavior. *Psychological Review, 66,* 183–201.

Fazio, R. H., Chen, J., McDonel, E. C., & Sherman, S. J. (1982). Attitude accessibility, attitude-behavior consistency, and the strength of the object-evaluation association. *Journal of Experimental Social Psychology, 18,* 339–357.

Flavell, J. H. (1963). *The developmental psychology of Jean Piaget.* New York: van Nostrand.

Greene, J. (1972). *Psycholinguistics.* New York: Penguin Books.

Kahneman, D. (1973). *Attention and effort.* Englewood Cliffs, NJ: Prentice-Hall.

Krosnick, J. A. (1988). Attitude importance and attitude change. *Journal of Experimental Social Psychology, 24,* 240–255.

Langer, E. J. (1989). *Mindfulness.* Reading, MA: Addison-Wesley.

Langer, E., Blank, A., & Chanowitz, B. (1978). The mindlessness of ostensibly thoughtful action: the role of "placebic" information in interpersonal interaction. *Journal of Personality and Social Psychology, 36,* 635–642.

McGuire, W. J. (1985). Attitudes and attitude change. In G. Lindzey & E. Aronson (Eds.), *Handbook of social psychology* (3rd ed., pp. 233–346). New York: Random House.

Norman, R. (1975). Affective–cognitive consistency, attitudes, conformity, and behavior. *Journal of Personality and Social Psychology, 32,* 83–91.

Petty, R. E., & Cacioppo, J. T. (1981). *Attitudes and persuasion: Classic and contemporary approaches.* Dubuque, IA: William C. Brown.

Raden, D. (1985). Strength-related attitude dimensions. *Social Psychology Quarterly, 48,* 312–330.

Shiffrin, R. M., & Schneider, W. (1977). Controlled and automatic human information processing: II. Perceptual learning, automatic attending and a general theory. *Psychological Review, 84,* 127–190.

Wells, W. D. (1987). Lectures and dramas. In P. Caffarata & A. Tybout (Eds.), *Cognitive and affective responses to advertising.* Lexington, MA: Heath.

Wright, P. L. (1973). Cognitive processes mediating acceptance of advertising. *Journal of Marketing Research, 4,* 53–62.

Author Index

Subject Index